PENG

dead man walking

Also by Kate McClymont

He Who Must Be Obeid (with Linton Besser)

KATE
with VANDA CARSON
McCLYMONT

dead man
walking

PENGUIN BOOKS

PENGUIN BOOKS
UK | USA | Canada | Ireland | Australia
India | New Zealand | South Africa | China

Penguin Books is part of the Penguin Random House group of companies
whose addresses can be found at global.penguinrandomhouse.com

Penguin
Random House
Australia

First published by Vintage in 2019
This edition published by Penguin Books in 2020

Cover illustration, 'Man Lying on Road' by Ethan Hundertmark / EyeEm,
courtesy of Getty Images
Cover design by James Rendall © Penguin Random House Australia Pty Ltd
Internal design by Midland Typesetters, Australia
Typeset in 12/15 pt Goudy by Midland Typesetters

Printed and bound in Australia by Griffin Press, part of Ovato, an accredited
ISO AS/NZS 14001 Environmental Management Systems printer

 A catalogue record for this
book is available from the
National Library of Australia

ISBN 978 0 14379 526 1

penguin.com.au

To Phoebe, Jack and Sophie

CONTENTS

A NOTE ON SOURCES

This book is based on dozens of interviews, including with associates of the main characters, some of whom, fearing retribution, have asked to remain anonymous.

Hundreds of pages of court transcripts, police statements of fact and police interviews, which were tendered across almost a decade of court cases, have been used. When I have attributed quotes to the main players in dialogue they are based on actual testimony, recollections offered or police interviews.

CHAPTER 1

THE SHOOTING

There had to be a word for this feeling of apprehension tinged with grief. Glassy-eyed, the tall, solid middle-aged man, his hair greying at the temples, gazed at the house across the road, ringed by a well-tended hedge. It was early evening and the intermittent rain had left the spring air redolent with the scent of wattle and jasmine from the neighbouring manicured gardens, looked after, no doubt, by a retinue of hired help.

On any other day, Haissam Safetli could have passed for one of Cremorne's many well-heeled inhabitants, a stockbroker, banker or lawyer. Only four months earlier he had been the general manager of Chan & Naylor, an accounting firm in the staid north shore suburb of Pymble, but he'd been fired for decking one of the partners. Since then he'd been doing some debt-collecting with his brother, Bassam, and now here he was sitting in a battered, unregistered Toyota Hilux with stolen numberplates on the precipice of becoming a paid assassin, and he was sure as hell there weren't many of them north of the harbour.

Safetli looked at his watch. It had just gone six and he was waiting anxiously for the return of the kid. Over the previous hour 43-year-old Safetli had said little as he and young

Christopher Estephan sat in the front seat of Safetli's old ute waiting for Michael McGurk to come home. Other evenings spent in wait for McGurk had come to nought and Safetli half-hoped this one would too.

His 19-year-old companion had prattled on about his girl-friend troubles; that he was behind in his rent. They talked about everything but what they would do if McGurk appeared. The .22 Norinco rifle, which they had spent the previous days grinding down in Safetli's shed, lay in a Stanley bag between them. Neither of them mentioned it.

Finally Safetli could bear it no longer. He got his wallet out of his jacket pocket and, fishing around for two $20 notes, sent Estephan off to a nearby bottle shop for bourbon. The dope they'd smoked a few hours before was wearing off and Safetli badly needed a hit of something to take the edge off his rising panic. How the fuck had it come to this, he asked himself as he watched Estephan head off down the street. Only months earlier he had a respectable job; now he was lying in wait to kill a man he personally had no truck with. Last night he'd actually wet the bed. He remembered sculling bourbon and slicing his arms. He wanted to feel everything. He wanted to feel nothing.[1]

Yesterday he had filled out his kids' passport applications. He had been practising forging his ex-wife's signature for the permission he'd need to take the children out of the country should he have to flee after this was done, but then he noticed that the form required his ex's passport details.

The passenger door of his ute opened. Chris Estephan was back. 'Shit, mate, I'm sorry but they wouldn't fucking serve me,' said the kid, closing the passenger door. 'They wouldn't believe I was over eighteen. Sorry, Hais.'[2]

The older man thumped the steering wheel. He had to have a shot to steady his nerves. All the money he'd lost trying to find someone else to do this fucking job, all the pressure, had driven him to drink – literally. He smiled wanly to himself at his own joke as he got out of the ute to find his second bottle of bourbon for the day.

He looked across the road again to McGurk's house. The street was as crooked as a dog's hind leg and the house sat on an awkward corner. The old wooden garage was down at the bottom of the street, and up the hill and around the bend, adjacent to the McGurks' tennis court, was the path to their home. Safetli had been looking at that fucking house, a cream-coloured pin-up for the surburban dream, for so long it nauseated him. He'd passed the hours watching tradesmen in the street come and go, and he'd followed a little brown and white dog as it jauntily paraded along the fence line of the house next to the McGurks'. For months Safetli had half-heartedly been surveilling McGurk. Shit, he'd even had sex in his car with his girlfriend, Krystal Weir, to pass the endless hours waiting for that arsehole to come home to his wife and four kids.

Safetli had been hired to do the surveillance by Lucky Gattellari, a former boxer who was now living the high life having become 'wealth adjacent' to uber-rich property developer Ron Medich. As Medich's right-hand man, Lucky was calling the shots. McGurk and Medich had had some sort of falling-out, was all Safetli knew. Gattellari kept hassling him, complaining that McGurk was costing Medich, 'the big boss', thousands of dollars a month and that Medich wanted him gone. Safetli was trapped in their deadly plan.

He set off down Cranbrook Avenue and round the corner to a little group of shops to buy the bourbon. At 6.10 pm he bought a half-bottle of Jim Beam. The price shocked him. The rich sure paid through the nose for the privilege of drinking in their fine suburb, he thought. As Safetli handed over his cash, the attendant went to put the bottle in a paper bag. Safetli stopped him – there would be no need for that. As soon as he was out of sight of the small group of shops, he opened the bottle and began swigging from it as he walked along. He decided to take the longer way back to the car. Before he came round the corner into Cranbrook Avenue, he glanced up and down the road to see if the coast was clear before relieving himself against a tree.

Safetli wiped droplets of rain from his glasses as he glanced up at the unlit lights bordering the tennis court at McGurk's house. They stood like sentinels, heads bowed in silent reproof at the horror lying in wait. As he took another swig he wondered if McGurk had arrived home while he was gone. Maybe the kid had done it. He realised Estephan wouldn't have been able to get in touch with him as they'd both left their phones behind when they'd set out some hours earlier from Safetli's home near Camden, 75 kilometres away.

As he rounded the dogleg in the road, his heart leapt. His ute was gone. Maybe it *was* done. But there was the battered old vehicle across the road. Estephan had moved it into a better position and was sitting in the driver's seat. There was a rectangular outline on the road marking the dry patch where it had previously been parked.

Safetli got back into the ute and offered the bottle to the kid. He hoped tonight was the night. He didn't think he could take much more of this.

Fifteen minutes later, at 6.25 pm, Michael McGurk's dark-blue Mercedes sedan turned from Spofforth Street into Cranbrook Avenue, pulling up outside the family home. For more than eight years the McGurk family had lived at number 11, 'Esslemont', a large, single-storey house with a grass tennis court and a swimming pool, for which McGurk had been fined after putting it in without council permission.[3] McGurk drove past his double garage and parked out on the street. Instead of providing a safe haven for the family to enter and exit the house, the garage had a variety of uses, from accommodation for a string of Indonesian nannies to storing McGurk's collection of knock-off luxury goods.

In the passenger seat of his car sat his son, who was days away from his tenth birthday. McGurk had collected him from a friend's house and then stopped to buy takeaway for dinner. If McGurk had been ten minutes earlier he and Safetli might have bumped into each other at the same little group of shops down the road.

McGurk opened the car door and twisted around to retrieve the barbecued chicken. Resting on his lap was a bag of hot chips, which he and his son had already started eating. He was felled by a single shot from a .22 Norinco rifle. The bullet entered his skull just behind his right ear and he fell onto the damp bitumen next to his Mercedes, his life's end framed by a cascade of deep-fried chips.

As McGurk lay dying, Safetli's ute careened down Cranbrook Avenue. The kid, who had lost his licence, was at the wheel, driving like a bat out of hell. They almost had a collision as they hurtled straight onto the Spofforth Street roundabout, then screeched up the hill to Military Road, where they were recorded on CCTV footage. The ute, with no e-tag, was photographed crossing the Harbour Bridge without paying the toll. As Safetli dismantled the rifle, he swigged the bourbon he'd just bought.

They took the exit that led to the Anzac Bridge and then looped around Blackwattle Bay, heading towards Annandale. Safetli ordered Estephan to pull over at a small car park at Bicentennial Park in Rozelle. On the bank of Rozelle Bay he flung the metal piece of the rifle into the harbour. Later, Estephan pulled into one of the breakdown bays on the M5 motorway and Safetli threw the wooden handle of the rifle over the high cement wall.

Back at his home in Elderslie, Safetli started smoking cones of cannabis to calm his nerves. In the rundown shed in his backyard, which doubled as a gym, he lit a fire in an old 44-gallon drum and threw in the long khaki coat he had been wearing, as well as his track pants and dark t-shirt. His teenage accomplice watched as the numberplates he'd stolen melted and twisted in the flames.

CHAPTER 2

THE SOCIOPATH NEXT DOOR

On the surface Michael Loch McGurk appeared to have it all: a loving wife, a seemingly perfect family – two girls and two boys who were ensconced in the comfort of a rambling family home in the desirable Sydney suburb of Cremorne.

But like the much-admired Picasso hanging in pride of place in McGurk's designer living room, everything about his life was an artifice. In the weeks before his death, I had begun to examine his murky world, but it wasn't until after his murder that the true depths of his wheeling and dealing came to light. McGurk was a whirling dervish who had spun his way through endless schemes of criminality and corruption and had left in his wake gross acts of treachery and betrayal. He was a blackmailer, a thief, a thug, an extortionist, a hedonist and a double-crosser par excellence. He was also ruthless and clever, and, like most successful con men, dynamic, charming and captivating. This made him a dangerous opponent.

Some neighbours spoke of his devotion to his family, that he would do anything for his kids. 'They were a Catholic family, a lovely family,' one woman told the *Sydney Morning Herald* at the time of his murder.[1] 'Forget the fact that they were millionaires, they were a fun-loving family, always respectful, no airs or graces,' her husband said. 'This is not the city's underbelly, this is just a quiet little suburb and this stuff isn't suppose to happen here,' he added.[2]

Another neighbour described McGurk as someone with a temper. 'The [family] are nice people but there have been odd bouts of strange behaviour since we moved in seven months ago.'[3]

In particular, neighbours reported that over the last few months they had overheard violent rows between Kimberley McGurk and her husband. One particular row had occurred in July. The McGurks arrived home late and had an argument in their backyard that lasted for hours. Friends also reported that relations between the pair appeared strained and Kimberley had become anxious and withdrawn. One neighbour, who lived in the block of flats next door, recalled his run-in with McGurk a few months back. A party that had started at lunch time continued until late at night, keeping everyone awake. The noise was compounded by McGurk putting up speakers around his tennis court. The neighbour went down to ask the revellers to tone it down. McGurk was belligerent and unreasonable, and threatened him. As soon as the neighbour said he would call the police, McGurk became a different person, agreeing immediately to bring the rowdy gathering to an end.

To the largely conservative parent body at the Sacred Heart Catholic primary school in Mosman, McGurk was also a divisive figure. One parent described the school community as 'suffocating and full of people who were pleased with themselves because they'd ended up in Mosman'. Most of the mothers didn't work and many spent their time shopping, talking about their renovations and 'living in the reflected glory of their Macquarie banker husbands', said the parent.[4]

McGurk was in his element. He was always at the school. He appeared to have no nine-to-five job as he hung around to have a chat with the mothers after dropping off his three younger children. (His older son had started high school.) Suddenly, though, he would be gone, dashing off overseas at short notice on one of his mysterious business trips. The McGurks certainly displayed all the trappings of wealth and appeared to lead a jetset lifestyle.

'You always knew when Michael McGurk was in the room,' said the parent. 'He was an attention-grabbing presence.' He could spin a great yarn and his tales of waltzing unannounced into an ayatollah's palace in Iran, or doing business in Mongolia, were delivered with a dash of élan.

There was gossip among the school's parents about where the McGurks got their money. 'He loved to give the impression he was doing very well for himself,' said one parent.[5] Some thought he was a bit shifty, and referred to him as '007'. Some admired his generosity to the school; others found his ostentatious bidding at its charity fundraisers crass. Was it an act of Christian charity to fly the much-loved elderly school priest to the Hong Kong Sevens Rugby tournament, or a naked attempt to bolster his children's standing?

McGurk always seemed to be able to get his hands on corporate boxes for sporting events, concerts and the like. In December 2006 he took a bunch of parents to a Robbie Williams concert. He'd got his hands not only on the hottest tickets in town but also on a much-sought-after corporate box with a bar, catering and waiters. One of the parents who went with him recalls that he parked at the nearby multi-storey car park at Fox Studios but rather than wait in the queue to exit, he drove the wrong way down the ramps, laughing all the way.

The contradictions baffled people. Here was a man who was clearly very wealthy, yet surreptitiously flogged fake Louis Vuitton handbags to school mums from the boot of his car. He even turned up on their doorsteps to deliver their designer knock-offs. He'd also been known to sell counterfeit Ralph Lauren Polo business shirts – a sideline that was halted when Customs seized 300 of the shirts from McGurk.

One thing the parents agreed on was that McGurk was a doting parent. A friend recalled weekends on Balmoral Beach with the McGurk family. While other parents began enthusiastically playing with the kids, then slunk off to sip coffees and thumb the Sunday papers, McGurk would muck around with the children for hours. He coached his kids' soccer teams and at the end of training would buy milkshakes for the whole team.

When the McGurk children were very small – in 2001 he had four kids under the age of five – he and Kimberley hired an Indonesian maid. McGurk started offering maids to his friends – at $15,000 a year for seven days a week work 'it's cheaper than daycare', he would boast.[6]

Certainly, some of the school parents saw just how charmless McGurk could be. Two fathers from Saint Ignatius' College, Riverview, the prestigious Catholic private school the eldest McGurk son attended, had invested money in a deal proposed by McGurk. When they politely asked him when they would be seeing some return on their investment, he suggested they meet for a cup of coffee to discuss the matter. At the meeting, McGurk slid a document across the table. It detailed the times and places their children had been for the past week. McGurk had had the kids followed to their music lessons, sports practices and knew what time they got home from school. 'Do you really want to pursue this?' he said.[7]

In short, McGurk was the sociopath next door.

'I reckon if you'd thrown the hat around, everyone would have chipped in for the hitter,' one of McGurk's former lawyers told me in the days after the Scot's murder.[8] It was a nightmare of a case for detectives from Strike Force Narrunga, the homicide investigation established to explore what looked like a professional hit. McGurk had been feuding with bikies, laundering money offshore, ripping off business partners in property developments, trying to blackmail businessmen and the Sultan of Brunei, using prostitutes to compromise associates, running mortgage and superannuation frauds, quarrelling with former Russian KGB agents, chasing up bad debtors for others using firebombing and beatings as incentives to pay up. He was a prolific user and abuser of cocaine and alcohol. He was in dire financial straits and was being pursued from the top end of town to the bottom over debts and rip-offs. As his mate Jim Byrnes, euphemistically known as a 'colourful Sydney business identity', told me the morning after McGurk's murder, 'I do understand that people who live by the sword sometimes die by the sword. McGurk had a lot of powerful friends who solved a lot of problems for him. Unfortunately, this [problem] wasn't one of them.'[9]

The commander of the homicide squad, Geoff Beresford, was asked at a press conference shortly after the murder if police thought it was a contract killing. The veteran copper told journalists, 'We are very open-minded at the moment, but what I can confirm is the deceased is very well-known to the police and there's quite a lot of avenues of inquiries that have already been established that we are pursuing with some vigour.' He added, 'This gentleman did have a lot of associates that are also known to us.'

This was police-speak to say there were any number of dangerous types who had a motive to do away with Michael McGurk.

CHAPTER 3

A WHODUNNIT FOR THE RICH AND FAMOUS

Michael McGurk knew he was a dead man walking.

On the morning of 24 August 2009, my mobile rang. It was exactly a month since the *Sydney Morning Herald* had run a front-page splash on the dubious exploits of the 'wee hustler from Glasgow', as one of his Scottish mates described him, and McGurk was calling to voice his displeasure about the latest article, 'A whodunnit for the rich and famous', which I had co-authored with my colleague Vanda Carson and had appeared in the paper that morning. It was our third story in a month focusing on the colourful criminal tapestry of McGurk's life, which appeared to be fraying at an alarming rate.

In a city obsessed with real estate and position, it was apt that at the heart of the Michael McGurk saga was a house. The house itself wasn't anything special – it had clearly seen better days – but the location was to die for. It just happened to have glorious views of the harbour and was located on the most expensive street in the country, Wolseley Road, Point Piper. Yet for some peculiar reason, the old mansion at 42a Wolseley Road was the subject of a flurry of lawsuits as well as a firebombing.

The house had once been owned by extraordinarily wealthy property developer Ron Medich and his wife, Odetta. Without ever living in it, the Medichs had sold 42a to Sydney society couple Adam and Sally-Anne Tilley. The Medichs had lent the Tilleys the money to buy the house and when the Tilleys defaulted on the repayments, they were sued. But not by the Medichs. Curiously, it was McGurk who'd chased the Tilleys for the money. Subsequently McGurk had broadened his legal attack to rope in Adam's well-known brothers, Simon and Ben.

In January 2009 McGurk was charged with the firebombing of the house. However, as our article that August morning revealed, the firebombing and a raft of other criminal charges against McGurk had been dropped. In a sea of ever-shifting allegiances, Medich took over the pursuit of the Tilleys.

The real battle, however, was between former friends Ron Medich and Michael McGurk. By that August they were at each other's throats via armies of lawyers. Each claimed the other owed him millions of dollars and, much to Medich's fury, McGurk had won the early skirmishes. On top of his own legal bills totalling $850,000, Medich had been ordered to pay his nemesis's court costs of $70,000.

The numerous threads of McGurk's scheming were alluded to in our story, which also featured abandoned arson and assault charges, a lawsuit against one of the richest men in the world, dealings in Russia, legal threats against former New South Wales premier Neville Wran and McGurk's extensive and ongoing court battles with Ron Medich.

That August morning McGurk, who had been seething at the beginning of the call, soon got his emotions in check. He indicated that he didn't give a toss about being described as a 'lender of last resort' or a would-be arsonist. He was, however, indignant at the suggestion that Ron Medich, his former business partner, was being portrayed as the victim. It was Medich I should be investigating, said McGurk, not him.

This wasn't the first time I'd heard this from McGurk. 'I don't think you understand what this guy is like and what he is capable of doing,' he said now with some vehemence.[1] He then told me that Medich had a 'hit' out on him and that Medich's lieutenant Lucky Gattellari was going to make sure the contract killing happened.

I thought McGurk was embellishing these supposed threats in order to eke out his revenge on Medich by manipulating me into writing another story. I didn't know at the time that he had only ten days left to live. Not only had I been forewarned of his murder, I had been given the key to the identity of his assassins.

Tersely, I told him that we couldn't write a story on his unproven allegations and that if he had something concrete he should give it to me. He promised to deliver me a tape recording by the end of the week that would reveal that Ron Medich was involved in bribing politicians, government officials and councillors to smooth the way for developments. He said the tape could bring down the government. I took this with a grain of salt. It sounded about as credible as his murder by contract killing.

Numerous attempts by Vanda and me to reach McGurk for comment before publication of our first article had failed. Even his mate Big Jim Byrnes didn't have his latest number; he muttered that McGurk was changing phones and numbers so often it was becoming impossible for people to keep track of him. This is exactly what McGurk was hoping to achieve.

McGurk's bail conditions for his assault and arson charges had been changed for a week from 19 July. He'd been given permission to report to police at Jindabyne, the closest town to the New South Wales ski resort of Perisher, where he'd taken his family for a holiday. It was later revealed that there was a plan to murder McGurk while he was at the snow, but the hitmen couldn't get themselves organised in time. Instead, on 24 July 2009, his last day at the resort, McGurk found himself on the front page of the *Herald*. Titled 'Point Piper feud, a fire bomb and a $17 million lawsuit', the story detailed an extraordinary chain of events embroiling some famous families. 'On one side of the stoush are the Tilley family brothers Ben, Adam and Simon. On the other is *BRW*'s rich-lister Ron Medich and his

wife, Odetta. Also caught up is Ron Medich's former associate Michael McGurk, who has been charged with firebombing
the house at the centre of the dispute, a charge he intends to
defend,' the article read.

McGurk assured his friends at the snow that there was
nothing to the story and that the charges wouldn't stick. The
way things turned out, it might have been better for him if they
had stuck.

When McGurk returned from his slope-side jaunt, he
received the messages we'd left at his office and with his associates. No doubt he was unhappy with the story, but he didn't
let on. Instead, with the con artist's supreme confidence in his
sales pitch, he said he wanted to meet in person. There was a far
bigger story, he said, but one that could not be discussed over the
phone. Could we have lunch?

On 29 July, Vanda and I met McGurk for lunch at Mad Cow
in the city. Wearing a well-cut navy suit and a crisp white open-
neck shirt, McGurk, who was fashionably late, slid into our
booth, which was upholstered in white leather dimpled with
canary yellow buttons.

Despite his recent holiday at the snow, his complexion had
a sallow tinge, and his receding greying hair and the hint of
jowls along his jawline made him seem older than his claimed
45 years.

Although we'd been told McGurk was furious about having
his alleged penchant for negotiation via firebombing splashed
across the front page of the Herald, he was charm personified.
Over the years I have dealt with my fair share of spivs and urgers,
and it was clear to me he was hoping to use us to his advantage.
If he could just turn our attention to the ill deeds of his adver-
sary, Ron Medich, there might be some upside in this for him.

His travails hadn't affected his appetite. He ordered the most
expensive item on the menu – the $68 Wagyu sirloin – and a
fine bottle of white wine. McGurk, who'd been to rehab several
times for drug and alcohol abuse, didn't touch a drop.

The first thing he asked was whether we were recording the
conversation. Although it struck me as odd at the time, given

his propensity for secret recordings I later wondered whether *he* had taped our conversation. Once we'd assured him that there were no secret recorders, McGurk embarked on a long explanation as to why Vanda and I were focusing our attention on the wrong person.

For the next hour or so he detailed a litany of complicated deals, dodgy developments and double crosses. Trusts, percentage points, foreign mining plays, caveats, put and call options were all terms that rolled easily off McGurk's tongue. His voice sounded like he'd once been a two-packets-a-day smoker who gargled rocks for breakfast. His accent was hard to pinpoint. His intonation seemed to be more East London cockney than Scottish brogue. McGurk's almost 20 years in Australia had added a mix of unmistakably flat Aussie drawl, most noticeably his pronunciation of his favourite word – 'dollar'.

As we ate, he was reluctant to talk about the widely rumoured existence of a tape recording. In the four days since our first story had appeared, numerous people had rung to tell us about the existence of this mysterious tape. When I asked McGurk about the recording, he took a sip of his mineral water and tried to change the subject. We persisted, recounting the various versions that had been related to us, in the hope that he would offer to set the record straight. He remained tight-lipped. The only thing he confirmed was that he had legally recorded his one-time friend and business partner Ron Medich. He couldn't help but add that there was some amazing material involving Medich's own corruption on the tape. He promised when the time was right he would provide us with a copy of the recording.

In the meantime he gave us a list of names of business and political figures and suspect deals that were worth looking at. I jotted down notes. He specified several New South Wales Labor politicians and one federal politician. Among the state Labor politicians he mentioned was Eddie Obeid. (Several years later Obeid was declared corrupt and, at the time of writing, the former Labor powerbroker is in prison for misconduct in public office.)

In particular McGurk advised us to concentrate on land the Medich brothers had bought from the CSIRO at Badgerys Creek. Ron and his younger brother, Roy, stood to make $400 million if this land was rezoned, he said. Lang Walker, another developer, had offered the brothers that amount but it was conditional on rezoning. McGurk also claimed that the former controversial Labor senator-turned-lobbyist Graham Richardson was on the Medichs' payroll and that Ron and Richardson occasionally lunched together at Tuscany, an Italian restaurant below Ron's office in Leichhardt.

According to McGurk, the rezoning of the Medichs' Badgerys Creek land had hit a snag, though, because Ron had 'blabbed'. Just who Ron had blabbed to or when he had blabbed was something McGurk was not keen on revealing.

After draining the remains of his hot chocolate, and making no mention of the bill, he stood to leave. He promised he would have further information for us soon.

As we waited to pay, Vanda and I chewed over possible scenarios as to how McGurk could have legally taped Medich discussing his involvement in political corruption. Who in their right mind would agree to such a thing?

That afternoon, McGurk rang me with a funny story he'd heard about Medich being set upon by his wife, Odetta, after she'd sprung him chatting to a young blonde the previous Saturday night. And by the way, we should pay close attention to Ron's associate Lucky Gattellari. If we ever wanted to find Lucky and Ron, we only need hang around outside their favourite brothel, Babylon in Chinatown, which they frequented most afternoons, McGurk said.

The following day he rang me again. This time the bonhomie was absent. 'Who did you tell that you were having lunch with me? Who did you tell?' McGurk's gravelly voice was frantic and angry. Within hours of the lunch, he said, someone had broken into his house and ransacked the joint. They were obviously looking for something. 'Things are getting out of control,' he said, his usual bluster momentarily gone.

He was rattled enough to go to the police – this was the second break-in, his office having been done over earlier that month. He also told them of a curious incident a few weeks before, when he'd seen two suspicious characters in a silver hatchback near his house. He wasn't to know how close he'd come to being murdered that night by the occupants of the hatchback.

McGurk was unnerved by the break-in and he was clearly worried that someone knew he was talking to journalists. That same day he rang his solicitor, Richard Allsop, and asked for an urgent meeting. McGurk walked the short distance from his office to Allsop's, which was on the seventeenth floor of Angel Place, a smart city tower that was home to lawyers, insurance and investment companies.

Allsop, the brother of the Chief Justice of the Federal Court, James Allsop, had had his share of interesting clients over the years but nothing had prepared him for a character as complex or as cunning as Michael McGurk.

McGurk handed him a sealed envelope, telling him that it contained a digital recording of explosive information about Medich paying money to government officials. As he handed over the envelope, McGurk warned Allsop not to open it, and to keep it somewhere safe as certain people were desperate to get their hands on it.

A former solicitor of McGurk, Andrew Williams, had also been given a copy of the recording back in February. Williams, a fast-talking, wisecracking solicitor originally from the Southern Highlands, was one of the merry-go-round of lawyers whom McGurk used, abused and didn't pay.

Williams had been fired in March when Medich's lawyers had made a pre-emptive strike, freezing McGurk's assets. McGurk was furious – this could have sent him to the wall. Although the orders were overturned, McGurk axed Williams and refused to pay the $120,000 he owed the lawyer's firm.

It was late in the afternoon on Thursday, 3 September 2009 when Williams was called out of a meeting in Brisbane. McGurk was on the phone, he was told, and his former client said it was urgent. Williams hadn't heard from McGurk for almost two months and because he'd been chasing him for fees he took the call.

McGurk was upbeat. 'Mate, mate, I really want to get together to talk about this money I owe you.'[2]

Naturally, Williams greeted the suggestion with enthusiasm. 'That'd be great. I'd really like to do that, Michael, I'd really like to sort it out. How have you been?'

In the circumstances, not so bad, said McGurk. He suggested they meet up the following morning. Williams explained he was in Brisbane but said they could speak first thing Monday morning to arrange a time. 'Yeah, mate, not a problem,' said McGurk and the pair enjoyed a laugh about something.

It was one of the last calls McGurk made.

Not long after dawn the following morning Williams was woken in his hotel room by a call from his personal assistant. 'Have you seen the news?' she asked. 'McGurk's been shot outside his home.'[3] Williams was stunned. He worked out that McGurk had called him only 20 to 30 minutes before his murder.

Williams arrived back in Sydney on the Friday night, surprised that police had not contacted him. Surely his number would've come up on McGurk's phone records. Then again Williams had seen McGurk on numerous occasions when he was juggling four different mobile phones and a pocketful of SIM cards.

On Saturday morning Williams called in at his regular café for his morning coffee. He picked up the *Herald* and almost choked when he saw the headline across the front page: 'It could bring down the government: secret tape blamed for killing'. Saturday's *Daily Telegraph* also screamed, 'Did he know too much? – execution bombshell: political corruption claims'.

Williams recoiled. He recalled McGurk telling him the recording was 'really hot' when he'd handed it over. McGurk had told him it was audio of Ron Medich, it was explosive, and the government could fall if it was ever made public.

'I thought if somebody has pissed someone off enough that there has been an Italian-style hit in broad daylight in Mosman, on a Thursday afternoon, in front of a kid, there's some seriously ugly people involved in this.'[4] He called a colleague who, months earlier, had spent five hours trying to transcribe the tape before she passed it over to someone else as the audio quality was so poor.

They agreed that they had to go to the police. But Williams was worried that the murderer could be keeping tabs on who was going in and out of North Sydney Police Station, where the homicide investigation was based. He rang his mate Robert Newlinds, SC, who had once acted for McGurk. Newlinds brokered a deal with police to meet Williams in a park in the nearby suburb of Waverton at 1 pm that day. Williams handed over the disc. No one asked about his conversation with McGurk just before his death or why McGurk had wanted to see him so urgently.

Of all the dirty little secrets that McGurk took to his grave, the existence of a supposedly explosive tape recording involving Medich and corrupt politicians and planning officials was without doubt the worst kept. For months rumours of it had been swirling in the groups in which Medich, McGurk and the Tilleys moved.

But would someone kill for it?

CHAPTER 4

McGURK'S EARLY YEARS

Michael Loch McGurk was born in Edinburgh at 2.20 am on 26 January 1964.[1] He was delivered in Eastern General Hospital, which was built in 1907 as a poor house and hospital, and was taken home to a one-bedroom flat in a tenement building in the docklands of Leith, an underprivileged district in the north of the city.

There were 16 families living at 9 Graham Street, four to a floor. The conditions were primitive, one bedroom and a kitchen, with McGurk's parents sleeping in a recess off the kitchen that was only wide enough for a double bed. There was no heating and no hot water, unless you were lucky enough to have a gas water system above the sink in the kitchen. Bathing was done in a tin on a Sunday night.

Michael's father, Eddie, a builder's labourer, was a hard man, prone to violent rages when he got on the grog. Graham Street, where the McGurks' block of flats was situated, had a shop on one corner and on the other a pub, which Eddie frequented all too often. A train line ran behind one side of the street, and the polluted Water of Leith, a small river which flows through to the sea, lay behind the other side.

Michael's two older brothers, Jake and Eddie, were twelve- and eight-year-olds when Michael was born, and were less than happy about having to make room for the howling brat their mother brought home from hospital. The stress of a crying baby further fractured the already troubled marriage between Eddie and his wife, Jane, and in 1966, when Michael was two, his mother took him to Glasgow to live with a man called Bob Rushford. Her older two sons were left behind with their father. Two years later she had a fourth son, Bobby, who was known as 'Cymbals' because of his protruding ears. When McGurk was six, Jane changed their surname to Rushford.

One of McGurk's in-laws said that McGurk had spoken of a horrible childhood with his alcoholic mother. 'He told of he and his brothers having to live in a boys' home for a while, and once he ran away and walked miles to see his mother, who just yelled at him for showing up,' she recalled.[2]

McGurk's stepfather, Bob, decided to chance his arm in South Africa, but after four years working on the railways in Johannesburg, the Rushfords came back to Glasgow.

McGurk was a tearaway kid, whose big mouth and quick temper were constantly landing him in hot water. By the time teenager Michael returned from South Africa, his oldest brother, Jake, now in his mid-twenties, was a feared hardman known as 'Hatchet' Jake McGurk. Much later in life McGurk joked to a friend about 'sending his son to Glasgow to stay with his brother so he could steal cars, take drugs and discover what life was really like'.[3]

After leaving school McGurk started as an apprentice electrician with a local council in Glasgow, but an arrest for shoplifting and rubbing up some local heavies the wrong way saw him head off to Europe in a hurry. Friends recall the young McGurk telling them he had to wear a disguise when he returned home for his grandmother's funeral, knowing there were men who still wanted a piece of him.

After a stint selling timeshare apartments in Spain, McGurk landed a job as a Mercedes-Benz salesman in the German city of Kaiserslautern, or K-town as is it is referred to by the 50,000 American military personnel based there. When an American officer came in wanting to buy a car, McGurk told him there was a special deal: if he paid cash, he could have the Merc for half its regular price. The soldier came back with US$50,000 and McGurk took the money, caught a cab straight to the airport, chartered a small plane and flew to the south of France. He brought one of his brothers over from Scotland and they promptly blew the lot. McGurk was proud of his chutzpah and later told mates that his flagship Australian company Bentley Smythe was named after the guy he fleeced in K-town.

After ripping off American servicemen in Germany, McGurk flogged brick-sized mobile phones in Los Angeles, before arriving in Australia in 1990. He was using the name of Michael Rushford, though three years earlier he had been calling himself McGurk. He was 26; he had blown everything he had earned and he arrived in Sydney with just $50 to his name.

Three days after his twenty-seventh birthday, in January 1991, Michael Rushford applied for a job at ECC Lighting in Ultimo, on the fringes of Sydney's CBD. He had just been sacked from a salesman's job at the Jaguar dealership in Hornsby on the city's conservative north shore. Customers had complained that to close the deal McGurk would promise to throw in extras such as a sunroof or air-conditioning, but that having handed over the money, not only were there no extras but McGurk denied point-blank ever making such promises.

Although his sales history was dubious, McGurk was brimming with self-confidence at the prospect of selling light fittings. After his interview with ECC's manager, McGurk asked with a cheeky grin, 'Well, are you going to hire me or not? Here I am! What are you waiting for?'[4] Within hours he was back on the phone: 'What else can I tell you to convince you to give me the job?'[5] The manager was impressed with this remarkable self-assurance. 'This guy Michael Rushford is going to be an amazing salesman,' he told the staff after giving McGurk the job.[6]

The Electric Construction Company was a large, privately owned New Zealand company, established in 1909 by the Thorburn family. In 1988 the company set up ECC Lighting in Sydney, hoping to get a foothold in the Australian lighting market. The Thorburns were popular with their employees and ECC was regarded as a great place to work. Such was the camaraderie that every Friday, the 20 or so staff would gather for a drink after work.

The arrival of McGurk changed everything. Although he soon became management's golden boy, other staff members did not warm to him. Kathy Field was working in the accounts department when he arrived. 'I didn't like him from the outset. He was smarmy and cocky,' she said.[7]

'He was a really horrible person,' recalled Paul Jeffery, the warehouse manager, who shuddered at the recollection of dealing with McGurk.[8]

McGurk could be great fun and he certainly had the gift of the gab. He entertained his colleagues with tales of having to flee South Africa and some scam he'd pulled in New Zealand. But how much of it was true?

'Within weeks we realised he was just a pathological liar. He would say whatever he needed to say to move on to the next stage,' said Jeffery, who went as far as erecting a warning sign about McGurk in his office: 'Rule one: Never believe anything he says. Rule two: Never forget rule one.'[9]

For starters McGurk had lied about his driver's licence – he didn't have one even though it was essential for his job. As a salesman, McGurk was mostly out on the road, promoting ECC's products – high-quality domestic and commercial lights – to architects, designers and developers. Nor did anyone quite know what McGurk got up to out of the office. One staff member who lived on the northern beaches of Sydney was driving home when she saw an ECC van pulled over on the side of the road. The boot was open and McGurk was nonchalantly selling flowers out of the back of his work vehicle. When staff queried his sideline as a florist during work hours, McGurk thought it was a laugh. 'Australia is fantastic, people just want to give you money,' he said.[10] He marvelled that he could make up a price: most of his customers were too polite to quibble.

On another occasion he returned from Canberra with a black eye, claiming he had been robbed at an ATM machine. No one believed him.

One day immigration officials arrived at the office looking for McGurk. He had overstayed his visa. He left the country, travelling first to Fiji and then returning via New Zealand. Upon his return management called staff into a meeting and told them that Michael Rushford would from then on be known as Michael McGurk.

When McGurk landed the company a million-dollar lighting contract at the luxury ANA harbourside hotel in the tourist hub of The Rocks, near Circular Quay, his colleagues were horrified to hear what he had done to secure the contract. 'He was always getting information to gain leverage,' said Paul Jeffery. 'To him everything was a means to an end.' McGurk had befriended some of the young apprentice electricians at the hotel and taken them out drinking. He'd spun them yarns about how he'd clock off early, or pretend to work overtime. The apprentices reciprocated, sharing tales of how they used their mates to claim they were at work when they weren't. The next day McGurk dobbed them in to their boss and they were sacked. 'He got the information and then crucified them with it,' said Jeffery.[11]

At ECC Lighting, the staff were shocked. Was there nothing this man would not stoop to in order to get ahead? McGurk was able to switch on the charm for his superiors in an instant, but other people were simply a means to an end. It was clear to his colleagues he felt not one shred of remorse about the apprentices who'd lost their jobs because of his actions. Yet still management could not see that his charisma was superficial and his ambition ruthless.

When McGurk was caught cheating on his expenses, no action was taken. Salesmen at the lighting company were issued with a company American Express card, which could only be used for expenses relating to work, or for costs incurred while on the road. But rules meant nothing to McGurk. Not only did he bill ECC for his nights out on the town, he was also caught double-dipping. McGurk received hundreds of dollars in cash as advances for entertainment expenses. When asked to justify the advances, he produced a pile of dockets. Kathy Field smelled a rat. When she rang the various establishments where McGurk had been, she discovered that the company had already paid via McGurk's corporate Amex card. She reported the fraud to management but as far as Field was aware, McGurk talked his way out of it.

The final straw for Paul Jeffery was when McGurk convinced management to give him a key to the new warehouse in Pyrmont, where millions of dollars' worth of lighting stock was held. Jeffery resigned immediately because he knew what would happen. Sure enough, at the next stock-take the numbers did not add up. There was a massive amount of missing stock which could not be accounted for.

In April 1993 McGurk bought a house in Winslow Street, Kirribilli, for $415,000. To his colleagues the sums just didn't add up: he'd been on a salesman's salary for two years and he was partying like there was no tomorrow even though he was engaged. The following year he married Kimberley McDonald, who worked at Mansours, a curtains and cushions shop on the north shore that was owned by her brother-in-law's family. But neither wedded life nor a bout of cancer, which resulted in the removal of one testicle, slowed McGurk down. Quite the contrary.

One of his friends, who knew him when he was living in Kirribilli in 1994 and 1995, said the Scot's stomping ground was the formerly working-class suburb of Balmain, and in particular the Cricketers Arms Hotel. At the time, the Cricketers Arms was a popular watering hole for petty crims and expat Poms. Even the bar's owner, Barry Wilson, was up to no good. Wilson, a mate of McGurk, went to jail in 1994 after he was busted for the brazen theft of two pallets of Westpac travellers cheques, worth $32 million, which he was getting mates to cash back in the Old Dart.

The friend recalled that on one occasion McGurk 'bought a massive amount of cocaine in a block for about $7000. I walked into the men's toilets at the Cricketers Arms and McGurk was holding the block under the hand-dryer frantically trying to dry it,' he said. 'It turned out he had accidentally dropped it in the toilet while he tried to cut it up.'[12]

McGurk's reputation among fellow drinkers was as a wide boy and a manipulator. He could be charming and fun but would then ask for favours and rarely repay them. 'He used to say, "If you do this for me I will do this for you," but he never came through on his end of the bargain,' said the friend.[13] Even McGurk's best mate, Frank Burke, used to admonish him: 'Why do you push people the wrong way so they hate you, when you are a nice bloke and could actually have people liking you?'[14]

For years McGurk's partners in crime were Burke, an impish, gregarious green-eyed Scouser who had emigrated from Liverpool, and a fellow Scot, Hamish Flucker Williamson, a small, solid man, always quick to laugh. Williamson could pass for your friendly suburban butcher, offering an unbeatable bargain on sausages.

'The Three Amigos', as they dubbed themselves, were rogues well known around the pubs of Balmain. 'Ah, fook it,' Burke was fond of saying, 'Let's go and get on the piss.'[15] McGurk would peel off hundred-dollar notes to shout drinks for the countless girls they chatted up. 'There was nothing like us on the make,' said Williamson.[16] The trio would jokingly introduce themselves as Fabulous Frank, Marvellous Mick and Handsome Hamish, Burke said, and they would end up 'partying for days on the run'. He recalled one time they'd ended up in the main street of Balmain at 5 am. The three just lay there 'laughing our heads off' until they fell asleep. When they woke it had been raining and on getting to their feet they found a dry outline of the patches on which they had crashed in their drunken stupor.

One of McGurk's favourite spots was Joanna's, a table-top strip club in a down-at-heel neighbourhood in the inner-city suburb of Surry Hills. One friend, who described the strippers at Joanna's as 'smoking hot', said McGurk always had girls with him, 'and they weren't always prostitutes'. His friend said, 'He was such a charmer that the girls from Joanna's, after they finished work, would go out to nightclubs with him.'[17]

McGurk sometimes took them to the Byblos nightclub in Darlinghurst, where he would claim he was a silent partner. 'He'd tell the girls what they wanted to hear,' laughed the friend. 'I could only go out partying with him once a fortnight or once a month. I couldn't keep up with him. He was like a whirlwind – if you went out with him, you'd be out for days on end.'[18]

Both Williamson and Burke recalled times when a tearful Kimberley would arrive on their doorsteps looking for her errant husband. After his coke- and champagne-fuelled all-nighters, McGurk would lie to his wife, saying he'd been interstate. He would go to a mate's menswear store in Redfern, which sold expensive suits at a discount, and simply buy a new suit and shirt and drop the incriminating clothes off to be laundered. But that sneaky little trick ended when McGurk didn't pay the huge bill he'd run up at the shop.

McGurk did come under suspicion for stealing from ECC's warehouse, but not before he had managed to squeeze a $50,000 advance on his salary out of the lighting company. He had also persuaded his bosses to sign bank documents fraudulently inflating his salary in order to get the bank to loan him money to buy the house in Kirribilli. But when McGurk was pressed for repayment, ECC finally saw what their staff had been trying to tell them. He was fired on 3 August 1993.

In a pattern that he was to repeat for the rest of his life, the betrayal of those who had gone out of their way to help him was compounded when McGurk instigated legal action in an attempt to buttress his crooked deals. When ECC sued him for the $50,000, McGurk counter-sued, saying that his advance was really a bonus and that he was entitled to $95,000. His boss was appalled. In 1996 the New South Wales Supreme Court ruled against McGurk. He failed to produce any documents and the court found his evidence 'unsatisfactory'.[19] With interest added, McGurk was ordered to repay ECC almost $70,000. Not satisfied, he tried his hand in the Federal Court. His case was thrown out and he was criticised for abusing the system.

'He was a Scottish Arthur Daley,' a friend said, referring to the unscrupulous wheeler-dealer in the British television series *Minder*. McGurk was always trying to ingratiate himself with others, flashing his money around and constantly big-noting himself. 'In the end I got sick of bailing him out of fights.' He realised, 'This guy is bad news.'[20]

After being fired from ECC Lighting, in 1994 McGurk established his own lighting shop, Winslows in Edgecliff Road, Woollahra. But the mundanity and responsibility of being a small-business owner did not suit the natural-born hustler at all. One of the things McGurk hated more than anything else was boredom, so after only three years he put the lighting shop on the market. The accounts were enhanced and McGurk rounded up Burke and Williamson and his other Pommy mates from Balmain to impress potential buyers with what appeared to be a thriving business.

He then used his networking skills to move on to something else. 'He was the consummate networker; he was just everywhere. If you ever said to Michael, "Do you know so-and-so?" if he didn't know them and he thought it was important, within forty-eight hours he had rung them up,' said a friend. He was persistent too. 'If they didn't take his call twenty times, he would call them twenty-one times. That's the sort of guy he was, absolutely determined.'[21]

Another one of McGurk's abilities was to sniff out who was who in the zoo. 'Every time he would walk into a room of people, he would work out who was the boss cocky and work on him. He had a fair bit of native Scottish cunning in him,' said a friend.[22]

Late in 1994, McGurk had heard on the grapevine that there was a business going cheap because its owner was stricken with terminal cancer. McGurk held out for a bargain basement price, sure that the vendor's limited life expectancy would work to his advantage. He was short of cash, having just bought Winslows, so he convinced three mates to stump up the $100,000 for the company, which manufactured steel handrails – something McGurk had no experience in, not that that fazed him. He borrowed his own $25,000 stake from another friend.

The business failed before the year was out and McGurk, who'd only repaid his mate a fraction of his quarter share, was already on to something new.

In 1995 Burke, who was a union delegate on a construction site, told McGurk there were some deals to be had over at a warehouse conversion in Pyrmont; McGurk talked his way into supplying whitegoods, furniture and curtains to the newly renovated apartments in the historic former Goldsbrough Mort building in Pyrmont. He would sell 'packages' to the new owners in the building, offering a discounted rate for fixtures and fittings as well as supplying refrigerators, ovens and dishwashers. He also ran a scam whereby, after supplying the whitegoods to the apartments, he arranged for them to be stolen. He would make an insurance claim and re-sell the 'stolen' goods.

Around this time McGurk met real estate agent Justin Brown, who was selling the units off the plan. Brown and McGurk got on: they were both ambitious, they liked to party hard and were salesmen with the gift of the gab. Brown introduced McGurk to South African-born Greg Magree, who was marketing the 45-storey apartment tower The Peak in nearby Chinatown. Magree and McGurk became friendly and McGurk bought nine Goldsbrough Mort apartments on spec, hoping he would make a few dollars as the property market rose. Because of his customary stretched financial position, McGurk used a put and call option. This means that you 'put' a deposit down – say 5 per cent – with the agreement – or 'call' – to pay the agreed price at a specified date. If the price falls, you lose your 5 per cent. But if it rises you can buy it for your 'call' price and then on-sell it yourself for much more. It allowed gamblers like McGurk, who never had the money, to bet on the next sure thing. McGurk boasted to his friends at the time that it was a 'great buy' and he was going to make a motza out of it.

McGurk kept some of the Goldsbrough apartments for years – his mother later stayed in one when she visited from Scotland – and he used them as crash pads after his all-night benders when he didn't want to go home to face a furious Kimberley.

While he was working at the Goldsbrough he attempted to make amends with a former business partner from the failed handrail company. He told this man he was putting a lot of curtains in the Goldsbrough apartments, so he could pay him back in curtains. But for the second time the man ended up out of pocket as McGurk only partially paid the curtain people, leaving his mate to stump up the remaining money owed.

McGurk continued to party. He would fly to the casinos in Cairns or on the Gold Coast at a moment's notice, get drunk and behave in an outrageous fashion, throwing furniture off a hotel balcony, destroying rooms and the like. 'He just had a wild spark in him,' an old friend said. 'Once he started drinking he would go crazy.'[23]

He was also an incorrigible playboy. 'Mick played up with the sheilas,' laughed Frank Burke. On one occasion when he was drunk, McGurk tried to chat up a gorgeous Norwegian girl at the Riverview Hotel in Balmain, Burke recalled. The woman's husband, who played rugby league for the Balmain Tigers, responded by breaking McGurk's nose. Hamish Williamson said, 'He had affairs – just one night stands. He'd be on a girl like a rat up a drainpipe if he got half a chance.'

When McGurk had money he was compulsively generous. 'Champagne Charlie, he was. He wanted everybody to have a good time,' said Williamson. 'And it wasn't just a cheap drop, it was vintage Moët at $300 a bottle.'[24] He once ran into some young Scottish backpackers at the pub who'd had their money stolen. McGurk told them to come round to his office next morning, where he gave them $10,000.

He had a constant supply of the party drug ecstasy. Friends saw him with up to 70 tablets at a time. He boasted that he organised importations through the airport, with couriers concealing the drugs in shampoo bottles, though nothing of the sort has ever been proven. Cocaine, however, was his drug of choice. Burke, Williamson and McGurk were once partying at a Melbourne nightclub when McGurk drunkenly demanded that one of the bouncers find some coke for them. The man refused but McGurk persisted and, with a fight brewing, his two mates had to drag him away.

Twice McGurk underwent the three-week drug and alcohol rehab program at the St John of God Hospital in Burwood, in Sydney's inner west. On his release he attended Alcoholics Anonymous with his customary – but temporary – zeal. During his bouts of sobriety he would stick to V energy drinks, but sooner or later he'd fall off the wagon, his poor impulse control and thrill-seeking behaviour always getting the better of him. With Burke and Williamson willing accomplices, the Three Amigos would lurch off on another ill-advised drunken adventure. Life for the two Scots and the Scouser from Liverpool was fun. 'There were thousands of occasions we have been laughing that much, you just couldn't laugh anymore. Screaming. We were sitting in First Class screaming laughing, and we were not on drugs or nothing, we were just taking the piss, laughing at whoever we were talking about,' said Burke.[25]

Although McGurk missed the birth of his third child because he was on a bender, Williamson said that he was a great dad when he was actually home, 'but the rest of the time he was on the bottle with us. He could drink for days and days. And then just quit and that was the end of it until the next time'.[26]

McGurk had little regard for the law. His driving record was atrocious. 'He drove like a madman. One time I went with him to the airport, and it took just ten minutes from his office to the airport,' said a former employee of the usual half-hour trip.

'He would zigzag between lanes and cross over double yellow lines. He would absolutely fucking fly. Like, ninety in a fifty zone.'[27]

Williamson told me that on one occasion McGurk asked him if he could sign over three points from his driving licence, saying that Kimberley had been caught speeding in a school zone. The next thing Williamson knew his driver's licence had been cancelled – he'd lost all his points. 'They gave it back because I was able to prove I was out of the country,' he said. The Roads and Traffic Authority (RTA) urged Williamson to report the matter to the police if he became aware of the culprit.

McGurk had a similar disregard for parking fines. Williamson recalled being in McGurk's Mercedes and noticing his registration sticker was half off and out of date. He told McGurk he'd have to get a new one. McGurk muttered, 'I'll get round to it.'

'The same day, he got stopped in College Street [in Sydney's CBD]. The cops took the plates off and said, "If you move that car, I'll be coming to see you at your house and I'll arrest you." He hadn't paid registration, fines, speeding tickets, camera offences.'[28]

His car was towed away and McGurk ended up paying $5700 in fines.

McGurk cheated at everything, even at sport. Frank Burke described a period when he and the Scot were playing golf every morning at Lane Cove Golf Club instead of going into the office like other north shore dads. 'We used to cheat that much, we would be screaming at each other,' said Burke. 'Every day we would say: "No cheating today, eh, we have to play properly," and I would either catch him cheating, or he would catch me cheating – we couldn't help it,' chortled Burke.[29]

Williamson was the inspiration behind one of McGurk's earliest get-rich-quick schemes: three-dimensional 'holographic' sporting cards. Williamson, a printer by trade, showed McGurk a prototype. When the card was tilted, the image moved. It could show a cricketer hitting a ball or a soccer player kicking a goal. McGurk thought they were brilliant and quickly made big plans to go global with them. Every kid would be digging to the bottom of their breakfast cereal box to get this action card of their sporting hero, figured McGurk. He persuaded cricket legend Tony Greig to come on board, but Greig soon realised McGurk was all hot air and the pair fell out. So instead Williamson and McGurk decided to go to the US to take their proposals to Upper Deck, a giant manufacturer of baseball cards.

In 1998 Williamson and McGurk flew to Los Angeles to talk to Upper Deck. McGurk had invested US$100,000 in the deal, much of it borrowed from Williamson's then girlfriend, Jill Taylor. However, their seed capital trickled away and Upper Deck wasn't interested.

McGurk was convinced – wrongly – that one of Williamson's Scottish mates, Sean McDonald, who had also been roped into the sporting card proposition, had ripped them off. He demanded McDonald return their investment money. McDonald not only refused but infuriated McGurk when he said something along the lines of, 'It'll be a cold day in hell when you get your money back.' McGurk leapt across the desk and punches flew. 'It was a good old-fashioned Glasgow fight,' said Williamson, chuckling at the memory.

According to Williamson, McGurk was always ready to take a dispute to a whole other level. In this case McGurk arranged for someone back in Scotland to put an empty petrol can on the bonnet of McDonald's brother-in-law's car with a note saying 'If your brother-in-law doesn't pay the money, your car will get torched'.

McGurk and Williamson did, however, manage to make some money out of the cards when they returned to Australia: they lined up a meeting with cereal company Uncle Tobys and signed a deal for $480,000. No sooner had McGurk got his hands on the $80,000 advance than he made one of his grand gestures, shouting the bar at the Sir William Wallace Hotel in Balmain.

Jill Taylor never did get her money back from McGurk.

A central figure in McGurk's life around this time was an unassuming disability pensioner, Richie Vereker. With his polyester shirts and loose cardigans, and a habit of wearing his glasses tucked into the front of his v-neck jumpers, Vereker flaunted a slightly shambolic untidiness reminiscent of John Mortimer's Rumpole of the Bailey. Certainly his penchant for a glass of plonk any time, night or day, was a characteristic shared by Rumpole.

Vereker's career as a conversationalist and relationship manager was a seven-day-a-week job. On Sundays he was found at 'choir practice', the tongue-in-cheek name given to his drinking group, which comprised lawyers, police and doctors. Apart from being a great raconteur and good fun, Vereker was one of Sydney's great facilitators. He knew everyone from the local councillor to senior Labor figures, including powerbroker Graham Richardson. His favourite watering holes were a trio of Sydney's eastern suburbs pubs – the Lord Dudley in Woollahra, the Bellevue in Paddington and the Woollahra Hotel. Drink coasters were handy to jot down the odd reminder or two, and there was always a quiet table for those confidential sessions during which Vereker advised his clients how to get things done on the QT.

James Richard Vereker was born in March 1941 – although some corporate records also list his birthday as April 1944 and 1940 – in Wollongong, a working-class Labor town where life once revolved around the steel mills and pubs. He came from a long line of Wollongong butchers, and followed his family into the meat industry, opening a string of butcheries round the town before running butcheries in the upmarket food halls of David Jones department stores.

Vereker owned the Oxford Hotel in Wollongong, from which a large SP bookmaker operation ran. Everyone who mattered – the police, union officials and the ALP heavyweights – were always looked after when they came to Vereker's pub. To Vereker one good turn deserved another – that's just the way things worked in the Gong.

Vereker's hobnobbing at the race tracks, where he had his own stint as a bookmaker, brought him an array of connections. He went into business with Ernie Smith, brother of the late legendary trainer Tommy Smith, and big punter Lionel Abrahams. Other business partners of Vereker were his racing mate, the well-known ad man John Singleton, and stockbroker Rene Rivkin, who later went to jail for insider trading. Their company, Aussie Pubs, owned a chain of pubs from as far afield as Mount Isa in outback Queensland to the Lake Jindabyne Hotel in the Snowy Mountains. But despite the joke that you can't go broke selling beers to Aussies, the hotel partnership was not a success and by the early 1990s Vereker was in financial trouble. In 1992 his meat supply business, Trendall Pty Ltd, which was based in Marrickville in Sydney's inner west, went into liquidation with debts of more than a million dollars, a sizeable portion of which was owed to the tax office.

In mid-1993 Vereker and his son, Trent, departed for Hungary to sell 'Aussie pies'. Sadly Hungary's appetite was for goulash not meat pies, and father and son were soon back.[30] On standby to lend a helping hand on their return were Richie's brother, solicitor Tony Vereker, and the property developer Bob Ell, whom Vereker had met in the 1970s when their sons were at school together.

As he held court in his favourite watering holes in Paddington and Woollahra, Vereker would receive a steady parade of people asking him to have a quiet word in a particular MP's ear, or to make an introduction to one of his pals with money. The extent of his network was illustrated by the experience of one business figure who recalled being invited to lunch by Vereker. Also in attendance was a senior manager with the City of Sydney Council and a retired police commissioner of dubious probity.

Vereker was friends with Kimberley McGurk's father, 'Fearless' Fred McDonald, a man with the gift of the gab and, like McGurk, a great salesman. Because of Vereker's connection to Kimberley's family, McGurk and he were close. Perhaps McGurk saw Vereker as a father figure. When Vereker suffered a stroke in 1998, which left him partially paralysed, McGurk visited him in hospital daily and offered him a place to work after his lengthy recuperation.

McGurk's affection towards Richie Vereker was understood and appreciated by McGurk's in-laws. Vereker was often spotted in the Bowlers' Club, an RSL-style social club in the city, sometimes alone, enjoying a quiet mid-morning beer. He would then catch the lift to McGurk's office on the ninth floor of the same building, where, fortified by grog, he would make cold calls about whatever scheme he had on the boil.

It was Vereker who was instrumental in providing McGurk with an introduction that would make the Scot – momentarily – seriously well-off. Part-way through the summer of 1997–98, McGurk was on the hunt for his next get-rich-quick scheme, when he was told about a place at 99 York Street that seemed to fit the bill nicely. A massive fire in the 13-storey block three years before meant that the owners of the Bowlers' Club, based in the building, had decided to sell ten floors. McGurk became involved after Vereker introduced him to Rocky Massaria, the CEO of the Bowlers' Club and a former head of the IT department at the New South Wales police. Massaria had approached Vereker to see if he could find a developer willing to buy the floors. By the time Vereker approached McGurk, he had already shopped the deal around to developers Bob Ell, Jackie Waterhouse and Robert Whyte, but none of them was interested. Then Vereker introduced McGurk to Waterhouse, who had property holdings in western Sydney worth $500 million. McGurk borrowed a deposit of $100,000 from Waterhouse through real estate financier Simon Levingston, and once again employed the strategy of put and call options to secure the ten floors.

McGurk wasn't exactly an obvious choice to buy the space. He didn't have any money or any experience as a developer. But he didn't give a damn about rules or regulations or ruining other people, and that made this the perfect business transaction for him.

Once McGurk had control of the Bowlers' Club building, he set to work breaking up the floors into offices and selling them off individually. He was able to use the money coming in from the sales to pay the Bowlers' Club for all ten floors. He ended up getting the floors for $18.5 million, a bargain. And the beauty of it was that he paid as he went. As he made money on one floor, he used it to buy the next.

It took him about a year to slice and dice the floors into offices and sell them off, and he maximised his returns by doing up each storey on the cheap, whacking in some partitions, and then selling off individual offices.

One of those working with McGurk was interior decorator Frank Slowiak, who installed partitions and walls for McGurk. Slowiak charged McGurk $12,000 for his work, but his requests for payment were studiously ignored by McGurk. Finally Slowiak decided to go down to York Street and ask the wily Scot for the money in person. When he politely inquired when McGurk was going to pay him, McGurk said calmly, 'I'm not going to pay you, and I will show you why.' He gestured for Slowiak to walk with him down a secluded corridor and then, looking him right in the eye, said, 'Look, mate, the reason I'm not paying you is I don't have to.'[31]

Slowiak was furious and told McGurk he'd see him in court, before turning on his heels and walking away. The next thing he knew he'd been king-hit from behind. The force of McGurk's blow knocked him to the ground, shattering Slowiak's glasses. 'By the time I got my whereabouts back, he had scarpered down the firestairs,' Slowiak recounted.[32]

Slowiak reported McGurk to the police and made a statement about the assault. But before charges were laid, McGurk's lawyer arranged for his client to pay Slowiak what he owed as well as interest, in exchange for Slowiak agreeing not to pursue the case.

As McGurk was in the middle of doing his office subdivisions in the building, he had one of his crazy ideas. His children's parties were something that he organised with great gusto. They were over the top and, more importantly, 'Everything was always bigger and better than everyone else's,' said a fellow parent.[33]

Towards the end of 2001 McGurk's eldest son was turning six. McGurk had eight go-karts shipped to the vacant top floor of the York Street building. The vast expanse of empty office space was transformed into a dodgem car circuit. The go-karts, with their big rubber tyres and roll bars, were the real deal. For the kids, it was pure magic. They smashed into each other and into the walls, leaving behind great black streaks where their tyres had gouged the walls.

'Michael was completely unconcerned by any damage that was occurring to the building,' said one of the parents. 'There were also some big rubber balls . . . Michael had this idea that there would be some kind of team ball game that involved the kids trying to move the ball around by bouncing it off the front of the go-kart.'[34]

'The party was out of the stratosphere in terms of novelty, fun and excitement,' said the parent.

It was not so much fun for others who had to deal with McGurk in the York Street building. He was a law unto himself. He didn't bother seeking permission of the owners' corporation when he made changes to the offices. He kept keys to people's offices, which worried some of the tenants, and at one point he blocked access to one of the floors after a fight with people on that floor.

Those close to the York Street deals say that McGurk bribed council workers for approvals to subdivide and sell off the offices as individual lots. The agent managing the sales was McGurk's old mate Justin Brown, whom he'd met during the Goldsbrough deal. Ninety-nine York Street was not a premier location, but it was only a block from the CBD's Queen Victoria Building and within walking distance of the major department stores. Demand for office space was good, and once McGurk had split up the offices in the building, he made a smart $7 million profit. Not bad for a boy from Glasgow.

The York Street deal was his first big break. He wanted everyone to know about the serious money he'd made. His excesses became even more extreme – this is when he bought his Mercedes convertible, hardly a sensible choice for a father of four small children.

But, again, McGurk had made the money at the expense of others. He had cut corners with the office construction by rounding up his mates from the pub and paying them a pittance to do work for which they were completely unqualified. Other tradesmen weren't paid at all. The wiring was done on the cheap, so for years afterwards there were disputes over the electricity bills. His Pommy mates put up dividing walls that didn't comply with council fire regulations. When you were supposed to use 16-millimetre gyprock, he told them 10 millimetres would do. When you were supposed to use fire-rated steel, he used non-fire-rated steel. When you were supposed to insulate the walls, he didn't bother. He knew what the requirements were, but if it saved him money by not doing it, he wouldn't do it.

Another person McGurk broke a promise to was Simon Levingston. Levingston had organised the seed capital for McGurk's deal on the Bowlers' Club and the agreement was that the pair would split the $7 million profit, with 45 per cent to go to Levingston and 55 to McGurk. But, as was his way, McGurk reneged on the deal. Once more, the dispute ended up in court. McGurk threatened to have Levingston run over with a car, but Levingston refused to back down. He maintained that McGurk had engaged in misleading and deceptive conduct by setting up a number of related entities and channelling the profits from the strata subdivision into those companies rather than giving Levingston his share. For his part, McGurk told the court that the 'horse had bolted' and it was too late to pay Levingston.[35]

Justice Brian Tamberlin of the Federal Court did not agree and in September 1998 he granted Levingston an injunction, meaning McGurk was restrained from selling off any more of the cheap office subdivisions.

The most tragic fate of all the people McGurk ripped off was that of his own brother-in-law, Richard McDonald, the youngest child of Noreen and Fred McDonald. Richard grew up in the middle-class inner-west Sydney suburb of Drummoyne with his four siblings, Deborah, David, Virginia and Kimberley. According to a family member, while Noreen often boasted about introducing her once 'wild child' Kimberley to Michael, other members of the family were concerned about Kimberley's flashy husband. Was he importing drugs? 'There was always banter between us that he was up to no good,' said one relative.[36] The fact that McGurk was making so much money so fast was a constant source of family gossip.

Richard McDonald, a caterer by training, became the warehouse manager at ECC Lighting when McGurk was working there in the early 1990s. McDonald had also worked with him in his lighting shop in Woollahra. When McGurk took over the floors in the Bowlers' Club, McDonald was employed as the property manager, with the promise of $200,000 for his initial work on the building and a cut of the profit once the sales were complete. When Levingston sued McGurk, it transpired that McGurk had installed his brother-in-law as the director of the companies he was using to hide money from Levingston. McDonald told the court he had no idea who the shareholders of those companies were.

Despite being family, McGurk refused to pay McDonald. 'Michael gave excuse after excuse. I'm just waiting for this caveat to come off the house. This went on and on and on,' said a close friend of McDonald.[37] McGurk would often fly into a rage and be verbally abusive towards McDonald. He would disappear for days on end leaving McDonald to face angry tenants or people who were chasing McGurk for money. 'It was very stressful,' said his friend.[38]

Sometimes McDonald was so skint that he borrowed money from his partner, Rachel Lewy, and her family. Rachel kept pleading with him to cut his losses and walk away but McDonald felt he'd invested so much time and effort he couldn't. His friend remembered how upset McDonald became when he found out that Richie Vereker had been paid $50,000 in cash and given an office in the York Street building despite McGurk telling McDonald there was no money available.

A relative recalled Richard and Rachel's anger on another occasion when they went to a family barbecue at the McGurks' Cranbrook Avenue house and saw major renovations were going on. 'So there was obviously money to support their life-style, but not to pay his brother-in-law,' said the relative.[39] And McDonald's friend recalled how furious Rachel's mother was when Kimberley turned up to a family function in a brand-new white Mercedes convertible, when McGurk had been telling McDonald that they were going through a slow patch money-wise.

In the end, the financial stress contributed to the breakdown of Rachel and McDonald's relationship and in 2003 McDonald left for South America to get away from it all.

'Everyone in the family knew McGurk had ripped him off. McDonald had gone to speak to Kimberley several times about it because he was really desperate. Before he went overseas, he managed to get $50,000 out of McGurk,' said the family member.[40]

McDonald went to Chile and then Bolivia to see Salar de Uyuni, the famous salt flats. He developed altitude sickness and when his condition deteriorated a Swiss tourist waited with him because he was unable to talk. She found a contact number for McDonald's sister, Deborah, and called Deborah to tell her that her brother was critically ill. The McDonald family tried to organise a helicopter to medi-vac him out but it was too late.

McDonald's mother, Noreen, was in Los Angeles on her way to South America to meet up with her son when he died. McGurk, who relished the role of an action man, jumped on a plane to bring Noreen home, drawing praise as the 'saviour' who went over to collect his mother-in-law. But other members of the McDonald family could not forgive McGurk for his treatment of

Richard. 'Richard was the greatest guy,' said his friend. 'It was so sad that his last few years were really, really hard for him because of what McGurk had done.'[41] His friend said that even while Richard was in Chile he kept calling and emailing, but McGurk did not respond.

'I spoke to Richard exactly a week before he died,' said his friend. 'He told me that Michael had destroyed him. Richard was given many, many excuses, time after time, from McGurk. I told Richard, "You have to cut your losses and move on."'[42]

But like many who were sucked into McGurk's treacherous orbit, it was too late.

CHAPTER 5

IT'S TAKEN LONG ENOUGH

I was at home with my family in Woollahra when the *Herald* news desk rang me around 7 pm on 3 September 2009. The desk had just received a tip: a Michael McGurk had been shot outside his Cremorne home about half an hour earlier.

I felt like vomiting. I immediately rang my editor, Peter Fray, and told him about my conversation with McGurk ten days before, when he'd told me there was a hit out on him and Ron Medich was behind it. 'I just can't believe this has happened,' I kept repeating.

Our police reporter Dylan Welch was on the way to the murder scene, as was our well-known sports commentator Peter FitzSimons, who lived only a few hundred metres away from Cranbrook Avenue. I rang Dylan and told him to ask the officer in charge to call me as soon as possible. Dylan kept trying to talk to Detective Inspector Mick Sheehy of the State Crime Command's Homicide Squad, but speaking to journalists was the last thing on the burly detective's mind. I also rang and left a message at the North Sydney Police Station.

For legal reasons we couldn't report that McGurk had told me he thought Ron Medich was going to have him killed. If

Medich sued for defamation, we would effectively have to prove that he was the murderer. However, Blind Freddy could tell from our front-page story on 4 September that Medich was a person of interest to police because of his ongoing legal feuds with McGurk.

A confronting photo accompanied the story. The front door of McGurk's blue Mercedes was wide open. Police floodlights illuminated McGurk lying on his back, his left foot pointing skywards, his right foot at an angle of 45 degrees. You could see that the soles of his polished black shoes were well worn; his navy-blue jumper had ridden up, exposing a glimpse of his pale stomach. A smattering of French fries surrounded his right wrist. Fortunately, the car door hid the pool of blood emanating from the bullet wound behind his right ear.

Neighbours said that his nine-year-old son had leapt out of the car and, screaming hysterically, had sprinted down the path towards the French doors which led into the kitchen. Mrs McGurk and her older son rushed out. They performed CPR on McGurk but he was already beyond help.

Night had blurred into day for Safetli in the hours after the murder. He welcomed the morning by breakfasting on Wild Turkey – the first glass of what had become a two-bottle-a-day bourbon habit. Fuelled by alcohol, he demanded that Krystal come to see him. In a grandiose gesture, he peeled off a few hundred dollars for a cab to bring her from her inner-city home all the way out to the boondocks, where Safetli shared a house with his mother and brother.

Safetli had previously big-noted to Krystal that he had secretly been a hitman for years. Krystal, a slight woman 20 years his junior, had taken no notice. He was a bullshit artist par excellence but she'd been happy to take advantage of his extravagant spending. He'd been splashing the cash at the Ivy, an upmarket nightclub in town. He'd spent thousands of dollars there before the murder.

Next to his bottle of bourbon lay the daily newspapers. Safetli passed them across to her. McGurk's brutal murder was plastered across the front pages. Having accompanied Safetli on numerous occasions to keep tabs on McGurk, Krystal knew in an instant that Safetli was responsible. And, with rising alarm, she realised he *knew* that she knew.

You might think that being named on the front page of the *Sydney Morning Herald*, a major metropolitan newspaper, as a person of interest in his former associate's murder would have made Ron Medich think twice about going to a very public lunch in his favourite restaurant less than 24 hours after his business enemy had been gunned down. And not just going to lunch, going to lunch with the very man who, it turned out, had organised the murder for him.

It was hard to tell whether Ron Medich had a tin ear when it came to the questionable characters with whom he associated, or perhaps he was drawn to like-minded unscrupulous souls. Whatever the case, by 2009 he had squandered millions of dollars on bad business deals, usually with not a shred of paperwork and with a changing cast of dubious partners.

Things had not gone well for Medich since he had split from his younger brother, Roy, following the sale in 2007 of their Norton Street Plaza shopping centre in Leichhardt for $112 million. When the brothers were in business together, Roy had tried to keep Ron's hangers-on at bay. Since then Ron had fallen in and out with a succession of shysters who'd leached away millions of dollars of his fabulous wealth. His dining companions were the best measure of which sycophant was benefiting from his millions at any given time. Medich was a creature of habit and invariably his dodgy new best friend and business partner would be eating and drinking daily at Medich's expense, while plotting the ruination of the jilted predecessor.

Much of the scheming was done at Tuscany Ristorante in Leichhardt, which sat just outside the Norton Street Plaza and served as Medich's office canteen even after the brothers had sold the shopping centre they had developed. As Medich was to later tell a parliamentary inquiry: 'Why would I run ten kilometres away when we can go downstairs, have our lunch and go back upstairs to continue working?'[1]

Having worked on the McGurk–Medich feud in the six weeks leading up to McGurk's murder, Vanda and I knew a hell of a lot about Ron Medich, right down to the brothels favoured by him and Lucky Gattellari, and where they liked to eat. Before McGurk's body had arrived at Glebe morgue, we were on Medich's tail, organising journalists and photographers to be in situ. No doubt Medich's wife, Odetta, was horrified and angry when, the morning after the murder, her picture was taken by a *Herald* photographer as she drove her black Porsche convertible into the Medichs' palatial waterfront digs. And when Ron's shiny black Mercedes-Benz E500 nosed out of their steep driveway, Ron was also photographed, and followed into the city, where more shots were taken as he stopped to collect derivatives trader Andrew Howard, who at the time described himself as Medich's financial adviser.

Given the circumstances, it was indeed surprising that Medich turned up to his usual lunch spot at Tuscany, which was open to Leichhardt's busy Norton Street. But turn up he did, and as he slumped into the curved beechwood chair in the restaurant he was visibly upset. He'd just been trying to park his Mercedes in the private section of the Coles supermarket car park underneath, but in his agitation he couldn't get his pass to work. He was pressing the button at the boomgate, desperate for someone to let him in. Erik Jensen, a young reporter at the *Herald*, appeared from nowhere and, since Medich's car window was down, asked if he had anything to do with McGurk's murder. 'I didn't do it. Fuck off!' squealed Medich heatedly.

'Do you know who did it?' persisted Jensen.

'How would I know? Christ almighty! You people are lowlife. You've upset me, you've upset my wife. Now, fuck off!'[2] The boomgate opened and Medich roared into his reserved car spot. Jensen watched as Medich, wearing a fine black cashmere sweater and black trousers, darted over to the service lift and made good his escape up into the shopping centre. A worker from a nearby business said Medich was in tears as he got out of the lift.

Perhaps it wasn't the best idea, either, to meet at a restaurant that was open to the elements on three sides. There were TV cameras, boom mikes, photographers and journalists out on the street watching the luncheon party. Apart from the media throng, the 438 bus kept rumbling by and the traffic was slowing down to see what drama was unfolding there.

As Medich relayed his woes about the intrusions of the press, 59-year-old Gattellari surveyed the gathered media out on the street. In his fashionably distressed Dolce & Gabbana jeans and a loose-fitting cream shirt, unbuttoned to reveal a tuft of dark chest hair, he was trying to keep his cool. A lick of thick black hair, which he wore parted down the middle, flopped lazily across his left eye every time he leant forward to check the caller ID on his mobile phone.

Medich and Howard sat with their backs to the street but Gattellari, on a banquette upholstered in olive-and-gold-striped corduroy, was directly in the firing line of the *Herald*'s photographer, only a couple of metres away. Every time he looked up, a camera shutter whirred. Howard, casually dressed in a red-and-white-striped business shirt and chinos, was deputised to step outside the restaurant and tell the media to clear off. He was not successful.

Needless to say, the previous night's slaying of Michael McGurk was the topic du jour. Ron's old silver Nokia mobile, with its classical guitar ringtone, was ringing continually. And if Ron's phone wasn't ringing, Lucky's or Andrew's was.

At one point Gattellari leant over and said quietly to Medich, 'Are you happy it's done?'

Medich grumbled, 'It's taken long enough.'[3]

As Medich looked with distaste at the media frenzy outside the restaurant, he whispered to Gattellari of his next plan – to intimidate McGurk's widow. 'We'll hold off on that for a while, there's too much interest at the moment. Just leave it alone.'[4]

Howard, then in his early forties, regarded McGurk as 'an evil little bastard'.[5] He had worked with McGurk until mid 2008, when he had rushed into the Scot's office after hearing a dreadful kerfuffle. He found McGurk wielding a cricket bat, which he had just used to break the arm of one of his employees. Loyalty was not only a fluid commodity in this world but one that was retained only if the price was right. Howard defected to the much wealthier Medich.

As they picked at their pasta and lamb cutlets and sipped their red wine, the men workshopped what response Medich could offer the press in the hope that it would make them pack up. Lawyers and mates were consulted. Howard disappeared upstairs to Medich's office and came back with a response crafted by one of the law firms then acting for Medich, Clayton Utz. Medich insisted there was no way he was facing the press again, not after what those pricks had put him through that morning. Howard, once again, was chosen to walk outside and hand over the piece of paper. It read:

> Recently, Mr Medich has been a party to proceedings relating to commercial matters in which Michael McGurk was also a party. Approximately three weeks ago, a significant part of one of those proceedings was settled amicably. Mr McGurk's murder is tragic and Mr Medich's sympathy goes out to his wife and children. Mr Medich has no further comment to make.

Strike Force Narrunga was established with veteran homicide Detective Inspector Mick Sheehy at the helm. Sheehy, in his late forties, had also done a lot of work on bikie gangs and narcotics. The tall, imposing detective was nicknamed 'H' after the friendly bigfoot Harry from the Hollywood film *Harry and the Hendersons*. Within hours of McGurk's murder, Sheehy was knocking on Ron Medich's door to check his whereabouts that night. Odetta wouldn't let her husband come to the door.

The homicide squad was divided into teams, and the roster assigned Team 2 the McGurk murder. Detective Sergeant Mark Fitzhenry was given the role of officer in charge. His job was directing the day-to-day work, allocating tasks and coordinating the investigation. At the time of McGurk's death he and Sergeant Richie Howe, a former butler, were in Albury, having attended court that day for a murder case. Fitzhenry had a fear of flying, and his fear was even greater when it involved small planes. Howe had been plying his colleague with beers all afternoon, trying to dull his anxiety. Fitzy, as he was known, was insisting he wanted to hire a car to drive the five and a half hours back to Sydney. They knew little about the McGurk job as they finally rolled on to the plane, and they certainly didn't know the murder would bind them together for years to come.

Amity was not a word that could be applied to any part of the Medich–McGurk relationship. For months Medich had been agitated about McGurk, especially after the Scot had had a couple of legal victories over him. Medich hated McGurk with such a passion that he was paying to have him spied on and followed. The role of gumshoes had been given to Hais Safetli and his brother, Bassam, who had been doing odd jobs for Gattellari, including collecting debts from people who owed Medich money.

The introduction to the Safetlis had come through Senad Kaminic, a former Bosnian soldier who was Gattellari's driver. Not only did the former pugilist have arthritis in his hands, and a tendency to get car-sick, but his propensity for cognac and a cigar when he got to work, followed by a long boozy lunch with Medich, required the services of a chauffeur.

In early March Gattellari met with Hais Safetli and handed him a photo, and McGurk's home and office details. Without telling Safetli why he wanted him followed, Gattellari said he wanted to know everything about McGurk – where he went, who he saw, what his routine was.

Within days Safetli was in the foyer of McGurk's York Street office looking at the nameplates of the various businesses within the building. A man with a Scottish accent was talking on his mobile phone about the English soccer results. Safetli pressed the button for the lift. McGurk, who had his suit coat draped over one arm, walked towards the lift. As the lift door opened Safetli could see McGurk's reflection in the mirror of the lift. Their eyes met. McGurk stepped back. Safetli pressed the button for the tenth floor and then turned around to see McGurk standing there watching him as the doors closed. McGurk had just come face to face with the man who would later kill him.

Safetli waited on the floor above McGurk's office for a while before going down a level. The door to McGurk's suite was ajar and Safetli could see a young woman at the reception desk. He listened as McGurk yelled and screamed about some problem with a bank transfer.

He reported the lift encounter to Gattellari, saying that McGurk seemed to be 'on guard'. Gattellari berated him for not listening to the conversation for longer.

During the Safetlis' first fortnight following McGurk, Bassam took numerous photos of their surveillance target, which he loaded on to a CD and gave to Kaminic to give to Gattellari. Bass was pleased with his efforts as an undercover operative, photographing McGurk as he reported to the Mosman Police Station and to his tailor. He proudly told Kaminic, 'There are photographs on here that Ron would be happy with.'[6]

But Ron wasn't happy. In late March Kaminic drove Gattellari to Medich's office in Leichhardt and waited outside while the two men spoke. According to Gattellari, Medich said, 'I need to put an end to this. I need some help from you. I need you to find someone to kill him for me.'[7]

Instead of telling Ron he was crazy, Gattellari replied, 'Are you sure about this, because there is no going back?'[8]

'Yes, I am absolutely sure,' Medich said. 'If you can find someone, I want him dead.'[9] For Medich, money bought solutions, and there was always a parasitical partner willing to do the dirty work so his own hands would remain clean.

As Kaminic drove Gattellari home that day, Gattellari told him to organise a meeting with the Safetlis. He'd recalled that at some

point over the previous weeks Bass Safetli had indicated that he
and his brother were prepared to go further than just intimidation:
'If you want anyone taken care of, it won't be a problem.'[10]

So a meeting was teed up with Haissam and Bassam, during
which Gattellari asked them, 'That comment you made about
going further with a job, is that still on the table?'[11]

He said the brothers looked at each other, went to the corner
of the room to talk in private, and when they returned said they
would take the contract.

The following day they said they wanted $300,000 plus
expenses for the hit.

'Fuck, that's a lot of money,' Medich complained when
Gattellari told him the cost of murder.

'If you don't want to pay it, let's forget about it,' said
Gattellari.

But Medich brushed aside the cost. 'No, it's all right. I want it
done,' he said. 'He's made a fool of me, the laughing stock of the
eastern suburbs.'[12]

Haissam Safetli, who would later minimise his brother's
involvement, offered a different version of events. He recalled
that in April 2009, Kaminic had asked him to accompany him
to Gattellari's house in Chipping Norton. With a cursory nod to
his wife, Pamela, the diminutive Lucky had ushered Kaminic
and Safetli into the kitchen, where Lucky was cooking pasta.
Without turning round Lucky said to Safetli, 'Because you
haven't taken this seriously, it's cost Ron a lot of money.'[13]

Safetli protested but Lucky cut him short. 'Listen, Hias,'
he said, as usual mispronouncing his name – Gattellari always
pronounced Hais's name as though it rhymed with ice instead
of ace – 'this is no fucking game. You didn't even know that the
fuckwit went to Brisbane.'

'How am I fucking well meant to know that?' said Safetli
angrily. 'You seem to know more about him than I do, so why do
you even need me?'[14]

Gattellari grabbed a bottle of Scotch and indicated for the
two men to join him at the kitchen bench. Without bothering

to inquire if they wanted a drink, Gattellari poured each of them a glass. Looking Safetli dead in the eye, Gattellari swirled his whisky in his cut-glass tumbler. 'I want him gone,' he said. Without taking his eyes off Safetli, he added, 'And I want you to do it.'[15]

Draining his Scotch in one gulp, Safetli claimed he said nothing, but pushed his glass forward for another. Looking back on that evening he said he realised that he had sealed his fate by that simple wordless act.

'You just tell me how much you need,' said Gattellari, leaving the room. Within a minute he was back with a calico bank bag. He reached inside the bag and pulled out a large envelope. 'Here's $50,000 and that will come off the $250,000 you'll be paid.'[16]

Safetli thought it might look crass to open the envelope in front of Lucky. Kaminic finished his drink, thanked Gattellari and steered his stunned friend out into the street. 'There is no panic,' said Kaminic in his thick Bosnian accent. They had driven barely a block before curiosity got the better of Safetli. Ripping open the top of the yellow business envelope, he saw five neatly tied bundles of crisp new bank notes. Each bundle contained $10,000. The thought crossed his mind that he should go back to Lucky's and return the money. But he looked again at those virginal bank notes, unsullied by the financial drudgery of everyday life and, closing the envelope, said nothing.

At that moment he knew in his heart there was no going back. One life had to end. It was either his or McGurk's.

McGurk was also paying people to do his dirty work. Knowing that Medich enjoyed his daily boozy lunch at Tuscany, a couple of months before his murder McGurk came up with a plan to have Medich caught drink driving. McGurk gave $5000 to a standover man connected to the Hells Angels to carry out his plan. He described Medich to him as 'the old cunt' with white hair, rimless glasses and wearing a black skivvy and black pants.[17] The 'accident' occurred just after 5 pm on 3 July 2009. As Medich drove home after a long lunch at Tuscany, a little Daihatsu Charade rear-ended his Mercedes on the corner of Sussex and King streets. Out of the car leapt a scary-looking man with a cap and a ponytail. He was wearing a black hoodie with the inscription 'Love Kills Slowly'. Despite being clearly at fault, the man insisted on calling the police.

The standover man was given a ticket for negligent driving and Medich, who was over the limit, was taken to The Rocks Police Station. He was breathalysed 46 minutes later. He was found to be 0.035 and was released without charge.

When Vanda Carson and I met McGurk for lunch on 29 July, McGurk was insistent that we look into this accident. He was convinced Medich had paid off the police or used his connections to get off the drink-driving offence. Needless to say he failed to mention his own role in orchestrating the crash.

Medich was enraged over the July crash, telling Gattellari that 'some arsehole' had run into him.[18] He swore that it was deliberate and that McGurk was behind it. It made Medich even more irritated about the fact that McGurk was still alive and kicking; still taunting him. 'What the fuck is going on? How long is this going to take?' he demanded of Gattellari.[19]

A little over a week after Medich's car was rammed into, Tuscany restaurant was the scene of yet another deal, though this one, surprisingly, had nothing to do with Medich's plans to kill McGurk.

It was early in the evening of 15 July 2009 when Ian Macdonald arrived at the restaurant. The minister for Mineral Resources, Energy and State Development had had a shocker of a day. That morning's *Herald* had referred to him as 'Sir Lunchalot' and had detailed the $150,000 that his wine advisory group, stacked with a number of his pals, had cost the taxpayer as the group ate and drank up a storm jetting around the state.[20]

While waiting for the other guests, Craig Murray and Bill Frewen – senior staff from an energy company – to arrive, Macdonald decided to drown his sorrows with the first of four bottles of Tasmanian pinot noir at $130 a pop. He knew that either Medich or the two government officials from the state-owned power company he had invited would be forced to pick up the bill.

Medich had ploughed almost $15 million into a group of electrical companies in which Gattellari was involved. But he wanted some bang for his buck in relation to these businesses and Macdonald might just be able to open a few doors. This was the second time Macdonald had organised a private intro-duction for Medich. The previous month George Maltabarow, the managing director of Energy Australia, had also endured Medich – and the bill – over dinner at Tuscany.

That July night as Macdonald tucked in to spatchcock and baby goat, Medich's unimpressive sales pitch to provide services to energy companies fell flat for a second time.

Because of probity concerns Murray and Frewen waved away Medich's offer to pick up the tab, but the two men were horrified when they saw that the meal for four of them at the suburban Italian restaurant had come to $850. Given the day's headline about the minister, they were gobsmacked that Macdonald was still up to his old tricks. The following morning Murray told his boss what had happened.

McGurk had told me that Medich had lunched with Macdonald four or five times in the latter part of 2008 with the expectation that Macdonald was about to be made planning minister. Although Macdonald ate at Tuscany weekly, some-times with Medich, sometimes with his now-jailed ministerial colleague Eddie Obeid, at a later corruption inquiry Macdonald was unable to provide a single receipt for any meal he'd ever had there. Nor were there charges on any of his credit cards to show that he paid.

Two days earlier Macdonald had asked Tuscany's owner, Frank Moio, to organise a girl for him. Moio passed on the request to

Gattellari and Medich, who shared a penchant for young Asian women, and often had a retinue of girls on tap for themselves and their mates – all paid for by Medich.

That night Gattellari had organised Cindy, Annie, Tiffanie and Cathy from whom Macdonald could choose. He selected Tiffanie, who had previously provided sexual services to men at Gattellari's request and had received payment from him for doing so.

After the dinner, with millions of dollars in potential contracts for Medich and Lucky's electrical company on offer, Medich drove the sloshed minister to the five-star Four Seasons Hotel. Senad Kaminic had gone ahead to install Tiffanie in a room at the hotel and was waiting to give Medich the room key to hand over to Macdonald. Gattellari, meanwhile, was transporting the 'lefto-vers', as Medich described them, to his boss's house.[21]

Room 1119 in the luxurious hotel looked straight on to the iconic Opera House. Not that Macdonald gave two hoots about the view from the $325-per-night room, for which Medich was picking up the bill. Once Macdonald had joined Tiffanie, she stripped to her underwear and lay on the bed. Macdonald, a tall balding fleshy man who had just turned 60, removed only his jacket and pressed himself on top of her. 'If only you knew who I am, you would be surprised,' he said before fondling her and kissing her roughly.[22] But that's as far as it got. Macdonald rolled off and fell asleep, snoring. Tiffanie telephoned Cindy, one of the other girls at the table that night, to complain that Macdon-ald was so repulsive he made her feel sick.[23]

Macdonald told a subsequent corruption inquiry that he had no idea that Tiffanie was a sex worker. There was much chor-tling in the public gallery when he told the inquiry, 'After the two Country Energy people departed, Ron Medich was at my table . . . and we had a discussion and I said I'd like a massage . . . do you think it could be arranged?' He said his wife was away at their country home and he asked Medich to organise the late-night 'remedial massage' in a hotel room as he had developed 'neck tiredness' during their dinner meeting.[24]

Questioned by his own barrister, Tim Hale, SC, Macdonald said he was anxious and upset and feeling 'unhinged' that day because people in his own party were leaking against him to force him out of government. 'You were upset because you had been described as Mr Lunchalot in the news media?' Hale asked.[25] Without a scintilla of irony, Macdonald replied, 'I think I was given a higher title than that. I think it was Sir Lunchalot.'[26]

Medich told the hearing that he had no involvement in the selection of the prostitutes for Macdonald, nor with determining what services they were to provide. He agreed that he drove Macdonald to the hotel, but grumbled he shouldn't have had to do that. But he said he didn't know if Macdonald was going to have sexual relations with Tiffanie. 'I don't know what relations she was going to have,' he said.[27]

Medich then said Gattellari wanted to bring the 'leftover girls' from the restaurant to Medich's house to 'show them the views'. Medich's own family was away on a ski holiday. It pleased him that the young Asian sex workers were awestruck by his mansion with its panoramic views across Sydney Harbour. Cindy told Tiffanie later that she had never seen anything like it.[28] A steep driveway wound down to the Medichs' four-storey all-white house. With its vast minimalist interiors, serviced via a circular glass lift, Cindy thought it was like a shopping centre. Out on the lawn by the harbour, several bronze sculptured dogs guarded the lagoon-like pool fringed with palm trees. Cindy also told her friend about the enormous garage, which had a rotation device so Medich's Mercedes would be facing the right way when he wanted to leave.

Cindy accepted an invitation from Medich to accompany him to Melbourne not long after the tour of the mansion. Medich's trip in late July 2009 was to meet Melbourne underworld figure Mick Gatto, who'd been acquitted of the murder of underworld hitman Andrew 'Benji' Veniamin in 2005. Since then Gatto had been operating a successful mediation and debt-collecting business, Gatto Corporation. He'd been hoping to score an 'introduction fee' if he could interest Medich in a

$300 million rescue of a troubled development in Chapel Street, South Yarra. Nothing eventuated.

There was also to be no happy ending for Macdonald: the day after his tryst with Tiffanie his wife found the electronic key from the Four Seasons in his trouser pocket. She rang Frank Moio at Tuscany, and Medich said that Moio thrust the phone to him to deal with her. Medich told the corruption inquiry that he couldn't remember what lie he had told to fob her off. 'I don't think it was an untruth, I think it was a porky,' said Medich.[29]

CHAPTER 6

THE SNOB MOB FROM BLUEBERRY HILL

'He's a skinny Tony Soprano who walks around in black skivvies,' said Sydney business identity Jim Byrnes of Ron Medich prior to the murder of Michael McGurk.[1] Medich's penchant for wearing black had also earned him the nickname Johnny Cash, after the famous American country and western singer who was known as 'The Man in Black'. In stark contrast, Medich resided in a house that was so white the dazzle from the afternoon sun reflecting off the water hurt your eyes.

At the time of McGurk's murder, 61-year-old Ron Medich appeared to have it all. The perfect house in one of the most prestigious streets in the country; a smart, attractive wife 20 years his junior; six children from two marriages; uniformed staff to wait on him hand and foot; mates like seagulls hovering at his beck and call for scraps of his extraordinary wealth. But while he had cents in the multi-millions, when it came to common sense he had almost nothing.

Behind his back, the old-money families of Sydney's eastern suburbs coined a cutting nickname for their nouveau riche neighbour: he was known as 'Cottee's' after the famous Thick'n'Rich flavoured ice-cream topping. He was the butt of jokes: 'How do you make a million dollars? You give Ron Medich $2 million.'[2]

The property developer's own barrister, Winston Terracini, SC, let slip a revealing insight while locking horns in court with Lucky Gattellari. 'You know very well he didn't make it on his own and you know very well he is not highly intelligent?' said Terracini.

'You are saying that, not me,' snapped Gattellari. 'You're calling Mr Medich stupid, are you? He can't be paying you too much.'[3]

Thirteen years before McGurk's demise, when Ron Medich's nattily dressed, chain-smoking younger brother, Roy, was interviewed by the *Herald*, Roy expressed the view that he and Ron would never leave Sydney's west. The glittering prize of an address such as Wolseley Road, Point Piper, was only for the 'snob mob of blueberry hill', he said disdainfully.[4]

In 1996 the *Sydney Morning Herald* interviewed Roy Medich for a story on millionaires from Sydney's western suburbs who, despite their fortunes, had stayed close to their roots. Although he was a millionaire many times over, it was reported that Roy Medich

> runs his multi-million-dollar business from a dingy, wood-veneered office off a car park on the polluted strip off Homepride Avenue in Warwick Farm. He and his brother, Ron, and his son, Anthony, sit near each other, desks pushed into a T shape. There's a big black leather chair each, and a secretary out in the front room. The door is always left open to save on expensive communication.[5]

While the public face of the Medich empire was dinginess personified, it was a different story in the homes they had constructed next door to each other in Cubitt Drive, Denham Court, an affluent suburb in Sydney's southwest. In Roy's garage was a fleet of cars – two BMWs, two Mercedes and an Audi. The *Herald* described Medich's mansion as:

> A pastiche of styles – high-gloss cedar furniture with an Eastern European passion for marble on the architraves and on the floors. There are acres of cream carpets, olive and burgundy drapes and faux waterwave wallpaper, and gold taps in each of the five bathrooms. Brass picture lights beam down upon a mini-gallery of Pro Harts and Norman Lindsay nudes, mingled daringly with David and Arthur Boyds.
>
> He's got a bit of a flair for design and worked out a lot of the colour schemes himself.
>
> 'Is it grape? Is it violet?' Struggling to define the colour of his own dining-room ceiling, he is suddenly self-conscious. 'It's purple, if you ask me![6]

Ron Medich's house next door was similarly grandiose. He had imported $1 million worth of furnishings and antiques from Europe for the seven-bedroom home, which had five separate living areas, a billiard room, tennis court and swimming pool. The chandelier in the foyer alone cost $160,000.

In 2003, however, Ron was won over by the pull of the glittering opportunities on offer on the harbour. His Cubitt Drive place was sold for $3.4 million, with all its furnishings and antiques, and he and Odetta joined the 'snob mob of blueberry hill' with their purchase of 42a Wolseley Road in Point Piper in Sydney's east.

For the uber-wealthy, Wolseley Road is one of the most prestigious addresses in the country; according to the *Wall Street Journal*'s 'Wealth Bulletin' it is one of the ten most expensive streets to live on in the world.

The Medichs bought their new house for $7.75 million from well-known fashion designer Lisa Ho and her then husband Philip Smouha, who had sold before restyling. The coffee-coloured mansion was a reno's delight: run-down, ugly and completely without style. But before the wrecker's ball could be let loose, Ron and Odetta had spied an even better house. Number 112 was in a more sought-after section of the road, and had a northerly aspect. The couple snapped up restaurateur Wolfie Pizem's pile for $15.3 million and spent a fortune on a redesign. They resold 42a, in a deal that would come back to haunt them.

Not that Ron would ever have left the familiar surroundings of the working-class suburbs in which he'd grown up but for the aspirations of his socially ambitious young second wife, Odetta.

The arrival of a 22-year-old blonde bombshell from Lithuania had changed everything for Ron.

Unsmiling immigration officials scrutinised the young woman as she waited to go through Customs at Sydney's international airport on 1 August 1990. According to her Russian passport, Odeta Chtouikite was born on 7 March 1968, in Kedainiai, Lithuania. Telling the official she was here for a holiday, he stamped her passport with a six-month visitor's visa.[7]

Only five months earlier Lithuania had declared independence from its former Soviet masters, and ambitious young folk like Odeta were seizing on the chance to escape their decaying, stifling hometowns for a better future elsewhere. Perched on the Nevezis River, Kedainiai was the tenth-largest city in Lithuania. The landlocked industrial town had a small expanse of pretty cobblestoned streets, but that didn't compensate for the acrid smell of sulphuric acid from a nearby chemical plant. Apart from having been a major Soviet air base, the town's only other claim to fame was that it was the cucumber capital of Lithuania.

Odeta Chtouikite met Ron Medich soon after she arrived. Exactly how she ended up in one of the least fashionable areas of Sydney, some 30 kilometres from the central business district, is not clear. Perhaps the Soviet sameness of the cheaply built, mass-produced homes in parts of Sydney's west made her feel at home. Some of Medich's associates uncharitably suggested she was Medich's cleaner or his mail-order bride. All agree that bantam-sized Ron Medich, then aged 42, was punching well above his weight. His surname meant 'bear' in Croatian, but Medich was more like a hamster – small, nervy and with a high-pitched voice that sounded like a jackhammer running out of petrol. In early 1990 he'd reached a generous property settlement with his first wife, Gail, with whom he had four children, Glenda, Denise, Pamela and Peter. And now here was this beautiful and mysterious young woman, about the same age as his daughters, draped adoringly over his arm.

When Odeta failed to leave the country on 1 February 1991, her six-month holiday visa having expired, the immigration department was soon on her tail. Medich's lawyers applied for an extension to her visa on the grounds that she was Ron's de facto partner, and the following month – in a scene straight out of the Gérard Depardieu movie *Green Card* – Odeta and Ron were taken into separate interview rooms by immigration officials to be grilled about their relationship. Medich also submitted a detailed statement regarding their relationship. He organised for a solicitor for Odeta, who in turn organised for statutory declarations to be obtained from the couple's close friends and relatives. On 29 July 1991 they provided the department with candid snapshots of them together in various social situations to prove they were indeed a couple. The pair argued they were 'emotionally dependent on one another'.[8] Medich in particular stressed his mental health would suffer if they were separated. He would experience 'considerable hardship if [Odeta] were forced to leave the country', he submitted.[9] But despite their best efforts, on 9 September 1991 an immigration officer knocked back the application, saying Odeta had been an illegal immigrant when she first applied to stay in Australia.

Nine days later, Medich's mother, Mandina, died aged 63. Medich was devastated. He worried that the decision he and Roy had made to install her in The Quay, one of the most expensive apartments in town, with panoramic views over the Opera House and Botanic Garden, had served only to isolate her from the people with whom she had grown up.

After his mother's death, Medich was even more determined to keep Odeta with him. The following month they tried to overturn the decision by appealing to the Federal Court. After a year of wrangling, in February 1992 the immigration department finally relented and Odeta was given a temporary entry permit. With her matrimonial status settled when she married Ron that December, the first thing the new Mrs Medich did was add an extra 't' to her first name.

Ronald Edward Medich was born on 11 April 1948, in the cane-farming town of Innisfail, in the far north of Queensland.

His father, Peter, and uncle, Lubo, had left behind the ruins of Croatia at the end of the Second World War. Refugees had to work for two years as a condition of their assisted passage to Australia. There were only three jobs on offer: the Snowy Mountain scheme, working on the railways out west, or cutting sugar cane. Refugees weren't given a choice and when the Medichs were assigned to the cane-cutting gang, their fellow migrants commiserated.

Coming from the cold European climate, Peter and Lubo found the heat in far north Queensland unspeakable. Work began at first light when the air was cooler, but the dew on the cane made the long cane-cutting knife slippery and accidents were common. And once the blazingly hot sun was high in the sky, the snakes began to stir and so did the bees. The work was back-breaking as the cane had to be cut as close to the ground as possible. Like other cutters, Peter resorted to spreading mutton fat along his limbs and binding his hands with cloth to protect the blisters which soon developed. The soot from the burning of the previous season's crop meant that when the cutters came home in the evening, their children were sometimes frightened by the apparition in black, broken up only by the whites of their teeth.

There was only one thing that made the gruelling job bearable and that was the money. The shortage of manpower meant that while the average weekly wage was £5, cane-cutters were paid a massive £30 a week. The farm owners complained that the workers were making more than they were.

Mandina Medich bore two sons in quick succession at Innisfail Hospital: first Ron, and the following year, in November 1949, Roy Anthony. Then, after their passage was paid off, Peter and Lubo moved their young families to Cabramatta, the Sydney suburb of choice for the waves of immigrants arriving from war-torn Europe. New arrivals were put up in Cabramatta's migrant hostels, and once on their feet many settled in the local area, some 30 kilometres southwest of the CBD.

With a burgeoning population on tap, people like the Medich brothers, who had an entrepreneurial bent, made a fortune providing housing and construction during the boom years of the 1950s and '60s.

One of Peter and Lubo's first investments was in a cinema in Cabramatta, with young Ron and Roy earning pocket money mopping the floors. By 1956 the Medichs had made enough money to build a brand-new second cinema in nearby Chester Hill. 'The pictures' were all the rage and their cinema was considered a modern marvel. It even had a 'crying room' for the mass of newly born baby boomers.

Peter and Mandina, like many migrants made good, had high aspirations for their children. Ron and Roy were packed off to board at one of the most exclusive Catholic schools in the country, St Joseph's College in Hunters Hill. Joeys' alumni have included a governor-general, a chief justice of the High Court, bankers, lawyers, a scrum full of rugby greats as well as three of the four Wiggles.

Ron was no great shakes academically but at sport he certainly followed the school's motto, which, translated from the Latin, means 'strive for better things'. The 1964 school yearbook records him as the singles champion in second division handball and squash. He also came second in the under-15 long jump, 90 yards hurdles, triple jump and discus. In his final year Ron made the first XI cricket team, which won the GPS premiership that year, as well as the second XV in rugby. Not bad for a scrawny son of a Croat immigrant at a school where they believed rugby was the game played in heaven.

Medich also made a lifelong friend of the choirmaster, cricket coach and discipline master Brother Vales, William Beninati. Medich lunched with him regularly for years after leaving Joeys, even when the old Marist brother had moved into a retirement home. Testimony given in 2017 at the Royal Commission into Institutional Responses to Child Sexual Abuse revealed that Brother Vales had groomed, drugged and sexually abused students at Joeys, where he had taught from 1955 until 1971. In the late 1990s he was charged over a sexual assault on a student but the charges were dropped. In 2013 police again attempted to prosecute the Marist brother for the 1968 sexual assault of a student but the 85-year-old was terminally ill and died a few months later.

After leaving school Medich trained as an accountant, but he and Roy soon went into business together, establishing Medich Enterprises, a property-developing company. By the time the brothers were in their late thirties they had built a minor empire, buttressed by strong connections with local and state government officials. Over the subsequent years they developed shopping centres, industrial estates and residential areas. Perhaps envious of their successes, many seemed to resent the brothers' ability to get things done. For instance, in the Camden area the Medichs bought a 300-acre farm from a former bookie, which they managed to get rezoned for industrial purposes as others around them had their applications refused. The Medichs' huge residential development in Denham Court was not only rezoned but the brothers were allowed to halve the size of the blocks.

With their growing wealth and power came political connections. The Medichs were courted by the state Labor Party, and the brothers returned the courtesy by not only joining the Liverpool branch, but becoming generous benefactors. Among their good Labor friends was frontbencher Eric Bedford, who was state planning minister from 1980 to 1984. It was Roy Medich who delivered the eulogy at Bedford's funeral in 2006. During the 1980s the Medichs would have been unaware that Eric Bedford and one of his staffers, Francesco Labbozzetta, had come to the attention of police. Labbozzetta was described as 'Il Capo' of the Australian mafia in the South Australian parliament. In December 1987 he was interviewed by New South Wales police. Among the many questions they asked him was, 'Would you care to tell us if you had any suspicions or knowledge of Mr Bedford receiving large amounts of money for development approvals or rezoning applications?'

'No, no suspicions at all,' replied Labbozzetta breezily. He also denied he had received money or benefits on Bedford's behalf.

In 1990 there were complaints of favouritism within Liverpool Council towards the Medichs' massive redevelopment of the El Toro Hotel in Liverpool. In 1972 the new prime minister Gough Whitlam had celebrated his famous 'It's Time' victory at the Medich-owned establishment. One local politician the Medichs were particularly close to was Liverpool councillor Pat Pantaleo. Then ABC stalwart Quentin Dempster reported on the connection between Pantaleo and the Medichs at the time. 'This council, Liverpool, has become embroiled in a bitter dispute over the conduct of this man, Pat Pantaleo, an influential Labor Party alderman, builder, developer and cement supplier,' Dempster told The 7.30 Report.[10] As Dempster explained, the council's own town planner had a problem with the Medichs' controversial plans for their company, Walstern, to build a motel next to their El Toro Hotel on the Hume Highway, on probably the busiest corner in Liverpool. While the planner had knocked them back, fighting on behalf of the Medichs was councillor Pantaleo, who had failed to disclose to council that he was in business with the Medichs. 'Both the Medichs and Pantaleo are directors and significant shareholders in another company, Gimbata Pty Ltd,' Dempster told his ABC viewers.[11]

Pantaleo admitted he might benefit through gaining a contract to supply cement for the hotel project. 'That in itself is not improper, nor is his relationship with the Medichs improper.

But what is wrong is Pantaleo's failure to declare his interest in Gimbata on the council's register of pecuniary interests,' said Dempster.[12]

Pantaleo, who had close connections to the New South Wales party machine in Sussex Steet, was subsequently found to have failed to disclose a pecuniary interest to the council. This was not related to the Medichs, but to his failure to declare an interest in a property in Scott Street, Liverpool, when it came before the council for development approval. Pantaleo was disqualified from holding any local government positions for 12 months, but some years later was appointed to a government board by his Labor mates.

Walstern, the Medich company redeveloping the El Toro Hotel, was later successfully pursued by the Australian Taxation Office (ATO) over attempts to bypass Australian tax obligations in a superannuation scheme promoted by their accountants. In 2004 the Federal Court described the 'New Zealand super-annuation scheme' as a 'miserable failure'. To add insult to injury the Medichs were also hit with fringe benefits tax on their contributions.

There were more howls of favouritism in 2002 when Roy Medich was caught doing a spot of over-enthusiastic weeding on an industrial site he owned out at Bringelly in western Sydney. Camden Council initially vowed to make an example out of him for the clearing on his land. It then changed its mind, arguing that a fine would be meaningless to Roy, and deciding that rather than prosecuting the multi-millionaire, it would pursue a more suitable 'ecological outcome'. Medich promised to revegetate the site and, according to council papers, 'agreed to apologise to and support council in publicising the matter as a public education campaign for raising awareness of conservation values'.[13] The council contended that having to be the public face of a campaign 'espousing conservation' and the impor-tance of local vegetation would be a good way for Roy to make amends. Mayor Geoff Corrigan disqualified himself from voting on Roy's punishment, if you could call it that, on the grounds that Medich was a donor to his campaign to get into the New South Wales parliament at the next election.

There was an anecdote about Corrigan's relationship with developers in the 1996 *Herald* article that had featured the Medichs. This tale referenced Tony Perich, a dairy farmer who had become a billionaire from property development. The reporter, Ali Gripper, recounted her attendance at a gathering at the Medichs' Macquarie Function Centre in the main street of Liverpool, and an encounter between the developer and the deputy mayor:

> Perich, clutching a glass of orange juice, leans in over Corrigan, deputy mayor of Camden Council. 'What do you mean it will take eight months? It could all be finished in six weeks if you put your brains to it!' he says. He's towering over Corrigan, browbeating him about the sluggish development approval for his new shopping centre. Perich looks formidable, and Corrigan looks cornered. 'All this mucking about,' [Perich] says, and strides off.[14]

Perich's browbeating of the Liverpool councillor was obviously grist to the mill for Corrigan, who was lavish in his praise for both Perich and Roy Medich in his maiden speech when he became the member for Camden in 2003.

The Medichs could never have foreseen the attention that would be focused – years down the track – on their 1996 purchase of land formerly owned by the federal government's peak scientific body, the CSIRO (Commonwealth Scientific and Industrial Research Organisation) at Badgerys Creek.

The CSIRO, under the chairmanship of the late Neville Wran, the former Labor premier of New South Wales, who later became Ron Medich's partner in a pizza business, had decided to sell a tract of redundant land as part of a restructure. In November 1996 the government body sold the 344-hectare property holding it had in Elizabeth Drive, Badgerys Creek, at the very time the federal government was acquiring land in the area for a proposed new airport. There was no auction and another Medich family company, Becklon, was the only tenderer.

It was a whirlwind deal. The Medichs registered the shelf company, Becklon Pty Ltd, on 22 October, became directors on 4 November and exchanged contracts two weeks later.

At that time Roy Medich was a government appointee to the Greater Western Sydney Economic Development Board, an organisation determined to get the Badgerys Creek airport up and running. Roy Medich denied his new land holding would cause a conflict of interest. 'If things fall into place I may make some money, but I don't intend to use my position on the board to influence any rezoning of the land,' he told a local newspaper.[15]

The land, which was zoned agricultural, was sold to the Medichs for $3.5 million, or about $10,000 a hectare. Local real estate agents estimated the price the Medichs paid was ludicrously low, at least half or two-thirds below the going rate. To rub salt into the wound, two years later the federal government paid 50 times that price – $500,000 a hectare – to acquire land for the proposed airport from the family of Tony Perich.

This rural block of land would prove to be a pivotal chapter in the lives of many in this story. Not only was it at the centre of McGurk's attempt to destroy Ron, but Roy and Ron would battle in court over it, as would Ron and Odetta.

That would all come later. Meanwhile, if Odetta thought a new life in Wolseley Road, the grandest street in Emerald City, would bring happiness, she was wrong. 'The Emerald city of Oz. Everyone comes here along their yellow brick roads looking for the answers to their problems and all they find are the demons within themselves,' wrote playwright David Williamson in his biting 1987 play of the same name.

So it was to be for the Medichs.

CHAPTER 7

McGURK'S DODGY DEALS

For a while Michael McGurk had a lot of empty office space at 99 York Street, but he soon filled some of it with his latest enterprise, the impressive-sounding Australian Telecommunications Consortium. In 1999 the dotcom industry was booming and McGurk wanted a part of it. In March of that year he visited Iran, where he found himself in a magnificent palace, smoking a water pipe with a bearded ayatollah. He knew nothing about Iran or telecommunications; nonetheless he was trying to convince the Iranians they needed to upgrade their fibre optic networks with more advanced technology to get faster internet speeds and an improved mobile phone network. McGurk smoothed the introductions by offering the Iranians gifts of little fluffy koalas and kangaroos. What he failed to mention was that the gear he was proposing to sell them was redundant telecommunications equipment from Israel, their sworn enemy.

McGurk made at least three visits to Iran but nothing came of them and no deals were made. So it was on to the next thing. He set up Planetel to develop an internet service provider, intending to float the company on the Australian stockmarket.

McGurk found a co-director in American Jim Betz, who seemed to be an expert on the subject. McGurk also managed to get himself introduced to Phil Green, the CEO of investment group Babcock & Brown. And to help deal with the high end of town, McGurk's mate Richie Vereker introduced him to PR man Marty Dougherty. A decade earlier, in 1987, Dougherty had been appointed to the Fairfax newspaper group as an editorial executive by Warwick Fairfax, whose family ran the newspaper empire that published the *Sydney Morning Herald*, *The Age* and other papers. 'Young Warwick', as he was known, paid a crazy $2.5 billion to seize control of the company, his bid bankrolled by the corrupt 'Last Resort' Laurie Connell and Connell's Rothwells bank. Both Rothwells and young Warwick's media empire would later fail spectacularly. Although Dougherty had secured a $3.62 million termination payment from his short-lived Fairfax gig, by 1994 he was bankrupt. Now, five years later, here he was helping out Michael McGurk.

According to Vereker, when the Babcock & Brown guys arrived at McGurk's renovated offices in York Street, they were most impressed by the extraordinary art hanging in McGurk's modest office. His mate Marty had borrowed some of pal Connell's million-dollar collection for the visit.

Babcock & Brown invested $23 million in Planetel. Soon they discovered that dealing with McGurk was a nightmare, and they offered him and Betz $5 million to walk away from the company. McGurk demanded $25 million. Hamish Williamson, who came to blows with McGurk over his refusal to accept the money, recalls telling him, 'Take the $5 million – you're never going to make that much money.' Three months later, in December 2000, Planetel collapsed and McGurk got nothing.

McGurk's reputation for violence and shady dealings involved burning business associates, so he was always on the lookout for new people to exploit and fresh schemes to keep his crooked little house of cards from collapse.

Although he followed Formula One, soccer – or football as he called it – was his great passion. He was a mad keen supporter of Celtic, the Glasgow team which competes in the Scottish Premiership; his silver Audi sported the numberplates 'CELTIC'. McGurk was desperate to own his own sporting team. In 2008 he and his mate Paddy Dominguez, who managed several high-profile sporting stars including soccer players Lucas Neill and John Aloisi, were hoping to win the bid for a new team to join Australia's A-League competition. McGurk's loan shark company Bentley Smythe was registered as the office and the principal place of business for the team they hoped to call the Western Sydney Wanderers.

Dominguez, who was born in Spain in 1972 but grew up in Ireland, had previously tried to get a Grand Prix swimming competition off the ground. For a short while McGurk was on the phone daily to Olympic swimming legend Ian Thorpe, but the plan for an international swimming competition went nowhere.

Fronting their bid for the soccer team was Lucas Neill, the captain of the Australian team. Former state planning minister Craig Knowles was approached by Dominguez and Australian soccer supremo Frank Lowy to chair the bid. Knowles knew nothing of McGurk's involvement nor how desperate McGurk was to come up with the $8 million needed to get the bid off the ground. McGurk also tried to persuade Bob Ell to back him, and behind the scenes he wined and dined the Socceroos. Through Greg Magree, McGurk organised VIP passes for the team to John Ibrahim's nightclub The Piano Room.

Several days after McGurk's murder, the Football Federation Australia (FFA) confirmed the funding approach to Ell but issued a statement saying the 'FFA was not aware at the time of any involvement from Mr McGurk'.[1]

McGurk's grand plans to be the owner of a football team never came to fruition despite his best endeavours. However, in 2012 the FFA finally announced a new team to compete in the A-league. Its name? The Western Sydney Wanderers.

*

One scheme which almost cost McGurk his life was a mysterious 'rubber tree' importation.

'You could smell danger in the air, you could just smell it,' said Frank Burke, recalling how he and McGurk had sat in silence in the back of a barely roadworthy taxi as it lurched through the narrow streets of Batam Island, one of the largest in Indonesia's Riau archipelago, and only a 45-minute ferry ride from Singapore.[2]

For fifteen minutes neither spoke as images of decay and bombed-out churches flew by like frames from a war-zone newsreel. It was 2003 and three years earlier Batam Island had been the centre of al-Qaeda and Jemaah Islamiyah terrorist attacks on Christmas Eve. As McGurk and Burke rode in the decrepit taxi, Burke couldn't shake a feeling of foreboding. 'What's the matter with you?' said McGurk defiantly.

'What's the fucking matter with me!' replied Burke. The very nature of McGurk's schemes meant that involvement in them entailed sailing close to the wind, but to Burke and Hamish Williamson, this one with the Indonesians was more dangerous than most.

Some of McGurk's associates insisted that 'rubber trees' was a code for a drug importation, others said it was a container-load of foreign currency. Exactly what the deal involved neither Burke nor Williamson would say, but whatever it was, the stakes were high. Williamson hadn't had a good feeling about the clandestine plan, telling McGurk he was 'dead gallus', Scottish slang for someone whose wicked deeds will lead them to the gallows. He bailed out of the rendezvous and flew home before the other two went to Batam Island. But as far as Burke and McGurk were concerned, this was nothing that bright lights, big drinks and a couple of babes couldn't fix.

McGurk and Burke had been dispatched to Batam Island by the Indonesian military for a clandestine meeting to finalise this latest dubious enterprise. Days earlier the pair had sat at a vast table covered in starched white linen and laid with a dozen gold-rimmed place settings in the private dining room of

Jakarta's Dharmawangsa, a luxurious boutique hotel in the most prestigious residential area of the city, waiting for a meeting that they were sure could reap them vast riches.

On the dot of 1 pm, McGurk's barrel-shaped Indonesian fixer, 'Hans', had arrived in his linen suit. The cigar-chomping Rosihan 'Hans' Yacub ran a business exporting dried flowers. He was a plumpish man of medium height and a dark complexion, with a taste for the good life, partial to linen suits, and as smooth as hell. Even though he always had thousands of dollars in cash on him, Hans never paid for anything.

Behind Hans was a group of high-ranking Indonesian military officials in their pressed khaki uniforms, shiny shoes and glittering regimental insignia. Oblivious to the exquisite turquoise silk panels lining the walls, the generals picked at the roasted foie gras with caramelised Thai mango and French caviar served with champagne. Burke, a feisty larrikin who'd been in more bar-room brawls with McGurk than he cared to remember, was appalled at his friend's obsequiousness; he was positively fawning over these pretentious military gits. Bowing respectfully, McGurk presented a general with rubies. 'This is for your wife, sir,' he said. McGurk's handsome cufflinks caught the light as, with a flourish, he offered diamonds to a second, and another received the finest Scotch whisky money could buy. Burke was unimpressed. 'Happy birthday!' he muttered in an aggressive tone as the gifts were handed over. McGurk glared at him.[3]

All up, the Sydney wheeler-dealer shelled out $800,000 to grease the palms of these Indonesian officials, but it seemed McGurk figured that was a small price to pay to get them on-side. After lunch the generals excused themselves and Hans ushered them to the door. Everyone was smiling and there was much shaking of hands. As McGurk and Burke waited for word on whether their scheme was on track, they whiled away the hours lounging on the blue-and-white-striped sunbeds by the Dharmawangsa's pool, working on their tans, sipping cocktails from coconuts, and pursuing nocturnal activities with the locals.

Within days word came through from Hans that McGurk had passed muster, and he was told to make his way to Batam Island to await further instructions. The military would provide protection for him there.

Having survived their taxi ride, under assumed names McGurk and Burke checked in to the best hotel Batam had to offer. McGurk was nervous so he and Burke changed rooms. McGurk became more and more agitated after he spent all afternoon and evening on the phone trying, and failing, to line up the rendezvous. Burke, tired of being holed up, demanded they check out the nightlife. McGurk said he'd noticed three men watching them as they went through the hotel lobby and Frank made fun of his mate's paranoia.

McGurk was an immaculate dresser who did nothing by halves, and now, even though they were on some godforsaken island, he ordered a limousine so they could arrive at the best nightclub on Batam in style.

As they knocked back a couple of cocktails there, McGurk and Burke pondered the delay of the meeting and wondered whether they were being set up. With a few drinks under their belt they tried their luck chatting up the young Asian woman singing at the piano, before moving on to some women at the bar.

Just as they were making in-roads with the ladies, the blood drained from McGurk's face. Three men had come into the disco. Although it was a steamy tropical night, the men were wearing ski jackets, beneath which they were obviously armed. They were scanning the crowd and they stopped when they spied Burke and McGurk. McGurk recognised them as the three men he'd seen in the hotel earlier in the evening. According to Burke, McGurk peeled off a wad of cash and gave it to the bar staff to distract the men. He and Burke bolted, collected their things from the hotel and fled.

Once they were safely on the ferry the next day, the two men roared with laughter, euphoric at having cheated death. Even before the vessel had docked in Singapore, rather than putting it down to experience, McGurk was already plotting how to recoup his $800,000.

But there are only so many times you can be dead gallus and get away with it. Six years later, in August 2009, Frank Burke received a call from a mutual friend. 'Listen, Franky, Michael really needs you. Someone's got to warn him, he's got himself into some really serious shit.'

Burke didn't want to know. All the nights on the town, all the laughs, the vintage champagne, the coke, the girls – it all counted for nothing when McGurk was short of a buck. As he had done to every friend he'd ever had, McGurk had betrayed his best mate. He'd taken $30,000 of Burke's money, claiming he would make a motza for him on a property development, the Regatta Riverside on the Brisbane River in Toowong, Queensland. But the ritzy apartment never materialised. McGurk had dudded him like he dudded everyone else.

Burke didn't call his old pal. Two weeks later the hustler from Glasgow was dead, and the list of people who had a motive to kill him was as big as a telephone book.

CHAPTER 8

KIDNAPPED

McGurk's 'rubber trees' wasn't the only perilous scam he had on the boil that involved Indonesia.

One mild autumn weekday in April 2005, pensioner Ray Simersall was pottering around in the garden of his Engadine home in the southern outskirts of Sydney when his phone rang. One of his contacts, Karl, wanted to meet him at 3.30 that afternoon. Simersall had recently taken a trip to Indonesia, after which his boss, Michael McGurk, had asked him to pass on a message to Karl and another contact, John. McGurk told Simersall that when he got back to Sydney he should explain to Karl and John that $240,000 was missing from their bank account because McGurk had had to pay it as a bribe to the Indonesian government. Simersall had duly delivered the message, so he was uneasy about the reception he would get from John and Karl at this meeting, but, always obliging, he said he'd be there in a jiffy.

Simersall was your grandfather from central casting. He was the very embodiment of geniality – twinkly eyes, thinning grey hair and a kindly air. Because he was of mature years and fairly nondescript, he was perfect for McGurk's latest criminal syndicate. Who would ever suspect such a charming, pleasant old gent was up to no good?

Simersall presumed – correctly, as it turned out – that his contacts wanted to talk to him about the missing $240,000. On his recent trip to Indonesia, he had transferred a total of $110,000 to Karl's account at the Arab Bank back in Sydney. The only problem was that John and Karl were expecting $350,000.

Simersall wasn't sure what John's last name was. Karl had two surnames, but Simersall didn't know which – if either – of them was real. The venue for his meeting with Karl was in a charmless coffee shop underneath a modern apartment block in the main street of Hurstville, a major commercial centre about 20 kilometres south of Sydney's CBD. Karl was at the coffee shop when Simersall arrived. Simersall explained to him what had happened.

A couple of weeks earlier Simersall had briefly assumed the identity of a retiree named Alexander Pails from Bellevue Hill. Armed with false identification, he had withdrawn $350,000, by way of a cheque, from Pails' superannuation fund. He had then deposited the money in a new account he'd set up in Pails' name at a different bank. His 100-point identification was a false driver's licence, a fake Medicare card and a forged Energy Australia bill. Days later, Simersall was instructed by McGurk to transfer all the money from that account to an Indonesian account.

In early March, McGurk provided Simersall with a plane ticket to Jakarta as McGurk needed 'Alexander Pails' to withdraw the cash in person. Accompanying Simersall on the journey was Hamish Williamson.

Williamson and Simersall were told by McGurk to buy two small suitcases and then drive to the Jakarta bank. Williamson waited outside in a chauffeur-driven car while Simersall, pretending to be Alexander Pails, transferred $110,000 to Karl's account back in Australia. He then withdrew enough money from the Indonesian bank to fill the two small suitcases with cash.

The next day he did the same thing until the account was empty. On both occasions, Simersall explained to Karl, he had taken the money, $240,000 in total, to McGurk's hotel and given it to McGurk and an Indonesian he knew only as Hans. McGurk had shoved a wad of cash at Simersall and told him to pay the hotel bill and have a bit of fun before flying home. 'That's all I know, honestly. I don't have the money,' Simersall earnestly told Karl now.[1]

Karl didn't seem convinced. 'Someone is going to have to pay,' he muttered darkly. Simersall left the coffee shop disturbed by Karl's accusatory tone and hoping to hell that if anyone was to pay it would be that bloody McGurk.

He hadn't got very far when Karl called out to him. 'John wants to speak to you. He's upstairs minding the baby and can't leave the apartment, so we have to go up to him.'[2]

As they caught the lift to the third floor, Karl was slightly more conciliatory, agreeing that it was probably McGurk who had ripped them off.

John let them in and indicated to the pair to sit across from him on the sofa, while he sat on an armchair. 'As I was just telling Karl . . .' began Simersall, but the rest of his explanation was cut off as a pillowcase was jammed over his head. He was wrenched backwards over the couch, and hurled onto the floor. A gun was put to his head. 'Hand over your fucking mobiles and then take all your clothes off,' said a voice Simersall didn't recognise.[3]

Naked and trembling, with the pillowcase blinding him, Simersall was made to kneel with his heels against the wall. He felt the cold, sharp edge of metal against his chest. Having worked for years in the meat industry, he knew straight away, by its unmistakable shape and weight, that it was a meat cleaver.

'Where's our fucking money?' screamed Karl.

'I don't know! I promise, I really don't know,' said the terrified 70-year-old man.

'Bullshit!' said Karl. 'You've stolen our money, you fucking thieving old bastard.'

Almost in tears, Simersall told them again he didn't have the money. 'For chrissakes,' he pleaded, 'I don't know where it is. Ask McGurk! Ask him!'

A blowtorch was held against Simersall's bare backside, singeing his hair and filling the apartment with an acrid stench. 'I am asking you again, where is the money?' said John, enunciating each word carefully and loudly as though Simersall was an idiot who hadn't understood the first time. Simersall's black briefcase was retrieved from his car. John and Karl rifled through his wallet, finding a bank card. 'What's your PIN number?' they demanded. After memorising it, Karl said they were off to see McGurk. 'If you are lying, this is going to end very badly for you. You have no idea how fucking bad it is going to be.'

With that, one of the men pushed Simersall to the floor and smashed his finger with the end of the gun. There was blood everywhere. 'Now look what you've done!' said John furiously. 'You're dripping on my bloody carpet.' He wrenched the pillow-case off and jerked Simersall's head towards the blood splatters on the carpet from his smashed finger.

John, still muttering about the mess, threw down a towel to protect his carpet. They hauled Simersall onto the coffee table, stretched out his arms like a crucifix, and tied each of his limbs to the legs of the table.

'You have three options,' said John. 'One: you can give us back the fucking money. Two: you can refund the money – sell your house, I don't fucking care. Or three, we are going to chop you up.'

Sobbing, Simersall told them to start chopping as he didn't have their money. With that John smashed the meat cleaver close to Simersall's left hand. 'You'd better bloody hope that McGurk confirms your story,' said John. With that ominous warning, John and Karl headed off across the Harbour Bridge to speak to McGurk.

Simersall tried to convince the other person left to guard him that he was telling the truth, but he gave up after a while and lay there shivering. He couldn't believe it had come to this. To end his miserable bloody life naked in this shithole of an apartment. He worried about his wife, Margaret. They'd been married for 49 years and she'd been through hell in the last decade. If anything happened to him, it would just about finish her off, he thought.

Nine years before, their eldest son had died of a heroin overdose, and only six months later their little granddaughter was orphaned after her mother also died of an overdose. Their youngest son had died in 2001. The poor bloke, an alcoholic, had passed away from smoke inhalation: he'd been boozed to the gills and had fallen unconscious with a cigarette in his hand.

Life hadn't always been bad, thought Simersall. He'd once had everything. He was a big earner, a self-made millionaire with an abattoir in Wollongong and a successful meat-delivery business. He and the missus had lived in a smart house in ritzy Vaucluse with a lifestyle to match. Those were the bloody good old days, before things went south in 1989 and they were declared bankrupt.

After his boys died, Simersall felt guilty. Their glamorous lifestyle was gone. They'd retreated to a modest house in Engadine. It was all they could afford and they struggled to make ends meet on the pension. That was until Simersall bumped into his old mate Richie Vereker, whom he knew from his Wollongong days. Vereker, whose connections were still unbelievable after all these years, had just the person who might be able to help Simersall out. Michael McGurk.

Simersall was introduced to McGurk's fraud in early 2003. Telling him what to wear so that he could be easily identified, McGurk sent him to meet John and Karl at a pub on Parramatta Road in Strathfield, just along from the railway station. The pair said they needed someone to bank a cheque for them as they had a mate who didn't want his wife to know about the payment. Simersall soon realised what they were up to but he was down on his luck and money was money. For the next two years he became a key member of a highly sophisticated superannuation fraud which netted McGurk and his mates millions.

Simersall never knew exactly how, but McGurk's syndicate had access to details of self-managed super funds. Pretending to be the policyholder, one of the syndicate's members would write to the fund requesting a withdrawal. They would notify the bank of the address the cheque was to be posted to. This would be repeated over a couple of weeks until the account was empty.

Simersall's role in the fraud was to identify houses that had easily accessible letterboxes. One method he had was to go to real estate agents and ask them for a list of properties available for rent. Knowing these houses or apartments were empty, he would use their letterboxes when the bank asked him for an address. When the cheque was sent, Simersall was on hand to remove it from the letterbox. Alternatively, he would use mailboxes at suburban apartment buildings popular with short-term renters, where the boxes were unlocked and easy to access, or where it was common for mail to arrive addressed to people who did not live there.

Once the first bank letter was received, Simersall could open a post office box and divert the mail from the address to the PO box. Australia Post's mail diversion service was also a handy tool for the syndicate.

When the cheque had been intercepted, the next step for the syndicate was to provide Simersall with a range of false documents to satisfy the 100-point identification needed to open a new account. McGurk's syndicate was able to produce false driver's licences, birth certificates, credit cards, Medicare cards, electricity and phone bills; it would even register fake business names with the Office of Fair Trading.

Armed with his own photo but in his victim's name, Simersall would open a new bank account in the name of the person to whom the cheque had been made out. For example, on 27 June 2003 'Justin James Davies' asked to withdraw $264,805 from his super fund. The cheque for that amount was posted to the address Davies supposedly supplied. One week later, using a $100 deposit, a St George bank account was opened in Davies' name using a forged driver's licence and birth certificate. The cheque, which had been intercepted by Simersall, was deposited in that account on 9 July 2003. A series of withdrawals were made and by the end of August the $264,805 was all gone.

The 'fraud kits', as they were known, were kept at a derelict house McGurk had bought with Justin Brown in 2002 at 26 Orlando Avenue, Mosman, a five-minute walk from McGurk's family home. After the cheques cleared, Simersall withdrew the cash and gave it to McGurk or his associates. One used the pseudonym John Adams, the other was known as Karl.

As Simersall lay tied up across the coffee table in the Hurstville apartment, the phone rang. It was John and Karl. They'd forgotten Simersall's PIN. It was a 45-minute drive each way to McGurk's place. On the way they had stopped at the ATM in the Shell service station on Military Road in Cremorne, just two blocks from McGurk's house. They emptied Simersall's account. Now Simersall was suffering what he had done to others.

It was edging close to midnight when John and Karl returned. Maybe the lack of funds in Simersall's account had satisfied them, maybe McGurk had put in a good word – whatever the case, they let him go.

That same night Detective Senior Constable Mathieu Russell was working the night shift with the Robbery and Serious Crime Unit when he had a call from the Police Integrity Commission (PIC). The PIC's primary function is to investigate crooked cops, but this call was different. They had just intercepted a phone call during which some male voices were talking about someone called Simersall being kidnapped and tortured at an address in Hurstville.

Hurstville Police Station was less than 2 kilometres away and two squad cars were immediately dispatched to the apartment block mentioned in the call. It was just after midnight. When no one answered the door at number 31, the police smashed it down. The apartment was empty but what police did find had them worried. There was a blood-stained blue towel and blood on the carpet. They found a briefcase with documents belonging to an R. Simersall. There were also two large plastic storage boxes in the apartment in which police discovered a treasure trove of impressively crafted fake identities: birth certificates, Medicare cards, key cards, rate notices, cheque books, deposit books and 19 driver's licences, all in different names. The fake IDs had one thing in common, the same photo of an elderly gentleman. Whoever the man was, his tanned complexion made him quite the chameleon, passing for an Anglo-Saxon ('Barry Bromley'), a Slav ('Tomislan Baric') and a Russian ('Alex Kernikov'), among others.

The police realised that they were looking at fraud kits – every piece of ID needed to pass the 100-point process introduced by the federal government to stamp out fraud – but scratched their heads when they found hundreds of thousands of dollars in obscure foreign currencies such as Nicaraguan córdobas, Argentinean pesos, Congolese francs and Bolivian pesos.

It didn't take too long for detectives to catch up with Ray Simersall, and as soon as they picked him up they recognised him as the man in the fake IDs. Back at Hurstville Police Station, Simersall said nothing. He'd had numerous brushes with the law in the past for stealing, driving offences, false pretences, having stolen goods and the like, and he knew to keep his mouth shut. His details, along with the names of the fraud kits, were circulated on the internal police system.

That would prove a godsend for one police officer.

The previous year, Kylie Stewart, a 26-year-old constable stationed at Mascot near Sydney Airport, had received a file from the Commonwealth Bank. The bank had a problem. The proceeds from stolen superannuation and insurance cheques were being deposited into new accounts that had been set up with fraudulent documentation at certain CBA branches. Constable Stewart's investigations throughout 2004 uncovered a similar pattern with other financial institutions. Although the banks had CCTV footage of the perpetrator at ATMs in Wynyard, Flemington Markets, Newtown and Hurstville, they didn't know who the old guy on the film was.[4]

By the beginning of 2005, Stewart almost had her man. On 28 January an elderly man had asked to withdraw $6800 in cash at the ANZ bank in Balmain. Because of the amount involved, the teller requested some identification. The retiree produced a driver's licence and a key card in the name of Brian Anthony Sturgess.

Nine days earlier a cheque from his MLC MasterKey Super account, totalling more than $60,000, had been made out to Brian Sturgess. At the same time, a phone sales business called MIC MasterKey was registered with the New South Wales Department of Fair Trading by a Brian Sturgess. MIC would look just like MLC to a bank teller in a hurry.

Three days later a new account in the name of Brian Sturgess was opened at the Maroubra branch of the ANZ bank. The 100-point identification criteria was passed with flying colours using the registration details of the newly set-up business, plus a Medicare card, driver's licence and a bill from Energy Australia. The account had been open for only a week and here was Mr Sturgess wanting to withdraw almost $7000 in cash. Odd, thought the teller. But when she took a close look at the driver's licence, her heart started racing. It had been issued on 1 January. The first day of the year was always a public holiday, so the teller knew the RTA could not possibly have been open to issue a licence on that day. 'Just a minute, sir,' she told the customer and ducked round to the manager's office to show him the fake ID. They rang the police. The teller calmly went back to the counter, trying her best to act as if nothing was amiss, to tell 'Mr Burgess' that it shouldn't be too much longer. Eventually, however, 'Mr Burgess' became agitated and rushed out of the bank, leaving the fake ID behind.[5]

When Kylie Stewart found out how close they had come to nabbing their guy, she was pissed off. Over the last three years this enigmatic elderly chap had stolen close to $2 million and police weren't any closer to catching him.

All that changed on the morning of 7 April 2005, when Stewart saw a notification on the internal police system. Sure enough, the photo posted by Hurstville detectives matched the dozen or so grainy images she had of her suspect. All that was left to do was join the dots in this series of ingenious frauds.

At 9.40 am on 16 June, Raymond Gerald Simersall, born 21 December 1935, was arrested by Sergeant Andrew Marks and taken to Sutherland Police Station, where he was charged with more than 50 fraud-related offences connected to the theft of 12 cheques totalling $2,043,518.26

Police offered Simersall a deal. If he could help them out with other members of the syndicate, maybe there would be a discount on his jail term. Simersall refused to cooperate. It wasn't until the end of 2006, when his trial was about to start, that he finally relented and told police he was willing to cooperate. The wheels of justice turn slowly, and another year passed before he sat down with his lawyer and Detective Sergeant Marks at Hurstville Police Station.

The mastermind of the fraud was Michael McGurk, Simersall matter-of-factly told Sergeant Marks. He had been introduced to McGurk by their mutual friend Richie Vereker. He described how all the fraud kits had been stored at 26 Orlando Avenue. Simersall said he had even lived there on and off, and so had another man, Hamish Williamson. Simersall explained to the police how it was his job to collect the mail addressed to his various aliases from the Orlando Avenue mailbox. Mail arrived daily relating to both the superannuation theft and a separate multi-million dollar mortgage fraud McGurk was also running.

At times bank employees would visit to check on mortgage defaulters who had listed Orlando Avenue as their home. Simersall was responsible for fending off inquiries, impersonating fictional residents with his disarming smile and, in some cases, changing the brass numbers on the apartment at the back to comply with whatever fake apartment number had been provided to the bank.

Sergeant Marks took notes as Simersall told him it was McGurk who had introduced him to John and Karl. He later recalled that Karl had given him a deposit slip for his security company. When I did a corporate search, the names Simersall had given the police, of the company and its directors, stacked up.

Simersall told police that he had transferred funds overseas and had been provided with air tickets to withdraw the money from these same foreign accounts. Simersall said he flew first class three times to Indonesia and Thailand to help transfer the stolen money back to Australia.

In March 2003, before his first trip with the syndicate, he transferred $900,000 in stolen superannuation funds from a Commonwealth Bank account to that of a Thai sports-goods and toy company belonging to the pseudonymous John Adams. John was in Thailand and he'd withdrawn part of the money from the Thai company, storing it in a 'backpack of cash'. It was one thing to get hold of it in Thailand but quite another to get it back to Australia. Days later Simersall boarded a Thai Airways flight to Bangkok, where he met up with John at the Millennium Hilton. Once there, Simersall opened bank accounts at Thailand's largest commercial bank, the Bangkok Bank, and at the Siam Commercial Bank. John took his backpack crammed with cash and deposited its contents into Simersall's accounts.

The ATM cards that the Thai banks had provided to Simersall were handed over to Karl and John so they could withdraw funds back in Australia. The syndicate was so busy laundering stolen cash that Simersall had been back in Sydney for only a week when he was told he had to return to Bangkok and open two more bank accounts. He informed the two banks, again the Siam and Bangkok banks, that he wanted to open new accounts as he had marital problems and his wife could access the two accounts he had opened the week before. The banks believed him and each issued him with another bank card, which he again passed on to Karl and John. Simersall told the police he'd spent a week at the Bangkok Hilton and had bought himself two suits, a pair of shoes and about six shirts.

His third and last trip was the one taken in March 2005, when he flew to Indonesia accompanied by Hamish Williamson; the fateful trip on which McGurk stole the $240,000, which led to Simersall's torture.

Of the $2 million he stole for the syndicate, Simersall's cut was a measly $25,000. McGurk had also promised him a share in a property development deal in South Australia which involved other members of the syndicate. But this never eventuated.

Other police were assigned to follow up Simersall's information. Their efforts were questionable. Local police went to the last address they had for Karl, in Auburn, only to find he was long gone. Checks with immigration showed that Hamish Flucker Williamson had first arrived in Australia on 4 November 2005, and had left the country on 7 September 2006. This meant he couldn't have gone to Indonesia with Simersall in March 2005 as Simersall was claiming. As it turns out the records were incomplete.

After McGurk's murder Williamson confirmed Simersall's account of the Indonesian trip. Williamson said he did accompany Simersall to Jakarta. He was surprised that there were such limited records of his movements because as a dual UK–Australian citizen he had been yo-yoing in and out of Australia for 20 years. Williamson said that McGurk had asked him to go into the bank with Simersall, and he had refused. 'I sat in the car, while Simersall went in,' said Williamson.[6] When Simersall emerged with the two bulging suitcases full of Indonesian rupiah, Williamson asked what he was doing. Simersall told the driver to take them to McGurk's hotel and then explained he was transferring money and that he was going to be cut in on a deal. Williamson turned to Simersall, warning him not to get involved with McGurk and Hans. 'What do you think I should do?' Simersall asked. Williamson replied, 'Whatever this money is, you should be thinking twice.'[7]

Not long after his arrest, Simersall went to see Williamson and told him about the kidnapping and torture. The pieces all fitted together for Williamson. The afternoon Simersall had been kidnapped, John and Karl had come over to Orlando Avenue looking for Williamson. Two Irish backpackers who were doing some dodgy deals for McGurk reported that John and Karl had turned up with a pillowcase and gun, demanding to know where Williamson was. When he heard they were looking for him, Williamson confronted McGurk. 'I said to McGurk, "What the fuck! What's going on here?"'[8]

McGurk was indifferent to Simersall's ordeal. He told Williamson that Simersall had stuffed up and there was really nothing McGurk could do to help him – he had brought it all upon himself.

'If those guys come in that door with a pillowcase, I will be telling them where you live!' Williamson angrily told McGurk. 'It's got nothing to do with me.'

Indignant at the idea that Williamson would direct them to his house, McGurk snapped, 'Hold on – there's kids involved.'[9] It was all right for other people to bear the consequences for whatever chicanery McGurk was up to, but the injustice of having his own family put at risk was a bridge too far in McGurk's eye. Williamson wasn't to know that when the police later came knocking, McGurk was only too ready to throw him to the wolves by falsely claiming that it was his friend Hamish who was up to no good and had stolen money from McGurk.

A few days after Simersall had spoken to police, Kylie Stewart, now working in Bourke in the state's far west, received an email from a young police colleague.

Date: Wednesday, October 24, 2007 10.43 am
Subject: SIMMRSALL [sic]
Hi Kylie, I made some inquiries with Michael MCGURK. MCGURK runs a property business in the city. He told me that he knew SIMMERSALL [sic] because he used to live in one of the properties managed by his company (he used to live there with some retirees). He told me that he had no business dealings with SIMMERSALL neither did he take part in any money transfers or frauds.

MCGURK told me that Hamish WILLAIMSON [sic] defrauded his company of $700,000 and have [sic] since fled the country. There are warrants out for his arrest.

MCGURK doesn't have any knowledge of [Karl] or John ADAMS.

Hope this helps.[10]

It's not hard to see how a young constable would be no match for a master con man like McGurk. No doubt he invited the constable into his expensive Cremorne home, passed the Picasso, and offered him a refreshment. Dripping with sincerity, he would have agreed that the name Simersall was vaguely familiar – offer a grain of truth, to make the story plausible. It would be hard for anyone to believe that such a well-dressed, charming man, who lived in such a lovely house and with a nice family, would be involved in any skulduggery.

And that was the extent of the police investigation into the criminal mastermind of this superannuation fraud, Michael McGurk.

Simersall, staring down the barrel of a long stretch in the slammer at a time when he should have been doting on his grandchildren, became increasingly desperate. He begged police to investigate further. What about the call intercepted by the PIC, which had tipped off the police to his kidnapping in the first place? Surely that would confirm his story and contain vital information the police could follow up?

On 16 January 2008, Simersall's solicitor, Craig Longman, wrote to the Crown prosecutor requesting that if New South Wales police were in possession of the audio recording capable of identifying Mr McGurk, as he had been instructed they were, a copy of any such recording and/or transcript was to be provided to his offices urgently.

A week later, Longman fired off another letter to the prosecutor. He had been instructed that the recording contained the voices of two of the suspects in his client's kidnapping, speaking to each other. He suggested that there may have been references to Mr McGurk during the recording, and that the recording was likely to provide evidence supporting his client's claim that he was kidnapped.

But it was to no avail. Despite his protestations that he was a mere foot soldier in McGurk's criminal network, Simersall was sentenced to four years in jail. He had stolen more than $2 million from 12 separate people. Only $82,000 was ever recovered.

At his sentencing, Judge Greg Woods of the District Court of New South Wales told Simersall that due to his lowly standing in the crime group, 'he was always going to be the "bunny" if the scheme came unstuck'.[11] It was Friday, 7 March 2008; exactly three years earlier Simersall had been in Jakarta handing suitcases of cash to Michael McGurk. 'This was an elaborate conspiracy in which the offender was a part,' said the judge sternly. 'It involved rather complicated arrangements within various institutions having the control of funds, and I would hope and expect that the police are quietly engaged in further enquiry into these matters.'[12]

Peering over his spectacles at the hapless Simersall in the dock, Judge Woods opined, 'It is a tragic aspect of this case that the offender is now seventy-two years of age; he certainly should have known better.' The judge continued, 'Police, after what I am satisfied are genuine enquiries made by them, are unable to charge anybody else. Nonetheless, it seems to me that the assistance which this man has given may be in due course of some use. I find it hard to believe that this matter will not eventually – perhaps after a matter of years – bring somebody else unstuck.'[13]

In his book *The Fast Life and Sudden Death of Michael McGurk*, Richie Vereker expressed surprise when Simersall, who had driven him around for eight years after his stroke, 'was convicted on dozens of counts of fraud and sent to prison'.[14] He omitted to mention that Simersall was committing those crimes on behalf of McGurk.

'It is absolutely disgraceful that my husband was the only one ever convicted over this scam,' said Simersall's wife, Margaret. 'We want to know why McGurk was able to get away with it all. I know [he] had friends in high places. Ray saw McGurk with some of them.'[15]

CHAPTER 9

THE MINIATURE KORAN

In the bone-chilling northern hemisphere winter of 2004, Michael McGurk and David Rahme, a property developer and construction manager, took a trip to Moscow. Rahme, with his wavy dark hair and silver-rimmed glasses, had been persuaded by McGurk to embark on the business opportunity of a lifetime. He could not have known that the object with which he was about to become entangled, smaller than a matchbox, would embroil him in a dispute with one of the richest men on the planet.

Normally he flew solo and didn't have partners, McGurk told Rahme and Canadian-born Hugh Millikin, an IT specialist and winter Olympian who'd represented his adopted country in the little-known sport of curling. Their children were classmates at the Sacred Heart Catholic primary school in Mosman and, as they were fellow school parents, he was, McGurk said, happy to make an exception in their cases. The breakup of the Soviet Union had given savvy middlemen plenty of opportunities to make a quick buck, he explained to them. Wealthy Westerners were willing buyers of all manner of Russian goods, from military hardware to precious religious artefacts. It was just a matter of getting your hands on the right ones. Two pieces of sophisticated technology developed by brilliant Soviet scientists had caught McGurk's eye, and he wanted to acquire the rights to sell them in Australia. Much of the technology had been developed as part of the Russian space program, McGurk told his two mates.

The first was a 'geo-radar', known as the 'Grot', which was a ground penetrating radar system used to detect water, mineral and oil deposits deep underground. McGurk explained that mining giant BHP had recently paid several million dollars for a similar machine from the US, but the Soviet model was superior and, at only $US25,000 each, Australian miners would be queuing up to get their hands on it. It could also be used by the military to search for mines, he told them.

The second was a thermoelectric cell, a tiny cooling system about the size of a credit card that could be used to extract hot air from confined spaces. Its potential was boundless, said the super-spruiker. If the two men put in $200,000 each, McGurk would let them have a piece of the action. Millikin and Rahme were both interested, but Rahme insisted on travelling to Moscow with McGurk to inspect the products before he and Millikin committed.

Opening the doors to these potential riches was fellow wheeler-dealer Viktor D'Jamirze. D'Jamirze was born in a migrant camp in country New South Wales in 1951, the second-eldest of seven brothers. As a primary school boy Viktor returned with his family to live in Russia for several years, before returning to Sydney, where his family elected to live in a highly secure compound in Toongabbie, in Sydney's west.

In his early fifties when he met McGurk, Viktor had long grey curly hair, which he tied back in a ponytail; an unfashionable moustache, which snaked down his cheeks like a handlebar; and he wore a gold chain around his neck.

D'Jamirze may have appeared an ageing hippy, but he was a whirlwind when it came to deals. His business record, however, was patchy. The Australian Securities and Investments Commission (ASIC) had banned him from being a company director for four years due to 'incompetence and lack of understanding of the duties of a director.'[1] He was bankrupt, as were four of his brothers. When asked to list the reasons for his bankruptcy, D'Jamirze's answer was, 'Because I have no money.'[2]

Viktor and his brother Vladimir, or Prince Vladimir as he liked to call himself, had first come to public attention in the mid-1990s. In a deal reminiscent of the plot of a James Bond movie, the D'Jamirze brothers and bankrupt billionaire Alan Bond tried to do a deal buying and selling osmium-187, which was being offered as a weapons-grade radioactive isotope used in the manufacture of Stealth bombers. However, according to the US Defense Special Weapons Agency, osmium-187 is frequently used in scams by con artists, who claim that it has nuclear weapons applications when it does not.

Bondy and his new Russian business partners also had a couple of side deals on the boil involving rare violins and the sale of roubles. The deals occurred at the time Alan Bond was looking dazed and crushed in the witness box, his brain so badly damaged, he said, that he could barely remember his own name, let alone where he might have stashed his multi-million-dollar fortune.

In May 1994, when Bond was claiming he was too ill to be in the witness box, his phone records revealed he was up all night making calls to Zurich, where the brothers D'Jamirze were staying, with the mouth-watering prospect of a deal potentially worth $4 billion. Vladimir D'Jamirze had told Bond he could get his hands on huge amounts of osmium-187 from contacts in the Ukraine. Bond deposited millions of dollars into a Swiss bank account to purchase the isotope. In his book *Going for Broke: How Bond Got Away With It*, author Paul Barry said the D'Jamirzes had stumped up $3 million as their seed capital for the deal. But their career as arms dealers came to nought, wrote Barry, as neither they nor Bond could come up with the US$2 billion needed to buy the 10 kilograms that was on offer, and the D'Jamirzes lost their $3 million.

Despite numerous commercial setbacks, for the enterprising D'Jamirzes there was always another deal just round the corner.

Viktor D'Jamirze and Michael McGurk's paths crossed in 2000 when D'Jamirze was selling precious stones and coins. D'Jamirze spruiked himself as smoothing the path of Australian entrepreneurs who wanted to trade with Russia. His family kept a permanent suite of rooms in the five-star Rossiya Hotel in Moscow, adjacent to the Kremlin. Viktor's clients tended to be those who didn't have any qualms about what he was trying to sell.

He claimed to be on first-name terms with several ministers, senior military commanders and officials in intelligence circles and had made a living of sorts over the years by providing introductions and doing deals. Like McGurk, Viktor always had his eye out for the big payday. When D'Jamirze was introduced to the thermoelectric cell and the Grot, he had just the investor in mind.

After D'Jamirze had delivered his sales pitch about the enormous potential of these products – both civil and military – McGurk could see nothing but dollar signs. 'Let's go to Russia to sign the agreement,' he told D'Jamirze with his customary enthusiasm.[3]

In October 2004 McGurk made his first trip to Moscow with Hamish Williamson. During their stay D'Jamirze flaunted his political connections by inviting McGurk and Williamson to join him at a wedding in one of Russia's most famous hotels, the Metropol. Guests at the wedding included Olympic gold medallists and high-ranking Russian government officials, as well as an empty seat for President Putin. McGurk disgraced himself by getting drunk and was unceremoniously carried back to his hotel room shortly after the main course.

The following day he and Williamson travelled to the dacha of Ludmila Volkomirskaya and her husband, both scientists who had worked in the aerospace industry. Ludmila demonstrated the Grot, which she calculated could detect objects up to 500 metres below the surface of the earth, whereas similar current Western technology could only measure to 20 metres. While the Grot could eliminate a lot of exploratory digging, it was so heavy-duty the operator had to wear a lead apron.

But McGurk and Williamson thought it was a winner. McGurk signed the contract with Viktor on the spot.

Next they visited Olga Vyacheslavna, the scientist behind the thermoelectric device. The small, rectangular grey brushed-metal box looked like a mobile phone. McGurk was equally impressed with this technology, telling the Russian scientists that when they visited him in Australia in a year's time it would have revolutionised the world. But McGurk's notoriously short attention span was soon diverted by another promising venture. D'Jamirze casually mentioned to him the existence of a miniature Koran. One of D'Jamirze's key Russian contacts was Inal Kochiev, an ex-colonel in the KGB. Kochiev sourced ancient artefacts, relics, precious stones and paintings, and D'Jamirze would match them with wealthy private buyers and museums. They split the proceeds.

Kochiev had a tiny object about the size of a matchbox for D'Jamirze to sell: a miniature Koran completed in 1576, when Queen Elizabeth I was on the British throne. It had 16 tiny orange and turquoise stones dotted around the outside of the silver case, in the shape of the hours on a clock face. The silver case was engraved with elegant Arabic script which translated as 'In the name of God the most merciful, the most compassionate.' Inside the case was a tiny leather-bound Koran with an insignia engraved into the front cover. Each octagonal-shaped page, only 7 centimetres wide, was handwritten in blue and gold ink on coffee-coloured parchment in minuscule, indecipherable Arabic lettering. 'I have inherited these books,' the retired KGB colonel told his friend. This was untrue. The retired colonel was almost certainly not a Muslim. As one person close to the deal said, 'He's an ex-KGB agent. Who knows how he would have got hold of all that stuff.'[4]

But how he'd come by the curious relic was of no concern to D'Jamirze. All that mattered to him was how he could dispose of it – and for what price.

McGurk became entranced by the romance of the miniature bejewelled Koran. He returned to Sydney with residual enthusiasm for the promise of riches from Soviet technology, and found investors Rahme and Millikin.

On their trip at the end of 2004, Viktor D'Jamirze organised for McGurk and Rahme to stay in another luxurious hotel in central Moscow, the boutique Alrosa. It had a discreet entrance and little or no signage announcing its presence. During the day, scientists would come to the hotel with their products. At night, Kochiev would arrive with a flock of dealers, bearing artefacts, paintings and sculptures. 'It was like going shopping. They were fishing to see what we were interested in,' Rahme said.[5] Most of the deals were done over copious amounts of vodka, regardless of the time of day. McGurk and Rahme were sick with hang-overs for the first couple of days.

McGurk, D'Jamirze and Kochiev also ventured out of the hotel to see a dealer who was selling paintings from the boot of his car. D'Jamirze warned McGurk not to buy 'under any circum-stance' as it was dark and difficult to see the paintings. 'Buying things in foreign currency in a dark alley is very dangerous,' he cautioned.[6] Heedless of his warnings, McGurk headed off down the alley and returned with a canvas of dubious authentic-ity for which he'd paid US$3000. 'It's an original Picasso!' he exclaimed, proudly unfurling a simple black-and-white charcoal etching with the famous 'Picasso' signature in the corner. Friends later recalled seeing the 'Picasso' he'd bought for his wife hanging in pride of place in the McGurk home.

The two men were in Moscow for about a week. It was only in the final days of their visit that Kochiev finally showed them the Koran. McGurk was sure it was the deal of a lifetime. Rahme was persuaded to pay Kochiev US$6000 as a holding deposit, with a percentage of the eventual sale he and McGurk made to be returned to Kochiev. Due to restrictions prohibiting items of cultural significance from leaving the country, Kochiev organised for the Koran, McGurk's 'Picasso' and some rare books to be smuggled out by a Russian diplomat working in the embassy in Dubai. McGurk had other business to attend to back home, so D'Jamirze and Rahme flew to Dubai to collect their precious cargo, which Viktor promptly popped into a plastic shopping bag.

When they returned to Australia McGurk wasted no time in finding a buyer for the miniature Koran. He claimed to have had interest from Lebanese president Rafic Hariri, but Hariri was assassinated in February 2005 before a deal could be done.

McGurk boasted that Tommy Suharto, the playboy son of former Indonesian President Suharto, was interested, as was the Kuwaiti ambassador in Canberra. But when he wanted to take the Koran to Canberra to show it to the ambassador, D'Jamirze insisted he accompany him. McGurk refused as he thought D'Jamirze's unkempt looks would hamper his sales pitch.

And so the custody battle began. The Koran had only been in Australia for a couple of weeks before McGurk and D'Jamirze were fighting over it. McGurk launched legal action in the New South Wales Supreme Court against Viktor D'Jamirze and Inal Kochiev. One of McGurk's associates remembers asking McGurk at the time, 'What have you got yourself into? Are you dealing with an ex-KGB agent?' McGurk replied, 'I think so.'[7] His friend then made a joke about the Russian mafia. Perhaps his friend's throwaway line made McGurk think twice, because within a week he had drawn up the will that would be relied on after his death four years later.

In typical McGurk fashion, the Koran deal was not on paper. Rahme later looked back wistfully: 'A lot of those negotiations, unfortunately, were left to McGurk to handle. They were always a bit bloody vague.'[8] McGurk claimed he had paid Kochiev the deposit so McGurk and Rahme could take the Koran back to Australia and sell it on behalf of Kochiev. D'Jamirze remembered it differently. He insisted he was the only one with a power of attorney to sell the Koran for Kochiev and that he had planned to sell it in Dubai. Hamish Williamson's recollection was that McGurk was 'trying to steal it' from D'Jamirze.[9]

Whichever version is true, the fight over the ownership of the Koran was to last for the rest of McGurk's short life. Initially, the court ordered it should be put in a safety deposit box in the Commonwealth Bank's Martin Place branch, which was considered neutral ground. If McGurk wanted to view it, D'Jamirze and his solicitor had to be there, and vice versa. The court later gave permission for McGurk, Rahme and Millikin to take the Koran to Singapore because there they had lined up a potential buyer – none other than the Sultan of Brunei.

Sultan Hassanal Bolkiah is an absolute monarch who, according to the oil-rich country's constitution, 'can do no wrong in either his personal or any official capacity'. He is one of the world's richest men, with a private fortune estimated to total at least US$20 billion.

McGurk's Indonesian contact, Rosihan 'Hans' Yacub, provided McGurk with an introduction to people with connections to the sultan. Two years earlier it was Hans who had organised Indonesian generals to provide protection for McGurk's 'rubber trees' scam, but they had ripped him off and then tried to have him killed on Batam Island. Now here Hans was again, greasing the palms of powerful people on behalf of the Scot.

On a steamy morning in April 2005 Hans, McGurk and the sultan's men teed off at the exclusive Royal Brunei Golf Club. The screech of monkeys from the lush expanse of surrounding jungle accentuated the exotic location. The three men dined that night at the neighbouring Jerudong Park and Polo Country Club, a private club used by the sultan and his family. The ornately decorated formal dining room, in shades of gold and royal blue, sat hundreds of diners. Classical Doric columns lined the walls and crystal chandeliers hung from the intricately painted ceilings. Elaborate woven carpets lay underfoot. On McGurk's right sat Brunei's transport minister, Pengiran Yakub Othman. On his left was Sunny Chai, a small, plump man who ran a chain of car dealerships and was well-connected to the royal court: he was the godson of the sultan's private secretary, Pehin Nawawi.

Like all good con men, McGurk made sure he didn't rush things. Instead, he trotted out his business history, embellishing

the details, telling his hosts that in the early 1990s he had travelled to Brunei with ECC Lighting to supervise the installation
of light fittings in the sultan's private residences (he had made
no such trip).[10]

It was only when the night was nearing its end that he
casually dropped the Koran into the conversation, almost as an
after-thought. He painted such an alluring picture of the object
that Chai arranged to meet McGurk the following day to discuss
it further. McGurk mentioned that the Kuwaiti ambassador to
Australia was interested in the Koran, and the sum of $US25
million was being discussed. With the sultan's net worth being
$US20 billion, McGurk and Hans figured that it was best to
start big.

When Chai said he was sure it was something the sultan
would be interested in, McGurk offered to sell him the Koran
for the knock-down price of $US8 million. He even offered to
sweeten the deal by throwing in a free 'biography of mystics'.

After his seemingly successful meeting with Chai, McGurk
flew back to Australia. On his return, photos of the Koran
were dispatched and complex negotiations with Sunny Chai
commenced. McGurk's timing couldn't have been better, said
Chai. The 58-year-old sultan was about to marry his third wife,
a stunning 26-year-old Malaysian newsreader. The exquisite
400-year-old relic would be the perfect wedding gift.

McGurk told Millikin and Rahme that they were on the
verge of clinching a deal that would make them all very rich.
They set up a company called Garsec; arrangements were made
for the Koran to be handed over to the sultan, and a Citibank
account in Singapore was opened to receive his payment of
US$8 million.

But nothing happened through 2005. The sultan's August
wedding to the young newsreader came and went. McGurk
made three trips to Singapore and six to Brunei, but he didn't
see the sultan, or any of his money. Not a patient man at the best
of times, he'd finally had enough. In February 2006, 14 months
after McGurk had first acquired the match-box-sized Koran,

Hans organised for a relative of the sultan to escort the Scot into the inner sanctum of the magnificent 1788-room royal palace in Brunei so McGurk could meet with Pehin Nawawi rather than having to deal with middleman Sunny Chai.

At the meeting Nawawi summonsed Chai and Transport Minister Othman. Chai began making excuses for why the sale had not yet come to fruition. 'Look, I must tell you,' said McGurk in a temper, 'if you want to lie, then be aware that we have the telephone conversations on tape.'[11]

After some discussion in Malay, the private secretary broke the bad news to McGurk. 'I recently told Sunny Chai that His Majesty has changed his mind and no longer wants the book.'[12]

McGurk was furious. With airfares, accommodation, legals and bribes, he'd spent close to $700,000, and had nothing to show for it. The only card he had left to play was an old favourite – a legal stoush. On 19 June 2006 McGurk launched in the New South Wales Supreme Court a supremely optimistic lawsuit: *Garsec Pty Ltd v His Majesty Sultan Haji Hassanal Bolkiah Mu'izzaddin Waddaulah the Sultan & Yang Di-Pertuan of Brunei.*

Perhaps McGurk thought that one of the world's richest men would find being sued unpalatable, and would buy the Koran just to get rid of him. But things didn't pan out that way. McGurk's partners in Garsec resigned. Rahme and Millikin didn't want to throw good money after bad. Millikin later summed up McGurk as 'a wheeler-dealer' who 'got involved in things that put him in difficult situations, and his dogged manner meant that he never let them go'.[13]

McGurk failed to convince the New South Wales Supreme Court that there had been a breach of the oral contract by Sunny Chai or Pehin Nawawi. The case was appealed all the way to the High Court and McGurk lost there, too.

But at the time of his death, he had still not given up. He'd come up with yet another plan to get the sultan to pay.

In 2006 Mark Burby, an English entrepreneur from Jersey, contacted McGurk after reading media reports about the aborted sale of the miniature Koran. Burby had successfully sued the sultan's sister-in-law and cousin over the failed UK launch of a Californian café chain, The Coffee Bean & Tea Leaf, and still had not received the compensation awarded to him by a British court.

In the meantime, Burby had stumbled across some information about the sultan's family that he knew could be very damaging to its members. Burby later told ABC radio that after McGurk flew to meet him in Jersey, he had no doubts about the Scot's motives. For one thing, Burby was shocked to discover that McGurk had hidden a digital tape recorder in his sock and recorded their meeting. Burby said, 'There's no short way around it. He was using that information, or was going to use it, to blackmail the sultan.'[14] Burby was sure that McGurk was planning to go to the media with the compromising material Burby had alerted him to unless the sultan completed the Koran deal.

After McGurk's murder, News Corp papers reported that Burby was seeking police protection in the UK as he had been days away from flying to Sydney to discuss with McGurk the material he allegedly had on the Brunei royal family. Burby had been gagged by the British courts from talking about this material, and the sultan had been forced to take action in the New South Wales Supreme Court to ensure McGurk did not carry out his blackmail threat. The details of exactly what Burby had uncovered still remain the subject of a worldwide suppression order.

After McGurk's death, the ownership of the Koran continued to be contested by not only D'Jamirze and his KGB mate Inal Kochiev, but by Kimberley McGurk. As for the current whereabouts of the miniature Koran itself, no one is saying. It was last heard of in that safety deposit box in the Commonwealth Bank in Martin Place. And Viktor D'Jamirze? He found a new partner to help commercialise his marvellous Grot: Moses Obeid, the son of former Labor powerbroker Eddie Obeid.

CHAPTER 10

THE ODD COUPLE

At any given time Ron Medich liked to be surrounded by young acolytes. One of those, for a time, was a young man called Paul Jason Mathieson. However, in Medich's world, being the 'favourite' could have deadly consequences – in the court of the king there are always other ambitious courtiers willing to do whatever it takes to depose the incumbent.

In November 2004, Paul Mathieson and his then wife, Nikki, smashed Denham Court's property record when they forked out $3.4 million for Ron and Odetta Medich's five-bedroom, four-bathroom house with cabana, tennis court and 25-metre heated pool sitting amid a hectare of garden.

The Mathiesons had actually bought the house 12 months before, but both parties had agreed to a delayed settlement. After meeting via the house purchase, Mathieson and Medich, despite a 30-year age gap, forged an unlikely friendship. Mathieson, impressed by Medich's wealth, admired the older man. The two quaffed copious amounts of red wine and stayed out late at places like The Establishment, the trendy Sydney CBD watering hole owned by the Hemmes family.

Unlike Medich, Mathieson was a self-made man. He was

the first in his family to finish high school. Mathieson was born in January 1975 in Warrnambool in Victoria to working-class parents who were employed at the local Nestlé factory – Paul's father worked there for 40 years. His parents doubled their shifts at the factory in order to pay for their son to live on campus while he studied at Macquarie University. Mathieson then did another degree at Bond University in Queensland, specialising in derivatives, options and futures. After graduating he worked in the financial industry, first with Japanese bank Daiwa in Melbourne, then as a research analyst specialising in industrial stocks at stockbroking firm Hogan & Partners in Perth. Subsequently he moved to Sydney, where he worked at ING.

His first business seemed a strange choice: a therapeutic massage service for the high end of town. Massages R Us opened two shops, one in North Sydney and the other near Wynyard Station. But perhaps corporate types were too stressed to take 20 minutes out for shoulder and neck massages – unfortunately the massage business was not as successful as he had hoped. Mathieson was broke and couldn't afford to pay the rent where he was living in the expensive suburb of Mosman; he retreated to his fiancée Nikki's parents' garage in the outer Sydney suburb of Hinchinbrook. His prospective father-in-law even chucked in a job for Paul – marketing manager at the Liverpool Catholic Club.

After six months of licking his wounds, Mathieson was back in the saddle, having scored a job at Next Financial, which offered innovative advice for clients investing in high-risk products. He upgraded his little MG sports car to a Porsche Boxster and, full of confidence, was ready to back himself again, launching Investment Evolution Global (IEG), which copied Next Financial's speciality of offering high-risk products for investors. Mathieson's clients had to outlay a minimum of $500,000 for investment products that previously had been available only to institutional investors. He also held seminars to market his scheme to wholesale sophisticated investors and financial planners.

Business boomed. The 29-year-old entrepreneur was making a fortune – it was time to move up in the world. Mathieson decided to splash out on a fancy house, and he had just the one in mind: Ron Medich's place in Denham Court, the Point Piper of the aspirational in Sydney's outer southwest suburbs.

Living life in the fast lane with Medich, Mathieson was keen to keep up. He traded his Porsche for a Lamborghini and regaled his friends with the expensive wines he'd shared with Ron in the expensive places they had dined. Mathieson spent more time with Ron than with his wife. Referred to by friends as 'the odd couple', the two were regular fixtures at the races and even travelled together to the horse auctions in New Zealand.

In June 2005, Mathieson launched his next venture: Amazing Loans, which was floated on the stock exchange in March 2006 at $2.50 a share.

Amazing Loans lurked at the bottom end of the lending business. With its shockingly high interest rates – up to 48 per cent – the company was regarded as a dodgy pay-day lender, meaning it handed out money to those who needed cash to tide them over to the next pay cheque. Only the desperate resorted to its loans – the target market was the unemployed and the distressed who couldn't get cash anywhere else.

The company was criticised in the Victorian parliament for lending $750 to a man with a brain injury. Another complaint involved a Melbourne woman who spoke limited English borrowing $1500 to fly to Samoa for her uncle's funeral and contribute to his burial costs. The Consumer Action Law Centre took action on her behalf against Amazing Loans for misrepresentation when she discovered she had to pay $4000 for her $1500 loan, which represented an interest rate of almost 54 per cent.

Despite A Current Affair chastising Amazing Loans for its predatory practices, the company continued to flourish. Its first shop in Campbelltown, a neighbouring suburb to Denham Court, was soon joined by six others throughout western Sydney. Six months after floating, its share price hit $7.50.

When Mathieson expressed an interest in expanding into Queensland and Victoria, his good pal Ron Medich was happy to oblige to get part of the action in this lucrative venture. In August 2006 he offered Mathieson a $25 million-loan facility at 10 per cent interest (rather more reasonable than the rates Amazing Loans charged). Mathieson immediately used $11.5 million of the loan to commence his expansion drive.

Unfortunately for the young businessman, within a few months a large spanner in the works materialised – in the form of Michael McGurk.

There is some confusion as to how Medich and McGurk first met. In a statement to police in March 2009, Medich said that he first met McGurk in 2006 during the Amazing Loans saga. 'I very [sic] stressed out at this time and I was recommended a solicitor Rob HUGH who in turn recommended Michael McGURK to try and recover my investment. McGURK helped me recover my investment in late 2007.'[1]

Interestingly, at the time of writing this police statement, Medich had a new acolyte, Andrew Howard (the man who went on to style himself as Medich's financial adviser). Already he was crediting Howard as being more effective than McGurk.

On another occasion Medich said he met McGurk in 2005 through Bob Ell and Richie Vereker.

McGurk's version was slightly different. He said he met Medich in 2006 when they were introduced by real estate agent David Vereker, Richie's eldest son.

However it was that McGurk and Medich met, at first relations between the two of them and Mathieson were all very friendly, with business being discussed at Tuscany over prosciutto, pasta and red wine. But McGurk was never able to share nicely for long. By 2007 he was desperate for cash and was being squeezed on every front. He had even resorted to forging documents in order to borrow money against his Cremorne home. Medich had money, and lots of it. In 2005 Ron and Roy had debuted in the BRW Rich List, which put their fortune at $135 million, and now, two years later, the brothers were on the verge of offloading their Norton Street shopping centre in Leichhardt for more than $100 million. McGurk realised pretty quickly that Medich was a goose, but a goose that laid golden eggs. Come hell or high water, McGurk was going to relieve Medich of some of his magnificent wealth.

Behind his back, McGurk cuttingly referred to Mathieson as 'Elvis' because of his safari jackets and sideburns. It was an Elvis classic McGurk had in mind to cleave Mathieson from his buddy Ron. 'Suspicious Minds' would do the trick.

In order to wedge out his rival, McGurk decided to sow seeds of doubt in Medich's mind about his Amazing Loans investment. He would tell Medich that Mathieson was cheating him; that Amazing Loans was almost insolvent; and ask Medich why Mathieson wasn't listening to his friend Ron's superior business ideas.

Medich had initially been excited about the potential 225 per cent return over four years from his investment in Amazing Loans. The company had plans to open 100 retail stores across the country and in June 2007 its shares peaked.

McGurk began to fuel Medich's discontent by asking him why Medich wasn't a director of Mathieson's company. After all, he had millions of share options as well as having advanced a $25 million loan facility.

McGurk would later tell the Federal Court that Medich had said, 'I can't be a director of the company due to my superannuation scheme, which is Ron Medich Properties as trustee for the Ron Medich Superannuation Fund.'[2] McGurk told the court that Medich did many of his share purchases and other finance dealings through his superannuation fund so as to reduce his tax. The disadvantage of holding shares through his superannuation fund was that he could not take a seat on a company board to look out for his investment. This meant he could not have a say in how Amazing Loans was run.

Medich began complaining that the company was opening shops in places he didn't like. By the second half of 2007 he seemed to be having second thoughts – thanks to McGurk – about letting Mathieson borrow more of the $25 million he had promised him. McGurk advised Medich he shouldn't lend any more cash until he had security for the money he had already lent. McGurk alleged Medich said, 'I want to get out of the facility agreement I have with Amazing Loans. I want to get out of the obligations to pay more money. I am sick of Paul Mathieson. He is a crook. He won't listen to what I have to say. I want the money that I've already paid to Amazing Loans returned.'[3]

Medich told the New South Wales police in a 2009 statement that he 'became worried' about his investment in Amazing Loans after he looked at the company accounts and 'thought that the company may have been insolvent'.[4]

McGurk's nagging about the viability of Mathieson's business had paid off: adept at ferreting out people's vulnerabilities, he had determined Medich's weak points. The businessman was both insecure and spineless. He allowed himself to be convinced that Mathieson was fleecing him. As would be the case with the Tilleys, Medich was only too happy to accept McGurk's offer to get his money back for him. The agreement with Medich was that McGurk could keep one-third of any amount above $14 million that he clawed back from Amazing Loans. McGurk got to work.

Not long before he was murdered, McGurk tried to explain the Amazing Loans deal to Vanda and me, telling us that he had merely been 'trying to unscramble an egg' of Medich's making. Between mouthfuls of Wagyu beef McGurk said, 'The reason I am telling you this is Medich and I still have an agreement he would pay me a third of what I could recoup from Amazing Loans.'[5] He talked of his successful negotiations with Paul Mathieson and that it was Medich who had dudded him.

It transpired that McGurk's idea of a 'successful negotiation' included the criminal offences of blackmail, extortion and demanding money with menace.

By September 2007, Mathieson had separated from his wife and abandoned Denham Court. He and his new partner, Imelda, an exotic Asian dancer he had met at Pure Platinum, a strip club in Sydney's busy Pitt Street, were paying thousands of dollars per week to rent a city apartment with panoramic views to the Blue Mountains in the west and Sydney Harbour to the east.

On the evening of Monday 24 September Mathieson had just poured himself a glass of wine and was about to have dinner when his phone rang. It was the concierge telling him that a Mr McGurk was in the lobby and wanted to see him.

Medich and Mathieson had already met that day over lunch at Dee Bee's café in Double Bay to clarify the funding of Amazing Loans. At 4.30 pm Medich had rung Mathieson to say he was sending McGurk around so that Mathieson could explain a couple of things to McGurk that Medich didn't quite understand.

Mathieson went down to the foyer. Half an hour later, he arrived back in his apartment pale and shaking. He felt physically sick and his dinner sat untouched as he told Imelda what had happened.

McGurk had started off with a couple of innocuous questions. Then he began threatening to destroy Mathieson. Medich wanted his money back. 'We will ruin your life,' growled McGurk in his toughest Glaswegian snarl. 'We will expose you in the media. We will report you to ASIC and you will go to jail.'[6]

McGurk had gone straight for the jugular because of his own dire financial circumstances. On 30 August Bankwest lawyers had written to Kimberley McGurk to tell her she had provided false information about her income, as well as false tax returns. They demanded she immediately repay her $3.2 million home loan. If she failed to do so, the bank threatened to seize the McGurks' family home and sell it from under them.

McGurk had committed a fraud to get the Bankwest loan in the first place and was being sued for more than $1 million for this sleight of hand. He had already used his house as collateral for an $840,000 loan. A caveat was registered on his house protecting the lender's interest. In order to present a clean balance sheet to borrow money from Bankwest, McGurk simply forged a legal document to remove the caveat. The furious lender slapped another caveat on the house, which met a similar fraudulent fate. This time McGurk forged the lender's signature and made up a non-existent Justice of the Peace who 'witnessed' the forgery. The caveat once again vanished. The furious lender was now suing McGurk over his $840,000 plus interest.

Here was McGurk a year down the track facing the grim prospect of losing the house altogether because of the financial trickery he'd performed behind his wife's back. It was now September and he had received a final notice from Bankwest. He needed to come up with a miracle. Also preying on his mind was that four days before receiving the bank's ultimatum, he'd learnt that Ray Simersall, a key foot soldier in his superannuation fraud, had given police a statement implicating him.

His multiple deceptions were threatening to ruin him. In the days following McGurk's visit, Mathieson rang Medich and also tried to make Medich's lawyer, Rob Hugh, see sense. It was all to no avail. Mathieson wondered whether Medich was withdrawing his financing to force Amazing Loans into liquidation. If it went into liquidation Medich would be the largest secured creditor; he could seize control of the company and do what he liked with it.

Mathieson felt he had no choice but to repay Medich's $11.5 million. He did so, but that wasn't enough for McGurk, who claimed Medich wanted a total of $20 million back. He wanted Amazing Loans to buy back his shares and options, but he wanted them repaid at a higher price than they were trading for.

Mathieson, concerned about his personal safety, organised around-the-clock security. Once that was in place he ignored Medich's and McGurk's demands.

McGurk told Medich that they would need to ratchet up the pressure on Mathieson by suing him. Medich was adamant he did not want to go to court so McGurk, who never shied away from a legal bout, volunteered to sort it out. This meant Medich would need to hand over his legal entitlement to the loans to McGurk.

On 31 October, for the princely sum of $1, Medich assigned his 115 million options in Amazing Loans to McGurk, who promptly hired city law firm Swaab to commence a lawsuit against Mathieson. McGurk also carried out his threat of going to the media. The day after acquiring Medich's options an article quoting McGurk on Amazing Loans appeared in Melbourne's *Herald Sun*. 'I'm concerned as to the solvency of the company,' he said. The article reported that an application to appoint an investigative accountant to the company would be heard by the New South Wales Supreme Court that morning. 'We'll be making our own investigations as to the disclosure made by Mr Mathieson, both to the ASX and through the press,' said McGurk in the article.[7]

That same day McGurk launched legal action against Mathieson. The young entrepreneur knew that they were holding him to ransom, that this was pure extortion. He also knew that at this point discretion was the better part of valour, and he agreed to pay $2.8 million to buy back the 115 million options Medich had assigned to McGurk. On top of that he gave Medich more shares to get him off his back.

To McGurk the $11.5 million he had clawed back plus the $2.8 million from the options meant he was above the $14 million threshold. Now he was in business. Medich still had shares. McGurk was entitled to a third of anything more he was able to extract from Mathieson. With more riches to exploit, McGurk was only just warming up with his threats to Mathieson.

Within months, Mathieson had had enough. He later told police that he had moved to Hawaii in February 2008 'to escape from Medich and his associates'.[8] There were other reasons. Amazing Loans had tanked. Its share price had fallen 90 per cent in a year and Mathieson was contemplating chancing his arm in the US market.

McGurk's prospective windfall from Amazing Loans was yet to come to fruition and Bankwest was still on his back. He managed to persuade Medich to advance him $3.8 million as commission for recovering Medich's money from Mathieson. As Medich was later to tell the Federal Court in one of his many legal stoushes against McGurk, McGurk said to him, 'I need $3.8 million in a hurry to pay off mortgages on my house and my wife is on my back: she wants me to get the mortgages paid.'[9] McGurk deliberately omitted that he had been sprung not only obtaining the bank loan by fraudulent means but doing so using his wife's name.

Having sold up in Australia, Mathieson spent US$3.5 million on a luxury tropical home on Hawaii's main tourist island of Oahu, in the picturesque east of Honolulu. His expansive lounge room looked out across a palm-fringed lagoon to the Pacific Ocean and the Diamond Head volcanic crater made famous in the TV series *Lost*. A pair of life-sized lion statues watched over either side of a paved driveway, which led through the manicured lawns dotted with palm trees up to the two-storey house. Mathieson's house had an impressive fortress-like six-foot stone wall and large wrought-iron gates. Perched prominently on the gate was a security company's red octagonal-shaped sign, a warning to the uninvited not to trespass.

Mathieson had been living in Hawaii for only three months when one morning in late May 2008 he received an email from McGurk in which he asked Mathieson to phone him. Mathieson was horrified. 'What do you want?' he emailed back.

'I want to meet with you,' McGurk said.

'What do you mean "meet with you"?' Mathieson said, believing McGurk to be thousands of kilometres away.[10]

'I'm in Hawaii,' McGurk replied.

Mathieson couldn't believe it. Given that the last time he had seen McGurk he'd been threatened, his first thought was to call the police.

Perhaps McGurk had intended to pay Mathieson an unannounced visit to his home but was put off by the security measures; at any rate, by the following day he'd convinced Mathieson to see him, assuring him that the venue would be a public place.

The Beach Bar of McGurk's hotel, the Moana Surfrider on Waikiki Beach, was selected and the pair chose a table overlooking the water and shaded by a massive 100-year-old Indian banyan tree. McGurk wore chinos and a pastel-coloured polo shirt and Mathieson, Hawaiian-style, was wearing shorts and a t-shirt. It was a tense meeting, but McGurk attempted to lighten the mood by ordering a bottle of chardonnay and a couple of club sandwiches. To outsiders the two men enjoying a drink looked like regular holidaymakers. But, as they say, appearances are deceptive. McGurk had flown to Hawaii, at Medich's expense, to persuade Mathieson to pay him $11.5 million in return for McGurk handing back Medich's remaining 275 million shares in Amazing Loans.

Mathieson didn't think he should have to pay for the shares, having handed them over to Medich for free the previous year. He would later allege that he had given them to Medich as part of an extortion attempt by McGurk in late October or early November 2007. 'That was the deal to stop them from coming after me and my family. So they extorted those shares from me,' he said.[11]

Mathieson said he didn't have the $11.5 million and as the meeting progressed, McGurk realised that he was telling the truth. But the Scot sensed an opportunity. Why not work both sides of the deal? By the end of their discussion, McGurk had accepted that Mathieson didn't have the money, but had persuaded him to meet again in a couple of weeks to nut out another deal.

McGurk's meeting with Mathieson took three hours, but in true McGurk style he stayed in Honolulu for a week – at Medich's expense. Things were looking up for McGurk. On 28 May Medich had transferred $4.4 million into his account to fund other dubious deals the Scot had on the boil. Even though Simersall had dobbed him into police, McGurk had charmed his way out of the frame. The pensioner was locked up over the superannuation fraud, but the mastermind was free as a bird and enjoying some rest and respite on a glorious island and someone else's dime. What could be better?

Back in Sydney, on 14 June he visited Ron and Odetta and told them a blatant lie – that he was negotiating to get as much as $25 million for the shares, when at the most Medich would be getting $3 million.

Three weeks after his first visit, McGurk returned to Hawaii and met with Mathieson again. McGurk complained about Medich, how demanding he was, how he expected company on the weekend. Perhaps it didn't cross his mind that Mathieson had filled that role only too happily before he was deposed by the conniving Scot.

McGurk assured Mathieson that he would be able to convince Medich to accept just $3 million in cash for his shares, provided that Mathieson secretly paid McGurk $8.5 million on the side over the next couple of years. Mathieson told McGurk that was fine by him. In actual fact, he had no intention of paying McGurk – or Medich – a single cent, but as McGurk was now planning to rip off Medich, he was happy to play along. He later admitted he was glad to see McGurk 'trying to screw Medich over'.[12] As far as he was concerned the pair deserved each other.

This meeting later formed the basis for Medich's accusations against McGurk in the Federal Court, where Medich alleged – quite correctly – that McGurk was double-crossing him and playing both sides of the deal by making a secret agreement with Mathieson.

But McGurk's act of bastardry fell apart because Odetta Medich smelled a rat and refused to sign the documents for the share transfer. McGurk was incandescent with rage. According to Richie Vereker, McGurk was overheard screaming about 'that interfering bitch'.[13] This led to him suing Medich, claiming that because of Odetta's actions and the drop in Amazing Loans' share price, he had suffered losses of $11.5 million. Mathieson's plan had worked a treat. His two enemies were now turning on each other.

The next time Mathieson spoke to Medich, relations between McGurk and Medich were frosty. On the evening of 5 February 2009, Medich had just greeted a dinner guest, businessman and dealmaker Albert Wong, when Mathieson, returning Medich's call, telephoned from Hawaii. He wanted to speak to Medich because his company, IEG Holdings, was trying to take over Amazing Loans. Like much else about Amazing Loans, this in itself was amazing: the child was gobbling up its parent. IEG's offer to buy out Amazing Loans' shareholders was due to expire on 13 February, and Medich owned about 7 per cent of the shares.

The conversation started out in a friendly enough fashion, with Medich asking Mathieson if he would be prepared to 'do a deal now' to buy out Medich's shares before the takeover offer closed a week later. But soon it began to turn nasty. Medich threatened Mathieson: unless he bought back his Amazing Loans shares for a decent price – he wanted $12 million – there would be hell to pay. Mathieson retorted that Medich was an idiot for missing his earlier chance to sell the shares for top dollar. Now $500,000 was all he would get.

He also accused Medich of sending McGurk to his apartment in September 2007 to threaten him. Mathieson said that if Medich ever threatened him again he would report him to the authorities. Warming to his theme, he shouted that he hoped both Medich and McGurk rotted in jail for all the dodgy things that they had done. 'I never want to speak to you again,' Mathieson said. Continents apart, receivers were simultaneously slammed down.[14]

Mathieson phoned McGurk straight away. McGurk was later to recount his version of this conversation during one of his Federal Court cases with Medich. McGurk recalled Mathieson saying to him, 'I've just had a telephone conversation with that lunatic Medich. He has told me that I better buy his shares from him or else. He threatened me with bodily harm if I didn't buy them. He told me that you [McGurk] are a crook and a shyster and that he didn't want anything further to do with you.'[15]

Of all the things they discussed that night, there was one that would have deadly repercussions. McGurk confided he was going to meet up with Medich the following day. He had devised a scheme to bring him down.

The next day, 6 February 2009, Michael McGurk secretly recorded his soon-to-be infamous conversation with Ron Medich.

One of the topics they discussed was Amazing Loans. Medich said he had spoken to Mathieson the night before.

'I had guests last night – Albert Wong was one of them – and when [Mathieson] fuckin' well rang . . . I just said to him, "Are you . . . would you be prepared to do a deal now before this thing happens?" That's what I asked him. And he went, "Oh, you sent McGurk over," and all this type of jazz. He's gone, "I hope you rot in jail" and all sorts of things like that, you know.'[16]

In his high-pitched whine, Medich raged about Mathieson's ingratitude. 'After everything I did for that moron!' he said bitterly.

McGurk waited until Medich had finished sounding off about Mathieson and then dropped his own little bombshell. He coolly informed Medich that Mathieson had spoken to him after his call to Medich. 'I'm going to tell you what he told me. He told me that you were running off at the mouth calling me a "lying, cheating fuck".'

'You?' Medich replied, his voice rising an octave.

'Yep, and that you told him I was a fraud . . . and that you're sick of me and that you are going to get someone to come and thump me,' McGurk said.

He also reported that Medich had threatened to put the 'bounce' on Mathieson and that he was going to use 'Lucky fuckin' Gattellari'.

'I didn't threaten him,' squealed Medich. 'He's a fucking liar. Do you believe that? I'm not that stupid. My phone's probably bugged, you know,' he said sullenly.

Medich then expressed concern that Mathieson might be talking to the police. On the tape he could be heard assuring McGurk he would never say anything stupid over the phone. 'I didn't say anything because, as you know, the phone could be tapped, right? So I was ultra-careful at anything I said, you know.'[17]

'I'm telling you now, I think, I wouldn't be surprised if he's talking to the fuckin' police now,' Medich was heard muttering darkly.

Medich told McGurk that Mathieson had said he hoped both McGurk and Medich rotted in jail. 'And he said it in such a nasty way,' said Medich, sounding seriously affronted. 'He was nothing without me. He was fucked, you know. He's a very ungrateful type of person. I'll have to see what I do about him in the long run, anyway, but we'll just stay quiet at the moment.'[18]

But three months later Medich's attitude to Mathieson had softened. By then Medich was consumed by his desire to destroy McGurk, and he needed Mathieson's help. In early May Mathieson was emailed a draft statement the Medich camp had written for him to sign. It was to be used in the police case against McGurk over some firebombings and assaults. Medich wanted Mathieson to detail the threats that McGurk had made. Needless to say, there were not only embellishments in the draft but serious omissions, especially about Medich's own role in the attempted extortion of Mathieson.[19]

A few days later, on 9 May, Mathieson updated McGurk about the draft statement and about a call from Medich which he'd found alarming. 'I don't want to say anything over the phone, but McGurk will be fixed up,' Medich had told Mathieson.[20]

Medich was desperate to get Mathieson to sign the statement and he suggested they meet. Mathieson, wary of the lot of them, agreed to see Medich in New Zealand. On 15 May 2009, Medich was having breakfast in his hotel's restaurant when Mathieson arrived for their meeting. Medich was keen to rectify the dispute with Mathieson and even offered to advance him much-needed funds, on the condition that Mathieson supply a statement to police.

'I'm going to fix him,' said Medich. Mathieson stared at Medich as he kept eating. 'Don't worry, he won't be a problem for much longer. It doesn't matter whether he gets locked up for the fire-bombing – either way, he won't be a problem.'[21] Andrew Howard and businessman Tim Alford arrived as Medich was talking about McGurk. Howard would later give evidence that Medich merely meant that if the arson case fell over, the back-up plans were to get McGurk for threatening Mathieson or possibly for tax fraud.

Mathieson took Medich at his word and started negotiations with Medich's lawyers about the promised advancement of funds. But talks soon broke down. On 29 June 2009, Detective Ray Hetherington, who was investigating McGurk for the firebombing and assaults, emailed Mathieson requesting a statement that he had been told was forthcoming. But in early August the detective was taken aback by Mathieson's response. 'Ronald Medich is the mastermind behind the crimes and was or would have been the major beneficiary if they had been successful. Medich provided the instructions/blessing for McGurk to extort money and threaten myself and then to firebomb the Tilley house,' Mathieson wrote.

It was only a fortnight before McGurk's murder, and here was Mathieson sending emails to different law enforcement agencies containing astounding allegations, including a statement that he seriously believed his life was in danger. The person he was afraid of was Ron Medich.

Medich was more than capable of having people murdered, Mathieson wrote. In the past the property developer had boasted of having people tortured to pressure them. And it was not just Mathieson who had been privy to such boasts, he said – the other directors of Amazing Loans could back him up.

In one email sent to a solicitor with ASIC on 18 August 2009, Mathieson reported that Medich had boasted about insider trading. Mathieson claimed to have witnessed Medich receiving inside information from a stockbroker, whom he named. Medich would then buy shares using information that was not known to the rest of the market. He also wrote in his email to ASIC: 'Ron often told the story in front of multiple people, including my fellow directors, that if he wants money off people he gets one of his henchmen to first slice off the finger above the knuckle and if they still don't pay he gets them to slice off the whole finger. He also told the story of how he had one person who owed him $70,000 hung by the feet over a cliff at the Blue Mountains. The person eventually paid. He also told the story of getting his henchmen to use a Bunsen burner under the testicles to torture someone who owed him money and said: "I mightn't have got my money back but at least he won't have any children!"

'Medich has told me he has contacts in the senior police and Ron has told many stories of how he has bribed government figures to get his developments through councils,' wrote Mathieson in his email.[22]

Extraordinarily, as Mathieson was relaying to Hetherington the threats he had previously received, he was threatened once again, this time by Lucky Gattellari. Mathieson was beside himself. He told Hetherington that Gattellari had been careful not to make the threat directly. Instead, Mathieson said, Alford had called him and passed on the message from Gattellari that the former boxer was contemplating flying to Hawaii to pay Mathieson a visit. Mathieson was so afraid of Gattellari that he reported his concerns to the Hawaiian police, who put Gattellari on a watchlist at Honolulu's airport.

Given that twenty-four hours before his murder, McGurk had told Mathieson of his plan to expose Medich the very next day, when Mathieson heard the shocking news, he was seriously scared.

CHAPTER 11

BIG JIM AND THE KRISPY KREMES

The blue Mazda 626 left a trail of burnt rubber as it took off from the apartment block in Redfern, mounted the kerb and tore through the streets. Hot in pursuit were several crowbar-wielding debt collectors who had been smashing the car. In the passenger seat was Maurice Terreiro and he was screaming at his girlfriend to drive faster. Terreiro later rang a friend in a state. 'He was completely freaking out,' said the friend. 'Someone was trying to kill him.'[1]

That someone was Michael McGurk, who was chasing Terreiro for money.

Within days of that night in June 2009, Terreiro's younger brother, Matthew, had his new SUV firebombed outside his fashionable Potts Point terrace.

A year earlier McGurk had lent $150,000 to Maurice Terreiro, who had been a Telstra technician before discovering there was a lot more money to be made on the fringes of the financial world. But Terreiro cut too many corners, made too many enemies, and by March 2009 he was bankrupt for the second time in a decade.

Terreiro had borrowed the money from McGurk for two months, and when he failed to repay the amount in full he was hit with astronomical penalty payments – $50,000 per month. Despite being on bail for assaults and firebombings, McGurk was desperate for money and was doing whatever it took to ensure the debt was collected. Terreiro might have scary friends like Felix Lyle, also known as Big F, the head of the Hells Angels, but as far as McGurk was concerned a debt was a debt.

A week after Terreiro's terrifying getaway in his girlfriend's Mazda, a group of men in suits was left speechless. Michael McGurk had just given a virtuoso performance that would have done Tony Soprano proud, said one of those present. The fresh-faced young man was beside himself at what he had witnessed. 'He sounded like he drank diesel for breakfast.' Laughing nervously, he added, 'I sure wouldn't want to be in Maurice Terreiro's shoes.'[2]

The ten men were financial advisors, also owed money by Terreiro, who had convened a meeting on level 53 of Sydney's MLC office tower to discuss their unscrupulous former colleague. On the boardroom table was spread a paper trail of Terreiro's bad deeds. Not only did he owe everybody in the room money for wages and unpaid commissions, the group of financial planners was also worried he had been forging their signatures on financial documents.

Maurice Elmar Terreiro was born in June 1965, in Masaka, Uganda. Aged ten he arrived in Sydney with his family after they were expelled from Uganda by dictator Idi Amin. The Indian family settled in Toongabbie, a working-class suburb in Sydney's west. Maurice was one of five children.

Terreiro was a heavy-set financier who fancied himself as a model of sartorial splendour, teaming his three-piece suits in shades of brown with tailored shirts, braces and a fob watch on a chain. He spent hundreds of dollars on Cuban cigars, which he kept in a humidifier in his office, and quaffed top-of-the-range cognac.

In a lot of ways Terreiro and McGurk had much in common. Both were foreign-born, from poor backgrounds and desperate to make it to the big time in their adopted country. Both men paraded the trappings of wealth but those trappings were largely a façade. And, like McGurk, Terreiro was a man short on both modesty and morality. Terreiro often bragged to mates that he had an IQ of 185 and could outsmart anyone. As to morality, he quipped to his friends, 'A conscience is overrated – it only keeps you awake at night.'[3]

Convening the meeting about Terreiro was Mark Schroeder, a short, slight, pale-faced man with rimless glasses and a school-boy look about him. Schroeder had previously been Maurice Terreiro's business partner in Financial Wealth, which had 50 advisers putting people into various investments and was raking in $400,000 each month.

As Schroeder was running through possible legal action they could take against Terreiro, in breezed McGurk, immaculately attired and brimming with bravado. He introduced himself and listened for a short time before interrupting. He scoffed at the tame options being chewed over by the group of suits before cutting to the chase. There was only one way people like Terreiro could be made to see reason, and that was McGurk's way. He claimed he was tracking Terreiro's mobile phone. He had people waiting outside the home of Terreiro's elderly mother in Toongabbie to catch him after Sunday lunch. He even offered to provide surveillance footage to those at the meeting.

He joked about certain 'people' having sledge-hammered Terreiro's Mazda the previous Friday evening. Those present were under no illusion that McGurk was referring to his own goons. He also said that while Terreiro and his girlfriend had escaped that time, they wouldn't be so lucky in future.

McGurk pulled back his crisp white shirt cuff to look at his Rolex. 'Damn, it's 5.30. I've got to fly!' he said briskly.[4] It was peak hour and he still had to cross the Harbour Bridge or his daughter would be late for her confirmation class at the Sacred Heart Catholic Church in Mosman, he said.

He tossed them a couple of mobile numbers, and told the other creditors to contact him if they found any more leads on Terreiro. Having delivered his bombshells, oblivious to the shock waves reverberating in the room, McGurk vanished into the night.

Exactly a year earlier McGurk had come to the aid of Maurice's brother, Matthew Terreiro. A letter dated 25 June 2008, on Bentley Smythe letterhead, read:

> Dear Matthew,
> We refer to your application for the property known as Hampton Court. We confirm that the loan is subject to a clear and irrevocable discharge of the entire facility from Suncorp-Metway limited which we understand will be forthcoming in the next seven days.
> Bentley Smythe Pty Ltd has the funds on call for Talmarc Pty Ltd to complete the purchase in the amount of $69 million. We trust the above meets with your requirements. Please don't hesitate to contact the undersigned should you require any additional information.
> Yours Sincerely,
> Per Michael McGurk, director, Bentley Smythe

Needless to say, it was all lies. McGurk didn't have $69 million to lend to anyone. But the letter would be used by Matthew Terreiro in a court case to prove that he had the funds for a deal he was trying to close on the Hampton Court Hotel.

The boutique nine-storey art deco hotel in Kings Cross, with its high ceilings and bay windows, had once been the first choice for rock stars and royalty visiting Sydney. Back in November 1957, it had attracted an excited throng hoping to get a glimpse of the world's most glamorous movie star, Elizabeth Taylor, and her latest husband, film producer Mike Todd. The newly married couple were holed up in room 718.

The hotel had also played a starring role at the Wood Royal Commission into Police Corruption in the mid-1990s. By then, in a dramatic reversal of fortunes, it was known as a sleazy drug-dealing joint. One dealer told the royal commission that he had a daily 12-hour shift at the hotel. He said that his activities were accepted by the publican, who had laid down a few ground rules: there were to be no fights between rival drug lords, and should patrons of the hotel become disorderly, the dealers were expected to act as bouncers.

In 2008 the owners of the Hampton Court were colourful Kings Cross identity Ferdie Nemeth and his Philippines-born wife, Virginia. Mrs Nemeth had brought the Hampton Court, and in particular room 718, the old Elizabeth Taylor suite, further notoriety. In 1998 a corruption inquiry found that Virginia Nemeth had understated the revenue from the hotel's poker machines by $1 million by bribing the government's poker machine inspector, with whom she was having an affair.

Fast forward again to 26 February 2008, and a business meeting was being held at Chifley Square in Sydney's CBD concerning the Nemeths' sale of the hotel. The business model for the sale was to convert it into upmarket apartments.

Two men strode through the expanse of pink marble in Chifley Square's foyer looking underdressed in matching ponytails and jeans. Up in the conference room potential investors were introduced to the first of these two as 'Jonathan Felix', a financial adviser. Jonathan Felix, it turned out, was in fact Felix Jonathan Lyle, at the time the president of the Hells Angels. The closest he had come to financial investment was dealing ecstasy tablets, mortgage frauds and the day-to-day running of an outlaw bikie gang. The other man was Lyle's son, Dallas Fitzgerald. At the time of the meeting, Fitzgerald was reporting to police weekly as part of his bail conditions after being charged over his involvement in one of the nation's most sensational cyber bank robberies, the $150 million Ocean's 11-style fraud on JP Morgan Chase.

Joining Maurice at the meeting was Dallas's co-accused, Matthew Terreiro. Matthew had a shock of white hair, and was taller and more polished than his older brother, who was known for his quick temper. Like his mate Dallas, at the time of the

Hampton Court deal Matthew was on bail over the Ocean's 11 case. (While Dallas would do time over the fraud, the case against Matthew Terreiro was later dropped.)

Matthew was excitable and loved to prattle on about his exploits; Dallas was contained and controlled, not one for small talk. He said little in meetings and, according to police, even less on a mobile phone. But when Dallas did talk, it was worth listening to. 'He just sits there taking it all in,' said one of those present at this meeting. 'He can break down figures and costs in his head. What I would need a calculator for; he will tell you off the top of his head.'[5]

In the course of the meeting Matthew and Maurice Terreiro claimed that their company, Financial Wealth, had been overwhelmed by interest from would-be buyers for the Hampton Court, and that there would be enormous demand for apartments in the redeveloped hotel, should the project go ahead. The mood was upbeat, though the financiers present from Bankwest felt that the consortium would have to advance the deal a lot further before the bank would consider lending it money.

In the early months of 2008 there were endless meetings with Lyle, Matthew and Maurice Terreiro in an attempt to stitch up the deal. Maurice's firm Financial Wealth was crucial because in order to get financing, the consortium needed to show that there was great demand for the apartments. The group of investors planned to develop the site into 102 units, with 48 car spaces, as well as a two-storey hotel with a 24-hour licence and 28 poker machines. The deal was expected to provide a windfall for all investors, yielding gross sales revenue of $100 million on the apartments and $22 million from the hotel.

The consortium also needed to show it had a buyer for the hotel licence. This lucrative licence most interested Felix Lyle. Not that it would've been in his name, as you had to be a fit and proper person to be the licensee. But that didn't worry him – the consortium had come up with just the man. A 22-year-old from Condell Park, who was still living in his modest family home with his mum and dad, signed to buy the $30 million pub through his company. According to family friends, the young man didn't have 30 bucks to his name, let alone $30 million.

The pre-selling of the unfinished apartments rocketed along, with Terreiro selling almost 20 per cent of them for between $700,000 and $1.1 million each. But if anyone had bothered to look closely at the would-be purchasers, they would have been left with the profound impression of dodginess. Some apartments were sold to people who did not exist. Many of the buyers were mysterious foreign companies and were paying via even more mysterious secret bank accounts or had contracts signed by fictitious lawyers.

The $22 million worth of pre-sales Maurice Terreiro obtained made the Hampton Court look like an extremely good investment. Baulkham Hills accountant and wealthy western Sydney property developer Dimitri Amargianitakis was persuaded to come in on the deal. But Amargianitakis soon realised he'd been dudded and his million-dollar investment had vanished. He sued Maurice Terreiro and Lyle for the return of his money. He received $250,000 and nothing more.

When Armargianitakis went back to court on 12 August 2008 to insist on the return of the rest of his money, representing the consortium was none other than Matthew Terreiro. Despite having no legal training, being bankrupt and on bail for money laundering, Terreiro played the role of a high-flying lawyer. Of course they were going to return the accountant's money plus interest, Matthew told Justice Paul Brereton of the New South Wales Supreme Court. The settlement on the hotel was imminent and then the money would be paid. As proof that the consortium was cashed up and ready to go, Matthew Terreiro produced the letter from Michael McGurk promising funding of $69 million.

When Felix Lyle and Maurice Terreiro failed to repay Amargianitakis, as ordered by the court, Amargianitakis moved to bankrupt them. Lyle's friend Jim Byrnes (whom a judge had once described as having 'a notorious reputation as a standover man and associate of major criminals'[6]) paid a visit to

Amargianitakis, offering a total of $50,000 in settlement of Lyle's debt. His offer was refused.

In March 2009, Maurice Terreiro and Felix Lyle declared themselves bankrupt. According to Lyle's bankruptcy records, the 'project manager' owed $1.3 million to the accountant, and had only $100 in the bank. Terreiro's creditors, who included his former employees at Financial Wealth, funded his bankruptcy trustee to investigate the possibility that Terreiro had money stashed away. McGurk held the same view, having been made aware that Maurice had been spotted behind the wheel of a top-of-the-range Mercedes sports car. Not long after penning his $69 million letter to hoodwink the court, McGurk was prevailed upon to loan Maurice Terreiro $150,000 at a very steep interest rate. But months passed and Terreiro was showing no intention of paying back McGurk's loan. He was still zipping around in his flash set of wheels and continuing to enjoy his extravagant lifestyle. McGurk was sure there was money somewhere and he wanted his share of it.

At the time of McGurk's murder in September 2009, Terreiro's debt to him had reached half a million and was still climbing. He never did pay back any of the money. Maurice Terreiro died suddenly on 10 January 2013, aged 47.

When Ferdie Nemeth, in his eighties, decided to divorce Virginia, one of the key assets was the Hampton Court.

In the wake of McGurk's murder Vanda Carson and I reported McGurk's threat to Maurice Terreiro as well as Terreiro's interesting underworld connections with people like the Hells Angels boss. Terreiro was one of the host of people wanting McGurk gone.

The day after details of the links between Terreiro and Felix Lyle were splashed across the *Sydney Morning Herald*, a silver Bentley glided to a stop outside the North Sydney Police Station. At 120 kilograms, with silver hair and designer glasses, Big Jim Byrnes heaved himself out of the driver's seat clutching a box of Krispy Kreme doughnuts, a gift for the police. His pony-tailed passenger, who didn't look quite so dapper, was Lyle.

Although he was a bikie boss, Lyle didn't care much for two-wheeled travel. His car of choice was a bright-red Bentley, the boot of which often doubled as a portable ATM, with wads of cash stashed inside. But on this occasion Lyle, who was bankrupt and without a licence, had accepted his mate Jim's offer to drive him. Big Jim and Lyle were business partners; their line of work – identifying distressed assets, distress being something of a speciality for the pair.

Lyle waited in the Bentley while Big Jim determined the lie of the land. According to Byrnes, he pressed the buzzer at the back door entrance, which read 'Police Only'.

'I am a big burly guy with a big box of doughnuts and they just let me in,' he said.[7] Having asked to see the 'Ds' in the McGurk matter, he was taken upstairs to the incident room, which was full of highly sensitive material, including photos of suspects on a large white board.

A young detective, who accepted Byrne's offer of a doughnut, asked Big Jim where he was from. 'Over east,' replied Byrnes. He asked how the McGurk investigation was progressing. 'I wasn't there to volunteer too much; I was more interested in how much I could get away with asking them,' Byrnes told me at the time.[8]

After chatting for a while about the case, the young detective inquired how long Byrnes had been at Rose Bay Police Station. Byrnes replied breezily that he was from Bellevue Hill and he wasn't a police officer, he was a witness. The detective almost choked on his doughnut.

Detective Sergeant Mark Fitzhenry was discussing some leads he wanted followed when he heard his boss Mick Sheehy say furiously, 'What the fuck is *he* doing here?' The other detectives hadn't recognised the hefty man who'd waltzed into the middle of the incident room with a box of doughnuts, but Sheehy had. His face flushed with anger as he rushed over to get Jim Byrnes out of the room.

Both Byrnes and Lyle were already well known to police. The intelligence on Felix Lyle's activities was voluminous to say the least: rumoured involvement in drug manufacture and distribution, with a sideline of violence.

In 2001 Lyle had been charged – he was later acquitted – with manufacturing speed. The New South Wales Crime Commission, the powerful investigative body that deals with serious organised crime, confiscated millions of dollars' worth of Lyle's property, including apartments in the exclusive harbourside suburb of Double Bay and the bandidos' HQ in Pyrmont, using proceeds of crime legislation.

Lyle was also charged with trying to extort $120,000 from a luxury car dealer, Terry Mullens. Those charges were subsequently dropped, but in 2013 the bikie boss was jailed for four years for serious fraud offences, drug supply and money laundering.

Also jailed with Lyle was the late Terrence Reddy, one of the last people to see McGurk alive. Lyle and Reddy, who was known as the Black Prince, had a sophisticated mortgage racket on the boil. They'd use the details of vulnerable people, including a woman with terminal cancer who later died, to get loans in their names, and defrauded financial institutions of millions of dollars using fake home loan documents with forged signatures to hoodwink the institutions into lending them money to splash on luxury cars and high-living.

It was believed that McGurk too was involved in this mortgage racket, and Reddy and McGurk had an urgent business meeting on the afternoon of 3 September 2009. Two hours later McGurk was dead.

CHAPTER 12

THE TILLEYS

In the pre-dawn darkness, at around 5.20 am on 20 November 2008, someone crept down the long, steep driveway leading to 42a Wolseley Road, Point Piper. Winding off to the right, the person passed a white house, the first of three that shared the driveway. The target was the middle one, a run-down three-storey latte-coloured confection of concrete and Italianate balustrades. Although the house, which couldn't be seen from Wolseley Road, was a knock-down job, it was right on the water and enjoyed a panoramic vista over Sydney Harbour.

The person was carrying two Molotov cocktails – a crude but effective home-made bomb. Having ignited and thrown the incendiary devices, the arsonist fled back up the steep drive, past an overgrown vacant lot, and vanished into the early morning darkness.

Adam Tilley and his wife, Sally-Anne, were woken by the noise and found flames licking against the window of one of their young children's bedrooms.

The Tilleys knew this was not a random attack and they had no doubt who was responsible. For months Michael McGurk had been pursuing them relentlessly. After taking over Medich's mortgages on the house, he'd launched legal actions, and when that had got nowhere he sent them a letter of demand saying he would sell the house from under them unless they paid what they owed.

In 2003, after Ron and Odetta Medich had had second thoughts about their $7.75 million purchase of 42a Wolseley Road, they had on-sold it for $12.5 million to Sally-Anne Tilley. The worst house in the best street had earned the Medichs $15,000 a day during their brief ownership.

The only problem was that the Tilleys couldn't really afford the house. They had to borrow $7.5 million from the Medichs to buy it, and then Sally-Anne obtained $6.5 million from the bank to cover stamp duty and legal fees. The plan was that the Tilleys and the Medichs would redevelop the site and pay back the Medichs from the profits.

In 2006 the vacant block of land immediately above the Tilleys' house, owned by Norm Carey, came on the market after the $400 million collapse of Carey's property group Westpoint. Ron Medich, Adam Tilley along with Tilley's neighbour at 42, hotelier Damien Reed, joined forces to buy 44 Wolseley Road, for $7.5 million. The trio intended to redevelop all three sites. Remarkably, Medich lent the Tilleys a further $8.65 million.

But the council knocked back their ritzy Burley Katon Halliday design to construct five apartments over four levels with garage space for 11 cars. The global financial crisis hit and a lot of developers were in serious trouble. Adam Tilley was one of them. He'd been depending on turning over the redevelopment quickly to pay Medich back. Now everything stalled and Tilley was in a bad way. The New South Wales Chief Commissioner of State Revenue was threatening to wind up Tilley's company over a $112,000 land tax bill; the bank was threatening to foreclose; his Terminus Hotel in Marulan was in dire straits; and Tilley was stuck with a $16 million debt to the Medichs.

As if things weren't bad enough for Tilley, an imposing man

at 6 feet 5 inches, into this nightmare waltzed the devil himself, Michael McGurk.

Having already convinced Ron Medich that he was a financial genius, after extracting an $11.5 million repayment of Medich's money from Paul Mathieson, McGurk volunteered to take over dealing with the Tilleys, a well-known eastern suburbs family whom Medich didn't have the stomach to confront about their debt.

From the outside it seemed the Tilleys had it all. They owned flash houses and were well-connected. Various members of the family had been involved in some slightly spivvy deals: business colleges, development sites, a wine investment business, hotels, smoking and weight loss treatments, debt collecting and nightclubs. Family patriarch Barrington Thomas Tilley always had a scheme or two on the boil. His two stretches of bankruptcy were a testament to his perpetual optimism, which tended to win out against the actual viability of his ideas. But Barry's failed businesses were no impediment to his confidence. A tall, handsome man with a constant tan, Tilley senior knew everybody. Not only had he been a buddy of the late media tycoon Kerry Packer, he was also mates with Richie Vereker and Kimberley McGurk's family. Everyone knew the knockabout Barry, so there was astonishment when the house of his eldest son, Adam, was attacked. Firebombings were not the eastern suburbs way of dispute resolution.

The three Tilley boys – Adam, Simon and Ben – were from Barry's first marriage to socialite Patricia McCoy. Adam, born in 1963, ran a mortgage-broking business. He and Simon, who was two years younger, did small-scale residential property developments.

The career path of the youngest, Benedict (Ben), was best described by the following 'job advertisement' in the *Sunday Telegraph* in October 2017:

WANTED: Babysitter for billionaire. Wealthy businessman living abroad requires good-humoured male companion. Must love casino games, the French Riviera, the Aspen snowfields, televised sport, the company of models, television personalities and some intense media executives. Expect to be on call 24/7. Must have an even temper, a passport and good sea legs. $5 million p/a. (Position now filled.)

For years Ben Tilley was the extraordinarily well-remunerated friend, companion and fixer of billionaire James Packer, having previously filled a similar role for the notoriously pernickety and demanding Packer senior. Although relations between Ben Tilley and James Packer were coolish in the wake of Kerry's death on Boxing Day 2005, within a couple of years the youngest Tilley son had inveigled his way into James Packer's life.

McGurk may not have felt favourably inclined towards the Tilleys as he had previously been rebuffed by Ben Tilley. In his book *The Fast Life and Sudden Death of Michael McGurk*, Richie Vereker claimed that when McGurk had yet another outlandish scheme – purchasing a casino in Bali – McGurk badgered Vereker to approach Ben Tilley seeking finance. Tilley said no.

Medich knew that taking on the Tilley family would win him no friends in the eastern suburbs, where they were well liked and knew everyone who was anyone. The entire Tilley tribe were Cranbrook old boys. Although Ron Medich was a Joeys old boy, Cranbrook, in Bellevue Hill, was within walking distance of the Medichs' house and was the school of choice for Ron and Odetta's two young sons. It wouldn't do to have unpleasantness between the two families.

On the other hand, money was money, and McGurk, the perennial outsider, didn't give a damn about offending the Tilleys. Nothing and nobody could come between him and the prospect of making a buck. So when Medich's solicitor Rob Hugh suggested that it would be preferable if McGurk rather than Medich raised with the Tilleys the large amount of money they owed Medich, McGurk leapt at the chance. The ink was barely dry on the trust deed – with the Medichs assigning the Scot their two sets of Tilley mortgages, one for $7.5 million and the other for $8.65 million – when McGurk set to work on the family.

It was June 2008, and Sally-Anne Tilley, in whose name the mortgage was, had promised to repay $8.65 million. It wasn't clear how she was going to repay that kind of money as she was working as a librarian at Kambala, a prestigious private girls' school in a neighbouring suburb.

When Sally-Anne didn't pay on the due date, 21 June, McGurk began a multi-pronged attack on the Tilley family. He placed caveats on every one of their properties he could find, which meant that none could be sold without his say-so. As well as a terrace house in Sutherland Street, Paddington, and the Wolseley Road house, he also put caveats on properties in Edgecliff and Pyrmont, which Adam Tilley jointly owned with his brothers. Those properties had been put up as collateral to secure Adam's loan with Medich. This heavy-handed action by McGurk dragged Adam's brothers Simon and Ben into the dispute.

On 24 June McGurk commenced an action in the Supreme Court, which gave Adam and Sally-Anne five days to pay before he would force the sale of their houses. But the months dragged on with no result. McGurk was in a perilous financial situation himself, so in November he issued further letters of demand against the Tilleys. When none of these bore results, he decided to up the ante. On 20 November, three days after his last letter of demand, Adam and Sally-Anne's house was firebombed.

As soon as he found out about the firebombing Tim Alford rang Medich to tell him what had happened. When Medich was questioned by Rose Bay police in the immediate aftermath of the arson, he said he had no idea who the culprit could be. Six months later, when he had well and truly fallen out with McGurk, the millionaire property developer had a different story. Medich told the police then that McGurk had said to him, 'The Tilleys are crooks and we need to take this to another level. I'll get some IRA guys and we'll put a gun in his mouth and then we'll shoot him in the leg.'[1]

He made this new statement to police on 9 April. The day before, Medich had received an adverse judgment in the Federal Court concerning McGurk and Amazing Loans.

Medich never did get the money back from the Tilleys. On 15 December 2010 Adam Tilley entered a personal insolvency agreement (PIA) with his creditors, who were owed more than $20 million. A PIA is a legally binding agreement via which you arrange to settle debts without becoming bankrupt. Tilley agreed to pay creditors less than 10 cents in the dollar over three years. The largest creditor was Medich, who would receive less than $1.7 million.

Other debts included $300,000 to Tilley's younger brother Ben. Hotelier Damien Reed, who was doing the Wolseley Road development with Tilley and Medich, was owed $800,000. Reed had suffered his own financial troubles with the collapse of his hotel group, Icon Hospitality, owing $60 million to the Commonwealth Bank.

Just before Christmas, Reed sold his house at 42 Wolseley Road for $11.75 million. Scott Barlow and his wife, Alina, whose billionaire Russian father, David Traktovenko, owned the soccer club Sydney FC, emerged as the buyer, having already spent $8.8 million buying the nearby vacant land that Medich, Tilley and Reed had acquired from Norm Carey after the collapse of the Westpoint Group.

It would, however, be another three years until the ill-fated Tilley house, on which the scorch marks from the firebombing could still be seen, was finally sold – for $10.65 million. After 91 days on the market, the buyer was Channel 7's commercial director and property mogul Bruce McWilliam. How much of the proceeds of the sale went to Medich is uncertain. As Medich complained bitterly to McGurk on the secret tape recording, 'Fuck that Tilley because, I mean, he's never put a zac into anything on the whole bloody thing.'

CHAPTER 13

McGURK'S FIERY MESSAGE

Just before noon on 20 November 2008, the same day as the firebombing of the Tilleys' Point Piper house, three men arrived at the office of valuers R.V. Dimond on the seventh floor of 99 York Street in the Sydney CBD.

Eddie Muscat was a handsome, affable, blond 73-year-old man who stood 6 feet 3 inches tall. Given his name and appearance, people were surprised when they heard his strong Greek accent. Muscat, a one-time sailing partner of King Constantine of Greece, had worked in real estate for as long as people could remember. His eyebrows knitted in concern when the trio burst through the door. Not bothering with even the most elementary of courtesies, they demanded to speak to Stuart Rowan, the company's principal valuer. 'McGurk has a message for him,' growled one of the men.[1] Muscat informed them that Rowan was out of the office. He politely inquired as to whether they would care to leave a business card and one of them shouted, 'Are you fucking stupid?! We don't leave cards. Here's our calling card.' Muscat was punched on the side of his head and in his face.

After receiving a call from his distraught colleague, the

diminutive Rowan hurried back to the office to find Muscat distressed and disorientated, his face red and swollen.

Rowan, who was in his mid-sixties, was frightened. He had been renting office space in McGurk's York Street premises since 2006, and in the past month or so McGurk had been pestering him to do a valuation of a property McGurk had bought at the quaintly named Hen and Chicken Lane in Perthville, 12 kilo-metres south of Bathurst, in the state's central west. McGurk had been tipped off that brothers Milton and Glen Naylor were about to lose their family farm in Perthville and after the Naylors were declared bankrupt, he swooped, offering their bankruptcy trustee a pittance – $450,000 – for the farm. But the Naylors thwarted McGurk's stingy deal by having their bankruptcy annulled after borrowing $620,000 from Fair Go Finance. McGurk went ballis-tic and did what he always did – sued – forcing the bankruptcy trustee to accept his higher bid of $685,000. As an extra slap in the face, he decided not to pay the last $80,000. McGurk simply ignored several court orders that he do so.

Having obtained the land, he tried to pull another swifty. A couple of months earlier he had tricked Ron Medich into paying twice for a property that he had found Medich near Port Douglas in northern Queensland. Now, in order to perpetrate this new fraud on Medich, McGurk told Ron that the Hen and Chicken Lane property was worth $3.2 million. He just needed a friendly valuer to triple the value of the Naylors' farm to back up his lie.

McGurk had a brainwave. He would get his tenant Rowan to do it for him. Rowan had fallen behind on the rent and instead of negotiating, McGurk went straight to bullying mode. He seized Rowan's computers and files and refused to give them back. Rowan was worried that McGurk, who had keys to all the offices on the floor, had been rifling through his valuations and stealing blank letterheads. Now, in early November, McGurk was hassling him to do the valuation on the farm at Perthville. Rowan refused point blank but, as he knew too well, McGurk did not take no for an answer.

Less than 20 minutes after the assault on Eddie Muscat, Rowan received a text message. It read: NXT TIME WIL B U DO AS U R TOLD 5PM OR IL B BACK. It was not well known that text messages could be sent from some payphones, and the menacing message Rowan received was later traced to a public phone box near the Queen Victoria Building, less than 50 metres from McGurk's office.

Later that day, McGurk himself called Rowan. 'You fucking well better finish the Bathurst valuation by five pm today or else you will be physically assaulted worse than what Eddie got,' he said coldly.[2]

Eddie Muscat and Stuart Rowan went to The Rocks Police Station. They were shuffled out the door, with the helpful suggestion that perhaps Rowan should just do the valuation.

Four days later Rowan received another text message from the same payphone. U DONT HAV THAT VAL DONE BY 9AM IM GUNA HURT YOU PROPER NO MORE WAITN GET IT DONE UR PROBS WIL GO AWAY.

Rowan was beside himself. He knew what kind of person McGurk was and he had seen what his henchman had done to Eddie Muscat. The next day he took his concerns to the police at Surry Hills, who helped him take out an interim Apprehended Violence Order (AVO) against McGurk. Rowan had already sent a letter to McGurk saying that in light of the escalating threats he would not be doing any valuation work for him.

At 9.45 pm that evening, 25 November, the police rang Rowan to tell him that his temporary AVO had been granted. He and his wife Tanya went to bed that night feeling reasonably happy that they would now be safe. That feeling was short-lived.

At 1.20 am the Rowans were woken by their fluffy white dog yapping frantically. Fireballs had reached the second storey of their home in Queen Street, Beaconsfield, and there was smoke everywhere. Six Molotov cocktails had been thrown at their house and at the house next door, which was also owned by the Rowans and was about to be auctioned.

Four fire engines arrived within minutes and the flames were soon extinguished. All up about $100,000 worth of damage was caused to the two houses and the auction of Rowan's house next door had to be postponed.

Rowan told the police that there was absolutely no doubt in his mind that McGurk was responsible. His suspicions were soon confirmed when police informed him that the incendiary devices used on his house were identical to the ones that had been deployed on a property in Wolseley Road only six days before. Rowan, who knew of the dispute between McGurk and the Tilleys, immediately saw the connection.

Rowan was a nervous wreck after the attack on his house. McGurk must have been really desperate because even though he knew police were investigating the firebombing, he did not back off. A black Mercedes, the same model as McGurk owned, was spotted on several occasions parked near Rowan's house in the days after the firebombing.

Around a month after the attack, Rowan was in his York Street office when a tall man with fair hair in a crewcut knocked on the door. The man, who was wearing a smart grey suit and tie, explained he was there to deliver some court documents relating to a valuation on a property that was subject to divorce proceedings. Rowan opened the door and was looking at the documents the man had taken out of his satchel and placed on the front desk in Rowan's office when, out of the corner of his eye, he saw the man produce an expandable metal bar from the satchel.

Rowan's head was beaten to a bloodied mess. His right eye socket was almost fractured and he required multiple stitches to his scalp and the side of his face.

Three weeks later Justin Brown, the high-flying real estate executive who had met McGurk around the time the Scot was buying up the Goldsbrough apartments in the mid-1990s, was attacked at his workplace. On the morning of 12 January 2009 a couple of tough-looking guys stepped out of the lift at Brown's place of work – CBRE in Bligh Street, in Sydney's financial district. The men brushed straight past the receptionist, saying they had an appointment to see Mr Brown. They knew exactly where to find him. They marched down the hallway, barged into his office and assaulted him.

By now Brown and McGurk owned a house in the south of France, and had done several property deals together. However, the pair had fallen out over the place they both owned in Orlando Avenue, Mosman, and Brown was embroiled in legal action against McGurk.

Three days after the assault, Brown, his pregnant wife and their young son lay sleeping in their architecturally designed sandstone and glass mansion in Mosman. The house enjoyed expansive views across Balmoral Beach and out through the heads of Sydney Harbour. Just before dawn, it was firebombed. The large hibiscus plant growing by the sandstone fence caught fire but the Porsche Cayenne and the grey Lexus SUV parked a short distance up the gently sloping driveway, and the house itself, were undamaged.

The incident bore all the hallmarks of the previous firebombings at Point Piper and Beaconsfield – the same accelerant and the same construction of the Molotov cocktail had been used.

Unlike the Tilleys and Stuart Rowan, Brown refused to talk to police.

Justin John Brown was born in February 1971 in St Ives on the affluent upper north shore of Sydney. Both his parents were Mormons and his father was a financier for property developers.

Brown eschewed his parents' faith but followed his father into the property world. By the time he was in his early twenties he was selling real estate at Century 21 in Neutral Bay. He joined Colliers around 1993 and met McGurk shortly afterwards, when Brown was selling the Goldsbrough apartments. Brown, a genial, round-faced fellow, and the ebullient McGurk hit it off from the start.

Brown had a meteoric rise through the ranks of Colliers and in September 2007 he was head-hunted to be the chairman of residential projects at CBRE, where his role was marketing and selling large city apartment buildings for big developers.

He was a polarising figure within the industry. Take the sale of apartments in The Hyde, which overlooks Hyde Park, the lovely rectangular stretch of green parkland in the centre of Sydney's CBD. The park, which was a race track in the colony's early days, is flanked on the western side by upmarket hotels and department stores. Along College Street to the east lies St Mary's Cathedral and the Australian Museum. A wide tree-lined avenue bisects the expanse of park. The Hyde, on the southwestern corner of the park, is a glitzy apartment block with spectacular views across Hyde Park and to the harbour.

In 2006 there was a scandal over the sale of the yet-to-be completed apartments in The Hyde. The sale process had started promisingly when a clutch of the city's wealthier citizens received a delivery of truffles accompanied by an exquisite gold-embossed invitation to attend a VIP inspection of Sydney's newest must-have address.

For a deposit of $10,000, prospective buyers were allocated times on the last weekend in October 2006 to inspect the various display suites. Those who'd put down their deposit first were to have first choice of apartments. But after walking the red carpet into the building, the well-heeled clientele, cheque books in hand, were furious. All the best apartments had been sold already. 'I was shocked at the ethics of that. It's a very odd way to do business. You can't help feeling that you needed to know someone to get in even earlier,' one disappointed prospective buyer told the *Herald* at the time.[3] It turned out that the person you needed to know was Colliers' Justin Brown, who had the marketing rights.

Brown had an eye for spotting an opportunity when it came to real estate deals he was handling. In the Chevron development in Melbourne's St Kilda Road, he had an interest in 17 of the best units through Lighter Quay Investments, a company incorporated in New Zealand, which Brown controlled. He also acquired an apartment in The Cove, the swish block designed by the late Harry Seidler. Finished in 2003, the 43-storey tower is on the fringe of Sydney's financial district and a couple of blocks away from Circular Quay. Many of the prime apartments on the prized northeastern corner were purchased by Brown's associates. Through his private company, Sharlotte Pty Ltd, Brown himself bought a spectacular unit on the seventeenth floor. Others to buy off the plan included the Yazbek construction family and controversial property spruiker Kovelan Bangaru.

South African-born Bangaru secured two of the best apartments in the building. In 2003 he paid a total of almost $12 million for adjacent penthouses on the forty-third floor. With his luxury Mercedes Maybach parked downstairs with his Porsche and other Mercs, Bangaru set to work decorating his prized apartments. Dinner guests could enjoy amazing harbour views courtesy of a revolving dining room. A retina-scanning device at his front door meant that Bangaru would never have to fumble in his pocket for his keys. According to the *Herald*'s gossip columnist Andrew Hornery, Bangaru had imported several $15,000 toilets from Japan 'which spritzed, buffed and fluffed one's derriere'.[4] But life turned sour for the former insurance salesman when he fled the country in 2005 after fleecing millions from 'mum and dad' investors whom he had persuaded to mortgage their houses to invest in his property schemes. He was jailed for fraud in August 2010.

In 2006 McGurk and Brown were not only close mates but business partners. That year McGurk took a leaf out of Peter Mayle's *A Year in Provence* and – with Brown, another property developer, Lance Hodgkinson, and London realtor and ex-Davis Cup tennis player Andrew Williams – bought a six-bedroom villa with a swimming pool next to the French property where Mayle had penned his 1989 bestseller. The men paid $2.6 million for the villa, which the four families planned to use as a base during the Rugby World Cup being hosted by France in 2007.

Needless to say McGurk fell behind with his contributions and the plan for the families to spend magical summer afternoons by the pool, sipping the local wine and enjoying the delightful views across the fields of lavender and grapes, never eventuated. Indeed, even before the Rugby World Cup came around, the relationship between the owners had begun to unravel.

On 12 August 2006, Hodgkinson, Brown and another property developer, Daniel Hausman, met at the Lord Dudley Hotel, just around the corner from Hodgkinson's Woollahra home. Brown was desperate for Hausman and Hodgkinson to buy him out of their multi-million-dollar joint ventures as he was under considerable financial pressure and urgently needed to find money for other real estate deals he had on the boil.

But Hausman and Hodgkinson weren't in any position to buy out Brown. Within 18 months both would be bankrupt. The three men were developing a large retail and residential complex in Miller Street, Cammeray, on Sydney's lower north shore, and an apartment building in the former Chevron Hotel in St Kilda Road, Melbourne. The St Kilda development, of which Brown owned a third via a company incorporated in the British Virgin Islands but administered in Hong Kong, was looking shaky.

Brown wrote out a one-page agreement at the pub and tried to rely on it as a binding agreement when he took his former mates to court. Even though the judge noted that 'It was brought into existence in a public bar over a number of schooners of beer,' Bernie Coles, QC, who was appearing for Brown, tried to argue that the 'Lord Dudley agreement' was clear to all three men.[5]

On 22 August 2006, only weeks before Brown launched his legal action against his friends, he emailed Hodgkinson saying: 'This is now beyond a joke. You play when it suits you to be a friend, however, you seem, particularly of late, to go out of your way to place me in difficult situations to advance yourself. That's not a friendship, and if this is not sorted as detailed above, I will treat our friendship in the same manner I perceive you too [sic] . . . non existent.'[6]

With that email the prospect of an idyllic holiday in Provence went down the drain.

Justice George Palmer found against Brown. Describing him as 'blunt, assertive and forceful, often to the point of being aggressive', the judge said he did not accept Brown's evidence, and ordered him to pay his former partners $1.5 million. Brown appealed the judgment and lost.[7]

It wasn't just Hodgkinson and Brown who were fighting over property. Brown and McGurk had also fallen out over the house they had bought at 26 Orlando Avenue, Mosman.

For years 26 Orlando Avenue was an eyesore to other residents in the street. McGurk had bought the run-down three-bedroom single-storey house for $905,000 in 2002 and he used it as the headquarters for his criminal dealings. Neighbours in the quiet suburban cul-de-sac, with its neat hedges and picket fences, suspected that the derelict house was used for all manner of skulduggery. Local children called it 'the haunted house' and were warned by their parents not to enter the building.

Two Irish backpackers who did odd jobs for McGurk, and were used as fronts in McGurk's companies when he needed them, lived at the house for a while, until the electricity and water were cut off as part of the dispute McGurk was having with Brown.

At some stage – it's not clear when – Justin Brown paid McGurk $750,000 for a share in the property, though his name was never placed on the title. The pair lodged a development application to build two townhouses on the 446-square-metre block. But just as he fell out with almost everyone he went into business with, McGurk also fell out with Brown, and in April 2008 Brown lodged a caveat on the Orlando Avenue title to protect his interest.

Hamish Williamson, who lived at the property on and off for years, said that Justin Brown was 'shit scared' of McGurk. McGurk decided to stop paying the mortgage. '[The house] was going to be repossessed. He did that to see if Justin Brown would come up with the [repayments],' said Williamson. In other words, McGurk wanted to see if Brown would blink first.[8]

Williamson was instructed by McGurk to go and have a word with Brown and tell him he had to sign his share in the property over to McGurk. When Williamson met Brown outside his city office, Brown sought his advice. 'What am I going to do with Mike? He keeps threatening to punch me in the mouth.'

Williamson's advice was to call McGurk's bluff. 'Do what we do in Scotland – threaten him back. If someone threatens to punch you in the mouth, you say, "Well, I'll punch *you* in the mouth!"'

Brown did just that, prompting McGurk to demand to know what Williamson had said to Brown.[9] Williamson said that after that Brown was 'obviously quite scared of [McGurk]'.

Even after McGurk's murder, there was a strange twist. Because McGurk had not met his mortgage repayments, HSBC took possession of the house and put it up for auction. This was the second time the bank had tried to sell the blot on Orlando Avenue's landscape. In November 2008, an auction to sell the house was cancelled at the eleventh hour because McGurk claimed the advertising had been misleading as it failed to mention that the property had development approval for two townhouses.

On 17 November 2009, almost a year after the previous aborted auction, 40 prospective buyers gathered in Mosman for the auction of 26 Orlando Avenue. Moments before it was due to start, the crowded room was informed that the sale had been cancelled. The realtor apologised, saying the agency had been told only an hour earlier that the house had already been sold on the instructions of the mortgagee and seller, HSBC. Other buyers had tried to make offers before the auction but the agency had been instructed not to accept those bids.

One businessman, who said he was willing to pay $1.7 million, told the *Herald* at the time, 'This is really unfair. Everyone should have been allowed to have made an offer.'[10]

'This is too fishy for words,' muttered a young woman to her partner. 'Most unprofessional,' he replied angrily.[11]

It turned out that the purchaser was Brown's long-term business partner and colleague at CBRE, Tim Rees, who had bought the Orlando Avenue eyesore via a company called Orlando Avenue Property Pty Ltd, a company that was established on the day of the auction.

The subdivision and development of the property went ahead and in 2012 Rees' company sold the two new townhouses. In August one was sold to Rees' wife for a bargain $700,000; it has since been rented at $1650 per week. The identical townhouse at 26b was sold two months earlier for $1,545,700 – more than double the price.

Exactly why Justin Brown refused to cooperate with police in the wake of his assault and the firebombing of his house remains a mystery, as does his interest in the Orlando Avenue property. But one of the more interesting emails to come to me – two days after McGurk's murder – was the following:

Hi Kate,

FYI. The police were totally unimpressed with Justin BROWN giving his 'word' that he would be making a statement in relation to the firebombing of his house . . . Justin BROWN was assaulted at his offices on 12 Jan 2009 in identical circumstances to Stuart ROWAN and then his house was firebombed three days later. BROWN's brother gave a statement in relation to assault but didn't even know his brother had his house firebombed . . . Who would let someone firebomb their house with pregnant wife and child inside and not make a statement unless they had something on them. BROWN is part owner of a house in the south of France with McGURK and someone from UK. McGURK had something on BROWN and openly bragged that he wouldn't be making a statement and he was right.

Anon.

The use of capital letters gave the missive the hallmarks of being written by someone in the police force.

CHAPTER 14

MUTUAL DESTRUCTION

It was 19 January 2009, and the McGurk household was quietly baking. The record-breaking heatwave made it too hot to do anything much, too hot even for the beach.

The grass, brittle and dry, crunched underfoot as Ray Hetherington, accompanied by a uniformed police officer, walked up to the McGurks' house. As McGurk answered the door barefoot, and in shorts and a short-sleeved shirt, his already heat-frazzled holiday mood was about to be destroyed. The week before his forty-fifth birthday, the feisty Scottish-born wheeler and dealer was under arrest.

There was little traffic as he was driven across the Harbour Bridge, silently seething in the back of the police car. He thought with bitterness of Medich, who right now was probably watching the first day of the Australian Open on his giant television screen. This predicament, thought McGurk, was all Medich's fault and the irritating, selfish arsehole would have to pay.

Four days had passed since the firebombing of Justin Brown's house. McGurk had been bragging to associates that he had something on Brown and Brown wouldn't be making a police statement. He was right – the wily real estate agent was still stubbornly refusing to talk to police.

Detective Senior Constable Hetherington, who was doing the McGurk investigation on his own, was worried. With or without Brown's help, Hetherington was of the opinion that McGurk's behaviour was escalating and something had to be done to stop him before he killed someone.

McGurk was taken to Waverley Police Station, where the tall, rangy Detective Hetherington read him his rights before charging him with two counts of maliciously damaging property by fire/explosive with intent to injure; two counts of common assault; one count of maliciously damaging property by fire/explosives; and one count of assault occasioning actual bodily harm. McGurk was fingerprinted, had his mugshot taken and was placed before the magistrate in the courthouse adjacent to the police station.

Due to the seriousness of the charges, the magistrate set McGurk's bail at a hefty $100,000. Because he wasn't able to come up with the money immediately, McGurk suffered the ignominy of being carted off in the prison van, where he had to spend the night in a cell at Silverwater prison.

By 10 the next morning Ron Medich had posted bail for McGurk, providing a bank cheque for $100,000. This meant that if the Scot disappeared, Medich would forfeit the money. Just what persuaded Medich to put up bail money for McGurk remains a mystery – their relationship was shaky at best. And gratitude was not a sentiment favoured by McGurk. Neither was trust. Almost as soon as he was released from custody he began to seriously turn his mind to destroying Medich.

McGurk's bail conditions included reporting to Mosman police three times a week; not approaching Rowan, Muscat or Tilley; and surrendering his passport. On a bright, sunny Monday morning on 2 February 2009 McGurk appeared at Waverley Court over the assault and firebombings. During the brief mention of the matters, the magistrate was told that the police were still working on their brief of evidence. But the preliminary facts were presented, accusing McGurk of firebombing the houses of Stuart Rowan and Adam Tilley. He was also alleged to have assaulted Rowan and Eddie Muscat. His $100,000 bail was continued.

Accompanying the Scot, looking considerably more relaxed with his suit coat slung over his shoulder, was Patrick Conaghan, a former detective and police prosecutor, and the latest of a very long line of McGurk's solicitors. And sitting on the wooden bench up the back of the court was the *Daily Telegraph*'s business reporter Peter Gosnell. He rushed up to McGurk and Conaghan as they left, asking them for clarification on some of the details. Telling his client he would handle it, Conaghan announced dramatically, 'Mr McGurk is a respected businessman, the allegations are unfounded and they will be defended to the death.' Little did he know how prophetic his words would be.

This was not McGurk's first time in Waverley Court. Just over three years before, McGurk had appeared at Waverley defending an AVO. In early December 2005, he had burst through the doors of a small lending company, Genesis, wanting to borrow $100,000 at 1 per cent per day interest for six weeks. It was for a property development, McGurk told John Constable, who owned the business. McGurk was rude and pompous, expressing surprise that Constable and his staff had not heard of him. There was something about him that was slimy and unpleasant, Constable recalled. When McGurk was told that the loan would not be forthcoming, 'he threatened to have my kneecaps smashed with a lead pipe', said Constable.[1] The threats continued, forcing Constable to take out an AVO. McGurk represented himself when the matter was heard at Waverley Court in January 2006. It took more than an hour for the AVO to be granted, and less than five minutes for McGurk to breach it. As Constable stood outside the courthouse having a cigarette, McGurk marched up to Constable and said icily, 'You do know that I know a lot of people. I know where you live. I am going to make you suffer.'[2]

Constable was shocked. As Stuart Rowan and others were to learn, an AVO meant absolutely nothing to McGurk. When

Constable reported this threatening behaviour, which constituted a breach of the order, the police merely cautioned
McGurk.

The day after McGurk's February 2009 court appearance, Peter
Gosnell's story in Sydney's tabloid *Telegraph* aired the dirty
laundry of all those involved in the Wolseley Road property
dealings. Under the headline 'Boss charged with firebombing posh Point Piper mansion', Gosnell made the connection
between Ron Medich and the Tilleys over 42a Wolseley Road,
though, he wrote, 'The link between Mr Medich and Mr
McGurk is not clear.' He did, however, note a curious fact: two
years earlier, Medich had assigned his 115 million share options
in low-end lender Amazing Loans to McGurk for just $1.

Ron Medich was livid about the story, screaming blue murder
at everyone, including Bob Ell. 'I've got about 5000 phone calls
from everyone I know,' Medich complained to McGurk.[3] All
he could think about was his own embarrassment, which only
added to McGurk's cold fury.

Odetta Medich had been in her husband's ear for months,
telling him that McGurk was ripping him off. At first, to Odetta
McGurk had seemed a cut above her husband's other sycophan-
tic sidekicks. He was smart, he dressed immaculately, he lived
in a nice house in the upmarket suburb of Cremorne, and had
a lovely wife and four kids. When McGurk took to dropping
into the Medichs' home, however, demanding that she and Ron
sign documents on the spot, Odetta became suspicious. She
soon decided that she was dealing with a Zegna-suited sociopath. Unlike Lucky Gattellari, whom she despised, it seemed
to her that McGurk was not content with simply being wealth
adjacent, he wanted their fortune and he didn't care who he had
to destroy to get it.

She was also irritated that McGurk had insinuated his way
into their lives. Particularly irksome was the way he treated
their boat as his own. Their Sunseeker Portofino 46, which

Odetta had bought on her Amex card for $1.2 million in 2006, was effectively taken over by McGurk. He later claimed in court that in 2008 Medich had verbally agreed to sell him a half-share of the boat for $350,000. Needless to say, no cash was ever forthcoming, but that didn't stop McGurk from passing the vessel off as his own to friends and associates. He was using the luxury craft, named after one of Medich's more successful racehorses, Flying Pegasus, to host bacchanalian parties. Odetta had seen a morning-after photo and it wasn't pretty – there were discarded heroin caps, empty beer and champagne bottles and used condoms. During one wild, drug-fuelled and drunken binge on the harbour, McGurk crashed the boat, causing about $80,000 worth of damage. Although he promised to pay, he made sure that in the end Medich footed the bill.

Odetta and Ron had signed the Tilley mortgages over to McGurk in May 2008. A couple of weeks later McGurk had arrived at their house claiming he was in a hurry and got them to sign a declaration of trust concerning two properties – one in the sleepy beachside hamlet of Gerroa, south of Sydney, the other in Mowbray, Queensland – without giving them a chance to read the related papers. He came again, on 25 June, trying the same tactic, this time about the Amazing Loans shares. All this rushing and urgency was unprofessional and peculiar, Odetta thought. She refused to sign the Amazing Loans shares over to McGurk.

Her refusal drove McGurk into a frenzy. In his office in York Street he would go into a wild rage at the very mention of her name. But he was careful not to betray his fury when he spoke to Medich about the difficulties she was creating.

McGurk would later detail in an affidavit that Odetta would not transfer the Amazing Loans shares because she thought her husband was hiding money from her. McGurk had asked Medich whether this was true. 'I don't want to tell her everything,' Medich apparently said. 'She's not going to be telling me how to run my affairs. She's only on there as a director because I put her on there and she is part of my superannuation fund . . .

Don't worry about Odetta ... she won't do anything stupid because she won't want to cut her nose off to spite her face.'[4]

Odetta Medich was only too aware of the saying 'a fool and his money are soon parted'. But that money was hers as well as her foolish husband's, and she was determined to safeguard it from McGurk's chicanery.

Not only did she refuse to transfer the shares in Amazing Loans, but towards the end of 2008 she decided to take a closer look at what else McGurk had been up to with her husband's cash. To find the answers, she embarked on a road trip to Gerroa. She wanted to see for herself exactly what McGurk had got Ron into.

A year earlier, Medich, who had suffered bouts of depression over the years, was unwell. In December 2007 Odetta suggested they go to Hawaii to help him recuperate. Before they left, he made the fatal mistake of entrusting McGurk with his power of attorney in order to deal with the Tilley matter and to look after some of his other interests.

This brief period was manna from heaven for McGurk – he had little sympathy for Medich's mental health concerns; his benefactor's weakness was something to be exploited. Despite it being the festive season when business normally winds down, in the last fortnight of 2007 McGurk managed to use Ron Medich's money to finalise the purchase of not one but two properties.

The first was in northern Queensland. If you drive 5 kilometres south of Port Douglas along a two-lane country road optimistically named the Captain Cook Highway, tropical resorts and holiday havens give way to lush cane fields, which in turn give way to dense bushland. It was here McGurk found an unassuming block studded with gum trees and overgrown grass.

In a letter he penned to Medich in October 2007, he described the block as 27.23 hectares of absolute beachfront located on the outskirts of Port Douglas. He also told Medich the property had been valued at $5.5 million 'as is' – in other words, without development approval – and at $4.4 million in a forced sale. McGurk had managed to screw the vendors down to the bargain price of $3.4 million. He and Medich would make a killing, he promised.

The truth was far from any of this. Lot 25, Captain Cook Highway, was technically a waterfront block, but it was also a floodplain fringed with a mangrove swamp. The nearest town was Mowbray, population 360, which was nothing like chic Port Douglas. Marking the entrance to this piece of 'heaven' was a dilapidated metal postbox perched precariously on a wooden pole, which itself had an unfortunate lean. Behind the postbox was a tiny fibro cottage surrounded by thick scrub. McGurk explained to Medich that the owner of the Mowbray property was in financial difficulty so Medich was in the box seat to snap up the property by paying $1.9 million to take over the mortgages. Medich then paid another $1.48 million to finalise the purchase and pay stamp duty and legal fees.

Medich would later claim that he had paid $6.03 million for the two properties when the total purchase price was actually just over half that amount. Bank statements revealed that $1.28 million had gone straight into McGurk's bank account.

The curious transaction was examined in March 2009 when Medich and McGurk were locked in legal battles in the Federal Court over, among other matters, the Tilley mortgages. Medich's barrister, Robert Newlinds, SC, observed then that there was 'something very strange' about McGurk's purchase of the Mowbray property. Newlinds questioned whether the former owner – one Cristina Lourdes Artillaga – had seen a cent from the forced sale, and whether it had ever been worth the millions McGurk claimed it was. 'Who knows what's behind all this? Who knows whether the actual owner is a victim or potentially a beneficiary of some scam? We don't know.'

Property records showed that Ms Artillaga had purchased the land for a mere $150,000 in 1987. But somewhere along the line she had fallen behind on her mortgage payments. McGurk took over both the mortgages on the property. Adding to the mystery, no one could find Cristina Artillaga. The only person I could dig up who went by her name had once been a runner-up in the 1968 Miss Philippines beauty pageant.

McGurk's taking control of the mortgages allowed him to get Medich to, in effect, pay twice for the property – with one payment he took over the mortgages, and with another – inflated – amount he bought the property he already owned.

Ms Artillaga's first mortgage on the property was with HSBC. An associate of McGurk, Theo Baker, had taken over the HSBC mortgage and had given Ms Artillaga a second mortage through his company, Freestyle Lending. In turn, McGurk bought out Baker's two mortgages using $1.9 million of Medich's money. This meant that McGurk became the mortgagee through his company Acett Pty Ltd, which appeared to have been established in October 2007 especially for this purpose.

Through documents tendered in court, it appeared that Theo Baker had received $250,000 and another business associate of McGurk, Clinton Sarina, $168,000 in connection to the Mowbray sale. McGurk's barrister, Alan Sullivan, QC, speculated that Sarina's payment might have been a 'finder's fee' for alerting McGurk to the sale. The court didn't hear that at the time McGurk owed Baker $250,000.[5] McGurk had borrowed that amount in July 2007 when he'd hit yet another financial spot of bother. (In 2001 Baker had ranked 142 on the BRW Rich 200 list with an estimated wealth of $130 million through his company, Powerlan. But the dotcom bubble burst and by 2002 Powerlan had debts of $142 million. Baker took to last-resort lending and, four years after McGurk's death, himself was bankrupted by the tax office, owing more than $17 million in a decade's worth of unpaid taxes.)

The valuation McGurk gave Medich of the property – between $4.4 million and $5.5 million – was preposterous for the rurally zoned land on which to this day sits a derelict house unable even to produce any rental income. At the time of writing, locals claim that the land is now worth only about $500,000.

For a businessman of Medich's experience, it was extraordinary that these multi-million-dollar deals with McGurk were done on not much more than a nod and a handshake. And after any handshake with McGurk, you'd want to check how many fingers you had left.

On 20 December 2007, only a day after McGurk had purchased the block at Mowbray for Medich, he snapped up another property for him. This property, on the aptly named Crooked River Road, was near Gerroa on the south coast of New South Wales. This time Richie Vereker, who in turn had been tipped off by a 'lawyer mate' in Kiama, alerted McGurk to the 1.9 hectare property, which was adjacent to the Gerringong golf course on one side and dairy farms on the other. The property had once been owned by Kiama Municipal Council, which had sold it in 2002 to a company called Palladian Pacific for $1.13 million after the homestead on the property was destroyed by fire. Using Medich's money, McGurk purchased it for $2.19 million, double the previous sale price.

McGurk told the Medichs it was going to be worth $200–300 million when the development was finished. To her horror, when Odetta arrived in nearby Kiama and inspected the records at the local council, she found that the land was only suitable for a couple of small environmentally friendly holiday cabins.

She recalled McGurk's rushing into their home telling them to sign documents but not letting them read them because he was late for an appointment. McGurk had explained at the time that the agreement they were signing meant he would lodge the development applications for Mowbray and Gerroa. In return he would get 50 per cent of the profits, after they deducted 10 per cent interest on the money Medich had put up. He would also be responsible for 50 per cent of the losses, he told them. He made no mention of the fact that buried in the documents he thrust at them to sign was an agreement that Kimberley McGurk would have 50 per cent ownership of both properties.

Odetta Medich quickly realised her husband had been tricked into paying double the amount for the two properties and that, to add insult to injury, McGurk had managed to install his wife as half owner. Not only that, but Odetta also discovered that McGurk had vastly inflated the price of Gerroa and had secretly pocketed $110,000 for organising the sale.

She was enraged. She told Medich he'd been a fool and that his actions were an embarrassment. She also briefed lawyers to start clawing the Medichs' assets back from McGurk.

She had another reason to watch her husband's actions like a hawk. Their marriage was on its last legs and Odetta was determined to protect their joint assets from being pilfered. Nor was it just the shifty Scot she had in her sights; she also needed to deal with Lucky Gattellari.

And so the Medichs' war with McGurk began. By March 2009 the two men were going at each other hammer and tongs over McGurk's alleged deception regarding the two properties.

'It would appear that the Mowbray property was acquired in a somewhat unusual manner which may not bear scrutiny,' said Justice Peter Graham on 8 April 2009.[6] And another matter puzzled the Federal Court judge. Medich claimed that for six months he had been demanding McGurk pay back the millions he had lent him, yet in January Medich had put up a $100,000 bond for the Scot over the firebombing charges. 'In other words, he's not particularly aggrieved by the man not having sent the money back,' the judge observed.

'Because he trusts him,' explained Medich's barrister, Newlinds. 'He has apparently continued to trust the person for longer than other people might have, but that's his case.'

'Could you help me?' asked Justice Graham. 'Over the relatively long history of the relationship between the principals, what happened that changed the relationship after the $100,000 was posted for the bond in January this year?'

'I can't point to it either,' Newlinds replied, 'other than, Your Honour might infer, just that someone gets pushed too far.'

'One might have thought that the protagonists would be assisted by getting together and learning to talk again. It might be a much more economic resolution of it than a full-blown battle,' noted the judge.[7]

But it wasn't a full-blown battle that was brewing. It was total annihilation.

CHAPTER 15

THE TAPE

Ron Medich had a lot on his mind as he walked through the marble and mirrored foyer of McGurk's York Street building on the morning of 6 February 2009. The bloody jumped-up Scot was causing him no end of grief. Yesterday had been a shocker. First of all, that irritating copper Hetherington had embarrassed him by accosting him in the street outside his Leichhardt office, pestering him for a statement about McGurk and the firebombing. Two weeks ago he'd had to front up to Waverley Court with a bank cheque for $100,000 to get McGurk out of the clink. Now Hetherington reckoned that someone had called Medich just after the firebombing in Wolseley Road. The detective also told him he should be careful of McGurk.

Medich told Hetherington that his lawyers had instructed him not to make a statement because of his ongoing litigation with the Tilleys. He then sat down for lunch at Tuscany with Graham Richardson, who had been collecting a hefty $5000 a month from the Medichs since July 2005 to help Ron and Roy get their ex-CSIRO land at Badgerys Creek rezoned.

Richo, a former minister in the Hawke/Keating government, still had great connections within Labor circles, which were handy because Labor was in power in New South Wales at the time. Medich barely listened as Richo filled him in on his lobbying efforts for Badgerys Creek; instead, he began to download to Richo about the grief McGurk was causing him. Richo mentioned the story in the *Daily Telegraph* three days before, on the Tilley firebombing and Medich's feud with the family.

'If you're involved in this, you could go to jail,' said Richo between mouthfuls.

'Give me a fucking break!' screeched Medich.[1]

To top off a truly bad day, last night he'd had Paul Mathieson yelling at him on the phone from Hawaii about him and McGurk going to jail for what they had done to Mathieson over Amazing Loans. How had he ever got himself involved with this crazy fucking Scot, he thought despondently as he rode in the lift to McGurk's office.

As the lift doors opened, the first thing Medich noticed was McGurk's attempts at self-aggrandisement: cascading down the wall by the lifts was a silver stream of nameplates, about a dozen all up, each embossed with the name of a McGurk company – Labocus Precious Metals, Control Risks International, Bentley Smythe. Pretentious little shit, thought Medich, before reminding himself that he had to keep his cool.

He took the corridor to the right and walked down to McGurk's office.

McGurk ushered him back up the corridor, suggesting that for privacy they should use the office of their mutual friend and solicitor, Rob Hugh, who was on the same floor.

Hugh was intricately involved in the machinations of both Medich's and McGurk's businesses and had acted for them jointly and separately. The solicitor had fingers in many pies. It was Hugh who'd drawn up the legal letters that McGurk sent to Adam Tilley, and it was Hugh who'd accompanied McGurk on his mission to Hawaii to talk sense to Paul Mathieson. Hugh was one of several people whom Medich blamed for introducing him to McGurk, and it was Hugh who'd introduced McGurk to Moses Obeid, the son of controversial Labor powerbroker Eddie Obeid. Hugh was close to the Obeids. In 1999 he swore a statutory declaration for Obeid, then Fisheries minister, which was used to exonerate Obeid over accusations in the New South Wales parliament that he had failed to declare a financial interest in his son Moses' company. Hugh was also a former business partner of Paul Obeid, another of Eddie Obeid's sons.

The waiting room in Hugh's office was decorated with floor-to-ceiling shelves stacked with ancient legal tomes whose impressive gold lettering no doubt lent assurance to prospective clients that the practitioner was well-versed in their contents.

It was 11.30 and Hugh was in court. McGurk asked the receptionist if they could use the solicitor's conference room for five minutes.

The purpose of the meeting, in Medich's mind anyway, was to work out a way to get McGurk out of his business dealings. McGurk was happy to oblige. The only question was his price. McGurk claimed that Medich owed him around $8 million for the work he had done. Medich's view was that he had already loaned McGurk millions and he wanted them back.

The way they both did business entailed very few of their dealings being in writing, so Medich should have been wary when McGurk offered to take notes of this meeting. As they sat down at Hugh's large conference table, the Scot took out a notepad and was fiddling in his pocket for a pen. 'I want to record it down, I'm going to take notes and I'm going to give you copies so you can take this. So we don't want to get into any misunderstandings later on,' he said.[2]

What Medich did not know was that McGurk had covertly switched on his small silver digital recorder. Crafty as always, McGurk had used the word 'record' so that afterwards he could claim Medich had given permission to record the meeting.

One hour and 37 minutes later McGurk switched off the recorder, confident that he now had the ammunition to 'take it to the next level', as he would describe what came next.

When Medich still didn't cough up the $8 million McGurk

had determined he was owed, McGurk thought a word in the ear of a village gossip about the tape's existence might provide him with the leverage he needed. A week after making the recording (though it was an audio recording rather than an old-fashioned tape, the participants tended to refer to this potential weapon of destruction as 'the tape'), McGurk mentioned to Richie Vereker on the quiet that he had a tape that implicated Medich, a state minister and a senior bureaucrat in corrupt planning activities. 'It's going to bring down the government,' McGurk told Vereker, adding that it would also bring down Ron Medich if he didn't pay McGurk what he was owed. When Vereker asked what was on the tape, he said McGurk replied, 'Everything the government doesn't want us to know about property developers, coming straight from the mouth of a property developer. It's damning, Richie, fucking damning.'[3]

Before long, the existence of the recording was an ill-kept secret in most of the pubs where Vereker drank. The problem was that no one knew what was on it. And the less the truth was known about the contents of the tape, the more the vacuum was filled by excited but uninformed speculation masquerading as knowledge. A planning minister was on the take; an official had asked for half a million dollars; the Medichs were buying their way to billions by bribing the planning department to rezone Badgerys Creek.

Vereker, possibly trying to play both sides of the fence, came up with just the person whom McGurk could use to advance the matter. 'I didn't want to help Michael with his extortion attempt – I wanted to deliver him to the professional, who would sort it out,' Vereker recorded in his book on McGurk.[4] The person he turned to was none other than Graham Richardson, who wasn't called 'the Fixer' for nothing.

'"Graham, mate," I said, "I've got a bloke up here who reckons he has a tape recording of Ronnie that puts the state government in the shit. He's talking about going public with it and I asked him if you could come in and hear it before he does something stupid,"' Vereker wrote in his book.[5]

Richardson rang Roy Medich, the more sensible of the two brothers, to discuss this potential nightmare with him. Roy suggested Richo should listen to the tape to see if there was anything on it that would be an embarrassment to the Medich family. Richo, who was out of town, made plans to come to hear the tape. Exactly when he did so is the subject of some uncertainty. Neither Vereker nor Richardson keep diaries so their best estimates were some time between 3 and 10 March.

Richardson was first to arrive at the Bowlers' Club, followed soon after by Vereker. The pair chatted about McGurk for a few minutes before McGurk arrived with a laptop on which he had the recording. Richardson, a no-nonsense man at the best of times, told McGurk to play him the best bit. McGurk fiddled around on the laptop trying to fast forward to the right spot. But when he hit the play button, Richardson couldn't hear a word that was being said. After 30 seconds, he told McGurk he was wasting his time and that unless he got the recording enhanced not to bother him again. As Richo was later to tell a parliamentary inquiry, 'I went there to ascertain whether or not the allegation that had been made to me over the telephone by Mr Vereker – i.e. that there had been a statement made on the tape that some planning officials had been bribed – I went to ascertain if that were true. What I ascertained was that no one could ascertain whether or not it was true because the tape was – and probably deliberately – blurred, garbled, whatever, so that I could not understand it. Once I knew I could not understand it, I saw no point in staying around.'[6]

Richardson told Vereker that Ronnie didn't have a worry in the world. He wouldn't need to pay McGurk $8 million because there was nothing incriminating on the recording.

When the recording was eventually transcribed, it was 20,000 words in length and if Richardson had listened patiently he would have heard some serious allegations of corruption.

Richardson's patronising comments about the quality of his tape incensed McGurk, who responded by launching a direct assault on Medich, sending him a threatening legal letter demanding payment.

As soon as Medich received the legal letter he contacted Detective Hetherington. It was 12 March, only days after Medich had been told that McGurk had the recording and that unless he paid McGurk $8 million, he would make it public.

Medich told Hetherington that in 2006 he had been 'very stressed out' about his $25 million investment facility in a company called Amazing Loans run by Paul Mathieson. Rob Hugh had introduced him to Michael McGurk. Because McGurk had helped him recover his investment in Amazing Loans, Medich said that his confidence in him increased and that he gave McGurk $3.8 million, as part of his commission, to pay off the mortgages on his home.

Medich then explained the complicated Tilley purchase of 42a Wolseley Road. Medich told police that when Tilley didn't repay his multi-million-dollar loan to Medich, 'I signed an assignation to give McGurk the power to recover the money or the actual property but only on my behalf. McGurk agreed to do this for nothing and there was no arrangement that he received any remuneration.'[7]

He said that around 11 on the morning of the firebombing he had received a call from his mate Tim Alford telling him that someone had poured petrol down Adam and Sally-Anne Tilley's driveway and set it alight. Medich told police that since McGurk had been charged with the firebombings and arson, Medich had discovered that the Scot had defrauded him on property transactions, and he was now in court trying to recover his money.

What was interesting was what Medich did *not* tell police. He made no mention of McGurk's most recent criminal endeavour – an $8 million extortion attempt. But while he didn't mention the possible illegality of McGurk's extortion attempt against him, he did cause McGurk to be charged with another offence.

On the last Tuesday in May 2008, while McGurk was doing a spot of standover work on Paul Mathieson in Hawaii, Will

Manning was in McGurk's office, where he'd been working for the last month. Manning's loosely defined job was to find either distressed people to whom McGurk could loan money at exorbitant rates, or distressed assets which his new boss could buy for a song. But Manning was a gambling man, and on that particular morning he was in possession of a red-hot tip.

Born in 1977 on a horse stud in the New South Wales country town of Cootamundra, Manning was the son of veteran racing identity Joe and his wife, Sally, a real estate agent in Sydney. Manning, a party animal, was friends with jockeys, polo players, developers, real estate agents and socialites. He'd done several stints as a real estate agent, and had been hired, along with Richie Vereker's son David, to flog Ron Medich's ill-fated house at 42a Wolseley Road. Will and David had found a willing but unfortunately impecunious buyer in Adam Tilley.

Manning's passion for the races had caused him a string of financial problems. Since 2006, five people had tried to bankrupt him, including Richard Wynne's hotel group over a $26,000 debt and Randwick rails bookmaker Henry Noonan, who was owed $50,000. In each case, Manning had somehow come up with the money at the last minute to stave off bankruptcy.

On that morning in May 2008, he had a surge of exhilaration – he was on to a sure thing, he just knew it. At the time Sydneysiders loved to gossip about their two rich kids, Lachlan Murdoch and James Packer. Only a month earlier, in the first week of April 2008, Murdoch had withdrawn his proposal for his private company, Illyria Pty Ltd, to take over James Packer's Consolidated Media Holdings (CMH), which owned major stakes in the website Seek and the pay television operator Foxtel. The deal had not gone ahead, but Manning had heard whispers around the traps that Lachlan Murdoch was coming back with another, higher offer. If correct, this would boost Packer's shares.

Manning called a stockbroker at ABN Amro and put in an order for a million Consolidated Media shares, at a cost of $3.6 million.

The fact that he didn't have an account was no impediment. Tiffany Boys, McGurk's young office assistant, had only been in the job for a week, but Manning instantly promoted her to Chief Financial Officer of McGurk's company Control Risks International. It might have had a grand title, but CRI, bank-rolled by money from Ron Medich, didn't actually do much. Now, however, the company was about to become a share trader, with Manning producing the necessary paperwork to establish a trading entity with ABN Amro.

Tiffany Boys was told to write a cheque for $1.3 million to cover the first tranche of shares. But when ABN Amro went to bank the cheque they got a nasty surprise. It bounced.

The stockbroker's boss called Boys to find out what the hell was going on. She assumed that Manning had authority from McGurk to buy the shares and she promised the money would be forthcoming. But the following day she had the unenviable task of ringing ABN Amro to say that they'd have to wait for McGurk to return from overseas to sort it out. That wasn't good enough, she was told. The bill had to be paid immediately. By 6 June, when the money still hadn't arrived, ABN Amro began selling the shares.

To add to Manning's woes, his sure thing was sadder than a beaten favourite. The Murdoch takeover offer never eventu-ated and the value of the shares sank, fast. ABN Amro sold Manning's order but the falling share price meant that McGurk's company was left with $2.87 million still to pay.

If the shares price had gone the other way, it would have been champagne and cocaine at the Ivy, with McGurk happy to foot the bill. But when McGurk returned from his Hawaiian trip in early June to find out what had occurred while he'd been away, he was livid. Almost purple with rage, the veins in his neck pulsing, he screamed, 'I'll fuckin' break his fuckin' legs! Who does that fucking fuck-knuckle think he is?'[8]

When Manning arrived in the office that morning, McGurk shrieked at him, 'This is a fine fuckin' mess you've got me in.' Grabbing a souvenir cricket bat signed by the Australian cricket team, he laid into the hapless young man, leaving Shane Warne's signature imprinted on Manning's broken arm.

McGurk's company was sued by ABN Amro, but McGurk dodged a bullet by successfully claiming Manning did not work for him and that he was a rogue trader who had gone off on a frolic of his own.

Manning did not file a defence in the case so a default judgment was obtained against him. When Manning failed to pay the judgment, in February 2009 ABN Amro moved to bankrupt him. Later that year the bankruptcy action was dropped. It seems that once again Manning found the money to settle the matter.

Manning was attacked by McGurk in June 2008, but he did not complain to police until March the following year. At the same time, 14 March 2009, Manning signed an affidavit for Medich to use in his legal battle against McGurk.

At some stage after he'd signed the affidavit, Will Manning was loaned $350,000 by Medich. It wasn't clear exactly when Medich had lent the money, but by early 2010 Lucky Gattellari – on Medich's behalf – was chasing Tim Alford for $200,000 and Manning for $350,000. When police raided Medich's home in October 2013, they found documents indicating that loans had been made to Manning and Alford, both of whom Medich had encouraged to give statements to Detective Hetherington about McGurk.

One of Gattallari's enforcers, Matthew Crockett, drove to the Manning family's horse stud in Cootamundra, to stand over Manning for the return of Medich's money. Manning wasn't there. On 3 February 2010, Gattellari sent Alford a text saying, 'Mr Alford, when am I going to get some cash?' Similar messages followed as the weeks went by. On 23 February, his text read, 'Tim, if I don't get some money today your dealings with me are over.' A month later: 'Do you believe that you have settled your obligation to pay, Tim? Well, my friend that's a shame.'[9]

On 20 April police intercepted a call from Gattellari to Alford. 'Tim, my phone calls are being tapped so I don't want anyone to think that I'm going to hurt a hair on your pretty little fucking head, you little prick.' In August 2010, Gattellari was on the phone to Crockett. 'If you get a chance, ring Senad. See if you can locate that little cunt, Tim Alford,' he said.[10]

When Manning was asked at Medich's trial about the money he owed Medich, he was vague to the point of being evasive. He was asked if Medich had ever lent him money. 'Yes,' replied Manning. He wasn't sure how many times, though, or how much he had borrowed. When pushed, he said he thought it was 'in the vicinity of $200,000'. Gattellari said it was $350,000. While Manning said he was certain he had paid the money back, he couldn't remember how or when, nor could he recall if Gattellari had been chasing him to repay Medich.

The prosecution quickly objected when Medich's barrister, Winston Terracini, put to Manning that he didn't get on well with McGurk. It was ruled to be irrelevant by the judge, who noted sternly that it wasn't McGurk who was on trial here.

'Curiouser and curiouser, to say the least,' said Chief Magistrate Graeme Henson, a droll, down-to-earth man with a keen sense of humour. It was 20 August 2009, and the magistrate was trying to unjumble the matter before him – *R v Michael Loch McGurk*: the charges against McGurk for the firebombings and assaults.

The Downing Centre Court complex, at the southern end of Sydney's CBD, houses the district and local courts. At the entrance to the building is a grand, vibrant circular swirl of colourful mosaics that spells 'Mark Foy's'. The former department store now dispenses justice. On the external walls, surrounded by falsely optimistic yellow mosaic tiles, are the names of departments long gone: 'Silks', 'Corsets', 'Hosiery', 'Gloves' and 'Mourning'. The latter is probably the most apt for the building nicknamed the Drowning Centre, in memory of all those hapless souls who head into court with their toothbrush packed, their goodbyes said, the prison van waiting.

Court 5.2 is one of the largest courtrooms in the centre and it's always a hive of activity first thing in the morning, with the flotsam of felons and their harried legal representatives. This last Thursday morning of winter was no different. There was a perpetual swoosh as the heavy wooden door to the fifth-floor courtroom opened and shut. Lawyers, their arms laden with folders, came in and out, their anxious clients in tow.

Chief Magistrate Henson waded through the list of 30 or so matters, trying to set dates, listening to excuses, chiding tardy lawyers, quizzing the police as to when the evidence would be made available and dispatching to other courtrooms cases ready to commence.

As the magistrate ploughed his way through the list, in no particular order, Michael McGurk sat calmly in a seat towards the back. Dressed in his customary expensive suit and shirt, he looked more like a lawyer than an accused. With his hands on his knees, he listened intently to the other matters as though there might be some information to be gleaned.

McGurk had a new solicitor. After representing the accused firebomber for six months, Patrick Conaghan, now a federal MP, had quit following a 'stand-up barney' with his client in the Downing Centre's café. 'What McGurk wanted me to do went against all my ethical standards,' he said, declining to elaborate.[11]

When McGurk's matter was finally called, there was confusion. Much to the irritation of Senior Constable Ray Hetherington, a young lawyer with the Director of Public Prosecutions (DPP) had decided to drop eight charges against McGurk. But McGurk's lawyer, Richard Allsop, seemed to have the only copy of all the charges. The magistrate looked at the bundle of documents, trying to work out whether *all* the matters were being dropped. The paperwork seemed to indicate that the firebombings of the Tilley and Rowan homes had been discontinued, as had the assault charges relating to Rowan and Muscat. Where did that leave the AVOs that valuer Stuart Rowan had taken out against McGurk? And what about the Will Manning assault case?

'Was your client ever charged with the offence?' said the magistrate, looking up from the papers in front of him. Up the back of the court, McGurk shook his head.

'It's been shoddily done and now it is a complete mess,' said Richard Allsop crankily.

Later, outside the court complex, a dozen steps above the hurly-burly of the Liverpool Street traffic, sitting in the pale winter sun at a café table close to the main entrance, McGurk was deep in conversation with Allsop. Signalling for Vanda and me to join him, McGurk let fly. Far from being relieved, he was furious. Furious with the police, but most of all furious with Ron Medich.

'It is clear Mr Medich has made some wilful misstatements to the police for commercial gain. He blatantly lied in his own statements to the police,' he said, stabbing his forefinger on the table top for added emphasis. His face was flushed with anger. 'Medich never disclosed to the DPP that I was not a beneficiary to the Tilley mortgage. He just beat the whole thing up to give me a motive,' he said, his voice rising.

Slipping into the language of lawyers, McGurk continued. 'We say Mr Medich is out to pervert the course of justice. We think the whole thing stinks.'

At this stage Allsop made his excuses and departed in a hurry.

McGurk continued. He said Medich was always boasting to him about his connections to government ministers, with the tax office, the Independent Commission Against Corruption (ICAC) and the police. According to McGurk, the majority of the statements police had obtained against him were made by people either employed by or indebted to Medich. Not only that but Medich had only turned on him in March, which just so happened to coincide with the Federal Court case. Besides, he added, the night before the firebombing of 42a Wolseley Road, McGurk, Damien Reed and a representative for Adam Tilley had come to an agreement about Tilley paying out the mortgage on 42a. 'Medich was the one who refused the agreement. He wanted more!' said McGurk.

McGurk also complained to me that Manning had only come forward 'after ten months to say I broke his arm with a cricket bat'. This coincided with Manning's offer to help Medich against him, McGurk said.

'The man is dangerous,' he said of Medich, taking a sip of water. 'Tilley has been told that Medich is going to get someone to bash him.'

The subject of the mysterious tape was broached again. 'What about that tape? When can we have a copy of that?' I asked McGurk.

'Soon, soon,' he replied non-committally.

I couldn't help but shake my head as I disappeared back into the bowels of the Downing Street complex. Outside, I was hearing a bizarre tale which was Sydney to a T: money, property, power and greed. Now I was heading into court again to hear exactly the same tale: a case that involved one of the very people McGurk had mentioned to us over lunch. Eddie Obeid's close friend John Abi-Saab was on trial for using a tape recording to try to blackmail a fellow councillor.

The similarities were remarkable: blackmail and a tape. Were these incidents a reflection of what was really happening below the superficial veneer of polite society? Trust and loyalty, it seemed, were invariably trumped by avarice and greed.

CHAPTER 16

A VERY SMART OPERATOR

Just a block east from developer Bob Ell's office in Sydney's financial district is one of his favourite dining spots – an upmarket steakhouse where the interior design is gentlemen's club meets abattoir. A collection of cow skulls hangs from the ceiling over the bar, and the large, curved pieces of pale wood that arc above the tables in a neat row make you feel as though you're dining inside the ribs of some long-extinct mammoth.

The Chophouse has a blokey atmosphere – a place to carve out deals over a bloody steak and bottle or two of red wine. One September day in 2009, eschewing one of its more private leather-padded booths, Bob Ell and his mate Richie Vereker were at a table chatting. There were three place settings but one of the white bread and butter plates, emblazoned with a small meat cleaver symbol, remained unsullied. The last of the luncheon trio was yet to arrive.

McGurk joined the table when Vereker and Ell had just polished off their first bottle of red. None of them could know that within 30 hours one of their party would be dead.

*

Robert William Ell, a former chippie, had made his billions slicing and dicing land for redevelopment. His company, Leda Holdings (named after the princess who was seduced by Zeus disguised as a swan), owned a number of shopping malls and had made a motza doing large-scale residential land developments in Queensland and New South Wales. Richie Vereker, on the other hand, had lost millions slicing and dicing meat carcasses.

Vereker was to Bob Ell what Ben Tilley was to Kerry Packer and, later, his son James – the affable, likeable one of the pair; Tilley and Vereker encouraging a modicum of tolerance from others towards Packer senior and junior, and Ell. 'Bob Ell made his fortune building brick walls, and talking to him is not unlike trying to talk to one of them,' was the opening sentence of a 1987 profile of Ell in the *Sydney Morning Herald*.[1] At Medich's murder trial, Ell offered nothing but monosyllabic replies. His most expansive answer was in response to a question about a call he had received from Medich on the replacement $100,000 surety Ell had put up for McGurk in April 2009. Asked what Medich had said to him, Ell replied, 'He said, "Mike's a cunt."'[2]

Described by an associate as 'a small, unsmiling' man, Ell is both admired for his ruthlessness and extraordinary achievements as a developer and despised by those who object to his aggressive business style and his stinginess. The joke around town is that when Ell and Vereker catch up for lunch, the billionaire is so tight he just buys one steak and cuts it in half.

Susie Carleton, the former owner of the Bellevue Hotel in Paddington, can attest to Ell's legendary parsimony. She said that Ell was only tolerated in her pub because he was Richie's friend and everyone adored Richie. 'He is the most terrific bloke,' she said. Richie never bad-mouths anyone and will do anything for you, Carleton said. 'He is Mr Fixit, he is an absolutely Sydney character.'[3]

I once reported a snippet about Ell's behaviour when he was living in the Harry Seidler-designed Horizon building in Darlinghurst, where he owned the entire fortieth floor. It was 2001 and Ell had whipped himself into a frenzy of self-righteous indignation about the failure of the front desk staff to treat him with the deference he felt that someone of his status deserved.

'At approximately 21.30 hours I was standing behind the concierge desk,' complained one concierge to his boss. '[Ell] started to hurl a barrage of insults to me and the concierges in general, and I quote: "You are fucking lazy pricks sitting on your fucking fat arses. You are here to push buttons and carry luggage," unquote,' wrote the concierge.[4]

A second concierge also filed a complaint. 'We the concierges are mature adults, we resent being called BOY this is a slang word from the American vocabulary meaning SLAVE. And as such we find the term derogatory and resentful [sic], as we are professionals in this field.'

Ell was only too happy to confirm that he had berated the front desk staff for not being more helpful. 'That's what concierges do, don't they?' Ell said to me. He added that because they were 'very lazy and wouldn't work', they had been fired.[5]

Ell is not a country boy at heart, even though he was born and raised in the New South Wales Hunter Valley town of Merriwa. He was born in December 1944 and lived in a modest weatherboard and fibro house on Bow Street until he was twenty. With its simple two-rung wooden fence and neat front lawn, the house looked much like all the others dotted along the quiet street. His passion was rugby league and he played a handy game for the Merriwa Magpies. He completed the last three years of his education boarding at De La Salle College in Armidale before coming home to work as a carpenter with his dad, who was a local builder.

Even as a young man, Ell watched his pennies. Earning eight pounds a week as a trainee chippie, he became the envy of the other young tradies in town when he saved up enough to buy the latest model Ford Falcon station wagon.

He met his first wife, Barbara, in his home town. At the time, Australia was recruiting overseas nurses. Babs, as she's known, a New Zealander and a couple of years older than Bob, was posted to Merriwa Hospital. Bob was barely in his twenties when they married and left for the big smoke. The only place they could afford to live was in a converted garage in Collaroy on Sydney's northern beaches. Babs nursed while Bob landed a job building apartments in Dee Why.

When Ell's aunt, Ella Mulholland, was interviewed in 1998, she said that her nephew 'always said he was going to be a millionaire' before he turned 40.[6] He was impatient for success, working his way up to foreman and then going out on his own buying up cheap houses, painting and carpeting them, and on-selling them for a tidy profit.

The Ells went to live in New Zealand for a spell, where Ell discovered how much money you could make buying factories and industrial sites. He either refurbished or knocked them down and erected in their place a row of cheap industrial premises.

What singled out Ell from others was his ability to spot a trend. 'He just has a fantastic gut feel for real estate; he knows when to get out when it's too hot,' said one industry figure.[7]

'He is a very smart operator. He knew what was required for the market, and he would do it,' said another.[8] He was often compared to Meriton's Harry Triguboff or Walker Corp's Lang Walker – men who knew what it took to get ahead and were tough enough to get there. Property development is not a business for the faint of heart. Ell's ethos throughout his career has been pretty simple: buy low and sell high; he's famous for his taste for distressed assets. 'If Bob Ell is spending money, he's probably doing it because the market is at the lowest,' said a real estate observer.[9] And he has ridden the market cycle with great skill. Twice he floated Leda, then, when times were bad and the price was in the doldrums, he bought it back again. For years now Ell has privately owned Leda Holdings. Its really big money came through major land rezonings and development approvals, where Ell often locked horns with councillors and state planning officials.

In the wake of McGurk's death, Ell launched a defamation action against one of his more vocal critics, Greens councillor

Katie Milne, who sat on Tweed Shire Council and had been opposing a $6 billion plan by Leda to build two 'mini-cities' for 11,000 residents at Kings Forest and Cobaki, which are close to the Queensland border.

In his statement of claim in his defamation case, Ell asserted he had been 'gravely injured' by a 'letter to the editor' Katie Milne had emailed to the Gold Coast Bulletin, the Sydney Morning Herald, the Tweed Echo, and several community groups in March 2010. The Echo, a weekly that printed about 20,000 copies, was the only media outlet to publish the letter, which claimed:

> The developer Mr Bob Ell has made massive donations to both the State and Federal Labour [sic] and Liberal governments as well as the last Council.
>
> The McGurk murder also raises serious concerns. According to Sydney newspapers Mr Bob Ell supplied $100,000 bail when McGurk was accused of firebombings and assault, though this was later dropped.
>
> McGurk was working for Mr Ell at the time of his murder.

For years Ell's developments in the Tweed area were bogged down by legal battles and problems with the local council, which was sacked in 2005 after it was discovered that six pro-development councillors had been recruited on to the council with the support of developers. In an inquiry into the council, conducted by Emeritus Professor Maurice Daly, the councillors were found to have been 'puppets' of the developers.[10] Daly found that the group was ignoring advice from council staff, instead giving approvals and concessions that were a substantial benefit to developers. He said ratepayers should have been told that $341,000 had been donated to Tweed Directions, an entity set up specifically to bankroll candidates who favoured business. The donations were made by developers with a vested interest in the area, including Bob Ell.

The McGurk allegations exposed Ell to 'hatred, ridicule and contempt', his barrister Terry Tobin, QC, told the court. Katie Milne's lawyer, Tom Molomby, SC, told the New South Wales Supreme Court that Ell had made 'massive' donations to state and federal political parties and had donated $80,000 to the group of candidates running for Tweed Council in 2004.

Ell's barrister said there was nothing illegal about Ell's $80,000 donation, and that people often donated because they had an interest in having someone elected who had a sympathetic vision.[11] Molomby also claimed that Ell tried to 'buy the favours of the state government and the local council by making large donations to political parties and election campaigns'.[12] He tabled a list of 15 donations totalling $165,439 made to New South Wales Labor by companies owned or co-owned by Ell between October 2005 and December 2007.

Justice Lucy McCallum was unpersuaded. She said that Molomby's use of the word 'buy' assumed 'that there is no such thing as a political gift and that all political donations are inherently corruptive. That is an opinion to which some members of the community may adhere but I do not think it is appropriate to treat it as a fact or an established premise for the purposes of determining Ms Milne's contextual truth defence.'[13]

The judge also found that: 'None of the documents in evidence, nor any inference that may be fairly drawn from them, reasonably sustains a finding that Mr Ell attempted to buy the favours of the New South Wales State Government and the Tweed Shire Council.' She found two of the six imputations pleaded by Ell were conveyed in the letter and were defamatory. They were that Ell had a 'scandalous association with the murdered man Mr McGurk' and that he 'conducted his business with regard to property development by employing a person with a reputation for violence'.[14]

The judge found for Ell but awarded the developer a paltry $15,000. 'The fact that he did not attend a single minute of the hearing speaks against his having suffered any real distress or hurt caused by the publication,' said Justice McCallum.[15]

The damages award might have been small, but the sting for Milne was having to pay Ell's legal costs, which were estimated to be around $500,000.

Five days after his defamation victory, Ell told a journalist from the *Gold Coast Bulletin* that Milne was not a 'fit and proper person to be a councillor'. The *Bulletin's* front-page headline on 13 March 2014 read 'Katie loses billionaire Bob battle: "I hope this sends her broke"'.

Milne sued both Ell and the paper. Her action against the *Gold Coast Bulletin* was dropped after the paper issued an apology.

In his May 2017 judgment Justice Stephen Rothman of the New South Wales Supreme Court wrote of Milne's lawsuit: 'It is hard to escape the suspicion that the defamation proceedings have been taken as a "tit for tat" exercise . . . Nevertheless, that aspect is not considered in the determination of the damages.'[16] Milne emerged the victor this time, and Ell was ordered to pay her $45,000.

In the 'letter' that ended up causing Councillor Milne so much grief, she referred to a decision Ell had made – to take over McGurk's bail. After relations between Medich and McGurk had deteriorated irreparably, Medich withdrew his bail money. He wrote to the court on 6 April 2009, saying, 'Since going surety on 20 January 2009, I have received further information about Mr McGurk in regard to his character and as a result I do not wish to be surety for Mr McGurk.'

On 15 April up to the plate stepped developer number two, Bob Ell.

Given his legendary miserliness, Ell's stumping up $100,000 bail for McGurk was out of character. Vereker was at a loss to understand Ell's generosity. 'I don't know what the deal was. Bob may have thought that since Michael had four kids, that it was the right thing to do. More likely, Bob saw it as a favour to me,' he wrote in his book.[17]

Vereker had done plenty of favours for Ell in the past. When Carleton sold the Bellevue in 2004, Ell was readmitted to the pub. Four years later Vereker and Ell were propping up the bar there when a man rushed in and yelled at Ell, 'Where's my money?'[18] He shouted that Ell had ruined his family, then he assaulted Ell, who was taken to St Vincent's Hospital. Afterwards, Vereker shuffled round the pub telling other patrons they hadn't seen anything and there was no need to talk to police.

Jim Byrnes told me that in mid-2008 he had struck up a friendship with McGurk when they were acting on the opposite sides of a dispute. McGurk was trying to collect $290,000 in unpaid rent from a tenant who had a chain of shops. McGurk arrived at this man's shop and began menacing Ell's tenant, who rang his man, Big Jim Byrnes, who demanded to speak to McGurk. Never one to take a backwards step, McGurk promptly offered to come round to Byrnes's home to extract the money from him personally. Byrnes was both irritated and amused by McGurk's approach. 'Do you know who you are talking to? Do your homework,' said Byrnes.[19] The pair agreed to meet the following day and they hit it off.

McGurk was always on the lookout for property deals for Ell, and he would collect a cut if those deals came off. One that did come off involved the Gladstone RSL Club in Queensland. McGurk got a spotter's fee when Ell made an $800,000 profit in 2006 after briefly owning the hotel. McGurk had hoped for a whole lot more but the council quashed their development plans so Ell on-sold.

McGurk was certainly holding himself out as Ell's right-hand man. One businessman told me of attending meetings in Ell's city offices with McGurk and Clinton Sarina. The businessman said Sarina and McGurk would take you into the main boardroom in Ell's office, where McGurk would order the staff around. 'He gave the impression he was a senior manager' and that 'he had sufficient clout to use the boardroom in that manner', he observed.[20]

McGurk was shameless in using Ell's name to organise meetings with distressed property developers who were hoping to stay afloat by selling part or all of their development to Ell. Ell would lend McGurk his 37-metre cruiser *Leda*, which had 11 cabins, two bars, a dining room and a theatre room with a wall-sized plasma TV screen. 'I've always liked boats,' Ell told the *Sun-Herald* in 2000. 'Some blokes buy planes and cars, but I like boats, I like the water. I reckon they are safer and better for relaxation and recreation.'[21]

The *Leda* has been the target of makeovers by women in Ell's life. When his girlfriend Gold Coast interior decorator Marie Stephens was on the scene, the boat became what one visitor described as a 'gin palace disco heaven, all black marble, flashing lights and mirror balls'.[22] Stephens later slapped a palimony suit on Ell, having signed a deed of separation from him in 1999. In 2001 he married his second wife, real estate agent Bridget McCarthy. The Gold Coast bling on the boat was soon removed.

McGurk was close enough to Ell to be given the keys to the *Leda*, which the Scot frequently used to impress school parents and mates. Several business people also recall meeting McGurk on board at Ell's 2007 Christmas bash. It was the one time of the year when Ell splashed out, and invitations to his legendary Christmas parties were keenly sought after by his favourite advisers, trade suppliers and business associates.

That warm summer's evening just before Christmas in 2007, the *Leda* set sail on Sydney Harbour later than planned as Ell was delayed travelling from the Gold Coast, where he spent much of his time at his Budds Beach mansion. The *Leda* was finally away, cruising in and out of the bays of the harbour as hundreds of guests spread out across two floors of open decks. Bankers, valuers, insolvency experts and lawyers crowded around the giant semi-circular bar that filled the full width of the boat as flickering images from a massive TV screen danced across an entire wall.

One insolvency expert recalled McGurk deep in conversation with a group of senior bankers from Westpac. He was talking excitedly about buying up a $35 million hotel in Surfers Paradise. He also boasted about his plans for a development project at Gerroa. He presented himself as a self-made man, worth about $10 million, said this man. 'He gave the impression he was on a winner with a bunch of projects about to make him more.'[23] The way he spoke, the man said, it was as if the Gerroa project was his alone – there was no mention that he was using Ron Medich's money.

After McGurk's murder, Ell put out a written statement saying that McGurk had never been an employee of the Leda group of companies and that 'At no time did Michael McGurk have a mandate to act for me.'[24]

He claimed that a doctor's appointment prevented him from going to McGurk's funeral. Vereker also decided – he said on legal advice – not to attend the funeral, which was held at the Sacred Heart Catholic Church in Mosman. The church, on Cardinal Street, formed part of Sacred Heart College, the school attended by McGurk's children.

As Vereker, Ell and McGurk tucked in to their steaks over lunch that September day at the Chophouse, things were looking up for McGurk. His criminal charges had been dropped. Vereker was keen to toast this fortuitous turn of events.

The celebratory lunch was the last time Ell saw McGurk alive.

CHAPTER 17

CRAZINESS AFTER THE MURDER

The murder of Michael McGurk was a huge story. It led every TV and radio bulletin; there were acres of newsprint on the killing; it was picked up overseas. Here was a man who claimed he had a tape that could bring down the government, who said he feared for his life, and subsequently was shot getting out of his Mercedes in one of Sydney's more affluent suburbs. As South Australia's *Advertiser* reported:

> It is the execution that has shocked Australia – a father gunned down in front of his 10-year-old son. It is also a murder with all the hallmarks of the TV crime series *Underbelly* – a tale of corruption and a double life. And now the web of intrigue is spun thicker. There are allegations of a plot to bring down two New South Wales government ministers, claims of government corruption, mystery tapes of conversations and possible investigations by Scotland Yard.[1]

In the days after the murder my phone rang incessantly; information flooded in. Not just about McGurk but about the whole carousel of characters to whom he was connected – the Medichs, the Gattellaris, the Verekers, the Tilleys, Big Jim Byrnes, Bob Ell, lawyers, accountants, valuers, mortgage brokers, standover men, government ministers, a former premier, and myriad dodgy bit-players who had come into McGurk's orbit. I could see this was going to be difficult for the police. McGurk had pissed off a lot of people.

Meanwhile, at the *Herald* we were struggling to keep up with all the tips. Not all of them were helpful. One man called with information so sensitive and sensational he couldn't possibly divulge it over the phone. I told him to come to the *Herald*'s office. A peculiar sight awaited me in the foyer: a gentleman of Mediterranean extraction with a blond wig perched on his head. The wig wasn't even on straight – it appeared to be back to front and it lurched at a dangerous angle across one eye. Despite it being a mild spring day the man was wrapped in a heavy trench coat. His failure to make any mention of his bizarre attempt to disguise himself only added to the general weirdness of the situation. His red-hot information was that in his job as a taxi driver he thought he may have once driven 'Mr McGerkin'.

One deep throat had gone to the trouble of buying a voice distorter. He rang with great information about Justin Brown. The distorted voice told me that recently he had seen Brown having a morning coffee with Eddie Obeid and his son Moses at their favourite café, Latteria in Darlinghurst. He'd overheard them talking about the Elizabeth Bay Marina (it transpired later that the Obeids had hidden their ownership of the marina) and a feud brewing between Moses' company Streetscape and the City of Sydney council over multi-function poles. The anonymous source with the voice that sounded like a crazed robot also reported seeing solicitor Hector Ekes with Moses Obeid and Justin Brown.

Looking back now it is remarkable how prescient the anonymous caller was. He detailed a number of controversial developments involving McGurk and his cronies. One of them he urged me to look at was the sale of union-owned Currawong workers' cottages in Pittwater, which were to become the subject of an ICAC investigation in which planning minister Tony Kelly was found to be corrupt.

It wasn't until 2013 that John Robertson, the New South Wales opposition leader, confessed that in March 2006 McGurk had offered him a $3 million bribe. In his then role as Unions NSW boss, Robertson was overseeing the sale of the Currawong cottages. Medich and McGurk were unsuccessful bidders. McGurk's introduction to Robertson had come via Moses Obeid, the son of then MP Eddie. There was uproar at Robertson's belated revelation. He had not reported the matter to police at the time, nor after McGurk was murdered.

My anonymous caller was fantastic and, after I thanked him profusely, I said, 'So, I can reach you on this number?' The poor chap nearly choked. He had gone to the effort of buying a voice distorter but his number had come up on my caller ID.

Given the information the mysterious informant had given me, I wasn't surprised when my calls to Justin Brown asking about his dealings with McGurk were returned by his lawyer, Hector Ekes, who said that his client had no comment to make owing to 'Supreme Court proceedings and the criminal investigation into the murder of Mr McGurk'. (Ekes knew first-hand just how volatile McGurk's associates could be. At the time of the Scot's murder Big Jim Byrnes was on a three-year good behaviour bond after taking to Ekes's office with a baseball bat. Byrnes, who blamed his actions on a 'brain snap', had his jail term reduced to a good behaviour bond on appeal.)

Two underworld contacts rang separately telling me to be careful. The day after the murder one said, 'I can't say too much on the phone but whatever you do, cover your back. These people don't give a fuck who they hurt.' Another said, 'This is just a courtesy call, but from what I've heard this is too big and you need to be careful. You don't want to end up like Juanita Nielsen.'[2]

A fortnight after the murder, late one night I came home to find a white envelope poking out of the mailbox. There was an

A4 sheet of paper inside. One of the first stories I'd written on the McGurk murder had been cut out and pasted onto the piece of paper – 'My lunch with a dead man', which detailed, without naming Medich, that McGurk knew there was a hit out on him and that he knew who had ordered it. Written above the cut-out article was 'lying slut'. Below was scrawled '303'. I took that to be a reference to a .303-inch calibre rifle cartridge. I was alarmed that these people knew where I lived. I tried not to touch the note too much and put it straight into a large envelope. The following day I contacted Detective Inspector Mick Sheehy, who was handling the murder investigation. No fingerprints came up on the note or the envelope and the police never did find out who was responsible for the death threat. If the purpose of the threat was to make me back off, it failed.

Instead of dissipating, the intrigue surrounding the murder of McGurk continued to grow, and at the *Herald* we continued to follow more leads and write more stories. McGurk's propensity to provide prostitutes as a way of blackmailing people was something several of his associates raised. After his murder, a dispute arose over $500,000 that McGurk had paid to brothel owners. McGurk's company Bentley Smythe had paid $500,000 to Anton Fabrications, a company which ran a brothel in Sydney's CBD. 'As I understand it,' Justice Julie Ward said in 2011, 'there is no dispute that the sum in question was paid.'[3] The question was whether the payment was a loan or 'the repayment on behalf of Mr McGurk of a debt that he had personally incurred . . . for remuneration in respect of prostitution services allegedly provided'. Neither of the brothel owners turned up in court and the liquidator of Anton Fabrications said the company was 'hopelessly insolvent', meaning there was no money to repay the McGurk estate even if it was decided it was a loan and not a debt.[4]

But the most persistent rumour in the wake of McGurk's demise concerned the existence of a tape, or tapes, and what they might contain, and they were on the front page of just about every paper in the country. There was intense speculation that the murder might be linked to disclosures on the tape about corrupt planning and development activities, and of bribes involving state and federal Labor politicians. McGurk had claimed that the revelations could bring down the New South Wales government and he had told me he feared for his life. Now he was dead.

The tape was also making a number of politicians extremely nervous. On 6 September, three days after the murder, Graham Richardson dropped a bombshell on Channel 9's Sunday evening news bulletin in an interview with veteran political reporter Laurie Oakes. 'Former Labor powerbroker Graham Richardson says McGurk demanded $8 million dollars not to release details of an audio tape, which is now the centre of a major political bribery allegation,' said the newsreader.

'He wanted money from Ron Medich and lots of it, millions of dollars,' said Richardson, who explained that Vereker had approached him about the explosive tape and had organised for him to meet McGurk for ten minutes six months before. 'There was McGurk, and he had the tape . . . He played it on his laptop. I listened,' he said. 'The critical part, where there was supposed to be allegations of bribery, was completely inaudible. There was nothing on the tape which you could understand, neither content nor names,' said Richardson, having listened to between 30 and 50 seconds of the 97-minute recording.

When Oakes asked him if he thought the tape would shed any light on McGurk's murder, Richardson replied, 'I would doubt it very much – you can't understand anything. Somebody like McGurk has a list of enemies as long as your arm so I would say that the police might be looking at a whole lot of people.' He added that about three months after he'd listened to the tape, he had given the police a statement about the matter.

Political pressure was mounting to hold an inquiry into what looked like a potential development scandal. Ron and Roy Medich stood to gain millions if the New South Wales government could be persuaded to rezone the brothers' block of land at Badgerys Creek. McGurk had dropped over to our office title deeds and other information about the Medichs' holdings at Badgerys Creek and nearby Bringelly. He had also made the point that Richardson stood to make a great deal via a 'success fee' if his lobbying efforts on behalf of the Medichs regarding the rezoning of their land came off.

Opposition leader Barry O'Farrell tried to round up the cross-benchers to support an inquiry into Labor's connection with the Medichs. 'At the heart of these allegations is a claim that massive windfall profits were made because of planning decisions made either by the minister or in the planning department,' said O'Farrell.[5] But the Labor government held firm. Police minister Tony Kelly said the opposition should stay out of the affair. The very idea of a parliamentary inquiry into corruption allegations raised after the murder of McGurk was 'ridiculous', said Kelly. 'They [police] should be allowed to get on with that murder inquiry and not be complicated by interference by politicians,' he told ABC radio. Asked if there were corrupt ministers in the New South Wales government, Kelly responded, 'I would have no idea. I've got no idea, in this particular case, whether any of these allegations are correct.'[6]

Kelly was later found to be corrupt in two separate ICAC investigations. Another Labor minister, Joe Tripodi, also had two corruption findings. Eddie Obeid had multiple corruption findings and was jailed. Ian Macdonald, the man Ron Medich was hoping would become planning minister also had multiple corruption findings, and spent 18 months in jail before his conviction was quashed.

The *Daily Telegraph*'s editorial on Monday 7 September observed: 'The death of Michael McGurk has lit up Sydney's great big elephant in the room: that something stinks about the way property deals are done in this town.'

That same day I was interviewed by Detective Sergeant Damian Loone at The Rocks Police Station. After some hours there I signed an eight-page statement – 'Statement of Kathryn Anne McCLYMONT in the matter of Death of Michael

MCGURK' – which would later be the subject of a legal battle between prosecutors and Ron Medich's legal team.

Later that day the ICAC announced that it would hold an inquiry into the tape after a referral from the New South Wales police. Vanda and I each received a summons to attend a compulsory examination or private hearing on 10 September. According to the summons, I had to bring:

1. Copies of all records whether written or audio recorded of all discussions with Michael McGurk.
2. Copies of all records whether written or audio discussions with other people spoken to you as a result of any discussion you had with Michael McGurk.
3. All material, including any audio tapes, provided to you by McGurk.

The barrage of unfortunate stories continued, most of them spotlighting Ron Medich's connections with the murdered man and Graham Richardson's connections with both McGurk and Medich.

There is no doubt that Richardson has been one of the most controversial politicians of his generation. In 1976 he became general secretary of the party's all-powerful New South Wales branch and in that capacity a kingmaker. Former federal opposition leader Bill Hayden, who was politically decapitated by Richardson and others in favour of Bob Hawke, said that Richardson had once explained his modus operandi to him: 'All decisions are democratically taken at a meeting of one: me.'[7]

In the early 1980s he featured in the Woodward Royal Commission into Drug Trafficking when it came to light that he had organised for his wife to be on the payroll of the Balmain Welding company.

He was 33 when he became a federal senator in 1983. After Labor narrowly won the 1990 election, Richardson was furious when he was denied his desired portfolio of Transport and Communication and was instead given Defence, and later – even worse – Social Security. He supported Hawke's ousting from the prime ministership in favour of Paul Keating in 1991 and his 'loyalty' was rewarded, finally, with the Communications portfolio. His closeness to media magnate Kerry Packer earned him the nickname Minister for Channel 9. In 1992 he was forced to resign from the front bench following a visa scam involving a friend of his, who was married to his cousin.[8] Two year later, in March 1994, he quit parliament for good, supposedly on health grounds. Within weeks he was the subject of allegations that businessmen had supplied him with prostitutes, which he denied.

At the time of McGurk's murder the former powerbroker was waging a prolonged legal battle with the ATO over a $2.3 million tax assessment from profits in a Swiss bank account. He claimed that the funds in the Swiss account were a gift from his close friend the late disgraced stockbroker Rene Rivkin, who was jailed for insider trading. Richardson reached a confidential settlement with the ATO in 2010, but a few weeks later it was revealed that in 1994 he had sent $1 million from his Swiss account to a bank in Beirut. My colleague Linton Besser and I later discovered that the Beirut account was operated by a close associate of Eddie Obeid and the million-dollar transfer was likely to have been Obeid's share of the mysterious Offset Alpine deal. When the Offset Alpine printing factory burnt down on 24 December 1993, the company had just taken out a healthy insurance policy and the share price went through the roof. Just weeks after the fire, Richardson directed that the $1 million be transferred from his account at EBC Zurich to an account in Beirut. Richardson told Linton and me he didn't recall the transaction but if he had transferred the money, 'It was under the instructions of Rivkin.'[9]

On 8 September the *Herald* revealed that only the previous month Richardson had personally lobbied the head of the New South Wales planning department over his refusal to rezone the Medichs' land. In a separate story, Richie Vereker, the go-between for McGurk and Richardson over the tape, was revealed to have been one of that year's biggest donors to the Labor Party.

A month before the New South Wales state election in March 2007, Vereker, who had suffered a debilitating stroke and was on a disability pension, had donated a whopping $75,000 to the state Labor Party. To put the figure in perspective, that year big Labor donors such as construction giant Grocon and Bob Ell's flagship Leda Holdings gave $55,000 and $39,000 respectively. In his spidery handwriting Vereker had signed his name on the donation form and when asked to declare whether the contribution was on behalf of an organisation or personal, he wrote in capital letters: PERSONAL. He signed and dated his declaration with '29-2-2007'. February 29 only comes around every four years, and 2007 was not one of them.

When the *Herald* revealed that Vereker had made this donation, one friend was quoted in the article as saying of Vereker, 'He doesn't have enough money to buy lunch' let alone donate $75,000.[10] It was an ill-kept secret among Vereker's drinking mates that he had donated the money on Ell's behalf. 'That $75,000 was Bob's money, for sure,' said one friend.[11] Another friend laughed, noting that 'Bob Ell is such a tight arse that for $75,000 he must have wanted half the state.'[12]

The Australian Electoral Commission declined to investigate the matter, saying, 'There must be evidence more substantial than just speculation.' One might have thought that is why an investigation was needed. Even had they looked into the gift, the fine was only a laughable $1000 anyway.

Ell denied that the $75,000 Vereker had donated was his. The billionaire developer said he didn't have a clue whose money it was.

CHAPTER 18

PARLIAMENTARY INQUIRY

With its floor-to-ceiling book shelves lined with weighty parliamentary tomes, the ornate Jubilee Room, once the New South Wales parliament's library, was the unlikely setting for the first public glimpse of one of the central figures in the murder that had been gripping the nation for just shy of a month.

By the end of September 2009, Premier Nathan Rees had been forced to abandon his opposition to a parliamentary inquiry into the Medichs and their dealings with planning officials or MPs over their CSIRO land at Badgerys Creek. Ron Medich was the last witness to appear on the first day of the inquiry, which began on 29 September. Medich, who had never been seen in anything other than black, appeared in a dark suit, white shirt and a mauve, patterned tie. He arrived as planning minister Kristina Keneally was testifying – rather triumphantly – that her department had not been persuaded to rezone the Medichs' land despite the persistent efforts of one Graham Richardson. She trotted out a line she'd used before about McGurk: 'A man I've never heard of, allegedly extorting people I've never met with, about land the government did not rezone.'[1]

She also had a swipe at the *Herald*, saying, 'Contrary to claims in the *Sydney Morning Herald* and by the leader of the opposition, Mr Barry O'Farrell – claims that neither of these parties has withdrawn – this land has not been rezoned.'[2]

While Keneally was on her feet, Ron Medich scurried up to one of the few vacant seats, in the corner of the front row. Roy, who was sitting in the third row, had given evidence before Keneally. The brothers did not acknowledge one another during the afternoon.

After watching both Medichs give evidence, it was apparent that Roy was the brains of the family business. With his distinguished salt-and-pepper hair and his Order of Australia pinned to the lapel of his pin-striped suit, he responded to questions with calm self-assurance, even when Liberal MP Greg Pearce tried to bait him over the Medichs' employment of Graham Richardson, a man who had been associated with more controversies than was socially acceptable.

'Why did you associate yourself with someone like Mr Richardson?' Pearce asked Roy.[3]

'I don't think that is a fair question,' he replied.

'You can still answer it,' directed Pearce.

'I have enjoyed Mr Richardson's company over many, many years. I mean, it is not an easy task these days to bring your matter before the government. Sometimes you need to get advice on which is the best way forward on a particular project. At the same time—'

'And he gave you that advice and assistance?' said Pearce, cutting in.

'I could pass things by him so that I would have a better understanding myself if I was doing something that was not as it should be in the way I was approaching government.'

Roy Medich also had the opportunity to complain of the unfairness of the media's 'witch hunt', which had blackened the Medich name and been 'very stressful on my family'.[4] After all his years of community service, it was all very hard to take, he said. Labor's Amanda Fazio, like Richardson a member of the right wing of the Labor Party, nodded sympathetically as Medich spoke.

Ron Medich blinked behind his rimless glasses as he took his place at the polished mahogany table, eyeing the eight-person committee with suspicion.

'Did you ever inquire what Mr Richardson was doing for the moneys that he was receiving?' Nationals MP Trevor Khan asked Ron.

'Well, he was supposed to be lobbyin', you know, and dealin' with the planning department, and liaising to find out what is going on,' Medich responded.[5]

'I hear that you say he was "supposed to". Did you make any inquiries as to precisely who Mr Richardson was speaking with?' asked Khan.

'No, because my brother was handling that,' said Medich.

Khan also quizzed Medich about his lunches and dinners with Ian Macdonald. Medich became flustered. He denied lunching with Macdonald and suggested it was mere coincidence they were in the same establishment at the same time. 'I was in at the restaurant where he was having a lunch, and the restaurateur there, Mr Frank Moio, I said to him that I would not mind, you know, havin' a word with [Macdonald] because I had not met him before. There was a reason why I would have liked to have spoken to him, and he organised that I could go over to the table, which I did.'

Medich made no mention of his dinner with Macdonald only two months before, during which he had tried to bribe Macdonald by providing the services of an escort in the hope of securing government contracts.

In his jumbled way Medich explained that he'd spoken to Macdonald only in passing because he wanted to ask the minister a favour since, as state development minister, he could put some funds into a company developing new cancer treatments. 'I was asking that on behalf of Albert Wong and Neville Wran. Because they were the ones that were raisin' funds for it. It is a company called Biosceptre.' Medich also volunteered that he was in a company called Tambour with entrepreneur Wong and former premier Wran, which had invested in the pizza business Doughboy.

Medich told the inquiry he didn't want to talk about the pizza company as it was another matter that was before the courts. 'I cannot say too much about it. I have been well and truly had things stolen from me,' he said as tortuously as ever.

Michael McGurk had inveigled his way into doing business with Wran and Wran's long-term business partner Albert Wong after being introduced to them by Medich, who told them McGurk would be acting on his behalf in Tambour. However, when McGurk was charged with assaults and firebombings, Wran did not want a bar of him. McGurk was persuaded to resign as a director of Tambour, though he remained the company's major shareholder, despite Medich claiming those shares really belonged to him. Then, in July, while McGurk was in Perisher on his family ski holiday, Big Jim Byrnes had turned up to a Doughboy company meeting at Wran's city office, claiming he was representing McGurk and had his proxies. Byrnes' instructions were to vote against the resolution to do a back-door listing of the pizza company. Medich was 25 minutes late to the meeting and, on seeing Byrnes, delivered a tirade against McGurk, calling him 'a crook and thief'. Byrnes also recalled Medich saying, 'He'll get his, don't you worry.'[6]

In the end Byrnes was not allowed to vote on McGurk's behalf and the pizza investment went ahead, with Wran's company investing in Doughboy. McGurk had told Vanda and me that he planned to commence legal action against Wran and Wong.

It was then Greens MP Sylvia Hale's turn to ask questions. Looking like the head teacher of a history department in her beige suit and navy shirt, Hale started innocuously. 'I want to ask you a question to clear the record, if I may?'

Medich stared at her blankly.

'Did you have any involvement in the murder of Michael McGurk?'

'You've got to be joking,' said Medich in a high-pitched, strangled voice. After taking a gulp of water from a white plastic cup, he snapped back at Hale, 'You're a shocker.'[7]

'That is an entirely inappropriate question!' barked Labor MP Amanda Fazio. The committee's chair, Nationals MP Jenny Gardiner, had said at the outset, 'In relation to the current police investigation into the murder of Mr Michael McGurk, I emphasise that this committee inquiry is not an inquiry into the circumstances of that crime.'

After Gardiner ruled the question out of order, Medich said angrily, 'I think this is a bloody disgrace.'

But Hale continued, this time asking Medich about Lucky Gattellari. She wanted to know if he'd talked to Gattellari about the tape.

'I cannot recall that I did,' mumbled Medich.

Hale went on, 'You presumably spoke to Mr Richardson about the contents of the tape?'

'No. Someone else rang my brother to tell him about it. Graham Richardson rang him because Richie Vereker, a guy, brought that to the attention—'

Hale cut his ramblings short. 'Did you ever discuss Mr McGurk with Mr Gattellari?'

'Not really,' responded Medich.

Hale persevered. 'You have never had any cause to mention any problems you may have had with Mr McGurk?'

Medich tried to palm off the question by suggesting that Gattellari only knew about the tape 'because he can read the press and everything else'.

Hale tried again: 'Apart from what he has been able to read in the media or hear on the television, you have never had any specific discussions with [Gattellari] about Mr McGurk?'

The struggling property developer then offered up a whopper. 'No, definitely not.'

Medich, clearly agitated, launched into another discursive, confusing rant about the tape and how McGurk had recorded it illegally. He said McGurk had said to him, '"Now listen, if you don't forget about this case and drop all these proceedings ... I'm going to go to the tax department, I'm going to say that I've got evidence on a tape, you know, that is going to bring the government down . . . I'm going to say that you blabbed all around town you've got political connections and things like that." So you know what I did? I went to the police because I knew that I hadn't said anything and I hadn't any dealings with anybody.'

It turned out it had taken some months for Medich to go to the police.

Medich also said that he had never heard the tape 'cos it's a load of crap'. It didn't appear to cross his mind that whatever crap was on the tape had come from his own mouth. Asked what was said about the director-general of planning, Sam Haddad, in the conversation that was taped, Medich replied, 'I do not know because I never heard the tape. Someone told me—'

Exasperated, Liberal MP Greg Pearce said, 'It was a conversation with *you!*'

Medich, looking cornered, said, 'I beg your pardon.'

Pearce repeated his statement. 'It was a conversation with *you*, so you must have heard the conversation.'

'Do you mean on the tape?' replied Medich.

'Yes,' snapped Pearce, barely containing his frustration.

Sitting in the room listening to Medich's apparent dim-wittedness, I wondered whether he was putting on an act. If he was the supposed mastermind behind the murder of McGurk, then surely the gig would soon be up.

Medich continued. 'What actually happened . . . all he said was did I know Sam Haddad? I said I knew of him. But I have never actually met Sam Haddad ever, or ever spoken to him.'

Amanda Fazio, flicking back her long dark hair, then threw Medich a Dorothy Dixer, asking him if he would like to comment on whether the media coverage of the McGurk matter had impacted on his business activities.

Medich, his voice quivering with indignation, leapt at the opportunity to protest his innocence. 'I think it has been very bad and I have been thoroughly disgusted with it because it is causin' me a few problems and a lot of upset, to be honest with you, because a lot of the stuff that has been printed in the press has been rubbish and untrue. Because I have cases runnin' at the present time I have to be very careful what I say. I have been told that if you keep your mouth shut it will go away, but this has extended a lot longer than I could have imagined.'

Taking another gulp from his white plastic cup, Medich concluded his evidence. 'I think this whole thing has been totally unfair.'

Earlier in the day, the softly spoken planning chief Sam Haddad had arrived at the inquiry with a phalanx of assistants. Asked about meetings he'd had with Graham Richardson, Haddad said he had not brought the details with him and that he was in the process of 'tabulating them'.[8] He spoke generally of a meeting with Richardson and Roy Medich early that month, but he had to be pressed several times for the specific date. There were ripples of incredulity around the room when the date was finally extracted. Roy Medich, Richardson and Haddad had met on 2 September, the day before McGurk was shot dead.

In his evidence, Roy confirmed that he and Ron had donated more than $200,000 to the Labor Party in the past four years. They had spent $2 million trying to get the parcel of Badgerys Creek land rezoned, which included having Richardson on a monthly retainer of $5000, but still the former CSIRO land remained rural despite its inclusion in a proposed employment zone in 2007.

It wasn't until a few weeks later that the star turn of the parliamentary inquiry made his entrance. Journalists were keeping a close eye on the public entrance of the New South Wales parliament in Macquarie Street for the arrival of Graham Richardson, but the Labor heavyweight had already slipped in through the back door and was ensconced at the mahogany table ready for action.

Adjusting his dark-green patterned tie as the cameras began to whirl, Graham Frederick Richardson took the oath and told the inquiry, 'I have a number of job titles but let's say "lobbyist" today.'[9]

It was a commanding performance. As soon as possible he put the boot into the *Herald*, scoffing at the fact that much had been made of his meeting with Haddad on 2 September, which, he suggested, was originally set for 31 August. 'The media, in particular the *Herald*, seem to make suggestions about these things that are improbable at best and ridiculous, and I have to put up with them on a constant basis,' he said.[10]

Richo threw little light on the subject at hand – dealings his clients Ron and Roy Medich may have had with state government or planning officials over their land at Badgerys Creek.

His business methods were an eye-opener. Apparently the written word was an anathema. 'Diaries I keep are up here,' he said, pointing to his head. 'I am my business. I just try to keep it in the head most of the time.' He billed his clients, who included Lang Walker, Bradcorp, Hardie Holdings and the Medichs, $5500 a month (including GST) but there were no contracts or even written agreements as to what was expected of him.

Richardson dispatched every question with bravado and an air of irritation that he was being subjected to this low-grade grilling by operatives not nearly as adept as he. Not a single question was asked of him about the tape recording, which was at the heart of the corruption claims.

The committee sent follow-up questions to each witness. All responded except for Richardson. His 23 October deadline came and went. On 4 November he rang to say that he wouldn't be providing any written responses. The committee was of the view that Richardson's answers could change the outcome of the inquiry, so on 11 November the chair wrote to him again requesting he give written responses by 19 November and if he didn't the committee could summons him to give further evidence in person. This was cutting it fine because the committee's report was due to be tabled on 20 November.

Momentous events occurred in New South Wales politics between Richardson's first and second appearance at the parliamentary inquiry, on 14 December. Earlier in the year, Premier Rees had moved to make lobbyists more accountable.

He had stunned the annual Labor Party conference in November by announcing a ban on donations from property developers. He also wanted the corrupt elements in his party removed, and, to this end, in a pre-emptive strike he convinced the floor of the conference to allow the New South Wales premier to pick his own cabinet. Rees immediately axed Ian Macdonald and Joe Tripodi. It was only 19 days, however, until party powerbroker Eddie Obeid and his acolytes wreaked their revenge. At 6.30 pm on 3 December 2009, three months to the moment since the death of McGurk, Rees's term of office as premier was over. That morning he had delivered the speech of a lifetime. 'Should I not be premier by the end of this day, let there be no doubt in the community's mind, no doubt, that any challenger will be a puppet of Eddie Obeid and Joe Tripodi.'

Within days, Ian Macdonald was back in cabinet.

These extraordinary developments were fresh in the minds of committee members when Richardson was recalled to give evidence less than a fortnight later.

Richardson's customary charm was noticeably absent at this second appearance. When asked by Pearce if he'd made contact with Labor MPs or officials in the last month, Richardson retorted, 'What would that have to do with the terms of reference of this inquiry?'[11]

Pearce replied, 'I ask the questions, Mr Richardson.'

Leaning forward to look at Gardiner, Richardson said, 'I am asking the chair whether that has anything to do with the terms of reference of this inquiry.'

Pearce shot back, 'Of course it does. It relates to influence and to your role as a lobbyist, or any other contact that you might have had with relevant ministers.'

It was dragged out of Richardson that he had spoken with both Obeid and Tripodi, and he agreed that they were among the prime movers of what committee member Trevor Khan repeatedly referred to as 'the defenestration of Mr Rees'.

'Do I take it that amongst the plotters we have got you speaking to [John] Della Bosca, Obeid and Tripodi?' Khan asked.

'A tremendous revelation!' said Richardson his voice dripping with sarcasm. 'Great work getting that out of me.'

Neither could the political fixer conceal his contempt at having to explain what was on the tape McGurk had played to him back in March. He told the inquiry he'd listened to less than 60 seconds of it and had demanded that McGurk 'play the bit that matters'.

'He plays it, it is completely and utterly inaudible and so I walk out on this lowlife because I am not prepared to spend an hour and a half listening to a tape with him. I did not want to spend a second or nanosecond more with him than I had to,' Richardson said.

Many people would find it 'absolutely inconceivable', said Sylvia Hale, that Richardson was not prepared to listen 'to more than thirty or sixty seconds of the tape, which potentially contains quite explosive information about—'

Before the Greens MP could finish, Richardson cut her off: 'I listened to the part that was supposed to contain explosive information and it would not have let off a bunger. I simply disregarded it because it was nonsense. It was a fake.'[12]

When Hale pointed out that there might be some public interest in what was on the rest of the recording, Richardson, whose normally florid face was by now puce with anger, said he couldn't understand why he was being grilled 'about a tape that I could not understand. I do not know what part of "I do not understand" you do not understand,' he snapped, throwing his palms skywards in frustration.

During Frank Sartor's appearance at the inquiry, the former planning minister said that he had been lobbied by both finance minister Joe Tripodi and Labor powerbroker Eddie Obeid over development projects.

When Eddie Obeid's diaries for the period were tendered before an ICAC corruption inquiry in 2013, they made for fascinating reading, especially when added to the dates which emerged during this parliamentary inquiry.

According to Obeid's diary, Richardson had met with him on 2 March 2009.

On 9 March, Richardson had met Sam Haddad.

On 10 June, Roy Medich had donated $13,750 to the ALP. Around this time he requested a meeting with Labor minister Joe Tripodi, which didn't happen.

The following day, Roy Medich's name and phone number appear in Obeid's diary.

Three days later, Richardson met Haddad again. Only days after that, Roy Medich met Phil Costa, then the water minister, to discuss Australian Water Holdings (AWH), a private company in which the Obeids were later found to have a secret share.

By early July 2009, the Medichs had been informed that their land at Badgerys Creek would not be rezoned by the government.

On 13 July, Richardson met Obeid at the Obeid family headquarters in Birkenhead Point, according to Obeid's diary entry.

On 22 July, Richardson again met Haddad.

On 2 August, the government announced the new Western Sydney Employment Area, and the Medichs' land was not on it.

Five days later, Richardson and Obeid met again at Birkenhead Point, and at 9 am on 28 August the pair met once more.

On 2 September, Richardson and Haddad met Roy Medich.

The following day, 3 September, McGurk was murdered, and within days it was revealed he had a tape recording he claimed was going to bring down the government.

On 30 September, the day after Ron and Roy Medich appeared at the parliamentary inquiry, Richardson met Obeid at his Birkenhead Point offices. Over the next weeks, during which time Richardson twice appeared before the parliamentary inquiry, he had three further meetings with Obeid.

Hopes that the parliamentary inquiry might reveal what was on this mysterious recording of McGurk's, and whether it had any connection to his death, turned out to be misplaced. It was not until five months after the murder that the tape's contents would be revealed, and even then the importance of Medich's utterances on the recording would be overlooked.

CHAPTER 19

ICAC: NOTHING TO SEE HERE

Medich was proving to be a goldmine for Sydney lawyers. On 1 February 2010 he had three legal teams on the go in various courtrooms across the city.

At the Supreme Court his lawyers were engaged in his ongoing battle with Adam Tilley. Seven kilometres away, at Waverley Local Court, he had another barrister, Doug Timmins, apologising to Magistrate Robert Williams for his client's absence over a drink-driving charge. On 7 December 2009, shortly before 10 pm, Medich was pulled over for a random breath test in Glenmore Road in Paddington. He was on his way home after a session at Tuscany. He failed the test and was arrested and taken to Waverley Police Station, where he recorded a blood alcohol concentration of 0.054.

When Medich's reading tested positive police heard him say, 'Oh shit, I knew that – no food.' Timmins entered a guilty plea on Medich's behalf. He told Magistrate Williams that his client was always 'very strict' about following this particular law. He didn't mention Medich's narrow escape six months earlier. Williams noted Medich's poor driving record, including seven speeding matters. He was convicted and fined $400.[1]

The first of February was also the opening day of the much-anticipated ICAC hearing into McGurk's infamous tape recording, and Medich had a team of lawyers representing him at the inquiry. Five minutes before the scheduled 10 am start, Medich and his legal team arrived, led by Ian Faulkner, SC, pushing their way through the waiting throng of journalists and members of the public to get to the door of the hearing room, only to find it was not yet open.

Graham Richardson slipped into a seat just in front of Jim Byrnes after the ICAC commissioner, retired Supreme Court judge David Ipp, QC, had commenced his opening remarks. The director-general of planning, Sam Haddad, and Medich nodded briefly to each other as the planning boss shuffled past to take a seat in the second row.

But within minutes it was clear – from the media's point of view, anyway – that this was going to be a fizzer. Commissioner David Ipp said that there was no evidence to support any of McGurk's claims of corruption. Nevertheless, he went on, it was important to have a public hearing to put an end to 'the unverified and unsubstantiated rumours and speculation of public corruption' that had circulated since McGurk's death and could cause a potential loss of confidence in the government and public administration. 'Such loss of confidence is harmful to the fabric of society,' Ipp intoned. 'For the reasons I have given, it is of great importance that the rumours and speculation be resolved and a main purpose of this public inquiry is to achieve this end.'[2]

The commissioner then outlined the scope of the inquiry, which included numerous allegations of corruption as presented by McGurk to various people. The first allegation was that:

Ronald Medich represented that he could make a corrupt payment to Sam Haddad, the Director General of Planning, as an inducement for favour to be shown by Sam Haddad in respect of a proposed development application relating to land owned by Ron Medich Properties Pty Limited

at 16 Crooked River Road, Gerroa. This allegation is
founded on an audio recording made by Michael McGurk.
Mr McGurk reported to various persons, including James
Byrnes, a business associate, and Kate McClymont and
Vanda Carson, *Sydney Morning Herald* journalists, being
that he had made this recording prior to his death.[3]

Ipp went on to say that the recording had been the subject of
extensive media reporting following Mr McGurk's death.

The second allegation was that:

Ronald Medich caused payments to be made by an intermediary to various Ministers of the Crown and Mr Haddad
as an inducement for favour to be shown in respect of
planning decisions affecting applications relating to land
owned by Ron Medich Properties Pty Limited and Roy
Medich Properties Pty Limited and known as the former
CSIRO site at Badgerys Creek. This allegation is based
on Mr Byrnes' account of a conversation that he had
with Mr McGurk. According to Mr Byrnes, Mr McGurk
told him that Mr Medich admitted making these corrupt
payments, or causing them to be made, and that he did so
during the course of the recorded conversation obtained by
the Commission. *Sydney Morning Herald* journalists Vanda
Carson and Kate McClymont met with Mr McGurk on
29 July 2009. Ms Carson has told the Commission that
Mr McGurk told them he had a recording of a conversation with Mr Ron Medich in which Mr Medich named
politicians, government officials and councillors who he
had paid to smooth the way for developments in which
he was involved.[4]

Another of the allegations was that a developer and former local
councillor had arranged to have property rezoned to financially
benefit a current member of parliament. While no names were
given, this was McGurk's allegation to Vanda and me about

John Abi-Saab, the former shire councillor who was found to be corrupt by ICAC in a previous inquiry, organising for the rezoning of a large landholding the Obeid family owned near Port Macquarie.

There were 12 allegations all up: that Medich had paid to get off his first drink-driving charge; that he'd been involved in insurance fraud; that he had bribed an unnamed former planning minister; and others.

Counsel assisting the commission, Jeremy Gormly, SC, said that the tape had been made on 6 February 2009, seven months before McGurk's murder, and that at the time the litigation between Medich and McGurk had not yet commenced 'but it was not far off'.[5] He also said that McGurk 'was apparently also under some financial pressure. There is evidence that he may have been under pressure from other quarters as well that are not of relevance to this inquiry.'

Kimberley McGurk told the commission her husband was stressed in the months leading up to his death, but had kept fears for his own safety from her.

At a compulsory examination Richie Vereker told the commission that he had met McGurk at the Bowlers' Club in York Street on several occasions in February 2009. He was asked what McGurk had said about the land in western Sydney and bringing down a government. Vereker answered, 'He said, "Ronnie's been opening his big mouth again. I've got info. I've recorded him, recorded the conversation and big enough to bring down the governments to do with the planning office [sic]."'

'Of greater interest in the investigation,' said Gormly, 'were some conversations that Mr McGurk initiated in the last six weeks of his life with the senior journalist Ms Kate McClymont, and her colleague Ms Vanda Carson.'

Vanda and I weren't called to give evidence. They relied on our evidence from the private hearing several months prior.

Gormly said, 'The reports given by Ms McClymont and Ms Carson of Mr McGurk's statements can be relied upon as accurate reports of what Mr McGurk said. The reports were based on notes made by the journalists. Some of the things that the journalists report that Mr McGurk said make allegations about the use of various political contacts to achieve private ends of benefit to the Medichs' and their interests. In addition, Mr McGurk is reported as making a scattering of allegations against various politicians and public officers. None, as I said, were supported by evidence, but to the extent possible from the allegation made, all have been examined and where investigation is possible they've been investigated. It's fair to say that much of his conversation with both associates and journalists has Mr McGurk directing attention towards Mr Medich.'[6]

In short, the content of the tape had not lived up to McGurk's grandiose claims.

Gormly went on to say that while the recording might suggest that Medich had either paid or was planning to pay Haddad for help with the Gerroa development, Medich had explained in the private hearings that he was just big-noting and that he had never met Haddad, let alone paid him. And the wealthy property developer's word appeared to be enough for the commission.

Only the softly spoken Tim Game, SC, representing the McGurk family, offered any resistance. Game took issue with the way the commission was dismissing the allegations on the tape. He insisted that McGurk's recording contained serious allegations of corruption, including those relating to the Badgerys Creek development, which were not contained in the transcript the commission was using.

'Our single point is if Mr Medich does say very significant things in this tape ... our concern has been that the significance of these things has not been appreciated.'[7]

He also said that the police transcript of the tape and ICAC's transcript of the tape were different and that ICAC's version was favourable to Medich and unfavourable to McGurk.

Medich's barrister argued that the tape should not be played at all. He was overruled.

Before the inquiry was halted to investigate the discrepancies highlighted by Game, an excerpt of the one-hour,

37-minute-long tape recording was aired. It related to Medich and McGurk's planned development at Gerroa, and which of them had better connections to get the approval through.

> Medich: Well, I've got connections there, too, so I don't care. If they . . . they can get it through, they can get it through, but I can get it through too.
>
> McGurk: Well, if you think that your, your, connections are better, then you should use your connections.
>
> Medich: Yeah, you still got to pay 'em though. They don't do it for nothing . . .
>
> McGurk: . . . In terms of the other connections that you've got, what do they do? Are they consultants or [unintelligible] councillor?
>
> Medich: You are right there.
>
> McGurk: To what?
>
> Medich: Sam Haddad, the whole bloody lot of them.
>
> McGurk: . . . I don't know Sam Haddad but you know him.
>
> Medich: He's the director-general, planning department. It comes to him before it goes anywhere else. The minister, he signed off on it.
>
> McGurk: So he'd be your connection?
>
> Mr Medich: Yeah.

On the face it of it, Medich was saying that he had connections with Haddad, the head of the department of planning, and that he paid him for results. Counsel assisting told the hearing that this assertion by Medich was 'untrue' and there was no evidence to support his claims.

'It seems to have been an assertion made by Mr Medich, but for his own purposes at that moment of the conversation with Mr McGurk,' Gormly said. 'The assertion may have been a mere boast, but more likely it was intended to fend off unwanted offers of help by Mr McGurk, which can be heard in the recording.'

The following day, nine excerpts of the tape were played, much to the irritation of the commissioner, who asked, 'How much more of this must we endure?'

The commissioner might have found it tedious, but most of us were enthralled by a fascinating glimpse into the relationship between Medich and McGurk, made at a time when one of them was planning to kill the other. Mick Sheehy, the head of the murder investigation, arrived just after 10 am with some other detectives. No doubt they were keen to observe one of their prime suspects as he gave evidence.

Medich was a frustrating witness: as usual jumping all over the place, shooting off on tangents, not answering the questions and interrupting.

'Be quiet, Mr Medich,' admonished the commissioner after Medich interjected 'Rubbish!' as Game raised the issues on the tape that suggested Medich had corrupt relationships.[8]

'If you do not stop interrupting in this way, I will take steps against you. Now, be quiet! Do you understand that?' said the commissioner crossly. 'Your job is to sit there and answer questions, not to interrupt, and the sooner you do that the sooner you'll be out of there.'[9]

Medich reddened and took a sip of water, but he was soon back to his quarrelsome self.

'I can tell you that the more you argue, the less the prospects of you being regarded as a reliable witness,' threatened the commissioner.

Medich was hard to follow at the best of times but under pressure he was almost incomprehensible. 'What you've got to understand, that when I went into this meeting [in which McGurk recorded the tape], we were shadow-boxing against each other, because I didn't trust him when I went into the meeting. It was recommended to me, I didn't even want to go to this meeting, but one of my lawyers said, "Try to go in there and find out what's happened with the money that he's misappropriated." And I went into that meeting . . . you can disregard anything that ever happened . . . I was not being truthful with Mr McGurk at all because I, as I said, I was shadow-boxing with him, as all I wanted to do was to fob him off.'

Medich explained, 'I was there for one, one reason alone and you can see how crafty he was during, during, you know, the whole tape that was going on and really trying to the stage of asking where, where is my money that he'd stolen.'

He also claimed that he wasn't really paying attention during the conversation with McGurk.

On another occasion he was asked if McGurk took notes. 'To be truthful, I wasn't watching him,' Medich said.

Something that piqued the commissioner's interest on the tape was Medich telling McGurk, 'If they don't put it through as asked, so I might bloody well bump them or something like that. Particularly if they're being paid or whatever.'

'So what did you mean when you said that you might "bump" them?' asked the commissioner.

'Well, belt them or whatever, you know. Like the firebombing, but the Tilley house got firebombed down at 42a Worsley Road.'

'So "if they don't put it through" – what does that mean?' Medich was asked.

'Well, if they don't get the results, that's . . . that's what I'm referring to.'

Somewhat incredulous, Commissioner Ipp pushed, wanting to know who 'they' were. 'Well, I was actually referring to Graham Richardson because Richardson was the one that spoke to me about it.'

Game also tried – without success – to probe Medich about 'the bump'.

Medich answered, 'I explained yesterday that people think if I'm a firebomber and doing these type of things; I might thump them or something if they don't get the job done that I'm paying them for. That's what I inferred.'

It was difficult to follow Medich's logic, but he appeared to be suggesting that people might think he was capable of bad things after reading Peter Gosnell's newspaper story about the firebombing. Only the day before the recording was made, Medich had become highly agitated after Richardson quizzed him about the *Daily Telegraph* article from 3 February 2009, 'Boss charged with firebombing posh Point Piper mansion'. Richardson had wanted to know if 'there were legs' to the story about the arson charges against McGurk, and the connection to the dispute between Medich and Tilley. Medich had expressed fears that publicity over the story could affect the rezoning of his Badgerys Creek land.

This still didn't quite explain the necessity of 'bumping' people.

'That Graham Richardson didn't get what result?' asked Ipp.

'Well, he was the lobbyist that was helping us try to get the properties through.'

'So, what, you tell me if he didn't get what through?'

Medich replied that it could have been 'Narellan, or the CSIRO site or other things that were happening that my brother was doing.'

It was still as clear as mud.

As to why Medich wouldn't cooperate with the police investigating the firebombing of the Tilleys' house, he was heard telling McGurk: 'I think I'm going to use the excuse that I'm in litigation against Tilley and I've been told by the solicitor not to make any statements.'

Even more peculiar, and hard to stomach, was Medich's self-serving response when he was asked if he was sorry for the trouble he had caused Haddad by making these outrageous claims to McGurk on the tape.

'Yeah, I do, I regret for him. And myself – the way we've been vilified over these whole issues, because my family's very upset about it too, the same as Mr Haddad's.'[10]

Medich was followed into the witness box by Graham Richardson, who said that he had worked for Roy and Ron Medich for years but that the 'arrangement ceased at Christmas'.[11]

Richardson confirmed that when Vereker had told him about the tape he was also told, 'Ron Medich had allegedly said some things that would bring the government down.' Richardson spoke to Roy, who said 'he'd appreciate it if I'd listen to the tape and just find out if there was any problem that was going to occur for the family'.[12]

Richardson said that when McGurk did play the relevant part of the tape, he couldn't hear any names, and certainly not Sam Haddad's. 'I thought it was a pretty lowbrow attempt to get some money out of . . . out of Ron Medich under duress.' He said he had met Haddad three to four times a year, but in all but one of his meetings with the planning boss someone else had been present.

'Now, Mr Richardson, you've heard that there's been an allegation that there's been corrupt conduct between Mr Medich and Mr Haddad, and that at one point you have been an intermediary for payments of money from Mr Medich to politicians or a minister, and to Mr Haddad?'

Richardson was outraged. 'It's nonsense. There is not a skerrick of evidence to support that in your words and it's highly offensive. I'm staggered that we've spent millions of dollars of public money and we're still here and we found nothing, nothing!' His voice rose on a flood of indignation.

After only half an hour in the witness box, Richardson swept out of the proceedings. 'Journalism, I'm told, is about a search for the truth,' he huffed. 'In this case, the truth simply didn't count, it was only a search for a story.'

What he wanted was an inquiry into this sorry state of affairs caused by Vanda and me, in which 'an enormous amount of public money – millions of dollars has been wasted'.[13]

After fewer than three days, the inquiry was at an end. Commissioner Ipp said that he believed Vanda and I had truthfully reported what McGurk had told us, but that ultimately the tape contained empty words from Medich. Ipp put the boot into the wealthy property developer, accusing him of creating 'public mischief' when he falsely claimed on the tape that he was bribing senior people in the planning department. Faulkner added that if there was a gold medal to be awarded for loose and inexact language, his client Ron Medich would be the winner.

Tim Game had tried valiantly to convince the commissioner that there was more to the tape than they were prepared to accept and that Medich was lying when he claimed that his words were innocent. He referred to Medich's statement on the tape: 'Well, at the moment this Labor mob mightn't be there for any longer than two years the way things are looking . . . you've got to get it rammed through now.'

'When you look at the whole thing, it goes a lot further than the limited life it's been given by counsel assisting,' said Game.

But it was fruitless. Nothing to see here.

The following day shock jock Alan Jones weighed in, saying, 'The result of the ICAC investigation into the McGurk tapes is damning – for the *Sydney Morning Herald*.'

Richardson later gave News Corp's *Sunday Telegraph* an interview. His considered view was that 'The *Sydney Morning Herald* had their big run over McGurk, and that turned out to be a massive fizzer.' And then it was on to New South Wales Labor, and the real power of Eddie Obeid and Joe Tripodi: 'They're friends of mine, but the idea they're running the cabinet is really silly,' Richardson said.[14]

He also poured cold water on the idea that there had been any corruption within the government or departments. 'Today's Sydney is straight,' he opined. 'It's pretty hard to imagine great corruption now.'[15]

CHAPTER 20

LUCKY

Within days of McGurk's murder the homicide squad had executed a search warrant at Lucky Gattellari's five-bedroom home in Chipping Norton, in southwest Sydney, where he lived with his wife, Pamela.

After two and a half hours police left with a number of weapons, including a .22 Ruger rifle, a popular model mainly used for small-game hunting and target shooting. In his bedroom, wrapped in a green towel, police found a double-barrelled shotgun, which Gattellari claimed was there because he was cleaning it. There were more firearms stored in his gun safe, which weighed a hefty 250 kilograms.

Although Gattellari had a permit for the Ruger, he had added to it an illegal device. A scientific officer with the forensic ballistics investigation section of the New South Wales police said the device fitted to the muzzle of the rifle was a silencer, which muffles the noise when a weapon is fired. The addition of the silencer made Gattellari's rifle a prohibited weapon.

Police did not find what they were looking for – and that was the weapon used to kill McGurk.

After police seized his guns, Gattellari was filmed outside his mock Tudor home angrily confronting a Channel 7 reporter, Robert Ovadia. Balancing a delicate fine-bone china teacup in his left hand, Gattellari berated Ovadia. 'Because a man has business dealings with a man, you guys are busting my balls. I've got fucking nothing to do with this guy,' said Gattellari of McGurk.

'You had a few fierce dealings with McGurk, didn't you, Lucky?' asked Ovadia, while the cameras were rolling.

'Take that, mate,' responded Gattellari belligerently, raising his middle finger as he stalked off, teacup in hand.

Lucky Gattellari was born in southern Italy in February 1950. Christened Fortunato, he was the youngest of seven sons. When he was three, his mother and her three younger boys set sail from Messina to join her husband and their four older sons, already in Sydney.

The Gattellaris' hometown, Oppido Mamertina, right on the toe of Italy's boot, was in Calabria, a stronghold of the Mafia. The criminal organisation had branches all around the globe, extending to Sydney, and due to their Mafia connections Lucky's older brothers and father were given jobs as soon as they arrived in Australia. Lucky's father, Giuseppe, worked as a loader at the Mortlake Gasworks and his sons were given cleaning jobs. The Gattellari family began a market garden in Bonnyrigg in Sydney's southwest, where land was cheap. Later, they owned a fruit and vegetable shop.

Lucky and his brothers were the first Gattellaris in many generations of illiterate shepherds to attend school. Lucky's older brother Rocky said he decided at an early age to be a 'bandito, a brigand. I would rob the arrogant families of *la signoria* [the establishment] and share the spoils with my brother.'

Instead, he became a champion bantamweight boxer. He won his first professional fight in September 1961 at the Sydney Stadium, though the evening was marred when Giuseppe was arrested as he tried to climb into the ring to present his son with a bouquet of flowers.

As Rocky's fame grew, his youngest brother, Lucky, was assigned the task of reading and replying to Rocky's fan mail, and lining up dates as he sorted through correspondence from adoring female fans, who often enclosed photos in their perfumed letters.

After finishing school aged 14, Lucky followed in Rocky's footsteps and also became a boxer. His burgeoning career helped him defer his service in the Vietnam War for a year. In April 1972 he defended his national featherweight title with a knockout victory over Aboriginal fighter Nev Williams in only 35 seconds. 'It was a dream punch, one of the best I have thrown in my life,' a jubilant Lucky said after the fight.

However, with the Gattellaris' boxing successes came the dark hand of the Mafia. In his autobiography *The Rocky Road*, Rocky Gattellari told of a local Mob boss arriving at the Gattellari family home after he became bantamweight champion of Australia.

He acknowledged that his world championship fight against Salvatore Burruni was a scam. 'I had never thought I would be part of a fix. It was against all my principles,' he wrote. There was a huge last-minute betting plunge on Burruni. Word had got out that the fix was in. Rocky claimed in his book that his manager drugged him, which enabled Burruni to knock him out.

In 1979, four years after Lucky finished his boxing career, he emerged from retirement for a Sunday afternoon fight at the Hordern Pavilion in Sydney as part of an entertainment billed as 'three hours of non-stop title fights'. He was opposing Barry Michael for the Australian lightweight title; the event was hosted by radio announcer John Laws, later known as the 'golden tonsils', and advertising guru John Singleton.

Rocky Gattellari, then aged 37, was the main event, fighting for the Australian featherweight title. In his autobiography, Rocky acknowledged that he'd only agreed to do the fight because he needed the money – his nightclub, Rocky's, in Edge-cliff in Sydney's east, was in difficulty. He lasted two rounds in his bout against Paul Ferreri before claiming after the third that he was paralysed by a pinched nerve in his neck, had hurt his hand and was quitting.

Lucky was knocked down three times by Barry Michael and wouldn't come out for the fourth round.

Both Gattellaris were in it for the money, but for the crowd, who had paid a colossal $200 (in today's terms about $650) a ticket, the clashes were an embarrassment. Commentators claimed the best fights of the night were between the spectators.

After retiring from boxing, Lucky had stints as a photographer, restaurateur, grocer, vigneron, thoroughbred trainer and Qantas steward. In 1975 the *Herald*'s Rod Humphries wrote of sportswriters being invited to a 'special luncheon in a mock-up Boeing jumbo jet' at the airport to be served by their new trainee flight steward, Lucky Gattellari. '"I've never been overseas," said Lucky as he cut the roast beef,' wrote Humphries. Gattellari said he had hoped to go to New Zealand to fight, but it had fallen through.[1]

Less well known were Gattellari's side careers, which emerged during his court appearances. They included a brothel owner, enforcer, drug distributor and money launderer. While boxing, he'd even toyed with the idea of going into the fashion industry. He had his 'heart set on opening a boutique to cater for the younger man's fashions', he told *The Sun* newspaper in 1971.

He also took the reins at the family's busy fruit and vegetable shop opposite Cabramatta's railway station. And this is where he first met Ron Medich, whose family owned the Cabramatta cinema.

At Ron Medich's appearance in September 2009 before the parliamentary inquiry into the dealings around his and Roy's land at Badgerys Creek, Ron's relationship with Lucky Gattellari was raised. 'The only relationship I have with Lucky Gattellari is that he came to me looking for funds . . . for friends of his that got into trouble,' said Medich.[2]

Medich explained that he had shares in companies of Gattellari and was taking mortgages over the loans. '[One] company is a major electrical contracting company called Rivercorp [Rivercorp had government contracts to install lighting in the federal parliament car park and for the governor-general's official residence in Canberra]. They had about three hundred employees. It was actually going into administration . . . If I did not put in the funds the company would have gone under. They were friends of [Lucky]. So we took some security and different things, and I have risked my money to put into these companies . . . What we are doing is trying to make these companies profitable,' squeaked Medich in his rapid-fire manner of speaking. 'I also helped him when he went to the Eling Forest Winery,' he said.[3]

In 2002 Gattellari opened the Eling Forest Winery at Sutton Forest in the New South Wales Southern Highlands. Former employees of the winery, which sat on 12 acres of rolling hills, described Gattellari as a fantastic host, vivacious, quite a character. 'Lucky enjoyed the Mafioso reputation,' said one.[4] Another recalled him getting a laugh out of his gangster act. 'He used to joke about it. At one vigneron's meeting at the Mittagong RSL club, Lucky said, in a joking way, that he didn't want to have to get his baseball bat out to the others.'[5]

When the winery won a local tourism award, an employee accompanied Gattellari to the presentation in Brisbane. Afterwards they went out to a nightclub and the woman was shocked to see that Gattellari had an armed bodyguard in tow. On this night, as on many others, he was shadowed by his towering mate Senad Kaminic.

At 6 feet 4 inches, with a barrel-chest and long hair tied back in a ponytail, Kaminic was a formidable-looking chap. He and Lucky made an odd pair, Gattellari barely reaching the shoulder of the former army sharpshooter. At this time Kaminic was running a business called Baron Security, and he was often by Gattellari's side. 'Whenever there were security issues or Lucky wanted some standover technique, that'd be Senad,' said a former winery worker.[6]

It seemed odd to the staff at the winery that the genial Gattellari needed a bodyguard at all. But there were lots of things there that didn't make sense. Cars were always coming and going, disgorging men who would have clandestine meetings with Gattellari. One person remembers a friend of the Gattellari family who had recently been acquitted of murder in Queensland lying low in the stone cabin at Eling Forest. On another occasion a person called Michael, who had just been released from jail, turned up. 'They gave him meaningless jobs around the place,' said the former employee, explaining that Gattellari was looking after this bloke.[7] A police dossier from that time linked Lucky and his late brother Antonio with major Mafia figures involved in marijuana distribution.

'Detectives rocked up at the door on at least one occasion when I was there,' said another former staffer. They were asking Gattellari questions. 'It was in relation to his business partner in Queensland, a guy called Louie.' He added that Louie was a drug dealer and 'they would bring money down and launder it through whatever company Lucky had'.[8] In 2008 Louie Gibson was jailed for 11 years for producing and trafficking the drug methylamphetamine.[9]

Another subject of curiosity to Gattellari's staff at the winery was his six mobile phones. This was years before the McGurk murder, but even then Gattellari was worried his phones were being tapped. One former employee recalled Gattellari had labels with the number of the phone taped to its back to remind him which one it was.

There were also whisperings among the staff when a truckload containing 'an amazing amount of premium wine', complete with an insurance valuation, arrived at the winery. It had been 'stolen' from Ron Medich's cellar. The inventory, which ran to about 65 pages, valued the wine at $330,000. Staff recalled Gattellari and two employees driving up to Medich's house in Denham Court to pick up the two tonnes of wine. It was hidden in a cellar in the stables at Eling Forest. 'There was Hill of Grace, Penfolds Grange Hermitage, rare Mount Mary Quintet cabernets and Petaluma,' one staffer said. Gattellari joked to his employees that despite the whole exercise being very cloak and dagger, his mate 'Ronnie' was more than happy with the result.[10]

There was much speculation about Gattellari's relationship with winemaker Michelle Crockett, especially when Michelle's then partner was found hanging from the pergola at their house. He had no pants on and cuts on his legs. 'We thought it was a bit suss,' said one of the former winery workers.

Michelle Crockett's son, Matthew, was later employed by Gattellari to do standover work and debt collection. He wouldn't comment when asked at Ron Medich's committal hearing about his mother's relationship with Gattellari. In evidence, Crockett admitted that he and Gattellari had been involved in the distribution of marijuana.

In 2005 the Eling Forest Winery went down the tube, owing creditors almost $500,000. The liquidator found that Gattellari hadn't lodged tax returns and his bookkeeping was a shambles. His failure to keep records, his possible insolvent trading, breaches of director's duties and failure to assist the liquidator were reported to ASIC. No action was taken.

This was not the first time Gattellari's business ventures had been unsuccessful. Despite the truckloads of money he and Rocky had made from their embarrassing fight in February 1979, within months both brothers were bankrupted over a $2634 debt to Heritage Liquor, related to Rocky's unsuccessful restaurant/ nightclub in Edgecliff. In the mid-1970s Rocky was also forced to sell his struggling restaurant at sleepy Berowra Waters on the Hawkesbury River. It must have been galling for him to see the Berowra Waters Inn become one of the most highly regarded restaurants in the world under its new owners, Tony and Gay Bilson.

Tony Bilson told the Sydney Morning Herald in 2008 that in all the years as a restaurateur his worst experience with a customer occurred soon after he and his then wife Gay had taken over the inn from Rocky. One day, a Sydney underworld figure arrived to dine with his wife and two children. 'Thinking

Rocky was still on-site, he asked for a beer,' Bilson said. 'We didn't serve beer, he was told, but champagne on arrival. Then he wanted Ben Ean and garlic bread. We had neither.' The colourful identity made his dissatisfaction known. 'He pulled a knife, a fight broke out, and the police had to be called. It was horrible,' recalled Bilson.

Gattellari's obvious lack of business acumen appeared to be no impediment to Ron Medich, who was always happy to stump up money for Lucky's unpromising get-rich schemes. In 2007 Gattellari and Medich went into a most unusual business: the Boomerang Funeral Fund. It planned to target Indigenous folk and get them to cough up weekly payments as funeral insurance.

Medich kicked it off with a sizeable cash injection of $857,000. Gattellari was chief executive, and Gattellari's gigantic sidekick Kaminic was one of the funeral fund's key personnel.

None had any experience in the industry – aside from Aboriginal elder Robert Lester who had some, but not all of it good. Lester had served on the New South Wales Aboriginal Land Council, where he had been publicly reprimanded for mismanaging a funeral fund five years earlier. This time round Lester promised to bring 16,500 members into the fund through his connections with the land council.

The funeral fund swiftly signed up about 270 members, who agreed to have $5 per week direct debited from their Centrelink accounts. Gattellari hoped to get up to 20,000 members, and ultimately to grow the fund into a general insurance company. It was even arranged that Amazing Loans would act as the 'collection agent' for Boomerang Funerals.

But less than a year after it began, the fund was forced by ASIC and the NSW Department of Fair Trading to stop offering its services. ASIC was advised that the Boomerang Funeral Fund was marketing a product that did not exist – there wasn't ever going to be a funeral at the end of it. Gattellari and Medich were forced to repay all the premiums they had collected because the fund was trading illegally.

In 2005 Gattellari had another crack-a-jack scheme to lose Medich money.

This time it was to develop land on the New South Wales south coast that was owned by the Wagonga Local Aboriginal Land Council (WLALC) in Narooma. Gattellari and Medich paid almost $200,000 in bribes to three executives on the council, with the expectation of receiving favourable land deals. The executives were council chairman Ron Mason, his daughter, Vanessa, the CEO, and the coordinator, Kenny Foster. The proposed developments on four council-owned blocks were eventually blocked by the New South Wales Aboriginal Land Council.

Gattellari and Medich put $126,000 into Vanessa Mason's private company. She told a 2012 inquiry into the WLALC conducted by the ICAC that she and Gattellari were in an oyster business together and the money was for business expenses. When asked how many oysters were ever produced, Vanessa Mason replied, 'None.'[11]

Kenny Foster, the de facto partner of Vanessa Mason's cousin, also received more than $30,000 from Gattellari in 2005, when he was on the payroll of the WLALC and at the same time responsible for negotiating with Gattellari and Medich. Foster stubbornly maintained that the payments were not bribes but were for his help with Gattellari's Aboriginal funeral fund. His claim was ridiculed by Gattellari. A prior *Herald* investigation had revealed that Foster had been accused of similar corrupt behaviour while he was an official at the La Perouse land council in Sydney. He was alleged to have received payments of $250 a week for two years until July 2002. The payments were made by a consortium of Sydney developers hoping to develop prime land at La Perouse.

At the ICAC inquiry, Medich angrily denied that he had given $50,000 in cash to Gattellari, which Aboriginal elder

Ronnie Binge collected from Medich's home in April 2005, or that any such sum of money was to be used for bribing land council officials. Gattellari told the inquiry that Medich had handed over the money after he explained to him that the Wagonga executives needed to be 'buttered up' to smooth the way with the land dealings.

'I totally deny that,' Medich said indignantly. 'I've never heard that word "buttered up" ever used in my life.' He also denied keeping large amounts of cash in his Point Piper home. He didn't even have a safe, he said, 'just a cupboard'.[12] When asked what his idea of a large sum was, Medich replied, 'The most I probably ever had at any given time might have been probably $120,000 or something like that.' There were suppressed giggles in the hearing room when Medich rushed to deny the suggestion that the $50,000 cash he had given Gattellari was in a mere paper bag. It was a 'shopping bag', he sniffed.

Medich wasn't helped when police records showed he'd forked out even more than the amount alleged at ICAC. On 8 April 2005, police from Rose Bay Police Station were investigating a robbery in Point Piper. With Ronnie Binge at the wheel, he and Gattellari had driven only 100 metres from Medich's home when they were pulled over by police, who were stunned to find $20,000 in cash in a brown paper bag in the front seat and $33,000 in the boot. According to police records from the night, Gattellari told them that 'a Ron Medich of 112 Wolseley Road, Point Piper had given him the money for a deposit on a subdivision development involving the Aboriginal Land Council'. Police went to Medich's house, where he verified Gattellari's account.

The pair's trip to 'butter up' the Narooma crew was delayed further when police discovered that Binge, also known as Ronald Jefferies, had been disqualified from driving for a year in 1993 and had therefore been driving unlicensed for the 12 years hence.

When it was his turn in the hot seat at the corruption inquiry, Binge disagreed that the $50,000 in cash was for bribes. He insisted it was an advance for travel expenses. 'Two nights at the most expensive motel in Narooma is not going to amount to $50,000,' quipped Geoffrey Watson, SC, counsel assisting the inquiry.[13]

The ICAC found that Medich was corrupt. Described as an unsatisfactory witness whose evidence 'was often evasive and unresponsive', the report also recommended the DPP consider prosecuting Medich for his role in providing 'corrupt benefits' to three former executives from the WLALC. The three – Ron Mason, Vanessa and Ken Foster – were also recommended to the DPP for possible prosecution for 'corruptly receiving benefits'.[14] Six years later, in October 2018, the DPP advised there was insufficient evidence to prosecute the Masons, Ken Foster or Ron Medich.

It didn't seem to occur to Medich that Gattellari never came through with a decent money-making proposition. In his little black book Gattellari recorded the progress of their various corrupt payments for the Narooma land deals and other schemes as at the end of 2007. It made for sorry reading. In his 'results' column Gattellari had recorded 'nothing' for eight of their endeavours; six were classified as 'fucked' (including the funeral fund); and the Narooma deal itself was recorded as 'screwed'. Yet despite Gattellari's tragic list, Medich went on to lend Gattellari a colossal $16 million to be invested in his struggling industrial electrical contracting and wholesaling businesses – businesses that would ultimately go the same way as the rest of Lucky's unlucky endeavours.

CHAPTER 21

FINDING A HITMAN

As 2009 dragged on, McGurk was still very much alive and Medich, an irritable man at the best of times, was peeved by the delay. 'Why isn't this fucking guy gone? I want him fucking dead. He's ruining my life and my marriage,' he ranted to Gattellari, who, in turn, took his frustration out on Haissam Safetli.[1]

In May Safetli met an old mate, Mr F, a Lebanese enforcer who was recently out of jail for kidnapping. Mr F had worked as a bouncer in Kings Cross and as he and Hais ate mandarins and drank coffee at Mr F's Condell Park home, Mr F boasted about the skulduggery he'd been up to in recent times. Safetli couldn't help himself. He was soon bragging about his own special mission for his 'big bosses' and asked Mr F if he could source some weapons for him.

Mr F could spot a sucker a mile off. Within days he claimed he had two weapons for $6500 each, but said he needed the $13,000 upfront. Safetli handed over the money. The following day Mr F did not produce the guns, offering the unlikely excuse that the woman who was delivering them had been pulled over by police on her way to his house. She'd managed to throw the guns out the window, said Mr F, but she was arrested for credit card fraud and couldn't go back for the weapons.

Safetli, downcast at this turn of events, spilt his guts to Mr F as to why he needed the firearms. When Mr F expressed interest in Safetli's assigment, Safetli quickly told him the contract killing would pay $150,000. Mr F sold him another gun for $10,000. Unfortunately, this one was a replica and had a mangled bullet wedged inside it from some other previous desperado trying to get it to work. Mr F took the gun back, promising to get Safetli a refund, which needless to say never materialised.

By now Safetli had spent $25,000 on guns with nothing to show for it. He went to his board at Chan & Naylor, telling them he was in serious trouble and that something dreadful would happen if he didn't pay back $25,000 to some 'bad people'. They lent him the money without any further questions, but on 13 May he attacked one of the partners in the Pymble account-ancy office. Not only was he fired, he was also charged by police. He never did pay back the firm's $25,000 loan.

In the end Safetli handed over $100,000 to Mr F as a down payment for taking on the murder of McGurk. Mr F used the money to feed his drug habit and for a deposit on a house.

Then there was Ahmad 'Joey' Samman, whom Safetli claimed he'd randomly met at a tyre shop in southwest Sydney that was owned by Safetli's cousin, Ghassan Bassal, who was later jailed over possession of the drug ice and stolen goods. Despite being an addict who was off his face most of the time, Samman too was offered the job of paid assassin by Safetli.

On 30 June Joey Samman, his brother, Nizar, and Nizar's then girlfriend drove to McGurk's house in Nizar's girlfriend's silver hatchback. Joey, who was armed, was planning to storm the premises, but when he got to the front door he decided against it and they went home.

On 9 July McGurk reported to police two suspicious charac-ters in a silver hatchback who had sped off when he confronted them. It was the Samman brothers. The following night Safetli and Joey Samman met outside McGurk's house. Earlier in the evening Safetli and Krystal Weir had been partying hard at the Ivy in the city. Safetli, fuelled by coke and alcohol, was revved up. He and Joey Samman exchanged about 90 text messages in which they eventually agreed to go to Cranbrook Avenue so Samman could kill McGurk.[2]

No fewer than three carloads of prospective hitmen congregated outside McGurk's house that night. At 10 pm Safetli and Krystal arrived. Waiting for them, parked just down the hill, were Chris Estephan and his mate Adam Chahine, Safetli's nephew. An hour later Joey Samman arrived and hopped into the back seat of Weir's yellow Ford Falcon. He was pumped up. He pulled out a pistol from under his jacket and complained to the couple about having to file down the bullets to fit in the weapon's magazine. He also whined about having to drive to the murder scene in his own car. He and Safetli discussed whether they should burn both the cars after the job was done. Samman was raring to go. 'Let's storm the house now!' he urged.[3] Safetli wasn't convinced that was such a good idea. They weren't even sure McGurk was home as the house was dark and quiet. Safetli paid Samman for his efforts and all three groups drove to their respective homes.

After this final aborted attempt, having received $40,000 from Safetli, the Sammans lost interest in committing the murder, leaving Safetli to find someone else. (The police statements of fact in regard to the Samman brothers were later tendered in court, but the refusal of a witness to testify led to the case against the brothers collapsing. Their lawyer, however, claimed that the Crown case was flawed from the start.)

In mid-July Gattellari, frustrated, demanded that Safetli tell him where McGurk was right at that moment. Safetli said he wasn't sure but that he was probably at home. Gattellari snapped, 'No, he's at the fucking snow; he's at Jindabyne! Ron said they are at the snow and that he doesn't want [McGurk] to come back from the snow,' roared Gattellari. He gave both Haissam and Bass a further $6000 to go down to Jindabyne to kill McGurk, but the Safetlis didn't get organised in time.[4]

Gattellari suggested that McGurk, a big user of cocaine, could be given an overdose to make his death seem accidental. Knowing that McGurk frequented the Ivy, Gattellari organised a membership for Safetli, which he used with gusto, often meeting up at the bar with Krystal and other mates.

As July drew to a close Safetli was getting desperate. He had been ripped off blind in his quest to farm out the murder and now much of the money for the hit was gone. Kaminic was constantly texting him asking how the 'rims' or the 'tyres' – their code for the murder – were going and Safetli would reply that he hoped the delivery would be soon.

Gattellari, under increasing pressure from Medich, organised for Safetli to sound out another prospective hitman. Safetli was told to meet a man who would be carrying a newspaper under his arm. Safetli went to the wrong place. The meeting was rescheduled and Safetli stood for two miserable hours under an awning outside the Malabar RSL Club sheltering from pouring rain. Finally a short, pudgy man, whom Safetli described as looking like George Costanza's dad from *Seinfeld* (except he had tattooed arms), arrived carrying a newspaper under his arm. The man at least sounded slightly more professional than previous candidates – he wanted to know about the security arrangements at the hit location and whether there were dogs. He also wanted $200,000, half the money before and half later.

This ageing hitman had been sourced by Ron Mason, who'd received bribes from Gattellari over the Narooma Aboriginal Land Council deals. Mason, Medich and Gattellari were lunching at Tuscany restaurant in Leichhardt when Gattellari took Mason aside. In desperation, he asked Mason if he knew anyone who might be interested in doing a contract killing. He needed someone 'bumped off' straight away as this unnamed person was costing Medich $100,000 a week. When Mason asked if the intended victim had a high profile, Gattellari reassured him that the person was a 'nobody'.[5]

'You must know any Aboriginal blokes around the place who are dying that don't have long to live?' asked Gattellari hopefully.[6]

Mason, no doubt thinking of enriching his own family, made arrangements to introduce Safetli to his daughter's father-in-law,

Henry Charles Landini. Landini was a career criminal, though if his rap sheet was anything to go by, not a terribly successful one. Between 1960 and 1998, 'Danny' Landini, as he was better known, had been charged on 60 separate occasions with the possession and supply of heroin and cocaine, and had served several stints in jail.

Mason later assured the court that Landini, whom Mason described as 'short and fat' and 70, planned to 'rip off' Gattellari, like all the other would-be hitmen. At least Landini appeared to be a better judge of character than Gattellari and his crew. He said to Mason of Safetli, 'Who was that imbecile I went to meet?'[7]

For his part Gattellari decided that Landini's fee was too expensive, and that he'd already outlaid too much. He thrust another $50,000 of Medich's money at Safetli and told him he had to attend Tuscany restaurant in Leichhardt. He warned Safetli that he was to make sure he introduced himself to Medich as 'the new guy' and to promise Medich that he himself could complete the 'job' in four weeks.

On his arrival at Tuscany, Gattellari directed Safetli to a table by himself at the back of the restaurant. It was the very same table at which Gattellari and Medich would be photographed the day after the murder. When Medich arrived, almost an hour late, Gattellari took him over to where Safetli was sitting alone. 'This is Hias,' said Gattellari, once again failing to get his hitman's name right. 'He's the new man,' he said with conviction. Turning to Safetli, he said, 'I explained to Ron that you can get this job done for us in four weeks.' Medich, who was wearing his customary all-black outfit broken only by a silver buckle on his belt, looked Safetli in the eye and said abruptly, 'Are you sure you can get this job done in four weeks?' 'Yes, a hundred per cent,' replied Safetli.[8] With that, Medich shook Safetli's hand and left to join a table of young women who were sitting with Kaminic and Gattellari. Safetli finished his lunch alone and drove straight to Krystal's house in the neighbouring suburb of Annandale. He relayed the conversation to her, and she said she'd do the job herself for a hundred grand.[9]

The countdown was now on. Safetli had four weeks and his options were limited. He decided to rope into his murderous scheme a newcomer, Christopher Chafic Estephan, the teenage friend of Safetli's nephew, Adam Chahine. By all accounts Estephan, who had left school at 15, entered the conspiracy to murder with some enthusiasm. He agreed to a payment of $30,000. He acquired the murder weapon, a .22 Norinco rifle, as well as a single-barrel shotgun, for which Safetli paid him $6000. In the month leading up to the murder, Estephan was at Safetli's house most days, where the two men smoked dope together.

On 19 August they decided that today was the day. Estephan stole some numberplates and drove his white van to Safetli's. They smoked dope for ten minutes, Safetli downed two glasses of straight bourbon and with a Stanley bag in the front seat packed with the rifle, they set off.

At around 2.15 pm, as they drove over to Cremorne, McGurk was on the phone to me. He wanted me to know that the following day the DPP was going to drop all the charges against him. I was surprised by this turn of events as the DPP's case seemed pretty strong. Once again he railed against Medich, saying that he had been set up. The problem with McGurk's version was that some of the people who had been assaulted, such as Eddie Muscat and Stuart Rowan, whose house was firebombed, had no connection to Medich. The only person with a connection to all the matters was McGurk. I told him I would see him the following day in court.

Safetli and Estephan arrived at McGurk's house at about 2.30 pm and parked across the road, sitting on the step of the sliding door of the van for a couple of hours. McGurk didn't show up so they went home.

In retrospect it seems crazy to have contemplated killing someone in the middle of the afternoon just as primary school kids were coming out of school less than 100 metres away. But Safetli didn't seem to be the sharpest tool in the shed.

A fortnight later, on 3 September 2009, he and Estephan were ready to throw the dice of death again.

CHAPTER 22

THE JOB IS DONE

On the morning of the murder, Gattellari and Kaminic drove back from Narooma, where Gattellari had been trying to advance his and Medich's development plans with the WLALC. Gattellari had asked to be notified the day before the murder was to happen so he could arrange to be in a public place with Medich and Kaminic. The previous day he had received a coded text message from Safetli promising 'the tyres' would be delivered the following afternoon.

Once back in Sydney, Gattellari and Kaminic joined Medich for lunch at a private room in a popular restaurant in Market City in Chinatown. At 2.48 pm Medich received a call from Detective Ray Hetherington to tell him that the criminal charges against McGurk had been withdrawn. Although he'd known about this for more than a week, Medich was still seething, and he complained bitterly to Hetherington that McGurk was costing him a fortune in legal bills. 'The bastard is down celebrating at the Chophouse restaurant having lunch as we speak,' Medich fumed.[1]

The three men finished lunch at 4 pm, by which time the contract killers were lying in wait outside McGurk's home.

Leaving the restaurant, Medich, Gattellari and Kaminic went down the escalators to the next level of Market City and disappeared along a corridor, through a door, past four large pink brocade armchairs and an enormous glass fishtank – into the familiar surrounds of the Babylon Sauna & Spa. The three regulars were ushered into the back rooms to receive their customary 'happy endings' from young Asian women.

Gattellari last heard from Safetli just after 3 pm. When they emerged from their rub 'n' tugs at Babylon both Gattellari and Kaminic checked their phones. There was still no word on the tyre delivery. At 6 pm Kaminic and Gattellari dropped Medich to meet one of his stockbrokers, Gerard Farley, in Bligh Street, not far from Circular Quay, and then headed home. Gattellari was pretty sure this was yet another false start. Safetli was big on promising but not so big on delivering.

At that same time Safetli was walking down Cranbrook Avenue to the bottle shop near McGurk's house for the fortification he needed for the job he had ahead of him. Within half an hour, McGurk's life would end. None of those involved in this half-arsed plot gave any thought to the fact that, down the track, the extinguishing of McGurk's life would result in the ruination of their own lives.

At 8.03 pm Bassam Safetli sent Gattellari a message saying, 'The job is done.'[2]

In the first three months of the investigation into Michael McGurk's murder, detectives Sheehy, Howe and Fitzhenry had pretty good leads on their main suspects, but they also had to eliminate many other potential suspects.

By the end of 2009 a number of sources had implicated Ron Medich, Lucky Gattellari, Senad Kaminic, Haissam Safetli and Christopher Estephan. One of those informants was Safetli's drug-addled friend Mr F. Another was Krystal Weir.

In December 2009 an investigation into the murder, codenamed 'Limbri', was authorised by the New South Wales Crime

Commission, which is used as an adjunct to police forces to help solve serious matters. There is no right to silence at the commission and it is a criminal offence to reveal, except to your lawyer, that you have even been summonsed to appear there.

At the beginning of January 2010 phone taps were authorised for the five suspects. From mid-June 2010 police also planted listening devices in Safetli's home. They intercepted numerous calls in which Medich ranted and raved to anyone who would listen about Kimberley McGurk. Much to Medich's irritation, Kimberley had not rolled over and given in to Medich's demands that she repay the millions of dollars which Medich claimed her husband had stolen from him. She was fighting him tooth and nail through the courts. Medich complained to Kaminic that Mrs McGurk was a 'bitch' who was even 'harder' than her late husband. 'The guy was a down-and-out crook . . . and she was complicit,' said Medich in one call.[3] In other calls Medich complained about his lack of success in ongoing legal disputes with her. 'She's not going to win,' said Medich, adding that 'sooner or later' she would understand that.[4]

To Gattellari he said, 'It's about fucking time she got the message. I can't keep going like this. I've even lost control of the house.'[5]

Medich was also heard whining to his mate and self-styled financial adviser Andrew Howard, who had previously worked with McGurk, about the amount of money he was paying lawyers for very little result. Howard, who was coordinating Medich's legal strategy against Mrs McGurk, stood to make $1 million if she could be forced to settle the cases. Howard later agreed in court that he knew that Mrs McGurk was a stay-at-home mother with four children who had nothing to do with her late husband's businesses. Decency was nowhere to be seen when there was a dollar to be made.

On the afternoon of 26 May 2010, Howard rang Medich with bad news. He'd been 'cleaned up' in court. Not only had the judge refused to extend the caveat he had lodged on the

McGurk family home, but Medich had been ordered to pay Mrs McGurk's costs.

'Oh yeah, fuckin' hopeless, but you know all as I'm doin' is incurring legal costs galore, you know, and these people are just not getting the job done . . . I mean to me that's most disappointing . . . I'm getting sick of solicitors, you know, I really am,' protested Medich, who then ordered Howard to convey to his solicitors how furious he was. 'I'm sick of the whole lot of all these people, because, honestly, how can they rack up bills of a million dollars on something they don't even succeed at, you know? . . . It's a fuckin' joke, you know . . . The only winners out of all of this are these fuckin' solicitors,' said Medich, adding that he thought all his lawyers were 'fuckin' hopeless'.[6]

In another call, Howard and Medich discussed ways of cutting off Kimberley McGurk's legal funding to force her to capitulate.

At the end of June 2010, Howard was heard telling his patron that Mrs McGurk needed a 'dose of reality'. 'She thinks she's going to walk away with money. That isn't the case,' said Howard, guffawing.[7]

Behind the scenes, Medich was keen for Kimberley to receive a more direct reminder of the error in carrying on her husband's battles. Medich instructed Gattellari that it was time to implement Plan B: the intimidation of Mrs McGurk.

Haissam Safetli was once again offered the role and, unbelievably, he once again turned to Mr F. The codename for the intimidation of Kimberley was 'the horses'. But things were different this time. Mr F had his own troubles with the police and the price of saving himself was to offer them a bigger fish. Mr F gave them Safetli. He told the police that not only had Safetli offered him money for the hit on McGurk, but now Safetli was asking him to threaten McGurk's widow. This was a major breakthrough for detectives from Strike Force Narrunga. Mr F's police handlers were hopeful that through him they could get enough information to bring in all those involved in McGurk's murder. Their newly recruited informant was instructed to assist Safetli in the intimidation, and to wear a wire.

On Friday 6 August police watched as Kaminic and Safetli walked seemingly aimless laps around an open-air car park in Liverpool. Kaminic was relaying further instructions from Gattellari about the timing of the intimidation. Gattellari wanted it to take place on 8 August because he and Medich would have the perfect alibi: they'd be in China.

Not that Medich was grateful for Gattellari's efforts to keep him out of the frame for their criminal enterprises. He criticised his friend for not booking flights that enabled him to be at the races on Saturday.

'Yeah, but we ... but we couldn't ... we couldn't, Ron, ya know? Cause we're not taking a holiday trip here ... the trip is based on certain things that need to happen at certain times,' explained Gattellari guardedly.[8]

'Yeah,' replied Medich.

Police were listening in as Gattellari continued: 'I, I can't just fuckin' decide to go on the ... on the drop of a hat.' He told Medich he hadn't been able to book the flights until 'other matters' were fixed. Medich knew exactly what he was talking about but failed to temper his petulance about the denial of a pleasure.

It was a winter's night, cold and dark, when detectives Fitzhenry and Sheehy came to warn Michael McGurk's widow that she was about to receive a visit from two men, one of whom they believed had killed her husband. Even though it was a 'controlled' operation, the police did not know whether Mr F or Safetli would be waiting in the dark to deliver the threat on that Sunday evening in August. At 6.30 pm, undercover police were monitoring Safetli as he went to collect Mr F and then headed to Cremorne.

Kimberley McGurk was doing the washing-up in an effort to keep occupied as she waited for the message to be delivered. There was a rattle at the back door. Her hands were trembling as she walked over to the same door her distraught son had rushed through screaming 11 months earlier. Was she now about to come face to face with her husband's executioner?

She was confronted by the chilling sight of a dark, thickset man of Middle Eastern appearance wearing a cheap, coloured wig and a hoodie pulled up over his head. It was Mr F.

'I am just here to pass a message to you, that's all,' he said in a foreboding voice. 'Don't be a con man like your husband. You know what you have to do, you know what I'm talking about.'[9]

'No, I don't,' she replied, trying to keep her voice steady.

The man said again, 'You know what I'm talking about. Do the right thing and don't be a thief like your husband. Pay his debts.'

Less than a fortnight later, on 20 August 2010, Medich happily trotted along to lunch with Bob Ell and their mutual buddy Richie Vereker. Medich assumed Plan B had been a success and that, as her representative, Ell would be outlining her capitulation terms. But instead of telling him about Kimberley McGurk's offering to repay the millions McGurk had stolen from him, Vereker and Ell had the hide to suggest that Ron should throw a couple of grand her way so he had clear title to Mowbray and Gerroa, the two properties they were fighting over. Kimberley's bloody husband had already made him pay double the amount Mowbray and Gerroa were worth, and here was his widow putting her hand out for more. Not only that, the two men told him to stop harassing Mrs McGurk. Medich demanded to know why on earth they thought he was harassing her. Unperturbed by Medich's huffing and puffing, Ell replied that there was only one person chasing Kimberley for money, 'and that's you, Ron'.[10]

Medich was livid. He later recounted the conversation to Kaminic, Gattellari and Crockett, who were dining at a nearby table while the boss talked business; and in an intercepted call with his daughter Pam later that day Ron belly-ached about Ell and Vereker 'going on and on' about Mrs McGurk. 'They are all a bunch of thieves,' he complained to Pam. When she asked if they were accusing him of being responsible for the threat to Mrs McGurk, Medich said, 'You don't need to worry about me.'[11]

But Medich was worried. If Ell and Vereker thought he was behind the threat then so must others. He became increasingly paranoid about the police. He'd asked Crockett to sweep his office and car to see if there were any listening devices. If there were McGurk-related matters to be discussed, he insisted on talking to Gattellari in a park or in the spa room inside the Babylon.

The police were closing in and friendships began to fray as panic set in. Kaminic and Gattellari weren't speaking, nor were Safetli and Estephan. Hais Safetli, in particular, was losing the plot. He was drinking like a fish and constantly high. Bass was worried that because Hais's relationship with Krystal had deteriorated rapidly since the murder, she might be talking. She was already in contact with the police – Safetli had harassed her so badly in the months after the murder that, on her behalf, they had taken out an AVO against him. When Hais heard she was thinking of going to Victoria to get away from him, he threatened that she would be dragged back quicker than she could blink.

In his sober moments Safetli knew that Chris Estephan and Krystal Weir could give him up and he seriously contemplated killing both of them. 'She knows too much, I need to get rid of her,' he confided in Kaminic. Because he'd fallen out with Estephan, Safetli told Kaminic, 'I can't go near [Estephan's] place – you will have to kill him.'[12]

By early September Safetli realised that the window of opportunity to kill Weir and Estephan had closed. The pair, as well as Bass and his nephew Adam, had been summoned for questioning at the Crime Commission. It was too late to dispose of anyone. The police were on to them. Now it was every man for himself.

On his birthday, 13 September 2010, Safetli, ever grandiose, contacted homicide detective Richie Howe, offering to give him 'god on a platter'.[13] It turned out, however, that god was a fool and the platter was of the plastic-tray variety: Safetli organised to meet Howe and his boss, Mick Sheehy, at a McDonald's on the Parramatta Road in the inner-west suburb of Five Dock.

Safetli later said his plan was to confess to everything and then take rat poison in the toilet of the golden arches. But the confession didn't go as planned because an argument arose with

Inspector Sheehy when, as was routine, he ordered Safetli to empty his pockets. Safetli couldn't believe it. He was an important man. He was central to the entire case and here they were ordering him around rather than listening to his every word. What he didn't know was that police had been bugging Safetli's house and had heard him confess to his family about the murder and the intimidation of Mrs McGurk. Big Mick wasn't in the mood for Safetli's histrionics; he'd been up all night dealing with the accidental shooting of a fellow officer. The police already knew about Safetli; what they needed were those further up the hierarchy. Safetli left the fast-food restaurant in a fury. He couldn't believe it. He'd been rebuffed by the police.

He sought legal advice that afternoon and, accompanied by his lawyer, confessed to the Crime Commission about his and others' roles in the murder of McGurk. His testimony meant the authorities had more than enough to charge both Safetli and Estephan with murder. Now they badly needed evidence to charge Gattellari, Kaminic and Medich. Safetli agreed to wear a wire. The only person he never volunteered to try to record was Estephan.

Two days later, on 15 September 2010, Gattellari organised a meeting inside his lighting factory at Chipping Norton. He thought the noise of the machinery would make it impossible for police to overhear what was being discussed. He was mistaken. As the conspirators talked about the police closing in on them, and their concern that Estephan would crack, Gattellari was heard urging Safetli to 'put his hand up' to save the rest of them: 'Listen to me. I swear to you on the lives of my children that if anything goes fucking wrong, your family will not suffer for it. Do you understand me?'

'You know I can get to you from in there,' Safetli replied.

Gattellari was furious, 'Fuck, why do you have to say that?'

Because, Safetli said, if he went down for the murder, 'I'm the only one that is fucked.'

Incredulous, Gattellari replied, 'Do you want us all to be fucked?'

Safetli pointed out that even if his family were looked after, if he went down for the murder, 'Mr Big is protected.'

Gattellari snapped, 'There's no Mr Fucking Big. There is no Mr Big.'[14]

Safetli said he wanted a written guarantee from Medich that his family would be taken care of if he took the blame.

'I'm giving it to you. I got the guarantee fucking yesterday. I'm giving it to you, I swear to God,' said Gattellari. 'I swear on the lives of my kids, your family will not fucking suffer. We need to get rid of this fucking mess, but do not admit to anything if the shit hits the fan.'[15]

Gattellari was offering promises to Safetli that would never be met, as he himself would soon find out.

In another conversation he advised Safetli that the rule of British law was in their favour. 'You're innocent until you're proven guilty beyond a shadow of a fuckin' doubt ... You've done nothin' fuckin' wrong,' he assured Hais.

'I have, Lucky, I am sorry but I have,' replied the contract killer. 'You've got to understand that in my position time is running out.'[16]

Medich, too, could see the writing on the wall and was already distancing himself from Gattellari. On 8 October, Medich's oldest son, Peter, was heard on phone intercepts apologising to Gattellari that his father wasn't going to be able to meet up at Babylon as arranged.

Two days later Peter again phoned Gattellari to say his father 'got caught up – he's not coming'.

On 12 October Estephan applied for a passport. But time had run out – for all of them.

CHAPTER 23

THE ARRESTS

The moon was still up as I sat in my car across the road from Ron Medich's house at 112 Wolseley Road, Point Piper. It was 5 am on Wednesday, 13 October 2010 – a year and a month since Michael McGurk's murder. The previous morning I had received a tip that the homicide squad was about to swoop on those allegedly responsible for McGurk's death.

I organised a confidential meeting with my editors to work out a plan. I didn't know for sure who police were going to arrest, where the arrests would take place, or what time of day they might happen. We discussed the logistics of how to cover the arrests. Our suspects were Ron Medich, Lucky Gattellari and Senad Kaminic.

Vanda Carson, with a photographer, was assigned to Gattellari in Chipping Norton. Another *Herald* reporter, Tom Reilly, and a photographer, would cover Kaminic, who lived in Liverpool. I assigned myself Ron Medich.

The next morning photographer Jon Reid and I sat in our respective cars in the darkness outside Medich's house. As we waited in the pre-dawn gloom, another car pulled up behind us. I thought it must be an undercover cop, but almost immediately my phone pinged. 'Hi, it's Natalie from online here. I am in the car behind you.' Natalie from online! This was meant to be a top-secret mission and now another reporter, who I had never met, was sitting in the car behind me.

As the sun began to rise, I hopped out of the car with my two accomplices, our family mutts, who had been lying low on the back seat. I'd barely walked a couple of metres before a parent from my daughter's school spied me from her car and pulled over, curious as to why I was walking the dogs at this hour. I confessed I was on a stakeout. 'Oh,' she said. 'Would you like to come in for a cup of tea?'

'No,' I spluttered, 'I can't come in for a cup of tea. A stakeout requires some degree of vigilance!'

At 7 am a flurry of household staff and construction workers began to arrive at Wolseley Road. The discordant architectural monstrosities which clung to the shoreline were like an archaeological dig marking the ebb and flow of family fortunes. The Point Piper way was to knock down the edifice reflecting someone else's dreams in order to erect a monument, in the prevailing style, to proudly parade one's own grandeur. I started to wonder whether I would have been better off wearing a fluoro vest and a hard hat rather than masquerading as a dog walker.

Three hours passed before there was any movement. At 8.15 am Gattellari sped away from his Chipping Norton house in his black Mercedes sedan. Vanda was momentarily confused because the Merc had a green P plate on the rear, but she followed it to Gattellari's lighting warehouse in the same suburb. Ben, the photographer, stayed at Gattellari's house.

Gattellari drove the length of the car park, on either side of which were a series of industrial premises. At the end of the lot he pulled up outside his premises and disappeared upstairs into the office attached to the warehouse. Vanda observed from a suitable distance.

Another hour passed. By then I was of the firm opinion that competent police officers would have made their arrests before their suspects left for work. Not that Medich actually had a proper job or did anything much but lunch at Tuscany.

Shortly after 9 am, Tom rang to say that Kaminic had emerged from an unprepossessing three-storey apartment block in Bathurst Street, Liverpool. Tom was nervous because Kaminic was nervous. Kaminic spent 20 minutes pacing up and down on the pavement talking earnestly on his mobile phone. Tom was in hyper-vigilant mode and noticed the same four cars discreetly doing laps of Bathurst Street. 'Gotta go, he's on the move,' he suddenly said, hanging up. Kaminic had got into a blue Volkswagen four-wheel drive and headed off at great speed.

It was now 10 am and I decided my tip-off about the arrests was rubbish. I had called it quits and was heading home to drop the dogs off before going to work when Vanda called. Hunger had got the better of her and she had snuck off to buy a pie at a Chipping Norton bakery. She couldn't believe her eyes when who should walk into the very same bakery but the unmistakable bulk of Detective Inspector Mick Sheehy. He queued up to buy a pie.

It was on.

I hurried back to Point Piper. Vanda returned to the warehouse just as Kaminic, followed by Tom, arrived at Gattellari's business premises. Only minutes after Kaminic arrived, a third car – a battered red Daihatsu – came screeching into the car park. Did these people always drive as though it was a life-or-death situation, or did they know something was afoot? At the wheel was a person we didn't know. He went into the building as well. Gattellari, Kaminic and Matthew Crockett were out on the verandah having a cigar and cognac. 'Christ, I didn't want to see this bloke today,' muttered Gattellari of the arrival of the man in the red Daihatsu.[1] He had been followed into the car park by a fleet of unmarked police cars and three police vehicles.

Suddenly it was all happening. There were police everywhere. Out of the black police vehicles, emblazoned with 'Public Order and Riot Squad', emerged men in armoured vests with guns pulled. Sheehy, Fitzhenry, Howe and other detectives, all wearing suits, disappeared upstairs into the building, where Fitzhenry told Gattellari he was under arrest for the murder of Michael McGurk.

After Fitzhenry cautioned him and produced handcuffs, Gattellari took off his watch and gave it to his son, Loren. He asked the accountant of the business, Kim Shipley, to arrange legal representation for him. A short time later the detective came back out with Kaminic, Gattellari and the Daihatsu driver.

Gattellari still had his reading glasses hooked over the front of his black t-shirt. He frowned but said nothing as he was ushered out of the building and placed in the back seat of an unmarked silver police car.

Kaminic was asked to sit on the ground so police could remove his white running shoes, which they placed neatly on the boot of a nearby police car. Unshaven, he remained on the asphalt of the car park watching the organised chaos around him. His widow's peak was rendered more prominent by him wearing his long greying hair pulled back in a ponytail.

The unidentified person driving the red Daihatsu turned out to be Haissam Safetli. The only photo we ever managed to get of Safetli was taken by Vanda on the digital camera which she carried in her handbag. She was shaking so much she forgot to put it on colour mode, so there is Safetli forever frozen in a black-and-white image looking off to the right with his manacled hands resting on the roof of his battered old hatchback as Richie Howe pats him down.

At the very moment police were arresting Gattellari and the others, 20-year-old Christopher Estephan, accompanied by his lawyer, was handing himself in at Kings Cross Police Station. He was charged with murder.

The police had made the decision to swoop that day because they were worried that Safetli was going to be killed. He was becoming so unstable that his co-conspirators were seriously spooked that he might give them all up. The original plan by homicide detectives was for a domino effect: Krystal Weir had provided assistance to police, and Mr F had rolled on Safetli, who in turn had given up Gattellari, Estephan and Kaminic. What they had hoped was that Gattellari would wear a wire and trap Medich. But fears for Safetli's safety meant they had to move earlier than planned.

Across town, Gattellari, Kaminic and Safetli were taken to Liverpool Police Station, where they were formally charged. In the year that had elapsed since the murder, never once had we heard the names Safetli or Estephan, yet here they were being accused of the murder.

Kaminic was charged with being an accessory before and after the murder. Gattellari was charged with soliciting to murder and being an accessory after the fact.

Meanwhile, back in Wolseley Road, it was quiet. I couldn't believe it. Was McGurk wrong in suggesting to me that Medich had ordered the hit? Then, about 40 minutes after the arrests in Chipping Norton, Medich came roaring out of his driveway in his black Mercedes. In hot pursuit were me and the mutts, the photographer and, bringing up the rear, Natalie from online.

Our trail ended at the Martin Place office of Medich's latest solicitor, John Bamford. Medich, dressed in his habitual garb of black v-neck sweater and black t-shirt, emerged two hours later with his son Peter, who had been working at the Chipping Norton factory and had witnessed the morning's drama.

As soon as he got home Medich organised a flight to Adelaide, departing that evening. Before he left he disposed of his mobile phone.

The horse-racing colours of yellow and white diamonds, yellow sleeves and cap were frequently seen on the tracks during the successful racing partnership of Les Samba and his buddy Ron Medich. And it was to the South Australian home of his racing partner that Medich fled following the dramatic day of arrests.

Once Medich had agreed to pay Haissam and Bass Safetli the $300,000 they'd asked for the contract killing, he told Gattellari that Samba would organise the cash.

The week before McGurk's murder, Medich and his dapperly dressed friend Samba were in New Zealand to sell their horse Guillotine, a half-brother of the Melbourne Cup-winning

Efficient. Within four months of Medich's dash to Adelaide, Samba was dead. On Sunday, 27 February 2011, around 9.40 pm, he was staying at the Crown Metropol Hotel at Southbank in Melbourne. He asked the front desk to have his silver Hyundai hire car brought up, and drove to Beaconsfield Parade in the inner-Melbourne beachside suburb of Middle Park, where he parked. He walked a short distance and stopped near a pedestrian crossing. It appeared that he was shot in the back as he tried to run. The killer then walked up to the dying man and shot him in the back of the head while he lay bleeding on the road. Ballistic experts later determined that two different firearms had been used to kill the 60-year-old.

Quietly spoken and well groomed, Samba turned out to have been a man with many secrets. At the time of his murder he was involved in money-laundering, race fixing and drug trafficking. One racing identity, who'd seen Samba at the Inglis thoroughbred sales on the day he died, told the Herald, 'There's a lot of people . . . who are shocked that this could happen to Les, but maybe they're being a bit naïve. Those people that knew Les well must have known he was a heavy hitter in areas that might be best described as "shady". When something like this happens, you can't help but think of that saying, "If you live by the sword you die by the sword."'[2]

Even his former son-in-law, controversial jockey Danny Nikolic, was quoted saying that Samba's death 'was a shock in one way, but not in another. You never expect anyone to be killed like that, but he did mix in a lot of unusual circles outside racing.'[3]

In a remarkable coincidence, Nikolic's brother Tommy lived in Beaconsfield Parade, about 300 metres from the murder scene.

In an unrelated incident, the following day police searched the Gold Coast home of Nikolic's other brother, John, a horse trainer who had previously been disqualified for doping a horse. (In June 2018 John Nikolic was arrested by Fijian authorities after a raid on his yacht Shenanigans. On board they allegedly found almost 13 kilos of cocaine worth up to $30 million, as well as ecstasy tablets, $20,000 in cash and guns and ammunition. Nikolic was subsequently sentenced to a minimum of 18 years in prison.)

Samba's own career as a horse trainer was cut short when authorities refused him a licence because of his underworld associations. After drug charges against him were dropped in 1995, Samba managed to keep living well beyond his means despite having no job and no discernible source of income. When Samba was investigated by the National Crime Authority (NCA) over his relationship with a known Italian Mafia figure, he was unable to explain the origins of the $1.2 million he spent between 1995 and 1998, much of it betting on and buying horses. Samba attempted to produce records to prove it was from gambling, but the NCA investigators soon proved most of Samba's records were false and that he was often overseas when he claimed to have been betting at a particular track.

No charges ensued although the ATO pursued him over the $1.2 million in undeclared income. Rather than fight the tax man, in 2002 Samba and his wife Deirdre were declared bankrupt.

Not that bankruptcy appeared to hamper Samba in the slightest. Even when he reputedly lost nearly $1 million, which was seized by police when they raided the premises of a suspected arms dealer, there was always plenty of cash to splash. So when Medich needed to source money for the murder, it was Samba to whom he turned.

Before his murder Samba, too, had been quizzed at the Crime Commission about the McGurk case. When the police executed search warrants at Medich's home and office on the day of his arrest, 'Les Samba' was one of the names listed on the warrants.

After Samba's murder, the Strike Force Narrunga detectives were informed by their Melbourne counterparts that Samba had on him a false New South Wales driver's licence in the name of Lester Turner. Airline records showed 'Mr Turner' had been flying to Sydney in the months leading up to the McGurk murder, including in late March, which was around the time Gattellari said he had collected the cash from Medich to pay the hitman who would get rid of McGurk.

Needless to say, Samba would have been a crucial witness at Ron Medich's murder trial. His own murder remains unsolved.

CHAPTER 24

THEY WANT YOUR FATHER NOT MINE

Lucky Gattellari might have savoured his cognac had he known that the liquor he was enjoying on the morning of 13 October 2010 could be his last.

Following his dramatic arrest he was taken into custody at the nearby Liverpool Police Station. Prominent silk Tony Bellanto, QC, a tall, courtly man with silvering hair and an expertise in matters criminal, was retained and he told the former pugilist that to fight charges as serious as the ones he was facing would cost Gattellari around $1 million.

Kim Shipley, still in shock after witnessing his colleagues' apprehension at gunpoint, went to see Medich that day to arrange the funding for Gattellari's legal fees. Medich was in a bad way. His hands were shaking, he was highly agitated and he was even more incoherent than usual. He was also adamant that he would not help. 'Don't be bloody stupid, it's their problem now,' he shrieked. When Shipley asked Medich if he was involved, he lowered his voice and replied enigmatically, 'Be careful what you say, the walls have ears.'[1]

Gattellari spent his first four days behind bars in a 'safe cell' at Silverwater Correctional Complex. He suffered from chronic claustrophobia and the initial shock of prison was overwhelming: 'It was probably the most horrific experience of my entire life,' he later said.[2]

The day after his arrest his matter was listed for a brief mention at Liverpool Local Court. He was absolutely desperate for Bellanto to apply for bail but his barrister explained that because of the seriousness of the charges, they were nowhere near ready to make the application. Bellanto informed the court that his client would make an application in a fortnight's time. The barrister did his utmost to emphasise to Magistrate Beverley Schurr just how severe his client's claustrophobia was and that he was having 'a lot of difficulties being confined'. Gattellari himself was not brought up from the cells for his brief mention.

Lucky was desperate and so was his family. That night his son Loren rang Medich's son Peter to tell his father to put $1 million bail money into Gattellari's lawyer's trust account. Peter Medich advised Loren that he didn't think that would happen but he'd pass on the message.

Gattellari's and Medich's sons worked together at the lighting factory and were friends. So when Loren didn't hear back from Peter, he sent him a text. 'What's going on, dude? . . . I get the feeling you are distancing yourself . . . just be straight up with me, man.'[3]

Both were reluctant to talk on the phone so they arranged to meet that night at the Zoo Bar in Leichhardt. Loren arrived with Matthew Crockett, Lucky Gattellari's enforcer. When Peter came in, they insisted he put his mobile phone behind the bar. Peter was affronted when Loren demanded to know if he was wearing a wire. He heatedly informed them that only a fortnight ago police had been asking his father to wear a wire and he had refused point blank.

Crockett told Peter they'd been asked to pass on a message that if his father didn't put the million dollars into Gattellari's lawyer's trust account, Lucky was going to tell police that Ron Medich was involved in the murder. 'The police don't want my father, they want yours,' Loren added with some vehemence.[4]

Peter Medich was angry and told them he didn't believe his father was involved. Loren was dismissive. He demanded that Peter ring his father right now to pass on the message. Peter said that even if he wanted to talk to his father he couldn't – his stepmother had thrown his dad's phone into the harbour. Nor could Peter speak to his father face to face as Ron had gone to Adelaide to stay with Les Samba.

Having visited his father in jail that day, Loren was shocked at the state Lucky was in, so he demanded that Peter get on the very next plane to Adelaide to tell his father in person that he had to help Lucky. That's what mates do for each other, Loren implored. Peter apologised, saying there would be no money forthcoming. Shrugging his shoulders, he added that there were no funds to be had, even for his dad, as Odetta had frozen all the accounts.

Gattellari couldn't believe what Loren relayed to him. 'Never in a million years did I think Ron would do this to me,' he repeatedly told Loren.[5] He had gone out on a limb to do the most horrific of deeds for this man; he had organised someone to be murdered because his friend had wanted it so badly. And now Medich was washing his hands of him. 'Unbelievable, fucking unbelievable,' he said as much to himself as to anyone else. When he finally comprehended that his closest friend planned to leave him to rot in jail, Gattellari told his son to pass on a message to Peter to give his father: 'Tell Ron to pack his bags.'[6]

After a few days of silence from Medich, and with no money arriving, Gattellari realised his best friend really had thrown him to the wolves. He was burning with anger. He told his lawyers to contact Detective Inspector Mick Sheehy. He was ready to talk.

And talk he did. Over the next few months, two investigators working full time with Gattellari took eight statements from the former boxing champ totalling around 550 pages. There was enough for two corruption inquiries and more than enough for murder charges.

'Certainly his evidence is exceptional,' Mick Sheehy said at a later court appearance. 'I have never had a statement of this length and duration.'[7]

Ten days after Gattellari started 'singing', the police had what they needed to bring in Ron Medich. On Tuesday, 26 October 2010, the property developer received the worst phone call of his life. His solicitor John Bamford was tasked with passing on the bad news that Mick Sheehy had informed him Medich would be arrested the following day. Bamford didn't want his client to endure the humiliation of what the Americans call 'the perp walk', when an accused, in handcuffs, is paraded before the media as they are taken into custody. So it was arranged that Medich would hand himself in at his lawyer's Martin Place office.

Just after noon the following day, Detective Inspector Mick Sheehy, flanked by Sergeant Mark Fitzhenry, arrived at Bamford's city office. Waiting for them was criminal defence barrister Clive Steirn, SC, a former detective, whom Bamford had arranged to represent Medich.

Medich, in his customary all-black regalia, arrived with Odetta.

'Mr Medich, I am placing you under arrest for solicit to murder Michael McGurk,' said Fitzhenry, the officer in charge of the case. He warned him that he didn't have to say or do anything, but if he chose to say anything it could later be used in evidence against him.

'Yes, I totally deny any of those allegations and I have nothing further to say,' replied Medich.

Fitzhenry handcuffed Medich and he was taken to the Sydney Police Centre in Surry Hills. At the same time search warrants were executed at his Point Piper home and his Leichhardt office.

Medich baffled the police. He'd just been charged with soliciting a murder, yet he prattled away to them about horses and racing. He had a red-hot tip for next Tuesday's Melbourne Cup.

He liked the look of Americain. None of the police took heed of Medich's lowdown. Americain won the cup by two and a half lengths.

It was late in the afternoon and as the hearings had finished for the day, the normally busy Central Local Court in Sydney's Liverpool Street was quiet as Steirn and Bamford walked up its curved sandstone steps. A throng of journalists filed into the courtroom for the appearance of the millionaire charged in connection with one of the country's most sensational murder cases. Those who hadn't managed to get one of the mismatched seats at the large cedar table that served as the press area had to sit in the public benches at the back. The dock was empty. Then suddenly there was Medich, larger than life via a video link from the cells of the nearby police centre.

Steirn requested bail, which was opposed by Crown prosecutor Mark Hobart, SC, who suggested that Medich had the motivation and the resources to interfere with witnesses. Hobart handed the magistrate a 17-page police statement of facts, telling him that the charge didn't get any more serious than this – a contract killing, the penalty for which could be a life sentence. 'The defendant is the mastermind of this conspiracy, soliciting to murder Mr McGurk,' Hobart said. 'It goes from him down to Gattellari and goes down to the people who actually did the shooting.'[8]

At this point, Medich sniggered and then said loudly, 'Bullshit! What a load of crap.'

Hobart went on, 'The Crown says there was a continuing dispute in relation to Mr Medich and Mr McGurk. Mr Medich had the motivation to kill Mr McGurk, and arranged to do so. He had the resources, he's a man of wealth and his position, as far as the Crown's concerned, is at the top of the pyramid of this killing.'

As the proceedings continued, Medich, who appeared not to understand that he was being beamed live into the courtroom, scoffed at the Crown's claim that two key witnesses – Gattellari and Safetli – would give evidence about the $250,000 he had paid for the murder. He also mumbled asides while he flipped through police documents.

There were fears that Medich, despite handing in his passport, had the means to flee, suggested Hobart. The magistrate heard that Medich had been overseas four times in the past year. 'If he wanted to, Mr Medich could easily have fled the jurisdiction,' said Steirn, who noted that his client had been given 24 hours' notice that he was going to be arrested. 'Arrests are normally done without prior warning, so this is exceptional,' he said.

Steirn claimed that the prosecution was weak and there was no independent evidence to support the Crown's case, just Gattellari's self-serving statement designed to deflect the blame from himself. Steirn also laid the grounds for what was to be the major plank of the defence case – that Gattellari owed Medich $16 million and therefore had his own motivation for trying to pin the murder on him. Steirn recounted Gattellari's recent demand that if Medich didn't pay him $1 million, Gattellari would 'dump' on him.

Crosses and double crosses and the co-accused pointing the finger at each other – the magistrate had seen and heard it all before. Despite Medich offering to put up $1 million in surety, and his younger brother, Roy, offering $500,000 in cash, the magistrate refused to grant bail because he was concerned for 'the protection and welfare of members of the community and to the victim's partner and family'.

There was much excited whispering at the journalists' table about this amazing twist to the case. Gattellari had rolled over and it seemed there was more to come. Earlier that afternoon the homicide squad commander, Detective Superintendent Peter Cotter, had announced that further information had come to light since the dramatic arrests a fortnight earlier: 'A number of people that we have charged . . . have obviously considered their options,' he said.[9]

There was to be an even bigger twist in the case as others of those arrested considered their 'options'.

CHAPTER 25

THE WHEELS OF JUSTICE TURN SLOWLY

A week after Ron Medich's arrest, his charge sheet had a new entry: 'That Ronald Edward Medich on 3 September 2009 did murder Michael McGurk.' The upgrade to murder meant Medich now faced the prospect of life imprisonment.

As they say in the criminal world, justice is what you get when your money runs out. And the reverse is true, money can hold justice at bay and the more money you have, the more abeyances you can buy.

Unlike Gattellari, Kaminic and Safetli, Medich had substantial financial resources at hand. After the property developer had been in custody for six weeks, his legal team made a bail application. His previous lawyer, Clive Steirn, was replaced with a leading barrister at the New South Wales criminal bar, Winston Terracini, SC, a shortish, bearded, barrel-chested man who bore more than a passing resemblance in looks and personality to his beloved British bulldogs – Bedford and his successor, Shackleton.

The son of a motor mechanic, Terracini was renowned not only for his brilliance in court, but also for his theatrical skills. Appropriately nicknamed 'the Terror' (or 'Terra'), Terracini was a defence assassin. The Terror's ferocious cross-examinations were virtuoso performances.

With Terracini now on his legal team there was much anticipation surrounding Medich's bail application. Bail apps, as they are known, produce more details about the matter at hand as the Crown has to convince a judge why the accused should remain behind bars, while the defence team pulls apart those claims.

It was 14 December 2010, and Justice Derek Price had been assigned to hear the bail application of the alleged mastermind in one of the state's most sensational murder cases. The courtroom was so packed that the court officer asked the media if they would mind sitting in the seats usually reserved for the jury. Roy Medich, his steel-grey hair brushed back, found a seat with his nephew Peter.

Terracini did not disappoint. 'They can't even tell you who shot the deceased,' he boomed. He was similarly scathing of a witness for the prosecution, Haissam Safetli. 'He's not sure what happened because he was drinking bourbon and under the influence of, or affected by, cannabis,' he scoffed.[1]

Just to emphasise the ludicrousness of the Crown's position in relation to the identity of the actual murderer, Terracini muttered melodramatically. 'Two alleged hitmen sitting in the same car who can't work out who has shot who.' This was not a strong case against his client: it relied on the testimony of others who had a 'very, very strong vested interest to implicate others to gain a reduction for themselves'.

On the video link, Ron Medich was seen coming through the door wearing a short-sleeve shirt, tracksuit pants and sandshoes, all in the same shade of prison green. The matter was adjourned briefly while the judge looked at material that had been handed up to him. When he came back to the bench, Medich was slumped on his chair, his pot belly protruding.

Terracini continued. Gattellari, the barrister said, had a 'dubious reputation' and connections to 'ne'er-do-wells'. As I sat in the court taking notes, the obvious question seemed to be, if Gattellari was a person of such ill-repute, why had Terracini's client been such a good friend and business partner with him over a long period of time?

Terracini didn't spare McGurk either: 'He was hardly an upstanding, decent citizen,' he said, making the point that plenty of people had a motive to kill him.

In opposing bail, Mark Hobart, SC, said that the case against Medich was strong and reiterated that the prospect of facing life imprisonment was a powerful incentive for him to flee the country. 'These are extremely wealthy people,' said Hobart, who added that the offer of $1 million surety for bail from Roy might sound like a lot of money, but it wasn't for the likes of the Medichs.[2]

Hobart once more expressed concern about Medich's ability to threaten witnesses. He said one of 'the most sinister aspects of this case' was that after organising the murder of her husband, Medich had paid the same group of people to threaten Kimberley McGurk.

But Medich did not have to spend Christmas behind bars. Bail was granted by Justice Price three days later. The judge thought it would be unfair for Medich to be in segregation, especially as his trial wasn't due to start until 2012. As it turned out, Ron had another eight years of freedom.

The judge formed the view that the case against the accused was not strong. Despite police having 22,000 telephone intercepts and 5400 hours of listening device surveillance, 'there is no recorded conversation that refers to the applicant [Medich],' the judge observed.[3] 'On the present state of the evidence [Medich] has in my opinion a reasonable prospect of a jury not being satisfied beyond reasonable doubt that he committed the offences with which he has been charged.'

Justice Price also noted the pragmatic observation of Terracini, who had said that if Medich was as 'well connected and powerful' as the Crown claimed, 'he could interfere with witnesses indirectly whilst in custody'.

Just how important Gattellari was going to be to the Crown was acknowledged by the prosecutor, who said the case against

Medich relied largely on Gattellari's evidence. 'I conclude that the Crown case is not strong but it is not so weak that it could be said it will inevitably fail,' Justice Price said. It was up to a jury to assess 'the honesty and reliability of Gattellari and the other co-accused', he said.

One matter to which the judge gave short shrift was Medich's submission that he needed to be out on bail in order to have regular contact with his stockbroker and up-to-the-minute information regarding the sharemarket.

Justice Price ordered Medich wear an electronic bracelet, stay within the confines of Sydney's CBD and the eastern suburbs, submit to a nightly curfew and report to police daily.

After his $1 million bail was secured, Medich had to wait for his electronic tracking device to be fitted around his ankle. Outside the court Terracini said his client was 'very happy' and continued to maintain that he was 'absolutely not guilty of anything'. Medich finally walked out of jail at 3.35 pm wearing his uniform of all-black. A sleek silver Jaguar whisked him away from the horrors of incarceration. It was 20 December 2010, and the 62-year-old was once again a free man.

Upon his release, however, it wasn't to Odetta at his harbour-side mansion that Ron Medich retreated. The couple's marriage had been in dire straits before the murder, but after the death of Michael McGurk it had gone into a death spiral and Odetta had commenced divorce proceedings.

In August 2010, just as he was paying for Kimberley McGurk to be threatened, Medich had rushed down to his local police station at Rose Bay in an agitated state, complaining that his own wife's aggressive behaviour was making him fearful for his personal safety. He was granted an interim Apprehended Domestic Violence Order until the matter could be heard in court.

On 2 September the matter was listed for hearing at Waverley Court, the very same place Medich had attended 18 months before when he had offered $100,000 in bail for McGurk to be let out of jail. It was also one day short of a year since he had dispatched his nemesis. So much water had passed under the bridge in the past year, most of it putrid. The murder of his tormentor had brought nothing but misery for Ron Medich. A shitstorm of unfavourable publicity had rained down on him. First, the existence of the tape had hit the headlines, then, before he knew it, he was being interrogated at Parliament House, having to explain there was nothing corrupt about his and Roy's planned development at Badgerys Creek. Sure, they were big donors to the Labor Party, but that was allowable in a democratic society. Roy was so pissed off with him he had demanded a separate time to appear and wouldn't even sit near Ron as they waited to give evidence.

Then there was the annoyance of the ICAC inquiry into the tape. But most irritating of all was that Kimberley McGurk had not paid him back his money. And only last week Bob Ell and Vereker had told him to lay off harassing her.

I listened as an aggrieved Medich complained bitterly to the police officer assigned the Apprehended Violence cases at Waverley Court. Everything was the fault of his ungrateful wife. He had given Odetta whatever she wanted and yet she treated him like shit. He whined that he was tired of her manner, always harassing and aggressive. Maybe this action would make her think twice, he told the police officer. The officer directed him towards the courtroom where his matter would be heard.

He had put on a lot of weight since McGurk had died. He hadn't bothered to wear a suit to the court; he was attired in his customary black regalia. He sat quietly in the front row of the court, his hands clasped between his knees, leaning forward listening to himself being referred to as the PINOP. In legal parlance this is an acronym for the Person in Need of Protection. Oh, the irony, I thought to myself as I looked over at Medich. Within weeks this PINOP would be arrested for murder.

Police phone taps indicated that the relationship between Odetta and Ron was absolutely horrendous; that their domestic situation was intolerable. Odetta, who was overseas a lot, shouted and screamed at Medich on the phone. Even the detectives listening were shocked at her array of swear words.

But there was a surprising twist. After speaking with Medich, the prosecutor informed the magistrate at Waverley that the PINOP wished to withdraw his application and that he currently did not, in fact, have any fears for his safety. There was no explanation offered for his change of heart. The magistrate told Medich that he was able to reapply for the order 'if any situation arises' in the future.[4]

Nodding, Medich left the courtroom, clutching his battered old Nokia phone in one hand, and walked off alone down Bronte Road.

After Odetta and Ron married in 1992, Odetta found herself struggling as the stepmother to four children who were only a couple of years younger than her. Her and Ron's first son was born in 1993; the second six years later.

Around this time Odetta completed a diploma in law. After graduating in the mid-1990s, she was employed by the same law firm her husband had used to fight the immigration department to keep Odetta in the country. She also worked briefly at the law firm Gadens before giving up her legal career in 2001.

One friend described the years when Odetta and Ron had lived in Denham Court as 'hell'. She was working in the city and the hour-long commute each way was killing her. 'She couldn't wait to get out,' said her friend.[5] She was frustrated with work, frustrated with life and sick of living next door to her in-laws, Roy and his wife, Trish, who had never warmed to the ambitious blonde. Friends claim that some of her husband's relatives talked about her behind her back as 'that mail order bride'.

Stifled by life in the western suburbs, Odetta was constantly in her husband's ear to move east, where there were people with whom they had so much more in common – that is, money, and pots of it. But her husband was perfectly happy with his lot in life. He had built his dream home in the area in which he grew up and he was comfortable there. Each day he and Roy worked together in their unpretentious office in Warwick Farm. It was a world he knew and loved.

After 12 years of marriage, Odetta finally got her way. Apart from the misstep of acquiring 42a Wolseley Road, which was offloaded without them ever living there, soon the Medichs were ensconced in the most expensive street in the country, in a four-storey modern monolith complete with minimalist furniture and a butler. It was a far cry from Denham Court, with its rolling hills and mock-Tudor McMansions.

Ron was a westie at heart and the uber-wealthy of the eastern suburbs interested him little. Odetta, on the other hand, turned her attention to improving her standing in the social set. She developed a passion for modern art, which provided her an entrée into the world of other wealthy collectors. On the walls of the Medichs' mansion was one of Australia's finest modern art collections, although not much of it was Australian. 'Odetta has an amazing eye,' said one friend. 'She had a unique collection of contemporary international work.'[6]

Ron had no interest in art, but Odetta was a member of the Art Gallery of New South Wales and a generous supporter of the Museum of Contemporary Art, where her name featured on a plaque in the foyer as a substantial donor. In 2009, before McGurk was murdered, she was appointed to a local committee for the Venice Biennale alongside other prominent members of the arts community including philanthropists Simon and Catriona Mordant, Morry and Anna Schwartz and Gene and Brian Sherman.

'Her prominence in the art world was all money-based,' sniffed a fellow collector.[7] 'She was just vulgar,' this person said. 'She felt she could buy her way into anything.' The collector recalled a behind-the-scenes tour of the Art Gallery of New South Wales for a hand-picked group of patrons and donors. 'Odetta was incredibly rude and kept talking loudly during the tour. Finally an official came over and asked her to keep her voice down. Rather than looking mortified, Odetta took no notice,' said the collector.[8]

A prominent art adviser said that Odetta's brashness and her use of her wealth to buy her way into society was off-putting. 'She wanted to be a leading figure in the arts world, and she was determined to spend her way there.'[9]

Friends of Odetta painted a picture of a complex, troubled woman who appeared smart and bright, full of self-confidence one minute but the next totally unsure of herself. She could be brash and rude as well as warm and generous. One thing on which many agreed was that underneath the polished veneer, Odetta was probably the unhappiest person they knew.

She liked to shock. One friend recounted the story of a girls' weekend at a friend's house in the Southern Highlands. Odetta decided that their hostess had a shockingly down-market shoe collection and she insisted on tossing every pair in the open fire. As the acrid smoke filled the room, a number of fellow guests thought it was hilarious, others were horrified. Back in Sydney, Odetta spent a couple of thousand dollars buying her shoeless friend an array of Manolo Blahniks, which she had couriered to the Southern Highlands.

'She was not a socialite, and had no interest in seeing herself in the social pages. She was actually quite down to earth and had something worthwhile to say for herself,' said one friend.[10]

Some spoke of how hard she had worked to get to where she was, while others described her as being a slave to money. At the time of McGurk's murder she was spending an estimated $25,000 per month on her lavish lifestyle.

For her fortieth birthday in March 2008 Odetta treated herself to breast implants. She'd already had work done on her lips. One friend who lunched with her after her birthday treat recalled the uniform swivel of men's heads as Odetta glided through a city restaurant, with her short dress, high heels, plunging neckline and her mane of blonde hair. Her profile picture on her Twitter handle said a lot: it was an image of her in the reflection of her oversized Chanel sunglasses.

She was swathed in designer black, sitting in the back seat of a limousine. Her make-up was flawless and in the pose she struck, her expressionless face, with her pouty lips, was tilted at a fetching angle.

The relationship between Ron and Odetta was troubled and volatile. They had little in common. She loved skiing, he hated it. He avoided the water, she loved swimming. He was keen on horse racing, she found it boring. The art of Australian painter Pro Hart was about as modern as Ron was comfortable with, while Odetta adored the work of acclaimed sculptor Anish Kapoor, modern German photography and cutting-edge contemporary Russians who mixed photographs, digital artworks, video and sculpture to create confronting art.

Her friends said that the two would yell and scream at each other, Odetta repeatedly reminding Ron that she had never intended to stay married to him for this long. For his part, Medich would splutter in fury at her ingratitude, claiming she would be nothing without him.

'What drives her is money and she watched Ron like a fiend,' said one of her friends, who added that Odetta could smell parasites a mile off and was always trying to wrench Ron away from his coterie of hangers-on who were keen to get their mitts on his rivers of gold.[11] 'Ron was a cliché of himself,' noted another in her circle. He lacked Odetta's intuition and perception and refused to see that 'the people he liked to have around were often bloodsuckers'.[12] Odetta was openly disdainful of her husband's friends. Her constant refrain to Ron in her Russian accent was, 'If you sleep with dogs, you're gonna get fleas.'[13]

One person had observed first-hand the hostility between husband and wife at a New Year's Eve party at 112 Wolseley Road a couple of years before McGurk's murder. Odetta was complaining loudly about the presence of Ron's 'bogan friends' as she jerked her head in the direction of Lucky Gattellari. She told a group of her guests that she just couldn't understand why Ron was hanging round with these people. They didn't care about him, they only cared about his money, she said. Fuelled by alcohol, the pair screamed at each other until Odetta took to Ron with an empty champagne bottle.

Whether it was the unwelcome publicity in the wake of McGurk's murder or her suspicion of her husband's involvement that finally put an end to the marriage is not clear. Perhaps it was a combination of both. Gattellari later told the court that part of Medich's motivation for ordering the murder was that he felt McGurk was making him 'a laughing stock in the eastern suburbs' and 'was ruining his marriage'.[14]

Odetta often complained that Sydney was not welcoming to foreigners; that she always felt like an outsider. She loved travel and took up jetsetting with enthusiasm. The months before McGurk's murder saw her extolling the virtues of Monte Carlo. That December she was in New York, but her plan to fly to Florida to attend North America's premier contemporary art show came to naught. 'I have missed Art Basel Miami this year!!!!!! I am sick,' she wrote on Twitter.

In January 2010 there was a ski trip to Aspen, the winter playground for the seriously rich. While Odetta was there she and Gattellari exchanged a series of ugly text messages. It was never clear what sparked the fight but she was convinced Ron had paid to have her followed, and rumours of compromising photos of Odetta on a gondola with two men in Venice became the subject of the heated messages. Gattellari would later claim that Medich only paid to have her followed in Australia, not abroad.

Odetta told Gattellari he was the 'worst human being' to ever cross her path. 'Please get the fuck out of our lives before I am back in Australia. I will make sure that your little Chinese prostitutes are out of this country or they better register themselves as sex workers for tax purposes.'

Gattellari responded: 'Thank you for your kind words I do think that living in the glass house you live in maybe you should watch the stones you throw I have some snap shots of overseas trips so how low do you want to drag this personally I don't give a fuck about you but I have the greatest regard for Ron and at present he knows nothing so if its a shit fight you wont you will find out just how disgusting I can get.'

Odetta replied: 'U r a moron!!!!! And a dumb one too ... get the fuck out of our lives!!!!!!!!!! I will make sure of it the moment I am back, u r a sick fuck!!!!!!!!'[15]

Gattellari said: 'Isnt that a bogan my dear Odetta you have picked the wrong moron to have a shit fight with because like you I grew up in the gutter only I got out of it unlike you.' He also texted: 'Just look over your shoulder now and then.'[16]

Odetta, whom Terracini later described as a woman of 'forceful linguistic skills', replied: 'Fuck off!!!'

'I don't think so my dear we will be joined at the hips,' Gattellari replied.

In March 2010 Odetta was back in New York, where her accent and attire melded with the hordes of nouveau-riche Russians feted as the art world's saviours amid the wreckage of the global financial crisis. In New York the name 'Medich' registered without the involuntary raise of an eyebrow. She no longer had to be on her guard as she enjoyed an exclusive art benefit and auction with the likes of playwright Edward Albee, contemporary artist Jeff Koons, and Mikhail Baryshnikov, the Russian ballet dancer who played Carrie Bradshaw's boyfriend in *Sex and the City*.

It was then off to Rome, followed by Tuscany, where she visited friends in their castle. In May she told friends she was looking forward to her trip to Moscow to attend a gallery opening. In July she tweeted: 'st tropez is so much better than miami!!!!! love love love st tropez!!!!!!'

By the end of July, Odetta needed a well-earned rest from her hectic international travels, spending some quality downtime checking on the refurbishments of her $5 million luxury apart-ment on the French Riviera, which were being overseen by Carl Pickering, an Australian-born, Rome-based designer. Her husband had never seen her bolthole, which she'd purchased under her maiden name, Odeta Chtouikite, in 2008 when her marriage was unravelling. Nestled between Nice and Monaco, the property was in Beaulieu-sur-Mer, a tiny seaside village which blazes with cerise bougainvilleas and heavily scented magnolia trees.

There was no small amount of self-interest in Gattellari's concern about how bad things were between Ron and Odetta as the police closed in. Just before his arrest he was recorded saying to Safetli, 'If the shit hits the fan, the other fucking bird will take charge of everything and we will all be fucked.'

Asked who he was talking about, Gattellari said, 'Ron's wife. She'll take everything, every fucking thing – he's already in divorce proceedings. She fucking gets involved in all of this shit and we are all fucked – all of us, right.'[17]

Upon her husband's arrest, however, Odetta declined to cooperate with the police, though she and Ron were by then at war. Even though the Medichs divorced in May 2013, they battled ferociously over their assets until November 2018, when the Family Court stamped the matter as finalised. By that time Odetta had left Australia permanently to take up residence in her glamorous apartment, which had featured in the high-status *World of Interiors* magazine under the title 'Riddle of the Riviera'.

In the weeks after Safetli, Gattellari and Kaminic were arrested, one after the other they capitulated and each agreed to give evidence against Medich in return for reductions in the lengthy sentences they were facing.

The jacarandas were in full bloom when Kaminic left Silverwater jail on 18 November 2010, having been granted bail the previous day. He was wearing the same clothes he'd worn when, five weeks earlier, he was arrested and charged with being an accessory after the fact to murder. With his grey-flecked beard, long hair and receding hairline, he looked a lot older than 42.

What wasn't known at the time was that negotiations were underway for the attorney-general to offer Kaminic an indemnity against the more serious charge of being accessory before the fact, which attracts a potential life sentence, in return for him testifying against Medich. Magistrate Allan Moore didn't appear pleased to have Kaminic 'at large', as he put it, but there was little he could do as the Crown had not opposed the Bosnian's bail application.[18]

'Mr Kaminic, you have bail and may leave the area. Don't waste it,' was Moore's parting suggestion as Kaminic disappeared from the screen.

After the matter finished I went to the registry at the Local Court in Liverpool Street to apply for the lengthy statement of facts that had been handed to the magistrate by the Crown. It indicated that Senad Kaminic was the driver and personal assistant to former boxer Lucky Gattellari. Kaminic was the person who had introduced his friend Haissam Safetli to Gattellari.

I was fascinated to read that Kaminic had received a $15,000 commission 'for arranging Safetli's involvement' in the job to threaten Kimberley McGurk. The statement of facts also stated that as the police net closed on the alleged conspirators Gattellari, Kaminic and Safetli, they were recorded discussing the possibility of murdering Christopher Estephan because they believed he could implicate them in the murder. I couldn't believe what I was reading.

But still there was no indication of who pulled the trigger on McGurk.

As I handwrote the statement – no photocopying is allowed in the registry – the magistrate came over to have a chat. Moore, a small man with a genial round face, gave the impression of world weariness. He remarked that the Crown hadn't wanted this statement to get into evidence, but 'too bad' he said, smiling as my hand cramped.

A couple of weeks later, on 9 December, Magistrate Moore was back on the bench, presiding over Gattellari's attempt to enter a guilty plea in relation to the charge of soliciting the murder of McGurk. For once, Medich sat quietly as the prosecution refused to accept Gattellari's plea. The reason given was that the police were yet to finalise their brief of evidence – they had 600 outstanding tasks still to be completed – and they couldn't accept a plea until all the loose ends were tied up. The police brief was already 5000 pages and growing, Magistrate Moore was told.

At the end of January 2011, Medich was back before the Central Local Court. He'd enjoyed Christmas a free man while his former pals endured the scant festive offerings of the prison system. Although his dapper dark suit with a white shirt and his mauve, patterned tie had replaced his penitentiary greens, he now had the ignominy of being referred to as 'the accused'. And as he squeezed onto the wooden bench at the back of the court, he found himself in the uncomfortable position of being surrounded by journalists who hadn't been able to nab a seat at the old cedar table. Sitting next to the father of six was his eldest son, Peter.

Father and son listened intently as the magistrate, Julie Huber, was told of the enormity of the work still to be completed by police. Nine officers were working full-time on the investigation into McGurk's murder. Although Safetli and Estephan had agreed to testify against Medich, neither man had admitted to firing the fatal shot. The pair, along with Gattellari, had been placed in top-secret special protection units in the jail system after agreeing to become Crown witnesses.

The wheels of justice turn slowly, especially in a case like this. Two and a half years after his client's arrest, Terracini expressed his frustration at the delays to Magistrate Beverley Schurr in the Downing Centre Local Criminal Court. 'We've been asking them to tell us who killed the deceased,' he said. 'I know that it's only a minor matter in a murder charge.'[19] It was June 2012 and the previous day the Crown had served another 650 pages of material.

Terracini said he wanted Mick Sheehy, the officer in charge of the investigation, to make himself available on 23 July to be cross-examined on when the completed police brief of evidence would be made available. 'We don't think it is too much to ask to let the accused know when it is going to be served,' Terracini told the court.

The Crown prosecutor replied that the brief was complete for the purpose of a committal hearing – the hearing that determines whether there is enough evidence for the accused to stand trial – and all that was happening now was the tying up of loose ends. Terracini asked whether the police thought that the matter of who actually pulled the trigger was a 'loose end'.[20]

At a mention in July 2012, Terracini raised the possibility that two unnamed journalists would have to stop reporting on the McGurk matter before it went to trial. 'In all probability one or both of them will have to give evidence,' Terracini told the court.[21] He was referring to Vanda Carson, who by this time was covering the case for the *Daily Telegraph*, and me.

Magistrate Schurr told Terracini she would have to obtain legal advice on the issue.

It was the first we'd heard of this.

CHAPTER 26

THE LAST MAN STANDING

Before Medich could face a committal hearing, the sentences of those giving evidence against him needed to be finalised. But Gattellari, Kaminic and Safetli couldn't be sentenced until every email, phone call, text message and piece of evidence relating to the conspirators had been nailed down by investigators, and one of the prosecutors had already warned that whichever magistrate heard the committal would need a week just to read the police brief of evidence.

While Gattellari and Safetli were behind bars, Medich was out on the town, footloose and fancy-free. On one occasion a reporter from the *Sunday Telegraph* spotted him leaving a city massage parlour not far from the luxury apartment he was renting, which looked down on the Gothic spires of St Andrew's Cathedral and the green patina of the aged copper roof of the nearby Queen Victoria Building. The display board in the parlour's foyer boasted of an hour-long $175 'erotic nude massage using oil and hot towel' which was guaranteed 'to relieve any tension'. When the reporter approached him, Medich's stress levels appeared not to have been relieved – he told the reporter to piss off.

By the time Gattellari's sentencing hearing took place in the New South Wales Supreme Court in February 2013, the former boxer had already been in jail for more than two years. The reputed standover man wept as he described again how 'horrific' being incarcerated was. He was still suffering from severe claustrophobia, as well as anxiety, arthritis, gout and haemorrhoids, having spent more than 200 days in Long Bay's punishment and segregation wing. 'Concrete and steel is all we see,' Gattellari said.[1]

He told the court his involvement in the death of McGurk was a terrible mistake he wished he could take back. 'What I did was wrong. What we did was wrong,' he said.

Justice Megan Latham asked him why he hadn't simply told Medich, to whom Gattellari said he felt indebted after years of business dealings, that he wouldn't be party to killing a man. He said Medich had paid him $140,000 a year for his help dealing with investments, and he stood to earn a hefty bonus if those investments were successful. But he denied that a financial reward was his motivation. 'Money can't buy that sort of help from me,' he said. 'It was misguided loyalty for someone who I regarded as a friend.' Medich was domineering and there was a lot of 'emotional attachment' to him, he explained. 'You can't buy that sort of friendship I had with Ron at that time.'

The former boxer also said he got caught up in Medich's obsession with having McGurk done away with. 'When we had McGurk followed . . . [Medich] would go out of his brain: "Why isn't this fucking guy gone? I want him fucking dead. He's ruining my life and my marriage."'

Gattellari, his voice quavering, said, 'I made the wrong decisions. I wish I didn't. I wouldn't be here answering these questions.'

Of his arrest, he said he'd felt an enormous weight lift from his shoulders. 'It was over.'

His brother Rocky told the court that the 'bubbles have all gone' from his sibling, while Bellanto said Gattellari had done everything he possibly could to make amends. 'This is a case of a good man with good values who momentarily lost his way out of misguided loyalty to a friend who was putting pressure and making demands on him.'[2]

But there were also signs that Gattellari's relationship with his police handlers was strained. The ex-boxer told the court that he had been given 'every assurance' by police that he would face the charge of solicit to murder rather than the more serious being an accessory before the fact of murder, which carried a potential life sentence. Yet the prosecutors insisted on the more serious offence. The court was told of the approximately 550 pages of statements Gattellari had provided to police; that the brief for the murder case was one of the biggest the New South Wales police force had seen for at least 11 years. 'Without doubt Mr Gattellari's evidence will be a substantial part of the evidence against Ron Medich,' Mick Sheehy said.[3]

Crown prosecutor John Pickering, SC, told the judge that Gattellari knew money had been paid to kill McGurk. 'There was not going to be any nice way for Mr McGurk to be murdered, whether it was done with a gun, a knife or a bashing . . . it was going to be a particularly violent and reprehensible attack.'[4]

Three months later, on 12 May 2013, Gattellari and his one-time assistant, Kaminic, sat side by side in the dock at the Supreme Court waiting to hear their fate, not exchanging a word or even acknowledging the other's presence.

If perpetually optimistic Gattellari was hoping he would be out of prison soon, he was mistaken. He was sentenced to a non-parole period of seven and a half years and a maximum sentence of ten years, making him eligible for parole in April 2018. Justice Latham said that although Gattellari had been of great assistance to police, his 'moral culpability is of a high order'. He had played a major role 'in a sustained effort to execute a man on the say-so of his employer'. 'Critical to the objective gravity of the offence is the offender's knowledge from the outset that McGurk was to be killed for money,' the judge said.[5]

Justice Latham went on to state that although Gattellari claimed to have gained no personal benefit from the murder, Medich had invested $16 million in various business enterprises of Gattellari. 'One compelling inference to be drawn . . . is that the offender acted at least in part in the belief that if he did not do Medich's bidding, he would be cut adrift from Medich's patronage,' she said.

Justice Latham gave Gattellari a 60 per cent discount on his sentence for past and future assistance in the matters, noting that his evidence had already prompted two corruption inquiries involving Medich.

Kaminic was sentenced to two and a half years. Justice Latham took into account that he would have to serve his time in protective custody and that he suffered from post-traumatic stress disorder after spending time in a prisoner-of-war camp during his military service in the Bosnian army when he was 20.

Safetli's guilty plea to the murder of McGurk and the intimidation of his widow was entered on 1 July. Safetli, who was in cells under the court, claimed he was unwell and did not want to appear in person, but Magistrate Jan Stevenson was having none of it. 'I want him here,' she said.[6]

His lawyer told the court that he had accepted full responsibility for his involvement and had agreed to give evidence against Medich and Estephan. Estephan? That's odd, I thought. The full import of what Safetli was doing soon hit me. Terracini had constantly baited the police and the prosecutors about their failure to identify the shooter. Four years had passed since the murder and, after all this time, here was Safetli sensationally offering up the kid as the cold-blooded killer.

Safetli's version was that upon seeing McGurk arrive home, Estephan had grabbed the modified rifle, got out of the utility and walked quickly over to the driver's side of the Mercedes. He'd shot McGurk behind his right ear, fatally wounding him. The tendered police statement of facts that accompanied Safetli's guilty plea said: 'The Crown cannot disprove the offender's assertion that Estephan was the shooter beyond reasonable doubt.' But nor could they prove it. They only had Safetli's word for it.

This was the first time I had set eyes on Safetli, a stocky, olive-skinned man whose short haircut gave his head a strange triangular shape. He sat staring ahead blankly as his solicitor said, 'This has been an extremely stressful time for him as well as his family.'[7]

Weeks later, when it came to his sentence hearing, Safetli's barrister, Murugan Thangaraj, SC, told the New South Wales Supreme Court that without Safetli's help police would have 'struggled to get to where they are'.[8] Thangaraj also spoke of his client's invaluable assistance in wearing a listening device for a month in September 2010, and recording conversations between Gattellari, Kaminic and himself in which the former boxer and Kaminic attempted to convince Safetli to 'take the rap' for all of them.

'The case against Mr Medich is now existing with the strength it does – or perhaps at all – with the domino effect of [Safetli] going to police,' Thangaraj said. Because of this, he suggested, his client should get a 60 per cent discount and 'a slightly lower sentence than Mr Gattellari'. The same Crown prosecutor as Gattellari had faced, John Pickering, agreed that Safetli had 'flushed out' Gattellari; but he also observed that Safetli was of limited use because of the few dealings he'd had with Medich. Of course, he could give 'significant evidence' against Estephan, Pickering said.[9]

Justice Megan Latham went through some of Safetli's personal history as he himself had recounted it to the court-appointed psychiatrist. Much of it was complete and utter tosh and it shocked me that Safetli's pathetic attempts at self-aggrandisement appeared to have gone unchallenged. He'd told the psychiatrist that he was born in Lebanon to wealthy parents, who had later brought the family to Australia. He said his father was a violent man who'd left them when he was 16. Haissam was educated at Punchbowl and Cabramatta high schools and studied electrical and mechanical engineering at university. I knew his university qualifications were a lie but surely so were his claims that he was a millionaire at 19 and had amassed a $50 million fortune by his mid-thirties.

There was no mention of Safetli's fight with the NAB, which had featured on the ABC's *7.30 Report* in September 2007.[10] On that occasion he and his then wife, Amanda, told the reporter that not only had they lost their own house but Safetli's mother had lost hers because the two women had given the bank personal guarantees to support Safetli's tyre business.

'I know in hindsight we should have checked these things, or I should have. My mother-in-law has limited English, limited reading. You walk into the bank, they give you a wad of documents, say a hundred pages, and the little tabs that say, "Sign here, sign here". And you do it,' Amanda Safetli said.[11]

'What both women claim they were never told was that they were, in fact, signing binding personal guarantees over the loans mistakenly made to Haissam Safetli's tyre business. Those guarantees would shortly afterwards see them each lose their homes,' the viewers were told.

'I had a husband who was a successful businessman who had a complete breakdown, who ended up in a mental health facility trying to take his own life,' said Amanda Safetli. Haissam added, 'I completely lost the plot. I lost my mind, I lost everything, I lost all feelings that I have left in this world.'[12]

It was interesting to hear that in November 2009, three months after the murder, Safetli was admitted to St John of God Hospital, the same private mental health clinic to which McGurk had previously been admitted. Safetli claimed to have been suffering from PTSD. This was his second admission, his first having been in 2005.

The court psychiatrist, who diagnosed him with post-traumatic stress and narcissistic personality disorders, was told by Safetli that suspicions he had that his wife was having affairs contributed to his 'downward spiral', which led to him abusing alcohol and cannabis.

The court heard that when it came to remorse, it was difficult to tell whether Safetli was remorseful for his actions or remorseful that he'd been caught. Had he made a calculated decision to help the police in order to obtain the best outcome for himself rather than because he felt genuine contrition?

'A deliberate killing for payment has always been regarded as potentially within the worst category of the offence of murder . . . In this case, the victim was shot in the presence of his nine-year-old son, outside his family home,' said Justice Latham.[13] She said the fact that the police could not prove who'd fired the fatal shot did not lessen Safetli's 'objective culpability for the murder'.

Safetli received a 60 per cent discount on his sentence for assisting police and an early guilty plea. According to the police statement of facts, detectives had installed a listening device in his home and heard him confessing to his family about his role in the murder and the intimidation. A search of his house found not only a will but letters to his children begging their forgiveness.

There were surprised looks exchanged as Safetli received a non-parole period of only six and a half years for the murder of McGurk and a further six months for the intimidation of Mrs McGurk. One of the homicide detectives observed drily that he would be 'working on this brief longer than Safetli will be in jail'.

He was right.

With the sentencings finally out of the way, the Crown could focus on the committal hearing of Medich and Estephan. The latter had admitted to being present with Safetli when McGurk was murdered but steadfastly refused to plead guilty to the murder.

Jan Stevenson, an experienced magistrate, was assigned the matter. She sat on the bench in courtroom 2, with an old-fashioned green office lamp illuminating the volumes and volumes of material in front of her. There was more behind her.

Before the hearing, Magistrate Stevenson had given Estephan a good talking-to. 'I am tired now and we haven't even started,' she sighed, resting her head on her hand.[14] Estephan, who appeared by video link from Goulburn Correctional Centre, looked like a young science nerd. He listened intently as the magistrate advised him 'in the bluntest terms I can' to consider his position. She warned him to take the advice of his legal team rather than listening to fellow inmates. 'People sitting in custody with you have not been successful in their defence. I just suggest to you, you are the one who serves the sentence.'

To Estephan's solicitor, Gordon Elliott, she said, 'Your client is the last man standing, and he's the youngest, and he is the one down the bottom of the ladder.' She advised that 'someone should have a deep and meaningful' with Estephan between now and his next appearance in court. 'At the end of the day, if he doesn't take some proper advice, he is going to be the biggest loser out of all of this and that is going to be tragic,' she said.

Elliott held firm. He told Magistrate Stevenson that his client would claim he did not know that Safetli was planning to murder McGurk on the night of 3 September 2009; that he merely thought they were carrying out further surveillance on McGurk. Elliott did not address the uncomfortable fact that a modified rifle had sat in a bag in the front of Safetli's ute between Safetli and Estephan.

Stevenson told Elliott that the 'chances of [Estephan] not being committed are amazingly slight' and that he would forgo the possibility of a 25 per cent discount on his sentence if he did not plead guilty to the murder before the end of the committal hearing.

Elliott had come to know Estephan's family through Estephan's uncle, Bakhos 'Bill' Jalalaty, who was currently in jail over a major drug conspiracy. The matter had received an enormous amount of publicity because Jalalaty's co-accused was Mark Standen, the assistant director of the New South Wales Crime Commission. Elliott, himself a former detective, had represented Standen, who'd received a sentence of 19 years non parole – triple that of Safetli's sentence.

On Monday, 5 August 2013, the much anticipated committal hearing in the Central Local Court began. As journalists queued to get a seat, Elliott quipped, 'As we used to say in the cops – another day, another collar.' Medich, dressed – unusually for him – in a navy suit and pink-and-blue-striped tie, appeared calm. Sitting next to him, wearing a pale-grey suit, a white shirt and shiny silvery-white tie and glasses, was Chris Estephan. His mother, Yolla, smiled and waved encouragingly at her son.

Before a single word of evidence could be heard, Terracini announced that his team would be seeking a suppression order on the testimony of half a dozen witnesses listed to give evidence before Gattellari and Kaminic, who were not expected to be called until halfway through the six-week case.

'In essence, we don't want publicity, and this case has generated an enormous amount of publicity – some of it factual, and other reporting has just been nonsense – but we don't want, as it were, reporting of these matters before the primary witness goes in the witness box,' he said.[15]

'Do I assume that you are seeking a suppression order so that the primary witnesses don't know what the other witnesses are saying?' asked Magistrate Stevenson.

'Exactly,' Terracini replied.

The no-nonsense magistrate indicated that she wasn't with Terracini on this. '*Prima facie*, I am against you in the interests of justice.' She told the court that one of the purposes of a committal hearing was to have the matter receive publicity so that other members of the public, who may have important information, could give it to 'the powers that be'.[16]

The journalists present were aghast at this development, and during a break in proceedings I suggested we brief a barrister to argue the importance of open justice. I sought permission to approach the bar table and told Magistrate Stevenson I was representing the media and that if there was such an application, we would like leave to get legal representation to challenge it.

When the court resumed the following day, the various media outlets had jointly engaged Tom Blackburn, SC, to represent us. He successfully argued that the principle of open justice was one of the most fundamental aspects of Australia's system of justice, and that the conduct of proceedings in public was an essential quality of an Australian court.

Terracini scoffed at this. The media, he said, were only about making money. 'The entire purpose is to publish, to broadcast, to increase their profits.' He wanted the suppression order for tactical reasons. He said there were 'connections' between certain events that his legal team had been able to make 'with a certain degree of meticulousness' and that he did not want Gattellari to know of these connections in advance.[17]

But the magistrate was on the side of open justice and finally, on 7 August, the committal hearing was underway.

Before the three crucial witnesses appeared, a cast of fascinating characters were called to the stand. The Crown's first witness was South American-born tradesman Daniel Costa, who claimed Gattellari had not only approached him to threaten Kimberley McGurk after her husband's death, but also took him to a mansion in Denham Court and suggested he rob it. The court heard that the house belonged to Roy Medich. Costa, who chewed gum as he gave his answers, said Gattellari suggested he make the robbery appear to be 'an insurance job'. Costa understood from Gattellari there was 'a problem between the Medich brothers'.[18] He said he had done neither of Gattellari's jobs.

Matthew Crockett was another witness. He told the court he had been paid thousands of dollars to act as Gattellari's enforcer. He'd gone overseas not long after Gattellari's arrest, but said he'd witnessed Peter Medich being told that unless a million dollars was paid into a specific account, Gattellari would implicate Ron Medich in some way in the murder of McGurk.

Crockett also told the hearing that in mid-2010 he was hired by Gattellari to travel to Canberra to threaten a man who owed money to Gattellari's business. 'Pay up or you will be taken care of,' was the threat he delivered.[19] When the Canberra man informed Gattellari that he intended to go to the police, Gattellari said he'd have the man kneecapped, Crockett claimed.

Another of his jobs had involved carrying out surveillance on Odetta. In her opening statement, Crown prosecutor Gina O'Rourke claimed that after McGurk's murder, Medich 'had Gattellari arrange surveillance upon his own wife', who was urging him to cut ties with Gattellari. Not that the thickset, monosyllabic Crockett got very far following Odetta. It appeared she was able to lose him in no time.

Gattellari gave evidence that the surveillance was arranged because 'Odetta was getting very troublesome to Ron.' He said, 'She was causing him all sorts of problems with companies, questions, accountants, and Ron wanted to find out if she was up to anything and wanted to know exactly what she was up to.'[20]

On one occasion Odetta was tipped off that Gattellari and her husband had taken some young Asian hookers to the Magic Millions horse sales on the Gold Coast. Medich angrily denied that this was the case but he packed off Gattellari and the two escorts. His furious friend was later heard on the phone taps complaining to Ron that he'd a shithouse day with the two young women tottering around in their short skirts and stilettos at Sea World.

Prior to his arrest Medich had been gearing up for an almighty divorce battle, and he had transferred shares to prevent Odetta from accessing his financial records. Gattellari said that some time after the murder a meeting was called at the office of Medich's tax lawyer, during which Medich 'wanted to alter situations with the companies so Odetta would no longer have access to the books'.[21] Gattellari said that all the shares and ownership of the companies were placed into one of his companies; Medich then took a fixed and floating charge over those companies, so he would have control of them.

On Monday 12 August, Crown prosecutor Gina O'Rourke called Fortunato 'Lucky' Gattellari. Gattellari was flanked by four armed guards, who delivered him to the witness box. He made no eye contact with Medich as he walked past him.

Gina O'Rourke, a slim woman with her dark hair cut in a stylish, short bob, was always immaculately attired and never wore shoes without a decently high heel. Although Tasmanian-born O'Rourke had been a Crown prosecutor in New South Wales since 2002, she was not well known among Sydney court reporters. While always polite to them, O'Rourke never seemed comfortable exchanging anything more than pleasantries. The police who worked with her thought she was brilliant. She was tough, efficient, smart and had a sense of humour. In 2015 O'Rourke was made a silk and three years later she was appointed a judge in the New South Wales District Court.

On that day in 2013, O'Rourke tendered Gattellari's five lengthy statements, as well as five volumes of telephone-intercept material.

'Mr Gattellari, on 31 July 2012, did you plead guilty to murder on the basis of accessory before the fact in the Central Local Court?' asked O'Rourke.

'I did,' Gattellari replied.[22]

'Were you then committed for sentence to the Supreme Court on 7 December 2012?'

Gattellari said he was and went on to agree he'd undertaken to give evidence against Christopher Estephan, Haissam Safetli and Ron Medich in relation to the murder of Michael McGurk on 3 September 2009 and the intimidation of Kimberley McGurk on 8 August 2010.

O'Rourke then reminded Gattellari that half his sentence discount was dependent on his assistance in giving evidence against Medich and others.

With that complete, she handed over Gattellari for cross-examination. Terracini stood, put a folder of notes on the lectern in front of him, flicked back his black gown, and turned to face Gattellari. Gattellari was smirking. It was as though he was taunting the Terror, saying, 'Bring it on.' The long-anticipated bout between the two professional brawlers was about to start. At stake was a man's freedom.

Within minutes Terracini was trying to assert his dominance. 'I think we better get a few things straight. We are not playing semantic games. You are a prisoner! You are here to give truthful evidence and, subject to her Honour's rulings, who doesn't allow unfairness. I ask them and you answer them, you got it?'[23]

'I understand,' replied Gattellari coolly, swinging his glasses in his hand.

'It is no good to be looking around trying to be a buffoon. Okay? This is—'

Before he could finish, Gattellari snapped, 'Getting down to name-calling ain't going to get you anywhere.'

Early on, Magistrate Stevenson was forced to intervene. 'Mr Gattellari and Mr Terracini – Mr Gattellari, in particular – it is going to be a long, tedious hearing if you try to have sport with Mr Terracini.'

Terracini quickly did his best to establish that Gattellari was a dangerous mobster who had once been known as 'Don Gattellari' and had stolen millions from his client, Ron Medich. Gattellari offered that whoever gave him that name had been watching too many *Godfather* movies.

Terracini also put it to Gattellari that he was falsely accusing Medich of wanting McGurk murdered when it was Gattellari who wanted McGurk out of the way. 'Because, over a period of time, [McGurk] became more influential and wanted Mr Medich to get rid of you. Correct?'

'You are telling the story. Carry on, you're doing a great job,' Gattellari replied mockingly.

Much time was spent going through the finances of Gattellari's group of electrical companies into which Medich had poured $16 million. From Medich's funds Gattellari had given his 24-year-old daughter a $100,000 loan for a house deposit; his brother Rocky had been 'loaned' $370,000. There were no documents setting out terms such as the length of the loans or repayment details. Of course, not a cent had been repaid.

'You are a thief, sir!' thundered Terracini.

'Coming from you, that's rich,' replied Gattellari, quick as a flash.

He was pushed as to whether he had been given any kind of authority – 'statement, fax, text, SMS' – to take the $100,000 out of a company account.

'I'm tired of this,' said Gattellari in frustration. 'Ninety per cent of everything I did for Mr Medich was illegal. We never kept any records of anything.'

Terracini goaded him about the $370,000 which his brother Rocky had received. Gattellari took great exception to Terracini's accusation that it was not a loan. Terracini had hit a nerve. 'You're going off the rails. You can leave my family's reputation out of this. You can concentrate on me but not my family,' he said heatedly.

'Don't threaten me!' Terracini shouted.

'"Threaten me"?' Gattellari said with feigned incredulity.

'Please, gentlemen,' admonished Magistrate Stevenson, 'back on track.'

When Terracini then offered Gattellari a break, he replied sarcastically, 'Not at all. Why would I want to miss any more of this?'

'So you didn't know the difference between the loan—'

Again Gattellari jumped in. 'I think let's get something straight. I was extremely under a lot of pressure at the Crime Commission. I was asked a million questions, I was afraid of being arrested for murder, there was all sorts of things, and if I made a mistake and say "We had a mortgage" and we didn't – so sue me.'

Terracini took Gattellari through his 'loans' book, remarking that people were tardy with their repayments. 'I am in jail, everyone's tardy,' said Gattellari.

Then it was on to Gattellari's other business interests.

'You were running a brothel, weren't you?' he was asked.

'Give me a break,' said Gattellari, rolling his eyes. 'If you are going to ask silly questions . . . I was never running a brothel.'

It seemed it was all a matter of semantics. Yes, Gattellari did have a silent interest in a Toongabbie establishment, but it was a massage parlour, not a brothel.

'In relation to the masseurs, did they have any qualification other than being in the nude?' queried Terracini, to stifled giggles in the courtroom.

Gattellari shot back: 'I never interviewed them so you tell me. Did you go there, did you?'

Ignoring him, Terracini pressed on, asking if the establishment 'involved predominantly Asian women who would apparently massage people without their clothes on?'

'That's what you say. I never saw them do that,' said Gattellari; he thought they were giving a massage.

Terracini then wanted to know about an alleged extortion attempt Gattellari had made on his client: the claim was that the ex-boxer had demanded $1 million not to implicate Medich.

'That is a load of absolute garbage,' said Gattellari heatedly. Leaning forward, he jabbed his finger on the table for emphasis. 'If I was going to extort Mr Medich for anything – honestly, one million dollars? The million dollars was mentioned to me by my solicitor, who said this case would cost me in excess of a million dollars to defend. He was the one who passed on the message to Loren to try and borrow a million dollars from Mr Medich to assist me. Considering Safetli and I put our lives on the line to satisfy his desires, we never believed for a moment he would say no. There was no extortion!'[24]

One of the more amusing exchanges between the two combatants concerned what exactly Gattellari did for work.

'I kept Mr Medich company,' he said.

Other than going out with Medich, what did he do?

'Very little,' he replied.

'Just wait. You used to go out with Mr Medich and, as it were, go to lunch, meetings, races. Anything else?'

'Brothels, massage parlours, the lot.'

Terracini, ignoring this jibe at his client's expense, pushed on. 'Anything other than that. Like work?'

'Depends what you classify as work. I classify being with Mr Medich day in day out as work.'

Telephone intercepts had confirmed much of this. Many of the two men's conversations were about whether they would have a massage before or after they had lunch. In one conversation Medich was adamant that the massage be after lunch as he didn't want to be covered in oil while he was eating.

As for the prominent silk's accusation that Gattellari was a standover man, Gattellari laughed. 'I couldn't stand over anyone. I'm only five foot six.'

At the end of the day my fellow journalists and I agreed the bout was about even. Certainly, the hoped-for knockout blow by the Medich team had not eventuated. But there was always tomorrow.

CHAPTER 27

ROUND TWO

Day one of Winston Terracini's stoush with Lucky Gattellari at Medich's committal hearing had garnered much publicity and there was a huge turn-out to courtroom 2 to see the second round. Terracini wanted to explore Gattellari's relationship with Kaminic, in particular what had caused a temporary rift between the two men.

Gattellari explained that 'Kaminic was under the impression that I kept some of the money Mr Medich gave me for the murder of Michael McGurk for myself.'[1]

'He apparently got annoyed?' asked the barrister.

'He certainly did,' Gattellari answered.

Gattellari claimed that over a period of time he'd handed Kaminic a total of $300,000 to give to Safetli for the hit.

'Obviously it goes without saying, no receipt?' Terracini inquired.

'Of course you don't ask for a receipt when paying for a murder,' Gattellari replied acerbically.

When he was asked how much Estephan was going to get, Gattellari said he didn't even know back then that Safetli had an accomplice, let alone his name. Later he was asked if he had ever spoken to anybody about having Estephan killed. Again he replied that he didn't know Estephan existed until the net was closing in and Safetli told Gattellari that he wanted to kill the kid. 'If you go to the recordings, you will find that in fact I saved Mr Estephan from Mr Safetli.'

He also denied asking Safetli to murder his former girlfriend, Krystal Weir. 'I asked Safetli to murder nobody,' retorted Gattellari. He seemed to have overlooked the fact that he was in jail for asking Safetli to murder McGurk.

Gattellari said that it was Safetli who had raised the possibility of killing Weir and Estephan. 'He was telling me he wanted to kill two people who knew about the murder, and that if he did that, he would not be in any trouble.' Gattellari said he'd told Safetli to get a grip of himself.

Terracini painstakingly took him through his initial statement to the Crime Commission before he was arrested, pointing out all the lies he had told. Finally Gattellari had had enough. 'I will answer your question this way: all answers given to the Crime Commission before I was arrested was in lieu of trying to keep myself, Senad Kaminic and Mr Medich out of the shit. We were all under investigation for McGurk's murder and I would have said anything at the time.'[2]

One of the answers he had given to the commision was 'I have asked nobody to kill nobody.'

To Terracini he said, 'Ask me a question in regards to the statement I made in the Crime Commission after I was arrested and then see which is the truth and which isn't. I can give you a blanket answer. All those questions you are picking there, the answer would be "Yes, I lied."'

Next, he was taken to a series of phone calls and text messages from when he was trying to recover money from 'that little cunt, Tim Alford'. Gattellari agreed that he wanted 'to put a bit of pressure on Mr Tim Alford' to pay his debts. Gattellari was adamant that it was Medich who had loaned Alford the money and he was merely collecting on his behalf. He said that Medich's instructions were to 'give that little bastard a slap in the face and get that money back for me'.

It was important that the defence show Gattellari to be a thug and quite capable of orchestrating violence all by himself. Gattellari said that Matthew Crockett and the other people he used for his standover work 'were always, always, under instructions no physical violence was to be used and no one ever did get touched, apart from Mr McGurk, unfortunately'.

He took great offence to Terracini quizzing him about his claustrophobia, which Lucky said had first arisen when he was about five. 'Claustrophobia doesn't happen every minute of every day – it comes and goes, unfortunately. Have you suffered from claustrophobia?' he asked Terracini.

'Sir, please don't ask me questions,' replied Terracini imperiously.

'Then don't quiz me on claustrophobia, because I suffer from it and I object to you making fun of it,' said Gattellari.

Terracini delivered a one–two blow with his next question. 'We have in our possession all of the material you presented to the Supreme Court, including your medical reports and also issues about your loving relationship with your wife, and whathave-you. How many times have you been to the Babylon massage lounge?'

Gattellari did not bite. 'Many times,' he answered.

Terracini was undeterred. 'How big are these little cubicles with these women in the nude?' he asked.

The claustrophobia was, retorted Gattellari crossly, all about knowing he could get out. 'I can be in a lift, as long as I know I'm going to get out. If I fear I can't get out of the space – that is when I am affected.'

Terracini, perhaps sensing he had struck a nerve, pushed on. 'In relation to apparently your loving faithful relationship with your wife as an outstanding family man, that couldn't possibly be the truth, could it?' he asked. He suggested to Gattellari he'd been a pimp. 'You used to take money from Asian girls and pass them on for sexual favours. That is the sort of grub you are – a pimp, living off the earnings of Asian women who may not even be able to speak English, and you traffic them,' Terracini's voice was raised. 'Some family man,' he muttered.

He continued. 'What was the truth about your personal life, Mr Gattellari? Do you want to listen to tapes where you are on lovey-dovey terms with your wife and the very next call you contact a whore?'

'You are very dramatic,' taunted Gattellari.

'Do you want to have the tapes played?' said Terracini, almost shouting.

'Mr Terracini, watch it,' rebuked the magistrate.

There were more questions about 'Asian ladies' and payments made by Gattellari. The former boxer retaliated by dropping Medich into his answers. The 'girls' were on the payroll of his and Medich's company, he said.

Asked how many girls were on the books, he answered, 'Six or eight, I think . . . Mr Medich had most of them – ask him.'

'Can you name one girl on a legitimate payroll other than getting cash payments for you working as a pimp?'

'As a matter of fact I can . . . The girl that Ron fancied most. Yeah, she was on a weekly wage from a company.' As an added dig at Medich, Gattellari claimed that Ron was paying for her education.

Attention was then turned to Gattellari's lack of business successes. He agreed he had no qualifications for anything and had been a previous bankrupt. Asked to name his successful business ventures, he declined.

Terracini suggested he'd been 'a hopeless failure' and 'a financial numbskull'. Under his breath, Gattellari muttered that the same could be said of Terracini's client. There was a wave of tittering through the public gallery. I looked across to Medich, who either hadn't heard or was pretending he hadn't.

Nor, the Terror suggested to Gattellari, were the 'loans' he had recorded in his diaries genuine. 'They weren't loans, were they? Were they? Were they?' bellowed Terracini.

'I don't think you were dramatic enough that time,' Gattellari taunted.

There was much laughter in the public gallery and among the media as Gattellari and Terracini went toe-to-toe, but at times it was too much for the Crown prosecutor. 'In relation to the cross-examination of Mr Gattellari, I know it may appear to be entertaining, but we are dealing with a murder committal and someone has been murdered; indeed, in front of their son,' said O'Rourke. 'I would ask Your Honour, with respect, if you could advise the public gallery and the media it is inappropriate to laugh during the course of cross-examination. It is quite inappropriate and offensive to the McGurk family involved.'

'I understand that,' replied Magistrate Stevenson soothingly. 'But at the same time, it has been a bit of sport. Counsel and Mr Gattellari have had some exchanges, and I can understand people laughing, because it is a spontaneous human reaction. I don't really think . . . that the fact a little boy saw his dad shot is ever . . . far from people's minds.'[3]

By day eight of the committal, Medich and Magistrate Stevenson had contracted chest infections. Gattellari's continuing cross-examination was delayed until the following Monday.

The prison van was almost an hour late on 19 August, when the third week's proceedings started. As he was brought up from the cells, Lucky had a good look at his former friend, deliberately staring at him for what seemed like a long time, as the guards walked him to the witness box. Medich stared straight ahead.

Terracini was soon back on Gattellari's retinue of Asian prostitutes, asking why he had made payments to 'people whose names are Candy, Mimi, Coco, Angela, Fiona, Chanel, Cindy, Yoko, Kandy, with a K'.[4]

'It is obvious you are running some kind of prostitution ring . . . you were a pimp.'

Gattellari fended him off. 'This is like being in a fifteen-round title defence,' he said.

Around mid-morning Gattellari dropped a bombshell. Asked what involvement Hais's brother Bassam Safetli had in the murder, Gattellari's response was completely unexpected: 'My belief was he had more to do with the murder of Michael McGurk than Safetli did, his brother.'

In Gattellari's statement to the Crime Commission on 19 October 2010, six days after his arrest, he said he'd asked Hais and Bass whether they would kill McGurk. 'There was no hesitation on Hais's and Bass's part, and it amazed me of their reaction, as if I had asked them to go and buy me a can of Coke or something. They did not ask for time to think about it or anything like that. They accepted on the spot. It didn't appear to me to be a problem for them to do this job.'

The brothers told him their fee for the murder would be $300,000.

Asked again by Terracini whether Bassam had played a role in the murder, Gattellari was unequivocal. 'I thought he was totally involved. I still do.' He suggested that Terracini should ask police why Bassam hadn't been charged over the McGurk killing.

Grilled about the money he gave Kaminic for the Safetli brothers, Gattellari was adamant that Medich had given him two sums of $250,000 on separate occasions. Some of it was for the murder, some for the electrical business. When Terracini said flippantly, 'Let's guess. There was nobody else present?' Gattellari replied angrily, 'When I'm handing that kind of money out to somebody for a murder, I make sure I have half a dozen witnesses with me. That makes a lot of sense!' [5]

It was difficult for Terracini to land blows about the kinds of people Gattellari mixed with. In relation to the Safetli brothers Terracini asked, 'What sort of people were you dealing with?'

'Well, you've dealt with a few, you tell me, I don't know,' hissed Gattellari.

'I'm a professional! You are a convict,' said Terracini. He persisted with this line of questioning. He wanted to know what it was about the Safetlis that made them potential assassins. Did Gattellari think a debt collector would, 'by some osmotic process', graduate to murder someone?

'My experience was very limited in that field so I didn't think I would put an ad in the *Herald*,' Gattellari retorted.

All he offered was that he'd formed the impression because of things Kaminic had told him about the brothers, but he did not elaborate.

Having sat through a torrid morning of questions, the court broke for lunch. After the break Gattellari joked with his guards that he would need to take his next Valium to get through the afternoon session.

He was asked about Roy Medich. Terracini said Roy had frequently described Gattellari as 'filth'. 'And he would have nothing to do with you, and he told his brother, who was far weaker in personality, he told his brother, "Never hang around with Gattellari," didn't he?'

Gattellari denied this, as well as Terracini's claim that Roy had called him 'a scoundrel' to his face.

Later, under re-examination by O'Rourke, Gattellari explained that over a lunch at Tuscany, 'Roy and Ron had some heated discussions' which left Medich 'quite irate and distressed'.[6]

He recalled Medich saying 'he'd like to teach that son of a bitch a lesson'. Gattellari claimed he and Ron had discussed getting someone to break into Roy's house at Denham Court, as he kept a lot of money at home. Gattellari insisted Ron didn't want his brother harmed in any way. 'He just wanted to put him in his place.'

Gattellari was in the witness box for five days. The Crown's star witness had been badly bruised by Terracini. But, importantly for the police and the Crown, he had not wilted under the sustained battering by the Terror.

The same could not be said for the person who followed.

Next up was Haissam Safetli. With his suit, rimless glasses and greying hair, Safetli, a tall, solidly built man, could have passed for the suburban white-collar worker he'd once been.

He agreed he had received a 60 per cent reduction on his sentence, having signed an undertaking 'in relation to fully and actively cooperating in criminal proceedings, including giving evidence in committal proceedings, trials, appeals and any retrial and attending conferences required by the office of the DPP against Christopher Chafic Estephan, Ron Edward Medich, Nizar Samman and Ahmad Samman and any other person charged.'[7] (In 2011 the Samman brothers were charged with conspiring with Safetli to murder McGurk. The following year the DPP dropped the charges.) It was then over to Estephan's barrister, Greg Farmer, SC.

Farmer, a calm and measured man, used to joke that he'd spent his entire professional life trying to live up to his mother's favourite challenge: 'Answer the question.' The well-liked barrister was appointed a judge of the New South Wales District Court in September 2015; he was on the bench for only eleven months when tragically he died unexpectedly.

At Estephan's committal hearing Farmer was being funded by Legal Aid, which had only provided enough money for him to appear for five days of the estimated month-long committal. Farmer compensated by reading each day's transcript so he could follow the matter. The person of most interest to him and to his client was Safetli.

Within minutes it was clear the Crown had a major problem. Safetli gave every indication of being a disaster in the witness box. After Farmer had taken him through the ludicrous circumstances of trying to confess to the police in a McDonald's and then kill himself with rat poison, the barrister went straight for an obvious weakness: Bass's involvement in the planning of the murder. 'You and Bassam had been asked together to do this job, weren't you?'[8]

'No,' replied Safetli, breaking into a strange giggling fit.

Asked why he was laughing, he replied, 'Because it's the truth.'

He continued to play down any involvement of his brother, while maximising Estephan's. His other tactic was to repeat, 'I don't recall.'

Asked how he knew he could trust Estephan to carry out 'a hit', Safetli replied, 'He told me he could do anything.'

Then there was Estephan's payment of $30,000. 'So you said to this nineteen-year-old man, knowing full well that the job was worth some $300,000 to you, that you would give him one-tenth of that amount to do the job?' Farmer asked Safetli.

'I didn't think of it that way,' replied Safetli. He denied that he'd planned the murder or shot McGurk. 'You wanted some nineteen-year-old hapless person who falls under your charms to be the fall guy?' said Farmer.

Safetli denied this too. According to Safetli, Estephan had done everything – sourced the murder weapon, hidden it in Safetli's shed without even telling him where it was, determined which car to take (Safetli's ute), stolen the numberplates for the ute, made sure the gun was in the car, pulled the trigger and driven the getaway car. Not only that but when they returned to Safetli's house, it was Estephan who'd instructed him to burn his clothes. The gallery was in stitches.

'You are making it up,' said Farmer.

'No, seriously, no,' said Safetli, accompanied by more laughter. The only person not laughing was O'Rourke, who sat stony-faced.

As Farmer was quizzing Safetli about his confession, a small, olive-skinned, well-built man in a blue t-shirt and jeans jumped to his feet in the public gallery. 'Yes, you did! You shot him, you piece of shit. You shot him in front of his son and you set up a nineteen-year-old boy for the murder.'[9]

There was mayhem in the court as officers rushed over, restrained the man and escorted him out of the court.

'Quite clearly that man is not to come back in here, whoever he is,' said Magistrate Stevenson. 'Anyone else who wants an outburst, I suggest you leave now, otherwise you will be going into the dock.'

Safetli muttered, 'That's his best friend.'

We didn't know it at the time but this bit player in an already crowded drama would later have a starring role. That was to be some years down the track; for now, however, Yolla Estephan, the mother of the baby-faced killer, was determined to find out who her son's champion was. Yolla, a plump, maternal woman who wore her dark hair in a ponytail or a loose bun, attended every day of the hearing, sometimes with her husband or other children. Chris was her oldest; she also had a son two years younger, and a daughter. He was such a good boy, never any trouble, she told me. She refused to believe he was anything other than innocent. He had been swept along by that dreadful man Safetli, and had only taken money to help her out. 'God bless him,' she said. The $30,000 wasn't going to 'touch the sides', as her family owed $2 million on their stockfeed/petbarn business, which they had since sold. Her husband hadn't worked since, she said. Every Sunday the entire family made the trip to Goulburn.

Yolla soon learnt that the interjector was a former cellmate of Estephan, and that Safetli had confessed to this man that he himself had pulled the trigger. Yolla latched on to the idea that the magistrate would be swayed by the man's outburst in support of her son.

The courtroom then heard that before supposedly enlisting his fellow dope-smoking 19-year-old mate to be the hitman, Safetli had handed over thousands of dollars to buy a gun from Mr F, a man who was well known in the Lebanese community for his underworld connections. Mr F, whose name was suppressed to protect his identity as a police informer, later gave the court the same story about the guns as he'd given Safetli: namely that he'd bought them, but a woman who was in the process of delivering them had tossed them out of the car window when a police car approached her.

'Give me break!' snorted Safetli, as Farmer ridiculed his other inept efforts to find a hitman. It wasn't, he said, as though 'I put an ad in the Trading Post.'

'It's not far from it, is it?' replied Farmer.[10]

When Farmer questioned Safetli about his academic qualifications, the wobbly wheels of his testimony fell off once and for all. His 'mechanical engineering' degree had, it turned out, entailed sitting a test at the Institute of Automotive Vehicles at Five Dock.

Farmer was incredulous. 'By mechanical engineering, do you mean motor mechanic?'

'Yes,' replied Safetli.

'You just did one test?'

Yes, replied Safetli.

'That was it, and you are qualified?'

'If I got all the test right, yes,' said Safetli.

Farmer asked him if he had any other qualifications. Not really, Safetli admitted.

'What do you mean by "not really"?'

'Driver's licence, motorbikes, stuff like that, forklifts.'

A short while later Farmer accused Safetli of 'being in love' with himself. Much to the amusement – and astonishment – of the journalists, Safetli replied with a straight face, 'I am quite good looking.'

The following day it only got worse. Farmer asked him, 'You've now twice taken an oath to tell the truth, is that right?'

'Yes,' replied Safetli.

'On the Bible?'

'Whatever he made me do, yes.'

'What religion are you?' Farmer asked.

'Muslim,' Safetli replied.[11]

Whatever credibility Haissam Safetli had remaining was shredded once the Terror got hold of him. Early on, Terracini asked him how he expected anyone to believe he had made a million dollars by the time he turned 19.

'As long as I believe it, that's all that matters.'[12]

Then there was the $50 million in assets he told the psychiatrist about. Safetli admitted that was an error, the shrink must've misheard him. It was $15 million not $50 million. When asked where it had all gone, Safetli told the court the NAB had sold him up. 'They foreclosed on everything. They sold every property, kicked me out of the house and everything,' he said earnestly.

'Why? Why did it all happen?' asked Terracini.

'I don't know. I had some major issues as a young man and they all caught up to me all at once,' said Safetli.

He struggled to explain why his brother had sent a message from his own mobile phone to Gattellari after the murder to say 'The job's done.'

'Did you and your brother accept readily to go and murder Mr McGurk?' asked Terracini.

'I did, but not my brother,' Safetli said.

'The problem with you,' opined Terracini, 'is you are so low you are prepared to implicate a fellow you think is a chump, like Estephan. Why would you want to bump [McGurk]?' Terracini had been waving his arms wildly. I snuck a look at Estephan, to see his reaction to being called a chump. He remained impassive.

Safetli said it wasn't his idea.

Terracini asked again, 'Why did you?'

'I took the money,' said Safetli. 'I knew I couldn't say no to it.'

Terracini asked him why not. 'You seem to have been able to say no to Mr Farmer and myself?'

Safetli was firm: 'To be honest, to Lucky I couldn't say no to him.'

Terracini pilloried the thousands of dollars Safetli had wasted – such as the $15,000 he'd paid Mr F for two handguns. He asked him sarcastically if the guns had pearl handles.

As Terracini goaded him about filling the coffers of 'these incompetents or hopelessly depraved drug addicts', out of the blue Safetli said, 'I tried to kill myself.'

'Well, you apparently tried to kill yourself about twenty times; you haven't succeeded?'

'I'm really bad at it,' Safetli deadpanned. There was a ripple of uncertain laughter in the courtroom.

Then it was on to Krystal Weir, Safetli's girlfriend at the time of the murder. He told the court that he didn't love Weir at that time. Terracini drily remarked, 'Perhaps that won't be passed on to her. But you were fond of her?'

Safetli said no.

But he had sex with her outside McGurk's house?

'I had sex with twenty women in a week sometimes.'

Terracini shot back, 'Along with the fifteen million.'

Safetli's response was bizarre. 'There is a big difference between six foot and five foot,' he said.

He was grilled by Terracini about burning his clothes after the murder. Terracini suggested that the only reason to burn them was to get rid of gunshot residue. Safetli claimed he had burnt them because that's what people did in the movies.

Terracini also interrogated Safetli about burning up to $130,000 of the murder money. Safetli had told the police he'd done it to expiate his guilt and had badly burnt his fingers in the process. For some reason, he couldn't suppress a smile during the exchange. Terracini sought permission to approach the witness. With a flourish he produced a magnifying glass. 'Turn them over!' he said, demanding to see whether Safetli's hands were scarred.

After determining there were no scars, he accused Safetli of being a narcissist, a fantasist and a big-noter, who pumped himself up in an attempt 'to be far greater than the miserable wretch that you are'. He also noted that Safetli had felt so riddled with guilt he'd accepted a further $50,000 to threaten Kimberley McGurk.

Apart from firebombing a car for insurance purposes, doing a spot of standover work, giving a false statement to a bank to obtain a home loan, not paying his taxes, Safetli claimed he was an honest man.

'What?' said Terracini, glaring at him. 'You are a thief; you're a firebomber, associated with a murder; you're a tax fraudster; you deceive banks. Are you kidding – you're an honest man?'

'In a business sense, maybe not,' replied Safetli. He agreed that he had firebombed a Mercedes to help Lucky Gattellari make an insurance claim. He also said that Gattellari had asked him to torch a boat for Medich, but he hadn't done that.

Safetli was given such a lenient sentence because he'd promised to give evidence that linked Medich to the murder, but it became clear that the only real evidence he had was his brief lunchtime meeting with Medich a month or so before the murder, when Gattellari took him to Tuscany and introduced him to Medich as 'the new guy' and Safetli had promised he could have the job done in four weeks.

Safetli's account of what had happened on the night of the murder left those in the courtroom shaking their heads. 'When you get to the area near Mr McGurk's home, did you have any plan, as it were? Some layout of how you are going to go about gunning this man down?' asked Terracini.[13]

'No, none whatsoever,' replied Safetli.

'You just rock up to somebody you are going to murder, and you don't even have any discussion between the two of you how it is going to take place?' queried Terracini.

No, said Safetli.

He said he knew 'what Chris was going to do, what he had to do and that was it'.

He claimed that Estephan had pulled out the rifle and there it lay on the front seat between them. 'We just sat there . . . [for] a couple of hours, to be honest.'

It sounded ludicrous. Terracini asked again what plan they had and Safetli replied, 'I left it all up to Chris.' The Terror was barely able to contain his amazement. Safetli added that Estephan 'asked me to come, and I came'.

'It was just a complete shock to you that he gets out of the ute and then he goes and shoots someone?'

'No, I knew what he was going to do when we left the house,' replied Safetli. But in the hours during which they sat outside McGurk's house, Safetli was adamant that not a single word was discussed in relation to their plan of attack should McGurk arrive home. And when he did so, in the blink of an eye Estephan was across the road. 'It happened so quick – he was there and he was back in – I didn't see,' said Safetli.

Terracini accused him of trying to distance himself from what had happened because he and Gattellari had set up Estephan.

Safetli replied heatedly that Estephan was no angel.

'We are not interested in angels, we are interested in criminals like you,' said Terracini slowly and deliberately.

'And him,' squeaked Safetli, looking across at 23-year-old Estephan sitting quietly in the dock.[14]

CHAPTER 28

THE EVIDENCE STACKS UP

The wooden benches in the courtroom were uncomfortable. Whether it was a deliberate decision by the court officers, who knows, but there was no padding on the bench on which the accused had to sit. One morning Medich arrived and stared at the seat. I suggested he should grab a cushion from one of the benches at the back. 'No, I figure I might as well get used to the discomfort,' he told me. I wasn't sure if he was preparing himself for jail or was just being stoic – there were still weeks of the committal hearing to go.

Safetli finished his evidence just before lunch on Monday 26 August. During the break, which was taken before the arrival of the next witness, Senad Kaminic, one of the court staff took pity on Medich and offered him an office chair. However, his comfort was short-lived as another court officer soon reclaimed it and Medich was back sitting on the wooden bench.

Senad Kaminic was a very tall man. Unlike the other witnesses who were in jail but had chosen to wear suits to court, Kaminic, still sporting his ponytail, was decked out in the prison clobber of green tracksuit bottoms and a sloppy joe. A Bosnian interpreter was on hand should he need assistance.

He agreed that he had received an indemnity from the attorney-general on 5 July 2012 and that he had pleaded guilty to being an accessory before the fact to murder and the intimidation of Mrs McGurk. He had received a non-parole period of two and a half years after receiving a 50 per cent discount on his sentence for his past and future assistance. Kaminic had started cooperating with police on 19 November 2010, five weeks after his arrest and a month after Gattellari had agreed to roll over.

Kaminic told the court he'd arrived in Australia at the age of 27 and had started doing security work. He'd met Safetli when he came to stand over him about a $17,000 debt. He described being at Gattellari's house in Chipping Norton in March or April 2009 when the Safetli brothers arrived and agreed they would 'finish off' McGurk. Hais had pointed his finger in the shape of a gun, Kaminic recalled. He said he was surprised: 'As far as I know them, they didn't appear to be capable of doing that.' The next day they had texted Kaminic their price. It was 'fifty on the front and two hundred and fifty when job is finished', said Kaminic in his thick accent.[1]

At first Hais planned to use Krystal Weir to give McGurk a drug overdose, Kaminic recalled. In another conversation Safetli told him Mr F would put a bullet in McGurk's head, but that Safetli had to put a bullet in too, because Mr F didn't trust Safetli.

Kaminic was aware of Hais Safetli's many false starts in finding a hitman. He also claimed he'd had a conversation with Bass, who'd said, 'Senad, Hais doesn't know what he's doing – his brain is not working. I'm out of this. I suggest that you get out of it too and stop this.' But Kaminic had already given Hais the down-payment of $50,000 from Gattellari – it was too late.

Kaminic said that although he was merely the messenger between the Safetlis and Gattellari, he went along with the murder plan because, 'Well, if somebody would break my legs or put bullet in my head then I would lose my job.' It was a weird and wacky world, I thought to myself.

The courtroom heard that about a month before they were arrested, Safetli told Kaminic he was considering murdering

Krystal because she knew too much. Safetli had also indicated that he wanted Kaminic to do away with Estephan.

In his statement to police Kaminic said, 'Hais once asked me whether he should kill Krystal or have her followed. I told Hais that I didn't know what she knew, and that it was his problem to sort out. I remember Hais telling me once that he had found someone to follow Krystal. I think I may have said something like, "If you want to follow her, then follow her," but I never told him to do anything with her.'

'Did Haissam Safetli ever say to you, "The young guy Chris is going to talk and we have to kill him." Did he say that?' Terracini asked.

'That's correct,' replied Kaminic. Kaminic told him again that it wasn't his problem and he wasn't going to do it.

In front of both Kaminic and Gattellari, Safetli had asked for $100,000 to kill Estephan, claiming he 'is the guy who killed McGurk and he knows everything'. Gattellari told him to calm down.

In his broken English, Kaminic provided a perfect description of his excitable friend Lucky. 'When Lucky talked he always put the hands around, and to me he is not screaming or yelling – that is normal to me. What you call that, I don't know.'[2]

He said he'd received $10,000 from Hais Safetli as part of the $50,000 Gattellari had given Safetli for the intimidation of Mrs McGurk.

At the end of Kaminic's second day in the witness box most of the public gallery left as there was boring legal talk about submissions and applications and which witnesses were scheduled next, so there was only a handful of people in the court to hear Magistrate Stevenson foreshadow the death knell of the Crown's case against Estephan. 'It goes without saying,' she said quietly, 'I am concerned about Safetli's evidence.'[3]

Prosecutor O'Rourke explained that Safetli had pleaded guilty only recently and they hadn't been expecting to use him. 'But I understand what Your Honour is saying.'

'I have major concerns, major concerns,' said the magistrate gravely.

The following day, day 16 of the matter, Kaminic described the call he'd had from Bass Safetli about an hour after the murder to say that 'the tyres are done'. Kaminic said that at first he had no idea what Bass was talking about because he had forgotten the code. 'Did you do a wheel alignment?' he asked. Bass Safetli replied, 'Yeah we did the whole lot. The job is done? You know what I mean?' It was only when Bass said pointedly, 'You know what I mean?' that Kaminic clicked he meant McGurk had been murdered.[4]

Kaminic didn't finish his evidence – he had diarrhoea. He'd mentioned that he was not well at the beginning of the day and Terracini promised he wouldn't be much longer. 'But he lied,' Kaminic said matter of factly.

The following morning I said hello to Medich as he came in. He smiled at me and said, 'By the way, we didn't like your story this morning.'

'Oh well. You win some, you lose some,' I replied. Medich looked at me blankly and kept walking.

Kaminic, minus his ponytail, returned to the witness box ten days later. His evidence was dynamite.

The Crown prosecutor asked him, 'Did you ever have a conversation with Mr Hais Safetli where he stated to you he actually shot Mr McGurk himself?'[5]

'Yes,' Kaminic replied. He explained that the day after the murder, on Gattellari's instructions he'd gone to Safetli's house to drop off $20,000 for Hais. When he arrived he found Safetli on his verandah big-noting about the 'job'. Kaminic said Hais was in high spirits, laughing and joking about the murder in front of Bass, his nephew Adam, and Estephan. In his thick accent Kaminic said those gathered were 'very proud, laughing' about the execution of Michael McGurk.

Kaminic, horrified, pulled Safetli to one side, only to be told they all knew. Safetli was boasting about everything: 'Gloves and no evidence or nothing and, on my best memory, he says probably was a bit of rain in his glasses – he needs to keep them clean.'

There was much discussion between the journalists as to whether Kaminic had said there was 'rain' or 'brain'. It had been raining lightly on and off on the night of the murder and in his statement to police Safetli said rain had sprinkled on his glasses. During a break in proceedings we asked what the court transcribers had taken down. It was 'brain'.

The brain/rain issue was raised by Magistrate Stevenson after Kaminic had left the witness box. She said she had written rain, and Terracini thought that's what he had heard as well. But Stevenson also noted that Kaminic was recounting what Safetli had said and because he was such a fantasist it could well have been brain. In the end it was settled that the transcript would record 'rain'.

Kaminic was pressed as to what else Safetli had said. He replied that Safetli told him, 'When he [McGurk] come, get out from the car, I hit him.'

This was extraordinary information.

According to the Bosnian, Bass Safetli was also in a jocular mood that day. 'Everyone thinks it was a professional hit,' he'd said to Kaminic. 'Look at these professionals,' he said, gesturing to Estephan and Hais. 'The idiot burnt his clothes when he got home, and the money in his pockets too.'

'You haven't told anyone about this before?' asked O'Rourke.

'No, never ever. I still worried about this,' said Kaminic. 'I was in the middle of everyone, everyone knows I got nothing from that, just trouble,' he offered.

O'Rourke said police would now take a formal statement about Kaminic's conversations with the Safetlis. Kaminic had just torpedoed whatever shreds of credibility Haissam Safetli had left.

If Haissam Safetli was an appalling witness, his cousin, Ghassan Bassal, who was brought from Cessnock Correctional Centre to give evidence, was even worse.

Gus Bassal was the very last witness on day 25 of the committal. He had provided the police with two statements, one in

November 2010 and another a year later. In his statements he'd detailed introducing the Samman brothers to his cousin as possible hitmen for the McGurk job. He had also recounted a conversation with Estephan, in which he said the kid admitted to being the shooter.

But in the witness box Bassal suffered a catastrophic memory failure. 'I know nothink,' he said repeatedly. He now couldn't remember any of the contents of his statements 'because I was on heavy drugs back at the time'.[6]

But he wasn't on drugs now? asked O'Rourke.

No, he told her. Not while he was in jail for possession of ice and stolen goods and the like.

So why had he been able to recall all these things while on drugs but now, when he wasn't drug-affected, he couldn't remember anything?

'I would have to get my brain checked out and ask the doctor – I really don't know,' he said.

'So the only reason that you can tell us as to why you have given this detailed five-page statement, and two years later as you sit before us in court that you can't recount anything, is because back in those days you used drugs?' asked O'Rourke.

'Yeah, heavy drugs. I used to sleep maybe one hour a week, if I was lucky,' replied Bassal.

'But you were able to provide this information or this statement to the police back when you were having one hour of sleep?' asked O'Rourke.

'Maybe that's what came to me at the time,' Bassal said unhelpfully.

Asked if the only thing he could remember was his name, he agreed, before adding, 'And my birthday.'

'And he knows when he is going to get out,' said Magistrate Stevenson drolly.

'A man never forgets his date of release,' said Bassal quickly.

The magistrate was not impressed. 'It is an extremely accurate statement for someone well affected by drugs. It is amazingly accurate ... Have you had any legal advice before you came here today?'

When he replied he hadn't, she suggested that he should.

O'Rourke, clearly angry, suggested, 'And you don't want to be seen by the guys back at the jail as giving evidence for the Crown.'

Bassal was roused from his torpor. 'Who's going to see me back at the jail? No one fears me! I don't fear nobody but my God.'

'I'm sure he will be very proud of you,' snapped O'Rourke.

On Friday, 27 September 2013, Magistrate Stevenson handed down her decision in relation to Medich. Gattellari had withstood the onslaught. He was strenuously cross-examined yet 'maintained his position', she noted. In committing Medich to stand trial for the murder, the magistrate said she was struck by how 'grossly amateur' the murder was; that it lacked a 'scintilla of professionalism'.[7]

She said that although there was no direct evidence or any intercepted phone conversations linking Medich to the murder, she was satisfied by the evidence of the Crown's star witness, Fortunato 'Lucky' Gattellari. She said the evidence before her was that the pair had enjoyed a strong bond of friendship and, as another witness at the committal, Gattellari's accountant Kim Shipley, had observed, they were 'joined at the hip'.

Gattellari was Medich's right-hand man and he had benefited from Medich's financial largesse. But the magistrate was puzzled as to why a businessman of Medich's experience had no documentation of his affairs. Gattellari, she said, had organised the murder and the intimidation as a favour to his friend. She accepted his evidence of receiving up to $500,000 in cash from Medich to organise the murder and the later intimidation of Mrs McGurk.

The magistrate said she was not persuaded by the proposition put forward by Medich's legal team that Gattellari was off 'on a frolic of his own'.

After committing Medich to stand trial, the magistrate asked him if he wanted to say anything, warning him that anything he said may be used against him at his murder trial.

Medich, who was shaking, stood to read from a prepared statement. His blue tie appeared to have been tied so tightly that the wings of his shirt collar were squished upwards. He looked and sounded as though he was being strangled. 'I am not guilty of these offences. I have always said so and that's all along from the beginning.'[8] In his high-pitched voice he also said he wasn't a violent person and he had never authorised or encouraged anyone to harm McGurk.

'I wish very much that I had listened more carefully to the encouragement and guidance of my brother, Roy, and my ex-wife, Odetta, who warned me about Gattellari. I should have taken their advice and ceased to have anything to do with him,' he told the court.

The paper he was reading from was shuddering because of his profound agitation. He went on to say he had suffered a nervous breakdown and had made some stupid financial decisions but that Roy had always 'picked up the slack'.

'I have never really had many friends nor been particularly good with my relationships – whether that is a result of some scepticism in others because they appreciate my wealth more than myself . . . but I have been told I am not a particularly good judge of character,' he offered.

'I understand the public perception that is out there. Why on earth was someone like me hanging around someone like Gattellari? With hindsight I should've avoided him like the plague.'

He explained that Gattellari had appeared to be 'a close supporter of me and a friend of mine. I have since found out that none of that was true.'

He expressed anger at the suggestion that he'd wanted Roy's house robbed. Not only was that 'preposterous' but Gattellari had threatened his brother outside Tuscany, said Medich. He said he had always tried to recover his debts by legitimate means and that it was 'laughable' he would use disreputable debt collectors.

'I can't understand for the life of me how I trusted [Gattellari], but he is a very, very cunning person,' he said animatedly.

Medich stated that he now realised Gattellari's entire world was propped up by his money. 'I propose to take whatever action I can to recover the stolen monies despite Gattellari's criminal attempts to hide those monies.' It was Gattellari, not him, who had the motive to kill McGurk, said Medich.

He expressed sympathy for Kimberley and her family. 'What happened to Mr McGurk and his family is a terrible and unwarranted thing and, as I have family like everyone, I have great sympathy for the McGurk family and what has happened to them.'

He ended on a personal call to arms. 'One thing that I do know is without question I'm not guilty of these charges and I will be vindicated. I will be vindicated no matter how long it takes, of that I'm certain. Thank you very much for letting me speak.'

CHAPTER 29

NO BROTHERLY LOVE

Despite Medich's warm words about his brother in his closing statement at his committal, all was not well between the pair. Within weeks Roy had launched a legal action in the Supreme Court against Ron over their land holdings.

Roy wanted a trustee appointed to sell their properties at Badgerys Creek and Bringelly because his brother was bad for business. 'As a result of Ron's arrest, criminal charges and ICAC investigations, the other members of the Badgerys Creek consortium have indefinitely suspended the activities of the consortium' until his older brother was no longer part of it, he said in an affidavit filed in the court.[1] He also said his brother's notoriety meant it was impossible to get the necessary rezonings. Although the ICAC had found no wrongdoing in its inquiry into corruption allegations contained in the tape, Roy Medich said the adverse publicity 'has compromised my ability to deal with the department of planning'. He also said that he and Ron did not have 'the same judgement or method of doing business. We are unable to agree on many things and we cannot work together'.[2]

For his part, Ron wanted his land to be separated off rather than sold. Justice James Stevenson refused to grant Roy Medich's request for an expedited hearing. Four years later Roy dropped the proceedings as they were going nowhere and costing too much money.

However, once again the Medichs were to strike real estate gold. In 2017 I got a tip-off from a political contact. The brothers had secretly sold their Badgerys Creek holding for a rumoured half a billion dollars to a Chinese company.

Weeks after Medich was told he was to stand trial for the murder of Michael McGurk, Estephan learnt of his fate. In a sensational development, the 23-year-old had his murder charge dropped. 'I just do not find that I can commit the accused [for the murder of Mr McGurk],' said Magistrate Jan Stevenson.[3]

Estephan, in his light grey suit and white shirt, was asked to stand. Yolla had her hand pressed to her mouth as the magistrate announced she was charging Estephan with being an accessory after the fact of murder, in that he had aided and abetted Haissam Safetli in concealing the killing. Estephan was also charged with unlawfully possessing three firearms. In dismissing the murder charge, the magistrate said that she was unpersuaded by the evidence of Safetli, who she described as a 'dangerous Walter Mitty character' and a 'fantasist'.

On the court steps, Yolla said through her tears, 'All our prayers have been answered.'

The Crown could have pursued the murder charge by way of an ex-officio indictment, but didn't.

In April 2014 Christopher Chafic Estephan pleaded guilty to being an accessory after the fact to murder. At his sentencing hearing Corrective Services psychologist Bruce Tolloch gave evidence. Estephan, he said, was naïve and overly trusting at the time of the murder and felt 'used and tricked' by Safetli but had been 'struck by conscience' afterwards.[4]

Estephan felt 'an extreme level of guilt, regret and remorse,' the psychologist said. He had also told Tolloch, 'I deserve to be punished.' But he was insistent that he had no idea that when they went to Cremorne that September night Safetli was going to murder McGurk.

Crown prosecutor Sharon Harris wasn't having a bar of it. She said the murder was 'in cold blood' and that Estephan 'made a conscious and voluntary decision' to assist Safetli. He had stolen numberplates for the car, had helped destroy evidence and had accepted a $30,000 payment for his efforts. And what about the hours they sat there with a rifle between them?

The following month Justice Geoffrey Bellew sentenced Estephan to a maximum of six years and five months' jail with a minimum non-parole period of five years. Justice Bellew accepted Estephan's claim that he did not know the businessman was going to be murdered. However, he rejected the suggestion that his role was entirely spontaneous. 'The offender's subsequent concealment of the offence took place over a long period of time,' Bellew said. 'He had ample opportunity to consider what had happened and to reveal it. I'm satisfied that the offender was motivated to become involved by the prospect of financial gain.'[5]

The judge rejected Estephan's claim that he had acted under duress in the form of threats from Safetli before and after the crime. Nor did he give weight to Estephan's claim he was suffering from severe depression and anxiety. Bellew said there was little or no evidence for when these conditions had expressed themselves or why.

Estephan received a 20 per cent discount for pleading guilty to the offences and for his remorse. His chances of rehabilitation were 'reasonable', said the judge.

The kid remained impassive but his family was distressed and angry. Yolla burst into tears. They had expected him to be released immediately. Estephan subsequently appealed the severity of his sentence. He was unsuccessful.

Estephan was released from jail on 12 October 2015. It was five years since he had handed himself in to Kings Cross Police Station and been charged over the murder of McGurk. At the time of his release, Medich's criminal trial for the 2009 murder hadn't even started.

Having been demolished as a witness of credit by Magistrate Stevenson, Haissam Safetli could not be used in any subsequent court case. It must have been the subject of considerable conjecture for subsequent jurors as to why the man who was widely believed to have pulled the trigger was never called to give evidence when Medich went to trial. They were told not to speculate.

Privately, the police were furious. On the grounds that he wasn't the actual murderer, Safetli had received an astonishingly lenient sentence – six and a half years for assisting with the murder, and another six months for intimidation. He had completely screwed them over. They wanted his sentence increased because his discount was dependent on his promise to give evidence against Medich, Estephan and the Samman brothers. That promise was now in tatters. The Crown did lodge an appeal to increase the sentence but for some reason the appeal was dropped. No explanation was given as to why.

However, there was another avenue. The evidence given by Kaminic and Gattellari during Medich's committal clearly implicated Bass Safetli, whether in a conspiracy to murder or concealing the murder afterwards.

Bassam Safetli was eventually charged with being an accessory after the fact, which attracted a maximum penalty of 25 years' imprisonment. In March 2015 his committal hearing was heard. Gattellari and Kaminic were once again the key witnesses for the Crown.

Gattellari, whose hair was now flecked with grey, explained that Bass had worked for his electrical business doing deliveries. 'Bassam was the one with the brains in the family. Without him there would be no murder. He was one hundred per cent aware that Hais was going to commit the murder,' Gattellari said.[6] He also told the court that Bass had done surveillance on McGurk and had provided Gattellari with photographs of his efforts. When Gattellari informed the brothers in July 2009 that McGurk was skiing, Bass had asked for more money so that they could travel to the snowfields and kill him there.

In May 2010 Kaminic and Gattellari weren't talking and Hais was becoming increasingly unstable. Bass warned Gattellari, 'You guys better sort this shit out or we'll all end up in jail.' After that Bass started keeping his distance and stopped returning calls. 'I think he saw the writing on the wall,' Gattellari said.

'I like Bass, he's a nice guy; I'm sorry he's involved in all this mess,' he said.[7] Bass, who was wearing an open-neck pink shirt and sporting a large diamond stud in his left ear, responded by making wanking gestures with his right hand.

'Don't feel sorry for us, just tell the truth,' shouted his wife, who was clutching her husband's other arm.

'If I was involved, so was he. If I am guilty, so was he!' said Gattellari angrily.

Bassam Safetli was slighter than his brother but still imposing. I looked at the veins bulging on the side of his shaved head. He was twitching with fury. I thought any minute he would rush over to make a lunge at Gattellari in the witness box.

Gattellari left the courtroom that day with a swagger to his step. He raised his eyebrows and grimaced, not in an unfriendly way, as he passed detectives Fitzhenry and Sheehy. Bass and his wife glared furiously at Gattellari and the police. 'They know the truth and they are just sitting there!' hissed Bass, looking over at the police.

Kaminic, sporting a buzz cut and wearing gold-framed glasses, entered court in his customary prison tracksuit with Velcro runners. He said he had given $50,000 in cash to Bassam and Haissam for the contract killing but that it was 'up to them' to decide who was going to do it. 'To me they were the same, they came together,' said Kaminic.[8]

Bassam Safetli was committed for trial. Three years later, in April 2018, on the first day of his trial he pleaded guilty over his role in the murder. All that bluster at his committal had been a farce.

He was arraigned in the New South Wales District Court on two charges: concealing the conspiracy to murder and concealing the murder itself, in that he didn't warn police of the plot or its aftermath.

At his sentencing hearing in June 2018 he told the court he hadn't alerted the police 'because he's my older brother. Out of stupid loyalty, I guess. It's made me sick in the stomach ever since I found out about the murder. If I could take it back, I would.'[9]

District Court judge Robyn Tupman handed Safetli a nine-month suspended jail sentence and a twelve-month good behaviour bond. Bass wiped away tears as the judge read out a letter he had written to the court apologising. 'My inaction has cost an innocent man his life,' he had written. 'I still to this day wish I had spoken out. I'm ashamed in myself and struggled to deal with the fact I could have stopped it. I am truly sorry for my part in this tragedy.'[10]

His performance back at his committal hearing stuck in my mind. What a bunch of liars this lot were. But Judge Tupman said she accepted Bass's claim that he did not believe Hais was capable of going through with the murder when he first learnt of the plot in April 2009. 'I accept that he tried to talk him out of it [and said to his brother], "We don't do that sort of stuff, that's not the way we were raised,"' she said.[11]

She also described his offences as 'relatively minor' and 'stale' and said he committed his crimes out of 'stupid loyalty to his older brother'.

While Haissam Safetli was available to celebrate his brother's narrow escape from a custodial sentence, having been released from jail by then, it's not known if he did. The pair no longer speak.

CHAPTER 30

THE TRIAL OF RON MEDICH

A date was set for Medich's trial. He would face the music on 25 August 2014. In July Medich made an application to have his matter permanently stayed. His lawyers argued that the fact two police officers, one of whom was Mark Fitzhenry, the officer in charge, had listened to Medich's examination at the Crime Commission meant their continuing investigation into Medich was tainted.

The Crown argued that the investigation was not tainted at all and pointed, in particular, to the evidence that nothing said by Medich had been used for any investigative purpose. This argument, which was the subject of suppression orders, went all the way to the High Court. The High Court rejected Medich's request that his trial be abandoned forever. Two years later, a new date was given: 11 July 2016.

There were endless minor legal skirmishes along the way. One concerned my being called as a witness. The Crown argued that they wanted to call me to give evidence about the relationship between Medich and McGurk. In particular they wanted the jury to hear McGurk's statement to me: 'I don't think you understand what this guy is like and what he is capable of doing';

as well as the fact that McGurk had told me Medich planned to have him killed.

The Crown argued that those statements were admissible under section 66A of the Evidence Act 1995 as evidence of McGurk's 'contemporaneous feelings, intentions, knowledge and state of mind'.[1] Justice Bellew, a tall, lean man with regular features and an air of crisp efficiency, noted that in criminal proceedings the court had to weigh up whether the probative value of the evidence was outweighed by the danger of unfair prejudice to the defendant. He ruled that my account of what McGurk told me could not be used. 'In the present case, the state of mind of the deceased is not a fact in issue, nor is it relevant to a fact in issue. For these reasons, that part of Ms McClymont's evidence identified by the Crown will not be admitted.'

I had a strained relationship with Medich. I knew he blamed me for much of the predicament he now found himself in. We had a nodding association and when we found ourselves outside court we would exchange brief, if awkward, pleasantries. On one occasion there was only one vacant plastic chair outside the Darlinghurst courtroom, where his trial was due to be heard. I could see Medich weighing up whether he could possibly endure the prospect of sitting next to me. It was going to be a long wait so he took the seat. I asked him, 'How's it all going?'

He said not so good and that he'd just had a colonoscopy. 'They stuck a tube down here,' he said, pointing to his throat. I figured he must've meant an endoscopy but I didn't say anything. He was still fighting with Odetta over the property settlement, he went on. He didn't want to go into too much detail, but she was a piece of work. I asked him whether it was true that he had a new barrister. 'Yes,' he replied, 'I've now got Mr Rampage.' I was puzzled. Rampage? Who could he be referring to? It turned out he meant Malcolm Ramage, QC, who never did appear for him.

The reasons for his supposed change of legal team later became apparent. It was May 2016, only two months before his trial was finally due to start. Medich had asked the court for a four-month delay because he claimed he did not have the funds to pay the estimated $1.8 million for his defence. Terracini and his junior barrister had withdrawn from the case after Medich had missed a deadline to deposit money into a trust account to cover the trial.

Medich told Justice Bellew that despite selling his Point Piper waterfront mansion for $37 million in 2014, he had run out of money and had been forced to borrow from others. Crown prosecutor Gina O'Rourke, SC, who had subpoenaed his financial records, cross-examined Medich about his current spending habits, which included hundreds of dollars daily – just on lunch. O'Rourke told the court that Medich had had access to millions of dollars in the past few years yet claimed he had no income. When Justice Bellew asked how Medich was funding his lifestyle, O'Rourke replied, 'We don't know, Your Honour.'[2]

The court heard that Mr and Mrs Medich were worth $88 million but their assets had been frozen while their legal battle continued. In September 2014 the Family Court had authorised Ron to have $2.9 million for his legal expenses, but by October 2015 he had gone through the lot, frittering it away on fine dining, holidays, massage parlours, paying his son Peter $120,000 a year as his personal assistant, leasing a $160,000 BMW and paying one lawyer $180,000 to liaise with his other lawyers.

Grilled about his daily lunch bills, some of which came to almost $700, O'Rourke asked, 'Haven't you ever considered eating in, Mr Medich? Cooking a steak? Having a salad?'[3]

Medich replied indignantly that he was forced to eat out because he used to have a chef and, besides, he had never learnt to cook. The court heard that on the very day Medich had lodged the application to delay his trial because he had no money he'd spent $300 shouting five people lunch at Sydney's Athenian Restaurant. Documents showed he'd also spent in excess of $33,000 on a luxury holiday to Hayman Island with his Chinese girlfriend.

Medich blamed his financial situation on Odetta, who, he claimed, would not give him 'one red cent'.

To say that Justice Bellew was unimpressed was an understatement. He was adamant: Medich would stand trial on the date set.

On Monday, 11 July 2016, the long-awaited trial of Ron Medich finally kicked off. In courtroom 2 at the Supreme Court's Darlinghurst complex a jury of six women and nine men took either an oath or affirmation that each of them would 'give a true verdict according to the evidence'. The jury was also told that because legal issues had to be resolved in the matter, the trial would be commencing on 25 July.

But two weeks later when the jury returned they were promptly discharged. Justice Bellew was absolutely livid. Five minutes before the trial was due to start, the defence was notified that there was an ongoing police investigation that could have an impact on a principal issue of the trial. Bellew didn't reveal the details of what the police investigation concerned, but he was scathing about the failure of New South Wales police to disclose details of the matter.

'It was not until the morning of the very first day of the accused's trial, and indeed only minutes before the proceedings commenced . . . that the material was disclosed to the accused,' said the judge.[4]

He noted that although the detectives who had investigated Medich's case had not been involved in this second investigation, it was 'inconceivable' that those detectives 'would not have had some knowledge' of the material.

'The unfairness visited upon the accused as a consequence of the late disclosure of the material will be obvious. He cannot be forced to go to trial in these circumstances,' said Bellew, who said he had no alternative but to scrap the current proceedings. In discharging the jury, Justice Bellew expressed frustration that Michael McGurk had been murdered almost seven years before but his family would be denied closure 'for a further period of time'.

Lengthy trials are difficult to schedule. Calendars of both the legal teams and judges are set a long way in advance. Also, judges don't like matters being left incomplete over Christmas, when often jurors have planned holidays, so a three- or four-month trial must start by September, or October at the latest.

By the end of the year it became obvious why the trial had been delayed. On 22 December Lucky Gattellari was charged with two counts of conspiracy to defraud Ron Medich of up to $30 million. Court documents detailed that Gattellari had conspired with two others between January and December 2013.

Just before Christmas Gattellari, dressed in green shorts and a matching t-shirt, appeared via video link from a small room in Long Bay jail. The magistrate was Robert Williams, who had previously had several dealings with Medich at Waverley Court. Gattellari leant back on a black swivel chair and shook his head cockily when the magistrate asked if he was unrepresented. 'Yes, I am,' he said, adding peevishly, 'In keeping with this farce of an investigation, they only gave me twenty-four hours' notice that I was supposed to appear before you guys.'[5]

He was told that a brief of evidence would be served on 2 February 2017, and that his matter would be mentioned again on 17 February. Gattellari shook his head in disgust. 'This whole thing is a farce,' he said again.

If it was a farce for Gattellari, it was a nightmare for the prosecution. Their case against Medich relied almost entirely on Gattellari, and now their star witness was under a very dark cloud.

It was an absolute scorcher when Medich's trial did at last commence on Monday, 30 January 2017. At midday the temperature hit 35 degrees and in the old courtroom in King Street the air conditioner wasn't working. Detectives Sheehy, Fitzhenry and Howe, in their suits, had beads of sweat on their foreheads as they squashed together in the small bench in the front row, just behind the Crown prosecutor.

Justice Bellew told the barristers that it wasn't going to get any better. 'So I am afraid we'll have to—'

'Sweat it out,' interjected O'Rourke.

The judge gave them permission to remove their wigs, and the sheriff's officers rustled up some old pedestal fans for the 15-member jury.

The judge explained that the law allowed a jury of 15 to be empanelled to guard against illness or other contingencies that might affect a lengthy trial. But only 12 of them would give a verdict. A ballot would be conducted at the end of the trial to determine which of them would deliberate on the verdict. 'I don't want to make it sound like some episode of *I'm a Celebrity . . . Get Me Out of Here!* because obviously it's much more serious than that, but that's what happens,' said the judge.[6] The only person exempt from the ballot was the jury's foreperson.

The judge also warned the jury that if any juror was caught conducting his or her own research outside the court, they faced a potential two-year jail term. Bellew observed that the case had attracted a great deal of publicity and was bound to attract further media coverage. 'Your responsibility is to ignore it,' he said. He also pointed out that the Crown bore the onus of proving the guilt of the accused and that 'the accused does not have to prove anything'.

'You must realise that as the jury in this trial you, and you alone, are the judges of the fact.' They must decide what evidence to accept or reject. His role, said the judge, was to provide legal principles that the jury would apply in the course of determining the facts of the case.

He warned them they were to speak to no one but their fellow jurors about the case. And by no one he meant family and friends as well.

With that, Gina O'Rourke, SC, opened the Crown's case.

'Ladies and gentlemen, the accused's name is Ronald Edward Medich. He is charged and faces trial in relation to two charges, one being that he murdered Michael Loch McGurk on

3 September 2009, and that on 8 August 2010 he intimidated the wife of the deceased, Kimberley McGurk,' she said.[7]

The Crown case was that Medich had participated in a joint criminal enterprise with other co-offenders to murder McGurk and intimidate his widow. The jury heard that Medich and McGurk had once been close business partners but had fallen out over a number of soured business and property deals. We were informed that by early 2009 Medich had allegedly told Gattellari, 'I need to put an end to this.' He said he wanted McGurk dead and that Gattellari was to organise the hit, the Crown prosecutor alleged. The two were embroiled in a number of messy legal action suits, with each accusing the other of owing millions of dollars. McGurk was shot only days after a firebombing charge against him was dropped.

O'Rourke also told the court that as McGurk's star was falling with Medich, the property developer turned to a long-term friend and associate, Fortunato 'Lucky' Gattellari. The evidence would show that Medich and Gattellari were 'joined at the hip' and that Gattellari's major role in Medich's life was 'to keep him company', O'Rourke told the jury.

Central to the actual murder of McGurk and the intimidation of Mrs McGurk was Haissam Safetli, who had also pleaded guilty. When Mrs McGurk refused to pay the millions of dollars Medich was demanding, Gattellari once again turned to Safetli, the court heard. Safetli subcontracted the intimidation to an associate, not realising this person was a police informant.

O'Rourke told the jury that she expected the credibility of the Crown's chief witness, Lucky Gattellari, to be 'extensively challenged' by the defence, but that he had only met McGurk four times and had no financial dealings with him.[8]

The following day Winston Terracini, SC, who must have been paid and was once again representing Medich, outlined the defence. 'The accused's case will centre round the criticism of the reliability, the honesty and in some cases the deliberate attempt to mislead you by the witnesses Gattellari and Kaminic.'[9]

He alerted them to the charges Gattellari was facing of trying to defraud his client. Terracini said Gattellari had been trying to extort 'many, many millions of dollars' from Medich. This was the second time Gattellari had tried to get money from the property developer, he told the jury. The first occasion was shortly after the ex-boxer's arrest in October 2010. The money had never been paid, and Mr Medich had never tried to influence anyone giving evidence, Terracini said.

He also said that the court wouldn't be hearing from either of the Safetlis or Estephan.

The opening witness called was Senior Constable Rebecca Pope, the first police officer on the scene. She said McGurk was lying on his back with a pool of blood surrounding his head. His car keys were on the roof of the car, and hot chips were on the ground near him. There were a couple of mobile phones in the centre console. An ambulance arrived shortly afterwards and she helped put a sheet over the body. Because it had started to rain she also helped erect a tent to preserve the evidence.

The autopsy report was then read to the jury. It concluded that McGurk suffered lethal brain damage caused by a .22 calibre bullet.

Straight after the lunch break Kimberley Francis McGurk appeared. Since the murder of her husband seven and a half years earlier Kimberley McGurk had never given an interview or even had her photograph taken. She was wearing a plain white blouse over dark trousers, her long dark hair loose. She seemed nervous, but gave her evidence in a calm, matter-of-fact manner.

On the day of the murder her husband had called at about 5.30 pm and offered to pick up their son, who was playing at a friend's house. He called again at 6 to say he had collected him and did she want anything from the shops. She asked him if he could pick up some grocery items. It was the last conversation she had with him.

Half an hour later her son ran up the side path of the family home screaming, 'Mummy, Mummy, Dad's been hurt. There was a pop and there's blood.'[10] She rushed out to find her husband lying on the road, one foot resting on the framework of the car door. She told the jury she saw a hole in the back of her husband's head. She moved her husband onto the ground and did CPR until the ambulance arrived. It was obvious he was dead, she told the jury.

Before her husband's murder, she told the jury, she was a stay-at-home mum who had little idea of her husband's business affairs. After his death, however, she became aware of a number of legal actions that her husband was fighting with his former business partner, Ron Medich.

The jury heard that between 7 and 7.30 pm on 8 August 2010 Mrs McGurk saw a dark shadow outside her kitchen window. 'I have a visual memory of his legs. He had very big legs,' Mrs McGurk said, gesticulating widely with her hands. She testified that the intruder told her she should do the right thing and not be a thief like her husband and pay her debts. When she asked what debts he was talking about, the man had replied, 'You know what you need to do.' 'I felt sick. I was shaking. I was very frightened for myself and my family,' she told the jury.

The prosecutor asked her if anyone else was chasing her for money apart from the accused. There was no one else but Medich, she said.

Mrs McGurk was only in the witness box for 20 or so minutes. She smiled and leant over for a quick word with the detectives as she left the courtroom.

It was then on to Lucky Gattellari.

The wooden dock was on the left side of the courtroom, directly opposite the jury. The media and the police were crammed into hard wooden benches in the middle of the courtroom, directly behind the bar table. The witness box, which was elevated, was in between the judge and the jury. Underneath the courts were the cells in which prisoners were kept until they gave evidence. They would emerge through an entrance right by the dock where the accused sat.

Gattellari arrived in a smart suit, a white shirt and a yellow patterned tie. As he came up from the cells, accompanied by guards, he glared at Medich for what seemed like an eternity. The dirty looks from Gattellari persisted throughout the afternoon.

Gattellari was in the witness box for eleven days, seven of which were spent sparring with Terracini.

The jury was played endless recordings of intercepted conversations. Gattellari was yawning, and strumming his fingers on his chin and then drumming them on the table in front of him. I was mentioned in one of the phone taps. Gattellari rang Ron to say he had some interesting news. 'Your number one fan, Kate McClymont, is running around trying to get dirt on you and me.'

Ron was heard saying in his customary shrill tones, 'That's unbelievable! All she has ever done is write rubbish in the paper.'

Gattellari replied with a laugh that I was looking for dirt on him and had rung someone at his lighting company.

At the lunch adjournment Medich apologised for speaking about me that way. I laughed it off and from then on whenever I talked to him I reminded him that I was his 'number one fan'. But Medich was so socially awkward he never knew how to engage in light-hearted banter.

The defence case was that Gattellari was a despicable leech who had 'milked' Medich for years.

'You were very, very concerned that monies you had stolen from Mr Medich would be uncovered, weren't you?' said Terracini, slowly and deliberately. Terracini also accused Gattellari of paying for the murder off his own bat.[11]

'No, that's not correct,' replied Gattellari evenly.

As the defence went through Gattellari's nefarious past, Justice Bellew granted him a number of legal certificates preventing his answers from being used against him in other proceedings. The certificates were for firebombing cars, cannabis supply, firearms offences, threats of extreme violence, pimping, a plot to break into Roy Medich's home, threats to Odetta Medich and defrauding insurance companies.

Under cross-examination Terracini was also keen to exploit the fact that Gattellari had been criminally charged for trying to extort money from his client. The court heard that just before

Christmas 2013 Gattellari was moved from maximum security in Long Bay jail to Cooma jail, and that in Cooma he and another inmate, drug trafficker Shayne Hatfield, had conspired to extort money from Medich.

'I've been charged, not convicted – I never will be,' retorted Gattellari.[12]

'You're a habitual liar,' Terracini said, raising his voice.

'I am not,' Gattellari said.

'You don't hold yourself up as an honest man, do you?' Terracini asked.

'I'm as honest as the next man,' said Gattellari.

Terracini looked away and shook his head as though in despair.

'I'm very anxious that we do something about trapping Ron,' Gattellari had written in his diary. 'I want Medich to show how guilty he is. That will ease my mental stress I'm feeling thanks to this fucked system.'

Gattellari confirmed he'd got in contact with notorious former police officers Roger Rogerson and Glen McNamara through Shayne Hatfield. The court heard from Gattellari that the plan was to trick Medich into paying $30 million for his silence at trial, then to renege on the deal and testify anyway. 'Roger Rogerson was going to get an offer to the Medich camp that for a certain amount of money I could be got at to not give evidence,' Gattellari said.

'You did not get any approval to do any of these things by police,' snorted Terracini.

'I did,' protested Gattellari.

'You made it up to convince and manipulate others to act on your behalf, so they would think they had some kind of protection from the police,' Terracini said.

'Incorrect,' Gattellari said. 'The original amount we discussed was ten million dollars before the committal hearing and fifteen million after the committal.'[13]

Terracini alleged that Rogerson was not interested in a scheme in which Gattellari would fake his own murder in return for money from Medich, as he had 'a reputation to uphold'.

I was interested to see Justice Bellew's reaction to Gattellari's choice of go-betweens in the attempted extortion of Medich. In July the previous year, when the Medich trial was due to start, Bellew had just presided over the murder trial of Rogerson and McNamara. In September 2016 he gave them life sentences for ripping off a young drug dealer, Jamie Gao, and then shooting him dead. He said both were party to the murder which was 'extensive in its planning, brutal in its execution and callous in its aftermath'.[14]

'It is clear that the offenders acted with complete disregard for the life of another human being,' said Bellew then. And in the midst of this planning for a murder they were – allegedly – trying to extort a fortune from another – alleged – murderer. At the first mention of their names Bellew allowed himself a wry, fleeting smile, but that was it.

The Medich trial took an extraordinary turn when Gattellari's former cellmate Hatfield was called to give evidence. Hatfield, who was solidly built with short hair greying at his temples and resembled a deranged Tom Hanks, was also charged with conspiracy to defraud Medich.

Before beginning his evidence, Hatfield was given an instruction by the judge about his rights. Hatfield, in his shorts and green prison smock, leapt to his feet. With his right arm bent into the shape of a spout, his left placed on his hip to form a handle, he began to sing 'I'm a little teapot short and stout', with the accompanying gestures, concluding with 'tip me over, pour me out'.[15]

The jury was sent out and Hatfield was threatened with a contempt charge, to which he replied, 'Well, I'll have to appeal that contempt with the "Hokey Pokey", Your Honour, and I will be instructing my lawyers to do that.'

The jury was brought back in and on their return Hatfield was asked by Terracini about the alleged extortion plot.

Hatfield asked Terracini if he knew the 'Hokey Pokey'.

Justice Bellew instructed Hatfield to answer questions directly, yes or no; Hatfield then answered all the questions that followed with 'yes or no'.

Terracini persevered but eventually he asked to make an application to the judge in the absence of the witness and the jury, who were sent home.

Was Hatfield mentally ill, Terracini, Bellew and O'Rourke asked each other.

O'Rourke said, 'His conduct appeared to be deliberate, calculated and manipulative.' The judge agreed.

The following day Hatfield appeared to have had a change of heart. 'I'd like to apologise for my behaviour yesterday,' he said.[16] It was as though a new person had turned up.

He told the court that Gattellari had asked Medich for $15 million but it had risen to $30 million. Gattellari told Hatfield the money would be paid via untraceable 'blue chip shares' and that the extortion attempt was being done with the full knowledge of the police. Hatfield, having enlisted the help of Rogerson and McNamara to aid in the negotiations, was promised a cut of the multi-million-dollar payout.

Hatfield wasn't the only problematic witness.

On 22 February, O'Rourke was forced to stop an examination mid-sentence when her instructing solicitor rushed into court and thrust a note into her hand.

'Your Honour, I am loath to do this but something very urgent has just arrived and it is a matter that I need to raise in the absence of the jury,' O'Rourke announced.[17]

As soon as the jury was out O'Rourke told the court that the federal police were holding a plane on the tarmac at Adelaide Airport. On board was Paul Mathieson, a witness crucial to the Crown's case. The prosecutor said that Mathieson, who now lived in Las Vegas, 'has, since last week, refused to speak to the police and he has indicated he went into hiding'. He claimed he feared for his life should he be forced to return to Australia to give evidence, yet somehow he had slipped into the country via Darwin in mid-February and now he was trying to slip out again.

Time was of the essence, said O'Rourke.

'Do I have the power to prevent his departure from Australia?' asked the judge.

The prosecutor said he had the power to issue a warrant, but first they had to serve a subpoena on Mathieson. 'I'm not trying to rush you,' she said, but 'we understand it's ten thousand dollars a minute' to hold up the plane.

Justice Bellew hastily signed the order for Mathieson to be served with a subpoena before the plane took off. Disobeying the subpoena meant a warrant for his arrest could then be issued.

But it was too late. By the time the judge's orders were sent to the Adelaide police, the plane was in the sky heading for New Zealand.

The jury was called back in and it was then left to Justice Bellew to read out the evidence Mathieson had given via video link at Medich's committal hearing four years earlier. He told jurors not to concern themselves with the reasons for Mathieson's absence.

The three men – McGurk, Medich and Mathieson – had a long and complex business relationship, which foundered after Medich had lent millions of dollars to Amazing Loans, the court heard. Mathieson said Medich and McGurk subsequently extorted him in an attempt to take control of the business and 'McGurk was sent as a hired thug from Medich to threaten me'.[18]

'Ultimately, the real person I was scared of was Medich, not McGurk ... McGurk was just being sent by Medich,' he had previously told the committal hearing.[19] McGurk had been dispatched by Medich to Hawaii, where Mathieson was then living, to stand over him. But, as was his way, McGurk had tried to double cross his benefactor, the court heard.

Mathieson had also said that McGurk, in a phone call on 5 February 2009, outlined his plans to secretly tape Medich. Mathieson said that McGurk was meeting Medich the next day and the tape of their conversation would be used 'to bring him down'.

In May 2009, Mathieson met Medich in Auckland. That was the meeting during which the property developer said he was going to 'fix' McGurk and that 'he won't be a problem for much longer'.

Sensationally, Mathieson had told Medich's committal hearing back in 2013: 'On the last day I spoke to McGurk before he was murdered, he said he was going to expose Medich the next day.'[20]

Another witness was allowed to have his name suppressed because he also said he feared for his life. He was a friend of McGurk. He gave the police a statement two days after the murder:

> Some time early this year, 2009, I was at Michael's office one night about 6 or 7 pm and we were having a couple of beers. During a conversation Michael said that he was still getting threatened by this Lucky bloke. He handed me a piece of paper and told me to start writing Lucky's details on to the paper.[21]

The witness wrote down Lucky's details. McGurk, he said, corrected his spelling from 'Gillardi' to 'Gattellari'. Medich was the one directing Lucky, McGurk told him, and the more McGurk continued to have successes against Medich in their civil actions, the more the Scot perceived his safety was at risk.

'Michael said, "If anything ever happens to me, make sure that the police get these details." I took that piece [sic] paper home and stored it in a safe location,' the man told the police.

As well as witness-wrangling difficulties, there were also problems with jurors. Just as Gina O'Rourke was about to start her closing address, there was a major problem.

One jury member had been discharged after only four days – his boss had threatened him with the sack if he was away for too long. His note read: 'Dear Sir, I have few messages from my boss. He said he is getting legal advice me beeng [sic] here. I am woried [sic] that he might give me hard time when I go back to work.'

After consulting with the Crown and the defence, the witness was discharged, on the grounds that his anxiety about his employment might impair his ability to concentrate on the evidence. Given the fact that his boss may have committed a criminal offence by not allowing his employee to do his civic duty, the judge asked for a further investigation into the matter.

There was a second, more serious, problem with another male juror. Towards the end of the trial, a senior Crown prosecutor not connected to this case alerted Judge Bellew to the fact that she was friends with a female solicitor whose husband was on the Medich jury.

This prosecutor, when put in the witness box, told the judge that her friend the solicitor had passed on comments her juror husband had made about aspects of the trial. She said her friend's words were to the effect that the 'Crown prosecutor's cross-examination was even firier than that of Mr Terracini'. This was in defiance of the order given by Justice Bellew that no discussions about the case were to be had with anyone outside the jury room.

The middle-aged juror was hauled into closed court and questioned by the judge. 'Have you discussed with your partner any aspect of this trial?' asked Bellew.[22]

'No,' he answered. He also denied he had discussed or made any comments on the differing styles of cross-examination between O'Rourke and Terracini. In open court the judge said the juror had denied breaching any of Bellew's directions. 'I find those denials somewhat difficult to accept,' said Bellew, adding that he had 'grave misgivings' about whether the juror was being truthful in his answers. He ordered the man be discharged. The remaining 13 jurors were told they must not have any contact with the dismissed juror for the rest of the trial.

The following week there was more. Again the court was closed to the media and the public, this time to inform the judge that the whistleblowing prosecutor had received a text message from the dismissed juror saying that he had never liked her anyway, and that she had never been able to keep her mouth shut because 'a large black cock' was usually in it. Those who'd remained in the room said that Bellew nearly choked when he got to the last words. He was momentarily speechless. He announced he was referring the matter to the police.

On 17 March 2017 O'Rourke made her closing address to the jury. She stuck a yellow Post-it note on the lectern in front of her to remind her not to rush her words; several times during the trial both the judge and the court transcribers had asked her to slow down her rapid-fire delivery.

'Lucky Gattellari is never going to be awarded Australian of the Year,' she said. 'But who do you go to if you want to arrange a murder and an intimidation? If you are the accused, ladies and gentlemen, you go to Lucky Gattellari. That is exactly what [Medich] did.'[23]

Her address ran over three days. She said several witnesses had given evidence that Medich was consumed by anger over McGurk fighting him in court for millions of dollars, when at every turn Medich was losing. He had turned to his friend Lucky Gattellari to get rid of McGurk on his behalf. Gattellari and Medich were close and their relationship grew even tighter after the murder of McGurk, which Gattellari had confessed to orchestrating on Medich's behalf.

O'Rourke painted a picture of Medich as a man consumed by his hatred of McGurk; and who, after his death, transferred his hatred to Kimberley McGurk. The jury heard that Medich was the only one who had a motive to murder McGurk and then to intimidate Kimberley when she didn't settle her late husband's legal actions against Medich. The prosecutor told the jury that the 'accused was guilty beyond all reasonable doubt' of both the murder of McGurk and the intimidation of his wife.

The following day it was Terracini's turn. He turned in a vintage performance. He opened with a list of 'The Lies of Lucky'. He joked with the jury that although there were so many, his team had reduced them to a manageable number. The jury heard a blistering tirade of insults about the credibility and character of the Crown's star witness.

Gattellari, he said, was a vile, wicked, evil, manipulative, lying, scheming scum whose 'infected fingers' had been used to 'rip off' everyone he had come across.

'His tongue is dripping with lies,' said Terracini, lingering with relish over the word 'lies'.[24]

'You can say something until you are blue in the face, it doesn't make it true,' he said of Gattellari's repeated claims that Medich had ordered, and paid for, the execution.

Terracini noted sarcastically that the 'spiv Gattellari' and his sidekick, 'the thug Kaminic', were so 'noble' that they claimed to have received nothing for their roles in the murder. With his voice raised, he described as 'fantastical' Kaminic's evidence that Medich's final payment for the murder was by way of a cheque for $150,000.

The organiser and prime mover of the murder was Lucky Gattellari. Terracini suggested that the jury find Medich not guilty on both counts.

Finally, after a lengthy summing up by the judge, the eight-week long trial was at an end. A ballot was held to decide which jury members would consider the verdict. The person who missed out would have to leave immediately and play no further role in the trial. A well-dressed, middle-aged woman with a fondness for pearls was discharged. Nicknamed 'Mrs Mosman' by some of the regular court attendees, she had taken copious notes and had listened attentively during the course of the trial. Her fellow jurors whispered their farewells as she packed up her things and left. The remaining seven men and five women of the jury gathered their folders and notes and in single file left the court.

At 12.50 pm on Friday 24 March the jury retired to begin deliberations. Medich spent many of the subsequent days at a nearby coffee shop. Reporters set up an informal roster to ensure someone was at the court ready to alert everyone else if anything happened.

On 1 April there was a flurry of excitement. But it turned out to be a note from the jury wanting to know more about a 'joint criminal enterprise' and the meaning of 'the proof of intention'.

The judge explained that the Crown had said of the joint criminal enterprise that Medich, Gattellari, Kaminic, Safetli and Estephan all had the relevant intention to murder McGurk. But the jury must ask themselves, were they satisfied beyond reasonable doubt that Medich intended that McGurk be killed? By 'intention', said the judge, it was just the ordinary English meaning of the word.

On Friday 7 April the jury asked for the judge to clarify the meaning of the phrase 'reasonable doubt' and also enquired as to what would occur in the event that a unanimous verdict could not be reached.

Finally, on 10 April, after two weeks of deliberations, the foreman of the jury said that they had been unable to come to a verdict on either of the two charges. The judge told them to try again. He advised each person to listen carefully and objectively to the views of their fellow jurors. 'In a calm and constructive way they may convince you to change your opinion. Please continue your deliberations,' said Bellew.

The following day came another question from the jury about the telephone intercepts. The judge explained that the Crown had tendered them as evidence of the close relationship between Gattellari and the accused. He said they were entitled to use their common sense to draw their own inferences after listening to the calls.

On Thursday just before 4 pm we heard that the jury was coming back with a verdict. Journalists who'd been covering the trial raced to the court. Mrs McGurk arrived. Medich's son Peter and daughter Pamela came too.

Justice Bellew announced that he'd received a note from the jury to say they were unable to reach a unanimous verdict and that was 'unlikely to change'.

In their note the jury explained what their numbers were, but Bellew did not share that with the court. Instead, he asked the foreman to enter the witness box. The male foreman, who looked like a school teacher or an accountant, confirmed he did not think further deliberations would help. The jury must have been evenly divided because if the numbers had been close Bellew could have sent them away to see if they could arrive at a majority verdict of 11–1.

'In the light of the content of your most recent note, and in the light of the evidence that has been given to me, I have come to the view that I must discharge you,' Justice Bellew told them.[25]

'That may cause some of you to have a number of different emotions – I don't want you to leave the court thinking that you have failed in your duty or responsibility.

'It has been apparent to me that at all times you have approached your task with great care,' said the judge, thanking them for their efforts.

A sheriff's officer ushered the jury out of the old King Street courtroom with its ornate, soaring roof for the final time. As he closed the heavy oak door behind him, a chorus of shouts could be heard from the departing jurors. It was impossible to tell whether their voices were raised in anger or jubilation.

After eight weeks of evidence and three of deliberations, Medich was back to square one. His legal fees, an estimated $22,000 per day for Winston Terracini, two junior barristers and two solicitors, would have been around $1.2 million, and that didn't take into account the weeks of preparation. With a hung jury he would have to do it all over again.

Mrs McGurk was in quiet conversation with the detectives, who looked shell-shocked.

Medich sat stony-faced in the dock while his daughter Pamela wept.

CHAPTER 31

NO HAPPY ENDING

After his disappointment at not being acquitted, Medich was told that the court system was unable to accommodate a trial in 2017. His new trial would commence at the beginning of 2018.

Justice Bellew warned Medich that he needed 'to get his house in order' and that he would not tolerate another attempt by the defendant to have the trial delayed because of funding issues.

In a mad rush of optimism, only weeks before his second trial was due to start Medich splashed out on an opulent sub-penthouse in a boutique building in Milsons Point. The $4.91 million purchase meant he could now look across the harbour at the fabulous house he'd once owned in Point Piper.

One thing Medich did not spend money on was clothes. On the opening day of his second trial, 30 January 2018, he was back in court wearing his favourite mauve, patterned tie. Eight and a half years had passed since that tie had enjoyed its first public outing – at the 2009 parliamentary inquiry where he'd been asked if he'd had any involvement in the murder of Michael McGurk. I thought back to his shrill reply then: 'You've got to be joking.' It wasn't exactly a denial.

Noticeably absent was Gina O'Rourke who, at that very moment, was being sworn in as a judge of the New South Wales District Court. This time the Crown prosecutor was Sharon Harris, who had been the junior barrister in Medich's previous trial.

A jury of 11 men and one woman was sworn in. Justice Bellew denied Terracini's application for 15 jurors, anticipating the trial would be shorter this time around. He told the jurors that it was 'no secret' the accused had stood trial in 2017 but they should ignore the fact that the previous jury had been unable to reach a verdict.

In her opening address Harris said that 'it was likely' that Haissam Safetli had fired the fatal shot on 3 September 2009. She told the court that neither Safetli nor Estephan would be giving evidence but they had both acknowledged their roles in the murder and had been sentenced.

Harris told the jury that Gattellari barely knew McGurk and had 'no reason of his own' to kill him. However, Gattellari was a 'close friend and confidant' of Medich and had enjoyed his financial patronage over many years. Gattellari's colourful business ventures, in which Medich had invested millions of dollars, included a funeral business targeting the Aboriginal community. She detailed the $16 million that Medich had poured into Gattellari's electrical contracting businesses after the murder.

The decision to have only 12 jurors was tested when one was absent on the second day. A sheriff's officer was dispatched to find out what had happened – the young male juror wasn't answering his phone. It turned out he had slept in.

The trial was similar to the previous one, though this time Paul Mathieson was persuaded to give evidence by audio-visual link. Mathieson was asked by Terracini if he had stolen shares and money from Medich. When Bellew told Mathieson his answer was non-responsive, he shouted at the judge. It was then put to Mathieson that he blamed Medich for his loss of a large amount of money. Red-faced, he yelled that it was 'total lies'. He angrily accused the judge of allowing Terracini to misrepresent what had occurred with Medich. 'He's ruined my life for ten years, Mr Medich. He's had people try to kill me. I've had the FBI. I'm under armed guard and this guy just lies. He should be—'[1]

Bellew ordered that the audio-visual link be terminated immediately. He instructed the jury to ignore 'that last outburst by Mr Mathieson' and told them it must not form any part of their deliberations. They were asked to leave the court. Once they were gone Terracini applied for them to be discharged because of the serious prejudice caused to Medich when Mathieson claimed that the accused 'had people try to kill' him. The judge refused his application.

It was Medich's seventieth birthday on 11 April, the day the all-male jury retired to consider their verdict. A month earlier, the sheriff's officer was bringing in lunch for the jury when the only female member told him she thought someone had been trying to take a photo of her when she was on the train that morning.

Her note to the judge said:

About 8.50 on the 13th of March 2018 I was travelling via train from [redacted]. At this time I was speaking on my mobile phone to a friend in Greek. While this was happening, I observed a male person who I would describe as being of Caucasian appearance, tall, thin build, grey hair, short, and was wearing a blue business shirt. He was aged in his 50s.

I was sitting in the vestibule area of the train and the male person was standing directly in front of me. About this time the male was speaking on a mobile phone and I heard him say something like, 'She's Greek.' The male then said something about Central, but I did not hear the rest. After the male finished speaking on his phone, I observed him to grab his phone on the ends with both hands and raise it to chest height as if he was about to take a photograph. I'm not sure if he took a photo or not. I don't think he took a photo as there was no flash.

I raised both hands to cover my face and moved to another part of the train. As the train reached St James station, I left the train. As far as I am aware, the male stayed on the train. I have never seen this male person before. Despite this incident, I'm not fearful for my safety. My husband will take me to and pick me up from the train station. I'm also willing to wear different clothes in order to change my appearance.

I also travel with other jurors. I mentioned this incident to the other jurors and they said it was all probably my imagination. At lunchtime I noticed the Sheriff's officer bringing in the lunches and I then told him what had occurred. The Sheriff told me not to talk about this while he went to get his sergeant. A short time later two Sheriff officers returned and spoke to me about this matter.[2]

On the basis of the note, Terracini requested that the juror be discharged because, logically, the only person she might speculate as being responsible for the incident was Medich. He said the Crown's evidence was that Medich had recruited people to conduct surveillance on his wife. Both these things could prejudice his client's right to a fair trial.

Sharon Harris disagreed but the judge decided the juror might still 'harbour concerns'. The female juror was discharged.

Judge Bellew decided to continue with 11 jurors. 'This case,' he later noted, 'has a long and, it might be said, tortuous, history'.[3]

This time the jury's deliberations appeared much less fraught. On Monday 23 April, after five and a half days, the foreman indicated to the judge a verdict had been reached.

The jury filed back into the room. A hush had fallen over the courtroom and the police looked searchingly at the faces of the jurors. The judge's associate read out both indictments and on each occasion the foreman answered 'Guilty'. The associate then asked the rest of the jury if they agreed with their foreman. They did.

Medich showed no reaction, but when he was asked to stand and Justice Bellew formally convicted him of the murder of Michael McGurk and intimidating Mrs McGurk, Medich, his faced flushed with anger, gave a short, sharp shake of his head.

As he sat back down on the hard wooden bench where he'd been daily for the past few months, the newly convicted killer hunched forward slightly with his hands on his thighs. He looked dazed.

Before he was taken down to the cells beneath the building, Medich removed the trappings of his life as a free man – wallet, keys, iPhone – and handed them to Terracini. There was silence in the court. Justice Bellew thanked the jury for putting their lives on hold for three months and they filed out of the courtroom.

The three police officers, Sheehy, Fitzhenry and Howe, were jubilant. Outside, Kimberley McGurk, her face etched with sadness, said, 'Today is a great day for justice and the jury system in New South Wales.' She expressed their gratitude to the police and the prosecutors from the bottom of their hearts for their extraordinary support and their sheer determination in bringing Medich to justice.

'The damage to my family will never be repaired but the result today will allow my family to move forward.'

Later that afternoon, with his favourite purple tie having been removed, Medich, his hands cuffed before him, was taken away in the prison van to his new residence.

On 9 May 2018, before he'd even had his sentence hearing, Medich filed a notice of his intention to appeal. At the time of writing the appeal is yet to be heard.

At his sentence hearing at the end of May, Crown Prosecutor Harris said Medich had shown absolutely no remorse for ordering and financing the contract killing and intimidation, which were at the upper range of seriousness and showed wickedness, greed and callousness. Rather than engaging in 'calm reflection' in the months leading up to the death and calling off the killing, Medich had instead demanded to know why McGurk wasn't already gone, she said.[4]

Adding to the horror of the execution-style murder, observed Harris, was that it was witnessed by McGurk's nine-year-old child.

Medich sat frowning as the prosecutor claimed that there was 'nothing more callous' than killing a man for money. '[Medich] wanted to put an end to what he perceived as an embarrassment ... and he didn't care how [McGurk] was to be killed,' she said.

'The facts show an extremely serious offence of premeditated murder for financial reward. The Crown ultimately submits that the objective seriousness of the offence of murder is such that the culpability of the offender can only be met by a sentence of life imprisonment.'

Terracini stated that his client maintained his innocence. He insisted that Medich was of prior good character and, even if given a lenient sentence, would likely be aged in his nineties when he was released. 'We don't deny that this is a very, very serious matter,' he said. He also pointed out that Medich did not deserve a life sentence, especially when one considered the sentences handed to others involved in the murder. Harris had argued that because Medich had a financial motive and was the only person to benefit from the killing, his actions were worse than others involved, including his former right-hand man, Lucky Gattellari.

Justice Bellew said the effects of the murder on the McGurks were 'catastrophic' and he found the family's victim impact statements disturbing and saddening. He didn't release the statements but felt that the McGurk family had lost their formative years largely as a consequence of what happened.

He announced that Medich would be sentenced on 21 June 2018.

There was no one from Medich's family to witness his ultimate fall from grace. On the other side of the packed courtroom,

Kimberley McGurk sat with homicide detectives to hear the sentence. Medich looked pale and tired. His shoulders were slumped and he stared straight ahead as Justice Bellew spent more than an hour delivering the reasons for the sentence he was about to give. When the blow finally landed, Medich shook his head.

Bellew had all but given him a life sentence. In sentencing the 70-year-old to a maximum of 39 years and a minimum of 29 years, for both the 2009 murder of Michael McGurk and the subsequent intimidation of his widow, Justice Bellew said that Medich's actions in ordering and financing the murder constituted an 'abhorrent and heinous crime'.[5]

The earliest date Medich would be eligible for parole was 26 February 2048.

Justice Bellew said that Medich's actions warranted a life sentence but that wasn't available to him. 'Even accepting the criminality of the offender is substantially higher than that of either Gattellari or Safetli, there is,' he said, 'a significant gap between the sentences imposed on each of them.' Bellew went on to say he had to pay proper regard to the 'parity principle'.

He also said it was important to note that the Crown had not brought an appeal against the sentences imposed upon either Gattellari or Safetli on the grounds of 'manifest inadequacy'. It appeared he thought they should have been jailed for longer.

In the end Ron Medich's phenomenal wealth had destroyed him. It had allowed him to pursue whatever his heart desired – and that included the execution of a rival. But all the money in the world would not be able to help him where he was going. There would be no glorious harbour views, no chefs, no cigars, no cognac, no Chinese girls and no happy endings.

CHAPTER 32

THE PRICE OF FREEDOM

No one walking into the Downing Centre courts was taking a second glance at the artwork on show. Inside a glass display case, a remnant of the building's previous incarnation as a department store, the word LOVE was fashioned out of large sandstone letters in granular layers of caramel and cream. If ever there was a place in which LOVE was almost totally absent, the Drowning Centre had to be it.

Nine years had passed since I'd had coffee outside these courts with Michael McGurk just after his firebombing and arson charges were dropped. The coffee shop where many a plea deal had been hammered out was long gone. I couldn't help but wonder whether McGurk would still be alive if the DPP had pressed on with those charges. Maybe Medich would have put an end to his murderous plans if he'd thought McGurk had a one-way ticket to the big house.

It was late October 2018 and I was heading into the court for the extortion trial of Lucky Gattellari, who was by now 68 years old. His co-ees – prison parlance for co-accused – were Shayne Hatfield (who'd sung 'I'm a little teapot' at Medich's trial) and Miss L, a former close friend of Hatfield, whose name has been suppressed.

There is always a lengthy queue to get through the security gates before the customary 10 am court start, and on this morning the queue was being held up by a thin, scruffy man wearing thick tracksuit pants, though it was a sparkling spring day. He was objecting to the confiscation of his goon bag – a plastic bladder full of cheap vino, which he must have removed from its cardboard box. The sheriff's officer assured him he could collect it on his way out. But that was the point, complained the scruffy man, he wasn't expecting to come out.

Exactly what the jury was going to make of this murky tale of murderers behaving badly was anyone's guess. Gattellari, the organiser of a contract killing, was on trial for attempting to double-cross now-convicted murderer Ron Medich using the services of two other murderers (lifers) with the assistance of a convicted drug boss. The Crown's chief witness was an armed robber.

Miss L, a slim, blonde woman in her mid-fifties, arrived wearing a perky black-and-white sparkly skirt. There was no sign of the third accused, Hatfield, who had apparently spent the last five days in his cell at Silverwater clothed only in underpants. As his state of undress was being discussed by his Legal Aid lawyers, suddenly Hatfield appeared by audio-visual link. He looked dishevelled and there was a certain craziness in his eyes.

The following day the trial was once again delayed by a wardrobe malfunction. When District Court judge Penelope Hock came on to the bench, Crown Prosecutor Darren Robinson said apologetically that although Hatfield was in court, his suit wasn't. Even though the jury would soon find out from the evidence that Hatfield was in jail, his prison attire was deemed too prejudicial for the jury to see. Just before she left the bench, Judge Hock, a self-confessed spelling pedant, notified the assembled barristers and their legal teams that her pet hate was the use of 'pled' when it should be 'pleaded'.

The next day, 24 October, Hatfield's suit arrived and all three accused pleaded 'not guilty' to the extortion charges in front of the newly selected jury. Unlike America, in Australia nothing is known about potential jurors, who are identified only by an allocated number. Three challenges each are allowed by the defence and the prosecution and they are made purely on instinct and gut feeling. A defence barrister once told me that he automatically rejected anyone carrying a copy of the *Financial Review* as they were unlikely to be supportive of criminal types.

On this occasion, an elderly chap had to be prodded by the young man sitting next to him when his jury number was called. He was later the subject of a challenge by the Crown, as was a bald, gum-chewing man wearing a bright yellow fluoro shirt and blue shoes.

Once the jurors had been selected, the Crown prosecutor read through a list of people who would be mentioned during the course of the trial and the jurors were shown a photo of an undercover police officer known only as 'George'. The names were read out in case any of the witnesses or lawyers were known to a member of the jury. A couple of jurors looked curious when Roger Rogerson and Glen McNamara were mentioned. But no one raised any concerns.

The jurors were told it would be a five-week trial and that after a short break the Crown prosecutor would begin his opening address.

But within minutes there was a note from the jury to say that one of them thought they may have gone to school with one of the witnesses. Judge Hock, a 20-year veteran of the bench who liked to keep a tight rein on her court, was not happy. She curtly discharged the jury. At 2.30 pm the same pool of jurors from the morning was brought back into the court. Several who had been rejected the first time round were picked – and rejected – again. They were told by the judge not to take it personally.

This time five men and seven women were chosen, including one woman whose long hair was an iridescent purple at the crown and bright pink at the bottom, and a tiny young woman who looked barely out of school.

The following day the trial was once again delayed. A juror was running late, one of the barristers had left his brief behind. Meanwhile, the Corrective Services officers spent ages working out where the three accused would sit. In courtroom 6.1 there were two docks for the accused. They were large enough to encompass a horde of accused plus guards. But Miss L refused to sit with Hatfield, and Hatfield refused to sit with Gattellari. Finally, the officers settled on Miss L and Gattellari, who rarely acknowledged each other during the course of the trial, being placed together in the dock closest to the judge.

The two docks were recessed rooms with sliding glass panels at the front. To get a better view of proceedings, the accused often had to lean out of their respective booths, giving the impression that they were keeping an eye out for the approach of a bus that might spirit them away from all this unpleasantness.

On the afternoon of the third day, the case was finally underway. The prosecutor explained that Gattellari was facing two charges of trying to extort money from Medich. 'It is the Crown case,' announced Darren Robinson, 'that in 2013, Lucky Gattellari . . . and Robert McCarthy formed an agreement to approach Ron Medich via members of his family seeking payment of money through representations regarding the evidence Lucky Gattellari was to give in Ron Medich's prosecution.'[1] Gattellari was trying to extort money from Medich by offering to change his evidence.

Robinson outlined the second plot involving Gattellari: a $30 million to $50 million demand of Medich made by Rogerson and McNamara. Hatfield and Miss L had been charged over this, but not the two former detectives. Maybe the DPP felt there was no point since the pair were already serving life sentences.

The members of the jury listened attentively as Gattellari's seven-and-a-half-year sentence over the McGurk matter was explained. His sentence, said Robinson, could be increased if he failed to assist in the prosecution of Medich. The sentence had expired in April 2018, but because of his extortion charges, the parole board had refused his pleas to be released. Gattellari was devastated.

Five years earlier, he'd kept his emotions in check when he was sentenced, but when he got back to his small cell in the segregation unit at Long Bay jail, he'd wept bitterly. According to his then cellmate, Bobby McCarthy, Gattellari felt betrayed by the system. He said that he thought he could 'just make it' through four or five years 'but at seven and a half years . . . I'm gonna be fucked, so fuck it'.[2]

He was also furious that Hais Safetli, the person he believed had committed the murder, had received a lesser sentence. 'The cunt that fucking pulls the trigger gets fucking five,' Gattellari told his cellmate.[3] 'That's what I call Blind Justice,' he wrote in his diary.[4]

As the years ticked by, Gattellari's fury with both Medich and the justice system consumed him. He was behind bars because he had no money and therefore no options. Medich, on the other hand, was using his vast riches to keep himself in the free world and had spent only a couple of weeks in prison.

Gattellari thought of little else but revenge and retribution. What price Medich should pay for forsaking the one friend who had done more than most friends ever would – organise a murder. Gattellari, who paced up and down his cell so much he said he'd 'walked to China and back five times', brooded on ways he could expedite Medich's downfall, and perhaps enrich himself along the way.[5]

He complained to detectives Fitzhenry, Sheehy and Howe that despite all the things he had done to assist them – his evidence had resulted in two findings of corruption against Medich – the one thing he asked for in return was continually denied to him. 'Because, as a Crown witness, life in jail is an absolute nightmare,' Gattellari later explained to the jury. 'I wanted to be moved to a jail where, with my condition of a chronic claustrophobic, I would have had a little bit of relief without being locked up twenty-two hours a day.'[6] The former boxer was desperate to be moved to Dawn de Loas Correctional Centre within Silverwater jail. Because it's a minimum security prison and offers TAFE courses and outside work release, in the prison world it's referred to as 'Club Fed, Silverwater'.

As the crucial witness for the Crown in Medich's continually delayed murder trial, Gattellari had to remain in maximum security. The longer Medich remained free, the longer Gattellari had to stay there. And his prison term was more arduous than most because he had to serve it in Long Bay jail's Special Purpose Centre, a maximum security institution for inmates requiring special protection. Gattellari's protection was taken so seriously that when he gave evidence at the 2011 and 2012 ICAC hearings he was brought in each day in a bulletproof vest.

In May 2013, when Gattellari was sentenced, Medich was only a few months away from the committal hearing that would decide whether there was enough evidence for him to stand trial for McGurk's murder. Gattellari knew only too well that Medich's fate rested on his performance on the stand. Even though Gattellari was behind bars, at that moment he held the upper hand. There was a small window of opportunity to put the squeeze on Medich. How much was the price for freedom?

Because all mail and phone calls are monitored in jail, Gattellari decided that his best bet was to get a message delivered to Medich in person by his cellmate, who was shortly to be released.

There was something familiar about Robert Harley McCarthy, the Crown's star witness in Lucky's extortion trial. I watched the diminutive, muscular man in his mid-forties, his olive complexion lined, as he strode past the two rows of the jury towards the witness box. Suddenly it hit me. McCarthy was the man who had caused such a drama while Safetli was giving evidence at Medich's committal hearing in August 2013. He'd leapt to his feet, yelling that Safetli was a 'piece of shit' who had shot McGurk in front of his son and had then set up Estephan for the murder.

The jury was told straight away that Robert McCarthy had pleaded guilty to his role in trying to extort money from Medich on Gattellari's behalf. He'd received a suspended sentence in return for giving evidence against his former cellmate. As McCarthy gave that evidence now, Gattellari listened intently, tapping his fingers on the wooden frame of the dock.

McCarthy told the jury that Gattellari was 'doing it quite hard' when he arrived at Long Bay after his arrest in October 2010. Lucky, he said, was 'very upset and angry'. He felt he had been left 'holding the bag'.[7] He'd helped organise McGurk's murder for Medich, but when he was arrested, the Medich family had refused to assist with his legal fees.

McCarthy's task was to deliver a note to Ron Medich's harbourside mansion in Point Piper. McCarthy explained to the court that he thought this was a bad idea as Medich was on bail for the murder and was probably under surveillance. Instead, he decided to drop a note at Roy Medich's home, some 45 kilometres away in Denham Court. But Roy had long since joined the 'snob mob of blueberry hill', having paid $7 million for an apartment in the eastern suburbs, and for years he'd been trying to offload his old house. He only checked in there irregularly so there the note lay for some weeks.

McCarthy was released from jail on 27 May 2013 but it wasn't until 13 July that Roy finally received and read the note. He rang the number on it, but once he realised the note was connected to his brother, he gave McCarthy the number of his nephew, Peter.

Via a video link from Perth, where he now lived, Peter Medich told the jury that he'd arranged to meet 'Bobby' that same day in a café in Norton Street, Leichhardt. Bobby had given him a handwritten note to read. It said that the evidence against his father 'wasn't worth a cracker' without Gattellari's testimony, and that for $10 million Gattellari would 'throw his testimony' at Medich's trial. The note also said that Gattellari 'wasn't scared of Winston "Fat Boy" Terracini', his father's barrister.[8]

Terracini urged Peter to notify the Crime Commission. On 18 July, five days after Peter had met Bobby, an investigation into the alleged extortion attempt commenced. The Crime Commission soon discovered that they weren't the only ones interested in McCarthy. Although he hadn't been out of jail for long, McCarthy was suspected of an armed robbery, and from early July 2013 the Robbery and Serious Crime Squad had been monitoring his calls and had placed tracking and listening devices in his car.

Strike Force Smedley, overseen by the robbery squad, was established to investigate the extortion attempt. An undercover cop, known only as George, was given the job of pretending to be an emissary for Ron Medich.

The case against Gattellari relied heavily on phone intercepts – both calls he made from jail to his brother Frank, and calls between McCarthy and George. In one call McCarthy explained that the extortion plot had its genesis in the fortnight after Gattellari was sentenced. George asked if Gattellari was planning to suffer amnesia at Medich's trial. McCarthy said, 'He's got to lie. He's gonna lie and he's going to make mistakes' and then it would all unravel. However, he was adamant that Gattellari 'was never going to move from the truth of his evidence'. He intended to take the money from Medich but tell the truth anyway, McCarthy told the jury.[9]

Although McCarthy thought the $10 million demand was completely over the top, he discussed with George the price of freedom. 'Hand the fuckin' lot over if it means you are going to stay free,' he said.

The jury was taken to conversations that McCarthy had had on 29 August 2013. This was the day Haissam Safetli was giving evidence at the committal and when McCarthy had created a kerfuffle by shouting from the public gallery that Safetli had fired the fatal shot.

The jury heard a phone intercept of McCarthy talking to his sister about being thrown out of court. Estephan's mother was 'naïve and gullible' and she didn't want her son to plead guilty to anything, McCarthy told his sister. He'd wanted to say to Yolla that while the kid wasn't the murderer, her son was 'still guilty of a crime'. He told his sister that he'd decided to say nothing because '[Yolla] thinks the sun shines out of his arse'.[10]

The economics of the murder contract were all wrong, according to McCarthy. 'He plays a role in one of the biggest murders in New South Wales' history and thirty k – that's all he gets,' said McCarthy.[11]

He told George that Estephan was 'a nineteen-year-old boy who got roped into something . . . but he never fuckin' shot the man'. He also told George that Safetli, 'the man who pulled the trigger', had a big mouth. The police didn't know 'but we all did', said McCarthy. What they all knew was that Safetli was the one who had murdered Michael McGurk.[12]

As the prosecution played endless phone intercepts, McCarthy rested his head on his arms. His heavily tattooed forearms were visible as he'd rolled up the sleeves of his black shirt. He told the jury that he hated hearing it all again – he wanted to put it behind him. Gattellari had been his friend and now Bobby was in the witness box giving evidence against him, well knowing that his evidence could lead to even more jail time for Lucky.

'He was a broken man,' he heard himself tell George of Gattellari's reaction to his sentence. 'A few of us gathered around him and helped put him back together.'

About Medich, McCarthy said, 'He's an idiot . . . they can bury his arse, fuck him. He should've fucking stayed loyal and done the right thing. What a . . . foolish man. He'll never get to spend a dollar again.'[13]

The most poignant comments concerned the fracturing of Medich and Gattellari's friendship. The jury listened as McCarthy told George, 'There's never going to be any trust between the two of them again.' I looked over at Gattellari. His mouth was set in a rigid line, but he wasn't looking at his former friend, another in the long line of betrayals in their dog-eat-dog world.

Outside the courtroom, McCarthy told me he felt bad about giving evidence against Gattellari. He said he hoped Lucky would understand and forgive him. 'I couldn't do one more day in there,' he said, explaining that he was the fourth generation of criminals in his family. His life had been a cycle of crimes and drugs and he'd spent 22 years, half of his life, in jail for armed robberies. Now he had a partner and a steady job organising maintenance workers and he never wanted to go back inside. As McCarthy gave evidence I sat next to his girlfriend, who was googling recipes for cheese muffins on her phone.

The McCarthy plot stumbled along. For months George kept seeking a meeting with Frank Gattellari, who was supposedly handling the negotiations for his brother. George pretended that his boss, Medich, the 'head honcho', was seeking more guarantees from Gattellari about changing his evidence. During their calls Gattellari was referred to as 'the big coach' and Frank as 'the assistant coach'. The police needed more concrete evidence about Lucky's involvement. George was constantly badgering McCarthy to 'bring along the assistant coach'. McCarthy eventually relented and on 17 December 2013 he took Frank Gattellari to Leichhardt to meet George.

Frank realised immediately that George was a cop, and the extortion attempt was over. Instead of his promised $200,000 cut, McCarthy was later arrested.

Lucky Gattellari was scathing of McCarthy's role in the plot. He had only one job to do and he botched it, said Gattellari. The plan was doomed once McCarthy involved Roy, 'who hated my guts', Gattellari explained to the jury. He said he knew Ron Medich 'better than anyone on this earth', and if Ron had thought there was a chance of not facing trial 'he would've grabbed it'.[14]

In the witness box he angrily denied that he had given McCarthy, whom he described as a 'career criminal', any authority to negotiate with the Medich camp, and that the price of $10 million was one McCarthy had dreamt up.

On 23 December, six days after the first extortion plot came to a grinding halt, Gattellari was shipped out of Long Bay jail. He was overjoyed, assuming he was finally going to 'Dawn's'. For security reasons prisoners are never given advance notice of their new location and it wasn't until he was in the prison escort van that Gattellari discovered, to his horror, that he was heading south.[15]

Cooma is at the foothills of the Snowy Mountains and in winter it's bitterly cold. The Cooma Correctional Centre opened in 1873 as a jail, but within a few years it was repurposed as a lunatic asylum. The wind whips around the buildings, and inmates complain they're chilled to the bone as the cold penetrates the towering granite walls. In one recorded conversation in June 2014, Lucky complained to Frank that it 'was minus five fuckin' degrees'.

In mid-2014 one of my underworld contacts, who had only recently been released from a lengthy jail term, told me of a rumour that Gattellari 'was going to be knocked' in Cooma jail. He even named the person who'd been approached for the task. Though it was prison scuttlebutt, I wanted never to have another McGurk situation on my hands, so this time I informed police. They assured me that Corrective Services would be notified and that Gattellari's safety was of the utmost importance to them.

Gattellari's new cellmate was Shayne Hatfield, who'd been arrested in May 2005 for importing enormous quantities of cocaine with the help of some Qantas baggage handlers. Six months before his arrest, a balaclava-clad Hatfield was photographed at his home surveying huge piles of cash worth more than $10 million. In December 2004, not long after the photo was taken, Hatfield's right-hand man had walked into the Crime Commission and given them all up. After Hatfield's arrest, police found $1 million in cash buried in his father's back garden.

Nicknamed 'Curly', Hatfield, a former pro-surfer, was initially declared unfit to stand trial. He was diagnosed with paranoid schizophrenia and confined to the psychiatric unit at Long Bay. At the end of 2007 his health had improved enough for him to enter a guilty plea. At his sentencing hearing Hatfield claimed he was 'directed by George Bush' to commit the importation. He also said that he had received messages through his television. His barrister explained that Hatfield could be 'apparently coherent' one minute and 'floridly irrational' the next. But the judge wasn't persuaded that Hatfield was delusional during his days as a drug kingpin importing large quantities of drugs from South America, which had required a considerable amount of organising and planning. In 2009 he was sentenced to a whopping 24-year term, with a non-parole period of 14 years. He appealed and one year of his sentence was cut off. Hatfield was due out of jail in May 2018, a month after Lucky. But here they both were now facing trial again and the prospect of several more years behind bars.

Gattellari's Cooma cellmate had serious underworld connections. Known as the 'Cocaine King', Hatfield's own drug syndicate had included former star footballer Les Mara, ex-detective Ian Finch and the late Michael Hurley, who was described in one royal commission as the head honcho of organised crime. After much discussion of Gattellari's plan, Hatfield hit on the bright idea of using the heft of his good friend Roger Rogerson to make an approach to Medich. 'Uncle Roger', as Hatfield was heard saying to Miss L, would be the last person Medich would suspect of being involved with the police.

On the outside, Hatfield was using his former friend Miss L to do his running around, and to pass messages to Rogerson and McNamara. Initially Rogerson wasn't interested, telling Miss L, 'I feel sorry for guys in prison, it would be tough,' but adding no amount of money could make him visit Hatfield in Cooma. 'I have a bad hip,' Rogerson told her.[16]

But Hatfield, who rang Miss L several times most days, told her to persist. Eventually Rogerson relented and promised to dispatch his offsider. On 29 March McNamara made the five-hour trek down the Hume Highway to Cooma to see if there were any legs to Hatfield's claim that he had a very worthwhile business proposition to discuss. After McNamara's visit, Gattellari wrote in his diary, 'So we are one step closer to making this happen and finaly [sic] sinking that scunk [sic] of passed friend of mine, but we are not there yet.' At the top of the page he'd written '35m'.[17]

The prospect of extracting millions of dollars from a wealthy property developer must have made Rogerson forget about his dodgy hip because the very next Saturday, 5 April 2014, he and McNamara drove to Cooma jail to nut out the details of the extortion plan.

Rogerson enlisted as a go-between Joe Prestia, a former bankrupt and wheeler and dealer who'd been to jail for drug offences. Prestia had been a major fruit and vegetable wholesaler in the 1980s and 1990s and had close ties to the New South Wales Labor Party's right faction. On 1 May, Prestia made contact with Roy Medich at the funeral of Neville Wran.

The next move was for Prestia to ask Roy if he could discuss a business proposition with him.

Roy Medich, his steel-grey hair perfectly coiffed, and his Order of Australia pinned to his dark-grey suit, told the jury that he thought Prestia wanted to talk to him about his plan to export dried mangoes. He said he was surprised, when they were later chatting in his office, that Prestia volunteered that he'd been to prison, a fact Roy said he had not previously known.

Prestia then handed him two notes. On the first were the contact details of McNamara and Rogerson. The second note, which was handwritten, was astonishing. 'I asked for your help with legal expenses and bail money and you turned your back on me and left me dead,' read the opening sentence.[18] Gattellari went on to say he would have protected his friend 'at all cost' and that 'neither of us would be in the shit if you had not been such a prick and tryed [sic] to shift the blame on me'.

Since Ron had refused to pay the $1 million Gattellari had asked for just after his arrest, and then the $10 million he'd wanted prior to Ron's committal hearing, the price had gone up. As Medich's murder trial approached, because of his 'games', the price was now $30 million. If that amount wasn't paid by 15 May, the price would be $50 million 'or go fuck yourself and you will die in gaol', the note read. 'It's the cost of being guilty.'

While the note wasn't in Gattellari's handwriting, it was clearly from him. There was a jibe in it at Terracini, who was referred to as a highly paid 'wig wearing fool'. The note concluded: 'This is no con and the man you are talking to speaks for me.' The method of payment was to be blue-chip shares in the name of Miss L.

But the 15 May deadline came and went. While Rogerson and McNamara were intent on extorting money from Medich, they also had a more deadly criminal enterprise on the boil. On Tuesday 20 May, Rogerson and McNamara lured student and drug dealer Jamie Gao to a rental space in Padstow and murdered him. They also relieved their victim of almost 3 kilograms of the drug ice.

That same day Miss L tried repeatedly to get in touch with McNamara. 'Yeah, well, he might have been busy,' said Hatfield as he chatted to her on the phone.

On the Sunday, five days after the murder, McNamara drove Miss L to Cooma to speak with Gattellari and Hatfield so they could advance the extortion plot. Miss L noticed that McNamara kept turning on the radio to listen to the news. There was an item about the disappearance of Jamie Gao.

During the visit, Hatfield said to McNamara, 'You don't look good, mate. Is everything all right?'

According to Miss L, McNamara was dishevelled and as 'white as a ghost'.[19] McNamara said he'd been ill since Tuesday and that he must've contracted a virus.

There wasn't much talk on the trip back. McNamara shouted Miss L lunch at McDonald's but he himself couldn't stomach eating. As they pulled into a car park at Kyeemagh, in Sydney's south, where Miss L had left her car, blinding lights were directed at them and there was 'lots of screaming and yelling'.[20] McNamara got out of the car, put his hands in the air and was arrested for the murder of Gao.

The following morning fishermen spotted Gao's body, wrapped in a blue tarpaulin, floating a few kilometres off Shelly Beach, south of Cronulla. That Monday night, 26 May 2014, there was a nationwide manhunt for 73-year-old Rogerson, and in one of the last calls he was to make as a free man, he was still plotting to extort Medich. Police, who had bugged his phone, listened with astonishment as he left a message for Joe Prestia's son, Roy. 'You've seen all the stuff on the news and whatever, it's fucking dreadful,' said Rogerson.[21] What was 'fucking dreadful', though, wasn't the execution of Gao but that his body had been found and Rogerson's mate McNamara had been arrested.

No doubt Rogerson was scheming for a bigger cut than the $2 million Hatfield had promised him, but he was arrested the following day and he and McNamara have since been jailed for life.

Several days after their arrest, Gattellari was heard complaining to Frank about this unfortunate 'hiccup'. He told his brother, 'This would have all been finished if it hadn't been for those other two fuck-wits.'[22]

Frank said he didn't think it was 'going to happen anyway', to which his brother replied crossly, 'Well, you're wrong. It's not going to happen the way you think it's going to happen. It's all been sorted out with the police so don't worry about it.'[23]

The phone intercepts provided a fascinating glimpse into family dynamics. Lucky was always upbeat, with a plan on the boil, whereas Frank, to whom Lucky spoke almost daily, was like Eeyore, the pessimistic donkey in 'Winnie-the-Pooh'. Frank had a sore throat, he's tired, he's got the flu, he's been a bit crook, his hand is sore, he's been done for drink driving.

'G'day, mate, how's it going?' asks Lucky one day in a call from Long Bay.

Frank whines, 'It's bloody hot here in Castle Hill. It's thirty-five degrees.' It's all right for Lucky, he says grumpily, 'You're near the sea, you've fuckin' got it made.'

'Yeah, that's right,' replied Lucky on another occasion. 'I'm livin' the dream, Frank, I'm livin' the dream.'[24]

Frank was right to worry. Although the extortion plot collapsed with the arrest of Rogerson and McNamara, two years later Hatfield and Gattellari were charged. It would take a further two years for them to face trial. Hatfield chose not to give evidence at his trial. On occasions he followed the proceedings intently; at other times he dozed, his head tilted back, mouth open. At one point, after the jury and the accused had left the room, Judge Hock told Hatfield's barrister that it wasn't a good look for Hatfield to be sleeping in front of the jury. His barrister, Roland Keller, replied, 'Your Honour, he is meditating.'

'Well, can you ask him to meditate with his eyes open?' said the judge primly.

At one point Hatfield called me over and gave me a note. On one side of the small square of paper he pressed into my hand he had written 'Song: What The World Needs Now'. Underneath was 'artist, Jackie DeShannon'. On the other side was 'Iris' by the Goo Goo Dolls. He said it was very important that I listen to these two songs if I was going to write about him. 'If you listen, you will know,' he said.

Hatfield was always up for a chat. He told me he had bumped into 'your mate Eddie Obeid' in the prison system and that the jailed former Labor MP wasn't 'a bad bloke'.

Ron Medich played the role of Banquo's ghost in the trial; as the unseen victim, his presence hovered over the proceedings. But one morning he made an appearance of sorts. On 5 November Hatfield told me that Medich had been in the prison truck with him that morning. This seemed highly unusual as Medich was in maximum security at Lithgow jail, which Hatfield explained was referred to as 'The Coffin' due to its shape and because it was cold inside. Besides, would Corrective Services allow Hatfield, who was on trial for trying to extort money from Medich, to be in the same prison van as him? According to Hatfield, Medich had volunteered that he was off to the Family Court – after eight years his and Odetta's poisonous property battle was still raging.

It was only a block to the Family Court. When I looked through the square glass inset in the door to courtroom 4D, there indeed was Medich in his suit and purple tie, sitting in the public seats at the back of the court. There was no sign of Odetta. However, there was no opportunity to talk to Medich as the court attendant would only allow parties to the matter to go in.

Gattellari was happy to chat as he sat in the dock waiting for the judge to come on to the bench or for the jury to arrive. He had rung me from jail in June 2014, wanting me to do a story about his poor treatment. I explained to him at the time that as Medich's murder trial was approaching, nothing could be written.

He handed me a letter which he had written to me but never sent. Gattellari's guards demanded to see it and, after reading it, allowed him to give it to me. It detailed his frustration at not being allowed to go to a minimum security prison. And look where his helping authorities had got him, he said grimly now, surveying the courtroom. He'd never planned to give false evidence about Medich and he thought the police were on board with his idea to trap Medich into paying a bribe so the whole case would move along faster. Besides, he told me, he couldn't afford to give false evidence because he ran the risk of being re-sentenced and receiving an even harsher term in prison.

He told me how unfair he thought it was that Bassam Safetli, who was the brains behind the murder, had been given a slap on the wrist and no jail time at all. If it wasn't for Bass, this would never have happened, he told me.

As for Estephan, 'He supplied the weapon, he's there on the night, he gets paid,' and yet he was already out of prison. 'Being in jail destroys you,' he said bitterly.

A month into the trial, Gattellari was finally on the stand.

'Never in a million years' did he expect Medich to abandon him, especially since Ron was 'the man who actually got me in that position', he said.[25]

'The whole thing was a circus,' he said of Rogerson's unilateral decision to demand $30 million and then $50 million. Those figures were 'absolute lunacy'; he knew Medich wouldn't pay that much. 'Rogerson was running his own race,' he said, and he suspected he planned to double-cross him once he got the money.

But Crown Prosecutor Darren Robinson pointed out that in almost every one of his diary entries in 2013 and 2014, Gattellari had recorded the figure of $35 million.

The former boxer explained that this was based on the power of positive thinking. It had nothing to do with the extortion demand and instead was what he aspired to earn once he was out of jail.

'My wife gave me a book by Florence Shinn called *The Power of Attraction*,' said Gattellari.[26] 'This book tells you that whatever you think about, whatever you dream about, whatever you want to happen to you, you need to think about it, write about it and state it as often as you can.

'What you set your mind to, eventually comes to you.'[27]

Gattellari angrily denied the prosecutor's suggestion that he'd intended to keep the money and had lied about planning to have the police arrest Medich after he handed over the millions.

'You wanted Ron Medich to pay for what he did to you,' posed Mr Robinson.

'Not correct,' retorted Gattellari. 'I had no intention of taking one penny from Mr Medich.' But he later admitted asking the police if he could 'keep half of [the money]' should Medich fall into his 'trap'.[28] The answer from the police was no.

The Crown prosecutor rejected Gattellari's claim that no one was going to receive any money from the scheme. 'I ask, rhetorically, who was going to tell Mr Rogerson that there was no money available once the trap had taken effect?' Robinson asked the jury. 'Was it going to be Mr Hatfield, who was apparently his nephew? Was Mr Hatfield intentionally going to deceive Roger Rogerson into thinking there would be money at the end of this venture?'[29]

'The plan always was that the money would be paid,' and divided up between the various participants, the prosecutor told the jury. Gattellari told the court that once he had the money from Medich, which he would hand to the police, he planned to renege on the deal and testify anyway. That way 'there would be no more delays in court . . . and we would all get along with our lives once and for all', Gattellari said.

Robinson told the jury that it was 'inconclusive' whether Gattellari 'had any intention to give false evidence'.

In his closing address, Gattellari's barrister, Maurice Gelbert, said his client 'had no intention whatsoever' of keeping any of the millions of dollars he was demanding from Medich. Instead, he was motivated by his desire to get out of the maximum security unit at Long Bay.

'Mr Hatfield's position was that he was involved because he was looking to ameliorate his incarceration conditions,' his barrister Roland Keller said.

After a six-week trial, the jury retired to consider its verdict. They did not have to decide on Miss L's guilt or innocence as she had become ill halfway through the trial and, after a week's delay, it was decided to proceed without her.

On 11 December 2018, after three days of deliberations, Gattellari and Hatfield stood as the five men and seven women of the jury filed back into the courtroom. The foreman announced that the jury had found Gattellari guilty of both extortion counts. He was visibly distressed.

Hatfield showed no emotion when he, too, was found guilty.

The following day the matter was in for mention to set a sentencing date. Gattellari was wearing his suit, but just an open-neck yellow shirt and no tie. The normally dapper dresser hadn't even done up the cuffs of his shirt. Every time I had seen Gattellari in court he had been cocky and pugnacious. Now he looked small and deflated and was trying to hold back the tears. He had cried all night. He said, 'I have no tears left.' He told me he didn't think he could do any more time in prison. 'They've broken me,' he said, looking down at his hands.

'We had such a great life,' he observed of his time with Medich. 'We really did. It was such a great life. Why did we ruin it? Why didn't Ron just leave it? Why did I do it for him?' The prison guards came to take him away.

That Sunday Gattellari asked one of the prison officers if he could give a letter to his family when they visited him because 'he would struggle to say the words to them'. The letter was 'very emotional', said the officer, who was worried about Lucky. 'He was visibly upset' but had assured the officer that he was coping with the verdict and was 'just sad for his family'.[30]

It was a cold and wet winter's afternoon in June 2019 when the cast in this long-running drama reassembled to learn of Gattellari's and Hatfield's fate. Lawyers, journalists, court watchers and Lucky's gloomy brother, Frank, were all present, as was Hatfield's 24-year-old daughter, who'd been just ten when her father was jailed. Even one of the jurors, a tall grey-haired woman in a blue overcoat, had shown up.

As we waited for Judge Hock to come on to the bench, Hatfield told me he was now in 'The Coffin' at Lithgow. He said Medich had looked blankly at him when he'd recently run into him in the jail. 'Remember when I did this at your trial?' prompted Hatfield, who said he'd once again performed his 'I'm a little teapot' routine. Medich was silent.

As she delivered her remarks on their sentences, Judge Hock appeared to have some sympathy for Lucky, and noted that he had served his entire jail term in 'extremely onerous' conditions that he had been desperate to escape. While this didn't excuse his behaviour, it did go 'a long way to explaining it', the judge said.

Towards 53-year-old Hatfield, she was less sympathetic. 'His motive was purely greed,' she said. His calls to Miss L showed Hatfield to be a man of 'considerable intelligence' who had manipulated and sometimes bullied Miss L, she continued. While Gattellari was the catalyst for both extortion attempts, it was Hatfield who was the driving force behind the second attempt.

'Stand up, please,' she said to Gattellari, before sentencing him to a maximum of four years and four months. But there was good news. His minimum sentence was half that amount and she was backdating it to six months before his release date for his role in the murder. He winked happily at Frank when he heard he would be released in six months' time, on 12 December 2019.

Hatfield received a minimum sentence of 26 months, which was backdated as well. His release date was 8 January 2020.

'It's better than I expected,' Gattellari told me from the dock. 'There is so much I need to tell you once I get out,' he offered. He was interrupted by the prison guard, a middle-aged man with regular features and square-framed glasses. 'Apologies, but our celebrity guest has to go now,' he quipped.

As I watched Lucky being led away, I wondered about the nature of truth and justice – noble concepts which, at the end of this decade-long saga, had only been reached in the most ignoble of ways. Morality and remorse were little seen. Instead, one after another, the self-serving participants had sacrificed their friendships and loyalties either to gain an advantage or wreak vengeance. Their mutual bonds, built up over years, took only a moment to be abandoned. At the heart of the murder and everything that flowed from it was the tawdry truth that it was every man for himself.

I was reminded of the shrewd observation by the late prime minister Gough Whitlam: 'The punters know that the horse named Morality rarely gets past the post, whereas the nag named Self-interest always runs a good race.'[31]

NOTES

Chapter 1: The Shooting

1 Police statement of Haissam Safetli, 12 October 2010.
2 Ibid.
3 Sue Hicks, 'Developer faces $1m fine', *Mosman Daily*,
   19 December 2002.

Chapter 2: The Sociopath Next Door

1 Georgina Robinson, 'Street execution: "fun-loving family"
   torn apart', *Sydney Morning Herald*, 4 September 2009.
2 Ibid.
3 Peter FitzSimons and Dylan Welch, 'There were sirens, lots
   of them', *Sydney Morning Herald*, 4 September 2009.
4 Confidential source, interview with Kate McClymont,
   September 2009.
5 Ibid., May 2010.
6 Ibid., September 2009.
7 Confidential source, interview with Kate McClymont and
   Vanda Carson, February 2010.
8 Confidential source, interview with Kate McClymont,
   16 March 2010.

9   Jim Byrnes, interview with Kate McClymont, 4 September 2009.

Chapter 3: *A Whodunnit for the Rich and Famous*

1   Michael McGurk, interview with Kate McClymont, 24 August 2009.
2   Andrew Williams, interview with Kate McClymont, 16 March 2010.
3   Ibid.
4   Ibid.

Chapter 4: *McGurk's Early Years*

1   The Leith Register Office in Edinburgh lists this as Michael McGurk's birth date, though there are references to it elsewhere as 1958.
2   Confidential source, interview with Kate McClymont, 10 March 2010.
3   Ibid., 22 June 2010.
4   Kathy Field, interview with Kate McClymont, 4 March 2010.
5   Ibid.
6   Ibid.
7   Ibid.
8   Paul Jeffery, interview with Kate McClymont, 23 February 2010.
9   Ibid.
10 Kathy Field, interview with Kate McClymont, 4 March 2010.
11 Paul Jeffery, interview with Kate McClymont, 23 February 2010.
12 Confidential source, interview with Vanda Carson, November 2009.
13 Ibid.
14 Frank Burke, interview with Vanda Carson and Kate McClymont, 18 March 2010.
15 Ibid.

16 Hamish Williamson, interview with Kate McClymont, 2 March 2010.

17 Confidential source, interview with Vanda Carson, November 2009.

18 Ibid.

19 *ECC Lighting Ltd v McGurk*, Supreme Court of New South Wales, 9 February 1996.

20 Confidential source, interview with Vanda Carson, November 2009.

21 Confidential source, interview with Kate McClymont, 22 June 2010.

22 Confidential source, interview with Vanda Carson, November 2009.

23 Ibid.

24 Hamish Williamson, interview with Kate McClymont, 2 March 2010.

25 Frank Burke, interview with Vanda Carson and Kate McClymont, 18 March 2010.

26 Hamish Williamson, interview with Kate McClymont, 2 March 2010.

27 Confidential source, interview with Kate McClymont, September 2009.

28 Hamish Williamson, interview with Kate McClymont, 2 March 2010.

29 Frank Burke, interview with Vanda Carson and Kate McClymont, 18 March 2010.

30 Keith Gosman, 'Hungarians rhapsodic over Aussie pies but Sydney firm folds', *Sydney Morning Herald*, 3 July 1993.

31 Janet Fife-Yeomans and Charles Miranda, 'A spiv and a shonk in a nice, shiny suit', *Daily Telegraph*, 12 September 2009.

32 Ibid.

33 Confidential source, interview with Kate McClymont, 22 June 2010.

34 Ibid.

35 *Levingston NB Pty Ltd v Michael McGurk & Ors*, Federal Court of Australia, 25 September 1998.

36 Confidential source, interview with Kate McClymont and Vanda Carson, March 2010.

37 Ibid., February 2010.

38 Ibid.

39 Ibid.

40 Confidential source, interview with Kate McClymont, 10 March 2010.

41 Confidential source, interview with Kate McClymont and Vanda Carson, February 2010.

42 Ibid.

Chapter 5: It's Taken Long Enough

1 Ron Medich, evidence, ICAC Investigation into the Conduct of Ian Macdonald, Ron Medich and others, 30 November 2011.

2 Kate McClymont, Vanda Carson, Dylan Welch, Erik Jensen, 'It could bring down the government: secret tape blamed for killing', *Sydney Morning Herald*, 5 September 2009.

3 Crown opening, committal hearing, *R v Medich*; *R v Estephan*, Sydney Central Local Court, 7 August 2013.

4 Sentencing of Gattellari, *R v Gattellari*; *R v Kaminic*. Supreme Court of New South Wales, 10 May 2013.

5 Confidential source, interview with Kate McClymont, 7 September 2009.

6 Senad Kaminic, evidence, committal hearing, *R v Medich*; *R v Estephan*, Sydney Central Local Court, 26 August 2013.

7 Lucky Gattellari, evidence, *R v Medich*, Supreme Court of New South Wales, 2 February 2017.

8 Ibid.

9 Ibid.

10 Crown opening, committal hearing, *R v Medich*; *R v Estephan*, Sydney Central Local Court, 7 August 2013.

11 Lucky Gattellari, evidence, *R v Medich*, Supreme Court of New South Wales, 2 February 2017.

12 Crown opening, committal hearing, *R v Medich*; *R v Estephan*, Sydney Central Local Court, 7 August 2013.

13 Police statement of Haissam Safetli, 12 October 2010.

14 Ibid.

15 Ibid.

16 Ibid.

17 Witness B, evidence, *R v Medich*, Supreme Court of New South Wales, 1 March 2018.

18 Crown opening, committal hearing, *R v Medich*; *R v Estephan*, Sydney Central Local Court, 7 August 2013.

19 Ibid.

20 Andrew Clennell, 'Minister defends $150,000 on wining and dining', *Sydney Morning Herald*, 15 July 2009.

21 Ron Medich, evidence, ICAC Investigation into the Conduct of Ian Macdonald, Ron Medich and others, 30 November 2011.

22 Geoffrey Watson, SC, opening address, ICAC Investigation into the Conduct of Ian Macdonald, Ron Medich and others, 24 November 2011.

23 Ibid.

24 Ian Macdonald, evidence, ICAC Investigation into the Conduct of Ian Macdonald, Ron Medich and others, 1 December 2011.

25 Ibid., 2 December 2011.

26 Ibid.

27 Ron Medich, evidence, ICAC Investigation into the Conduct of Ian Macdonald, Ron Medich and others, 30 November 2011.

28 Cindy, evidence, ICAC Investigation into the Conduct of Ian Macdonald, Ron Medich and others, 25 November 2011.

29 Ron Medich, evidence, ICAC Investigation into the Conduct of Ian Macdonald, Ron Medich and others, 30 November 2011.

Chapter 6: The Snob Mob from Blueberry Hill

1   Jim Byrnes, interview with Kate McClymont, 20 July 2009.
2   Janet Fife-Yeomans, 'Medich: Australia's richest killer',
    Daily Telegraph, 28 April 2018.
3   Lucky Gattellari, evidence, committal hearing, *R v Medich*;
    R v Estephan, Sydney Central Local Court, 20 August 2013.
4   Ali Gripper, 'The Golden West', *Sydney Morning Herald*,
    11 May 1996.
5   Ibid.
6   Ibid.
7   *Odeta Chtouikite and Ronald Edward Medich v Minister for
    Immigration*, 4 November 1991.
8   Ibid.
9   Ibid.
10 Quentin Dempster, *The 7.30 Report*, ABC TV, 28 May
    1990.
11 Ibid.
12 Ibid.
13 Kate McClymont, 'Turning new leaves', *Sydney Morning
    Herald*, 19 October 2002.
14 Ali Gripper, 'The Golden West', *Sydney Morning Herald*,
    11 May 1996.
15 Allan Cleaver, 'Row over Medich's land buy', *Liverpool
    Leader*, 18 December 1996.

Chapter 7: McGurk's Dodgy Deals

1   Jacquelin Magnay, 'Rules of the game changed for Knowles',
    Sydney Morning Herald, 10 September 2009.
2   Frank Burke, interview with Vanda Carson and Kate
    McClymont, 18 March 2010.
3   Ibid.

Chapter 8: Kidnapped

1   Ray Simersall, police statement, 30 May 2007.
2   Ibid.

3 The account of Ray Simersall's encounter with John and Karl is taken from his police statement.

4 Police statement of Detective Senior Constable Kylie Stewart, 10 September 2007.

5 Ibid.

6 Hamish Williamson, interview with Kate McClymont, 2 March 2010.

7 Ibid.

8 Ibid.

9 Ibid.

10 Court document, *R v Simersall*, District Court of New South Wales, March 2008.

11 Woods, J, Remarks on Sentence, *R v Simersall*, District Court of New South Wales, 7 March 2008.

12 Ibid.

13 Ibid.

14 Richard Vereker, *The Fast Life and Sudden Death of Michael McGurk*, Allen & Unwin, 2010, p. 21.

15 Margaret Simersall, interview with Vanda Carson, 22 October 2009.

Chapter 9: The Miniature Koran

1 CBD column, *Sydney Morning Herald*, 7 February 1995.

2 Colleen Ryan, 'Bond and the fixer family', *Sydney Morning Herald*, 25 February 1995.

3 Viktor D'Jamirze's affidavit, *Garsec Pty Ltd v Smirnoff & Ors*, Supreme Court of New South Wales, 26 May 2005.

4 Confidential source, interview with Kate McClymont, March 2010.

5 David Rahme, interview with Kate McClymont and Vanda Carson, 9 March 2010.

6 Viktor D'Jamirze's affidavit, *Garsec Pty Ltd v Smirnoff & Ors*, Supreme Court of New South Wales, 26 May 2005.

7 Confidential source, interview with Kate McClymont, March 2010.

8   David Rahme, interview with Kate McClymont and Vanda
    Carson, 9 March 2010.
9   Hamish Williamson, interview with Kate McClymont,
    2 March 2010.
10 Michael McGurk affidavit, *Garsec Pty Ltd v His Majesty
    Sultan Haji Hassanal Bolkiah Mu'izzaddin Waddaulah the
    Sultan & Yang Di-Pertuan of Brunei*, Supreme Court of
    New South Wales, 2006.
11 Ibid.
12 Ibid.
13 Matthew Benns, Vanda Carson and Leesha McKenny,
    'This is ripping through all of them: a family grieves',
    Sun-Herald, 6 September 2009.
14 Mark Burby, interview with Meredith Griffiths, PM,
    ABC radio, 10 September 2009.

Chapter 10: The Odd Couple

1   Ron Medich, statement to police in the matter of Michael
    McGurk charged with arson offences, 12 March 2009.
2   Affidavit of Michael McGurk in the matter of *Ron Medich
    Properties v Bentley Smythe Pty Ltd & others*, Federal Court of
    Australia, 25 March 2009.
3   Ibid.
4   Ron Medich, statement to police in the matter of Michael
    McGurk charged with arson offences, 12 March 2009.
5   Michael McGurk, interview with Kate McClymont and
    Vanda Carson, 29 July 2009.
6   Paul Mathieson, interview with Vanda Carson, September
    2009.
7   Ben Butler, 'Backer bid to probe Amazing Loans', *Herald
    Sun*, 1 November 2007.
8   Paul Mathieson, email to ASIC, 18 August 2009.
9   Affidavit of Ron Medich in the matter of *Ron Medich
    Properties v Bentley Smythe Pty Ltd & others*, Federal Court
    of Australia, 25 March 2009.

10 Paul Mathieson, evidence, *R v Medich*, Supreme Court of New South Wales, 24 February 2017.

11 Ibid.

12 Ibid.

13 Richard Vereker, *The Fast Life and Sudden Death of Michael McGurk*, Allen & Unwin, 2010, p. 142.

14 Paul Mathieson, evidence, *R v Medich*, Supreme Court of New South Wales, 24 February 2017.

15 Affidavit of Michael McGurk in the matter of *Ron Medich Properties v Bentley Smythe Pty Ltd & others*, Federal Court of Australia, 25 March 2009.

16 Recording made by Michael McGurk, exhibit, ICAC Investigation into allegations of corruption made by or attributed to Michael McGurk, February 2010.

17 Ibid.

18 Ibid.

19 Paul Mathieson, evidence, committal hearing, *R v Medich*; *R v Estephan*, Sydney Central Local Court, 10 September 2013.

20 Paul Mathieson, statement to police, 26 February 2010.

21 Paul Mathieson, evidence, *R v Medich*, Supreme Court of New South Wales, 24 February 2017.

22 Ibid.

Chapter 11: Big Jim and the Krispy Kremes

1 Confidential source, interview with Vanda Carson, 24 September 2009.

2 Confidential source, interview with Vanda Carson and Kate McClymont, 24 September 2009.

3 Mark Schroeder, interview with Vanda Carson and Kate McClymont, 24 September 2009.

4 Ibid.

5 Confidential source, interview with Kate McClymont and Vanda Carson, May 2010.

6 Elisabeth Sexton, 'Notorious: Byrnes foiled by eagle-eyed judge', *Sydney Morning Herald*, 8 July 2010.

7   Jim Byrnes, interview with Kate McClymont, October
    2009.
8   Ibid.

Chapter 12: The Tilleys

1   Ron Medich, statement of a witness in the matter of
    Michael McGurk charged with arson offences, 9 April
    2009.

Chapter 13: McGurk's Fiery Message

1   Stuart Rowan, interview with Kate McClymont,
    5 September 2009.
2   Ibid.
3   Susan Wellings, 'The Hyde of it all', *Sydney Morning Herald*,
    20 October 2006.
4   Andrew Hornery, 'Penthouse to prison', *Sydney Morning
    Herald*, 5 January 2008.
5   Palmer, J, judgment, *Brown & Ors v Hodgkinson & Ors*,
    Supreme Court of New South Wales, 8 April 2009.
6   Ibid.
7   Ibid.
8   Hamish Williamson, interview with Kate McClymont,
    2 March 2010.
9   Ibid.
10 Kate McClymont and Vanda Carson, 'McGurk house sale
    provokes anger', *Sydney Morning Herald*, 18 November
    2009.
11 Ibid.

Chapter 14: Mutual Destruction

1   John Constable, interview with Kate McClymont,
    11 September 2009.
2   Ibid.
3   Recording made by McGurk, exhibit, ICAC Investigation
    into allegations of corruption made by or attributed to
    Michael McGurk, February 2010.

4   Affidavit of Michael McGurk, in the matter of *Ron Medich
    Properties v Bentley Smythe Pty Ltd & others*, Federal Court of
    Australia, 25 March 2009.
5   *Ron Medich Properties v Bentley Smythe Pty Ltd & others*,
    Federal Court of Australia, March 2009.
6   *Ron Medich Properties v Bentley Smythe Pty Ltd & others*,
    Federal Court of Australia, April 2009.
7   Ibid.

Chapter 15: The Tape

1   Recording made by Michael McGurk, exhibit, ICAC
    Investigation into allegations of corruption made by or
    attributed to Michael McGurk, February 2010.
2   Ibid.
3   Richard Vereker, *The Fast Life and Sudden Death of Michael
    McGurk*, Allen & Unwin, 2010, p. 200.
4   Ibid., p. 201.
5   Ibid.
6   Graham Richardson, evidence, NSW Parliamentary Inquiry
    into Badgerys Creek Land Dealings and Planning Decision,
    14 December 2009.
7   Ron Medich, statement of a witness in the matter of
    Michael McGurk charged with arson offences, 12 March
    2009.
8   Lucky Gattellari, evidence, committal hearing, *R v Medich;
    R v Estephan*, Sydney Central Local Court, 13 August 2013.
9   Confidential source, interview with Kate McClymont,
    October 2009.
10 Ibid.
11 Patrick Conaghan, interview with Kate McClymont,
    11 June 2019.

Chapter 16: A Very Smart Operator

1   Suellen O'Grady, 'Why Bob Ell isn't just another brick in
    the wall', *Sydney Morning Herald*, 18 February 1987.

2   Robert Ell, evidence, *R v Medich*, Supreme Court of New South Wales, 28 February 2017.
3   Susie Carleton, interview with Kate McClymont, March 2010.
4   Kate McClymont, 'Ell's bells, good help is hard to find', *Sydney Morning Herald*, 13 April, 2013.
5   Ibid.
6   Stephen Downie, 'High-flying Magpie, Ell's helicopter the sound of success', *Daily Telegraph*, 3 April 1998.
7   Confidential source, interview with Kate McClymont, March 2010.
8   Ibid., September 2009.
9   Ibid., March 2010.
10 Emeritus Professor Maurice Daly, Tweed Shire Council Public Inquiry, first report, May 2005.
11 *Ell v Milne*, Supreme Court of New South Wales, March 2013.
12 Ibid.
13 McCallum, J, judgment, *Ell v Milne*, Supreme Court of New South Wales, 7 March 2014.
14 Ibid.
15 Ibid.
16 Rothman, J, *Milne v Ell*, Supreme Court of New South Wales, 8 May 2017.
17 Richard Vereker, *The Fast Life and Sudden Death of Michael McGurk*, Allen & Unwin, 2010, p. 185.
18 Confidential source, interview with Kate McClymont, September 2009.
19 Jim Byrnes, interview with Kate McClymont, 4 September 2009.
20 Confidential source, interview with Kate McClymont, 20 March 2010.
21 Alex Mitchell, 'Ell of a way to swan around', *Sun-Herald*, 20 August 2000.
22 Confidential source, interview with Kate McClymont, 12 January 2010.

23 Confidential source, interview with Vanda Carson, September 2009.
24 Bob Ell, statement, 11 September 2009.

Chapter 17: Craziness After the Murder

1 Sam Rodrigues, 'A classic tale of murder, corruption and intrigue', *The Advertiser*, 8 September 2009.
2 Juanita Nielsen, a publisher and conservation activist, was last seen in Kings Cross in July, 1975. Her body has never been found.
3 Ward, J, *Bentley Smythe Pty Ltd v Anton Fabrications Pty Ltd*, Supreme Court of New South Wales, 18 March 2011.
4 Ibid.
5 Barry O'Farrell, interview, ABC radio, 7 September 2009.
6 Tony Kelly, ibid.
7 Bill Hayden, *Hayden: An Autobiography*, Angus & Robertson, 1996, p. 160.
8 'History of relative damage, the Richardson resignation', *Australian Financial Review*, 19 May 1992.
9 Kate McClymont and Linton Besser, *He Who Must Be Obeid*, Random House, 2014, p. 97.
10 Kate McClymont and Vanda Carson, 'The murky world of Mr McGurk', *Sydney Morning Herald*, 19 September 2009.
11 Confidential source, interview with Kate McClymont, 20 March 2010.
12 Ibid., 12 January 2010.

Chapter 18: Parliamentary Inquiry

1 Kristina Keneally, evidence, NSW Parliamentary Inquiry into Badgerys Creek Land Dealings and Planning Decisions, 29 September 2009.
2 Ibid.
3 Roy Medich, evidence, NSW Parliamentary Inquiry into Badgerys Creek Land Dealings and Planning Decisions, 29 September 2009.
4 Ibid.

5 Ron Medich, ibid.
6 Jim Byrnes, interview with Kate McClymont, 4 September 2009.
7 Ron Medich, evidence, NSW Parliamentary Inquiry into Badgerys Creek Land Dealings and Planning Decisions, 29 September 2009.
8 Sam Haddad, evidence, NSW Parliamentary Inquiry into Badgerys Creek Land Dealings and Planning Decisions, 29 September 2009.
9 Graham Richardson, evidence, NSW Parliamentary Inquiry into Badgerys Creek Land Dealings and Planning Decisions, 19 October 2009.
10 Ibid.
11 Ibid., 14 December 2009.
12 Ibid.

Chapter 19: ICAC: Nothing to See Here

1 Kate McClymont and Belinda Kontominas, 'So many hearings to attend, so little time', *Sydney Morning Herald*, 3 February 2010.
2 David Ipp, transcript, ICAC Investigation into Allegations of Corruption Made by or Attributed to Michael McGurk, 1 February 2010.
3 Ibid.
4 Ibid.
5 Jeremy Gormly, transcript, ICAC Investigation into Allegations of Corruption Made by or Attributed to Michael McGurk, 1 February 2010.
6 Ibid.
7 Tim Game, transcript, Investigation into Allegations of Corruption Made by or Attributed to Michael McGurk, 1 February 2010.
8 Ron Medich, transcript, Investigation into Allegations of Corruption Made by or Attributed to Michael McGurk, 2 February 2010.
9 Ibid.

10 Ibid.
11 Graham Richardson, transcript, ICAC Investigation
into Allegations of Corruption Made by or Attributed to
Michael McGurk, 2 February 2010.
12 Ibid.
13 Kate McClymont and Geesche Jacobsen, 'Medich claims
created public mischief: ICAC', *Sydney Morning Herald*,
4 February 2010.
14 Claire Harvey, 'Inside Richo's world', *Sunday Telegraph*,
30 May 2010.
15 Ibid.

Chapter 20: Lucky

1 Rod Humphries, 'Lucky Flying High Again', *Sydney
Morning Herald*, 20 February 1975.
2 Ron Medich, evidence, NSW Parliamentary Inquiry into
Badgerys Creek Land Dealings and Planning Decisions,
29 September 2009.
3 Ibid.
4 Confidential source, interview with Kate McClymont,
26 February 2010.
5 Ibid., 27 February 2010.
6 Ibid.
7 Ibid.
8 Ibid.
9 Chesterman, J, *R v Gibson*, Supreme Court of Queensland,
21 November 2008.
10 Confidential source, interview with Kate McClymont,
26 February 2010.
11 Vanessa Mason, evidence, ICAC Investigation into
Wagonga Local Aboriginal Land Council, 29 February
2012.
12 Ron Medich, evidence, ICAC Investigation into Wagonga
Local Aboriginal Land Council, 1 March 2012.
13 Ronnie Binge, evidence, ICAC Investigation into Wagonga
Local Aboriginal Land Council 29 February 2012.

14 Report, ICAC Investigation into Wagonga Local
    Aboriginal Land Council, September 2012.

Chapter 21: Finding a Hitman

1   Crown opening, committal hearing, *R v Medich*; *R v
    Estephan*, Sydney Central Local Court, 7 August 2013.
2   Statement of police facts, Ahmad Samman and Nizar
    Samman, 20 December 2011.
3   Ibid.
4   Police statement of Haissam Safetli, 12 October 2010.
5   Ron Mason, evidence, committal hearing, *R v Medich*;
    R v Estephan, Sydney Central Local Court, 29 August
    2013.
6   Ibid.
7   Ibid.
8   Police statement of Haissam Safetli, 12 October 2010.
9   Ibid.

Chapter 22: The Job Is Done

1   Ray Hetherington, evidence, *R v Medich*, Supreme Court of
    New South Wales, 23 February 2017.
2   Crown opening, committal hearing, *R v Medich*; *R v
    Estephan*, Sydney Central Local Court, 7 August 2013.
3   Andrew Howard, evidence, *R v Medich*, Supreme Court of
    New South Wales, 8 March 2017.
4   Ibid.
5   Ibid.
6   Ibid.
7   Ibid.
8   Lucky Gattellari, evidence, *R v Medich*, Supreme Court of
    New South Wales, 2 February 2017.
9   Kimberley McGurk, evidence, *R v Medich*, Supreme Court
    of New South Wales, 31 January 2017.
10 Robert Ell, evidence, *R v Medich*, Supreme Court of New
    South Wales, 28 February 2017.

11 Intercepted calls, tendered as evidence, *R v Medich*, Supreme Court of New South Wales, 8 March 2017.

12 Senad Kaminic, evidence, committal hearing, *R v Medich*; *R v Estephan*, Sydney Central Local Court, 27 August 2013.

13 Haissam Safetli, evidence, committal hearing, *R v Medich*; *R v Estephan*, Sydney Central Local Court, 21 August 2013.

14 Lucky Gattellari, evidence, *R v Medich*, Supreme Court of New South Wales, 3 February 2017.

15 Ibid.

16 Ibid.

Chapter 23: The Arrests

1 Police intercept, committal hearing, *R v Medich*; *R v Estephan*, Sydney Central Local Court, March 2013.

2 Kate McClymont and Tom Reilly, 'Heavy hitter much preferred the shadows', *Sydney Morning Herald*, 5 March 2011.

3 Rod Nicholson, John Kaila, 'Samba talks of mystery meeting two hours before his murder', *Herald Sun*, 6 March 2011.

Chapter 24: They Want Your Father Not Mine

1 Kim Shipley, evidence, *R v Medich*, Supreme Court of New South Wales, 21 February 2017.

2 Lucky Gattellari, sentence hearing, *R v Gattellari*, Supreme Court of New South Wales, 11 February 2013.

3 Peter Medich, evidence, *R v Medich*, Supreme Court of New South Wales, 14 March 2017.

4 Ibid.

5 Lucky Gattellari, evidence, *R v Gattellari*; *R v Hatfield*, District Court of New South Wales, 17 November 2018.

6 Ibid.

7 Mick Sheehy, evidence, sentence hearing, *R v Gattellari*, Supreme Court of New South Wales, 11 February 2013.

8 Bail hearing, *R v Medich*, Sydney Central Local Court, 27 October 2010.

9 Kate McClymont, Vanda Carson, Geesche Jacobsen, 'Police arrest "mastermind" of the McGurk murder', *Sydney Morning Herald*, 28 October 2010.

Chapter 25: The Wheels of Justice Turn Slowly

1 Bail hearing, *R v Medich*, Supreme Court of New South Wales, 14 December 2010.
2 Ibid.
3 Price, J, judgment, *R v Medich*, Supreme Court of New South Wales, 17 December 2010.
4 Magistrate Robert Williams, Waverley Local Court, 2 September 2010.
5 Confidential source, interview with Kate McClymont, 13 March 2010.
6 Ibid.
7 Ibid., 22 May 2010.
8 Ibid.
9 Ibid., October 2009.
10 Ibid., 13 March 2010.
11 Ibid.
12 Confidential source, interview with Kate McClymont, October 2009.
13 Ibid., 13 March 2010.
14 Lucky Gattellari, evidence, *R v Medich*, Supreme Court of New South Wales, 3 February 2017.
15 Lucky Gattellari, evidence, committal hearing, *R v Medich*; *R v Estephan*, Sydney Central Local Court, 20 August 2013.
16 Ibid.
17 Haissam Safetli, evidence, committal hearing, *R v Medich*; *R v Estephan*, Sydney Central Local Court, 21 August 2013.
18 Magistrate Allan Moore, bail hearing, *R v Kaminic*, Sydney Central Local Court, 17 November 2010.
19 Directions hearing, *R v Medich*, Downing Centre Local Criminal Court, 19 June 2012.
20 Ibid.
21 Ibid., 24 August 2012.

Chapter 26: The Last Man Standing

1 Lucky Gattellari, evidence, sentence hearing, *R v Gattellari*, Supreme Court of New South Wales, 11 February 2013.

2 Rocky Gattellari, ibid.

3 Mick Sheehy, ibid.

4 Ibid.

5 Latham, J, judgment, *R v Gattellari*; *R v Kaminic*, Supreme Court of New South Wales, 10 May 2013.

6 Magistrate Jan Stevenson, plea hearing, *R v Safetli*, Sydney Central Local Court, 2 July 2013.

7 Dennis Miralis, plea hearing, *R v Safetli*, Sydney Central Local Court, 2 July 2013.

8 Haissam Safetli, sentence hearing, *R v Safetli*, Supreme Court of New South Wales, 1 August 2013.

9 Ibid.

10 Haissam Safetli, interview with Nick Grimm, *7.30 Report*, ABC television, 8 September 2007.

11 Amanda Safetli, ibid.

12 Ibid.

13 Latham, J, judgment, *R v Safetli*, Supreme Court of New South Wales, 9 August 2013.

14 Magistrate Jan Stevenson, committal hearing, *R v Medich*; *R v Estephan*, Sydney Central Local Court, 26 July 2013.

15 Winston Terracini, SC, committal hearing, *R v Medich*; *R v Estephan*, Sydney Central Local Court, 5 August 2013.

16 Magistrate Jan Stevenson, ibid.

17 Winston Terracini, committal hearing, *R v Medich*; *R v Estephan*, Sydney Central Local Court, 6 August 2013.

18 Daniel Costa, evidence, committal hearing, *R v Medich*; *R v Estephan*, Sydney Central Local Court, 7 August 2013.

19 Matthew Crockett, evidence, committal hearing, *R v Medich*; *R v Estephan*, Sydney Central Local Court, 7 August 2013.

20 Lucky Gattellari, evidence, committal hearing, *R v Medich*; *R v Estephan*, Sydney Central Local Court, 21 August 2013.

21 Ibid.

22 Ibid., 12 August 2013.
23 Ibid.
24 Ibid.

Chapter 27: Round Two

1   Lucky Gattellari, evidence, committal hearing, *R v Medich*;
    R v Estephan, Sydney Central Local Court, 13 August 2013.
2   Ibid.
3   Magistrate Jan Stevenson, committal hearing, *R v Medich*;
    R v Estephan, Sydney Central Local Court, 14 August 2013.
4   Lucky Gattellari, evidence, committal hearing, *R v Medich*;
    R v Estephan, Sydney Central Local Court, 19 August 2013.
5   Ibid.
6   Ibid., 21 August 2013.
7   Haissam Safetli, evidence, committal hearing, *R v Medich*;
    R v Estephan, Sydney Central Local Court, 22 August 2013.
8   Ibid.
9   Vanda Carson, 'Fury in McGurk public gallery', *Daily
    Telegraph*, 22 August 2013.
10 Haissam Safetli, evidence, committal hearing, *R v Medich*;
    R v Estephan, Sydney Central Local Court, 21 August 2013.
11 Ibid., 22 August 2013.
12 Ibid.
13 Ibid., 26 August 2013.
14 Ibid.

Chapter 28: The Evidence Stacks Up

1   Senad Kaminic, evidence, committal hearing, *R v Medich*;
    R v Estephan, Sydney Central Local Court, 26 August 2013.
2   Ibid.
3   Magistrate Jan Stevenson, committal hearing, *R v Medich*;
    R v Estephan, Sydney Central Local Court, 27 August 2013.
4   Senad Kaminic, evidence, committal hearing, *R v Medich*;
    R v Estephan, Sydney Central Local Court, 28 August 2013.
5   Ibid., 9 September 2013.

6 Ghassan Bassal, evidence, committal hearing, *R v Medich*; *R v Estephan*, Sydney Central Local Court, 11 September 2013.

7 Magistrate Jan Stevenson, committal hearing, *R v Medich*; *R v Estephan*, Sydney Central Local Court, 27 September 2013.

8 Ron Medich, evidence, committal hearing, *R v Medich*; *R v Estephan*, Sydney Central Local Court, 27 September 2013.

Chapter 29: No Brotherly Love

1 Roy Medich affidavit, *Roy Medich Properties v Ron Medich Properties*, Supreme Court of New South Wales, 16 April 2014.

2 Kate McClymont, 'No brotherly love: Roy Medich wants Ron out of Badgerys Creek deal', *Sydney Morning Herald*, 26 April 2014.

3 Magistrate Jan Stevenson, committal hearing, *R v Medich*; *R v Estephan*, Sydney Central Local Court, 15 November 2013.

4 Lema Semander, 'I'm guilty, I must be punished', *Daily Telegraph*, 11 April 2014.

5 Bellew, J, judgment, *R v Estephan*, Supreme Court of New South Wales, 30 April 2014.

6 Lucky Gattellari, evidence, committal hearing, *R v Bassam Safetli*, Sydney Central Local Court, 20 March 2015.

7 Ibid.

8 Senad Kaminic, ibid.

9 Bassam Safetli, sentence hearing, *R v Bassam Safetli*, District Court of New South Wales, 3 June 2018.

10 Tupman, J, sentencing, *R v Bassam Safetli*, District Court of New South Wales, 18 June 2018.

11 Ibid.

Chapter 30: The Trial of Ron Medich

1 Bellew, J, judgment, *R v Medich*, Supreme Court of New South Wales, 9 December 2016.

2   Directions hearing, *R v Medich*, Supreme Court of New South Wales, 20 May 2016.

3   Ibid.

4   Bellew, J, judgment, *R v Medich*, Supreme Court of New South Wales, 25 July 2016.

5   Emma Partridge, 'Assassin's creed', *Daily Telegraph*, 23 December 2016.

6   Bellew, J, *R v Medich*, Supreme Court of New South Wales, 30 January 2017.

7   Crown opening, ibid.

8   Ibid.

9   Defence opening, *R v Medich*, Supreme Court of New South Wales, 31 January 2017.

10 Kimberley McGurk, evidence, *R v Medich*, Supreme Court of New South Wales, 31 January 2017.

11 Lucky Gattellari, evidence, *R v Medich*, Supreme Court of New South Wales, 14 February 2017.

12 Ibid., 6 February 2017.

13 Ibid.

14 Bellew, J, sentencing, *R v McNamara; R v Rogerson*, Supreme Court of New South Wales, 2 September 2017.

15 Shayne Hatfield, evidence, *R v Medich*, Supreme Court of New South Wales, 28 February 2017.

16 Ibid., 1 March 2017.

17 Gina O'Rourke, *R v Medich*, Supreme Court of New South Wales, 22 February 2017.

18 Paul Mathieson, evidence, *R v Medich*, Supreme Court of New South Wales, 22 February 2017.

19 Paul Mathieson, evidence, committal hearing, *R v Medich*, Sydney Central Local Court, 10 September 2013.

20 Ibid.

21 Name suppressed, evidence, *R v Medich*, Supreme Court of New South Wales, 22 February 2017.

22 Bellew, J, *R v Medich*, Supreme Court of New South Wales, 17 March 2017.

23 Crown closing, ibid.

24 Defence closing, *R v Medich*, Supreme Court of New South Wales, 22 March 2017.

25 Bellew, J, *R v Medich*, Supreme Court of New South Wales, 13 April 2017.

Chapter 31: No Happy Endings

1 Paul Mathieson, evidence, *R v Medich*, Supreme Court of New South Wales, 28 February 2018.

2 Bellew, J, judgment, *R v Medich*, Supreme Court of New South Wales, 13 March 2018.

3 Ibid.

4 Sentencing hearing, *R v Medich*, Supreme Court of New South Wales, 30 May 2018.

5 Bellew, J, judgment, *R v Medich*, Supreme Court of New South Wales, 21 June 2018.

Chapter 32: The Price of Freedom

1 Darren Robinson, opening address, *R v Gattellari*; *R v Hatfield*, District Court of New South Wales, 25 October 2018.

2 Robert McCarthy, evidence, *R v Gattellari*; *R v Hatfield*, District Court of New South Wales, 29 October 2018.

3 Ibid.

4 Exhibit, *R v Gattellari*; *R v Hatfield*, District Court of New South Wales, October 2018.

5 Lucky Gattellari, evidence, *R v Gattellari*; *R v Hatfield*, District Court of New South Wales, 16 November 2018.

6 Ibid., 28 November 2018.

7 Robert McCarthy, evidence, *R v Gattellari*; *R v Hatfield*, District Court of New South Wales, 26 October 2018.

8 Ibid., 29 October 2018.

9 Ibid.

10 Ibid., 26 October 2018.

11 Ibid.

12 Ibid.

13 Ibid.

14 Lucky Gattellari, evidence, *R v Gattellari*; *R v Hatfield*, District Court of New South Wales, 27 November 2018.

15 Lucky Gattellari, police interview, 7 September 2016.

16 Miss L, police statement, 28 July 2014.

17 Exhibit, *R v Gattellari*; *R v Hatfield*, District Court of New South Wales, October 2018.

18 Ibid.

19 Miss L, police statement, 28 July 2014.

20 Ibid.

21 Exhibit, *R v Gattellari*; *R v Hatfield*, District Court of New South Wales, October 2018.

22 Ibid.

23 Ibid.

24 Ibid.

25 Lucky Gattellari, evidence, *R v Gattellari*; *R v Hatfield*, District Court of New South Wales, 29 November 2018.

26 Florence Scovel Shinn wrote about 'The Law of Attraction' in her book *The Game of Life and How to Play It*.

27 Lucky Gattellari, evidence, *R v Gattellari*; *R v Hatfield*, District Court of New South Wales, 29 November 2018.

28 Ibid.

29 Darren Robinson, closing address, *R v Gattellari*; *R v Hatfield*, District Court of New South Wales, 4 December 2018.

30 Case note report, NSW Department of Corrective Services, 16 December 2018.

31 Gough Whitlam, *The Daily Telegraph* (UK), 19 October 1989.

ACKNOWLEDGEMENTS

First and foremost I would like to thank Vanda Carson, who spent endless months feverishly researching the astonishingly murky worlds of Michael McGurk and Ron Medich. This book could not have been done without your superlative sleuthing skills.

Over the years so many people have come forward to share information about the central characters and to them I offer sincere thanks. I am especially indebted to Frank Burke and Hamish Williamson for their rollicking tales of adventures and misadventures with McGurk.

To the homicide detectives – Mark Fitzhenry, Richie Howe and Mick Sheehy – what a journey it has been.

Thanks also to the hard-working lawyers (for both the prosecution and the defence) as well as the judicial wisdom of Justice Geoff Bellew, Judge Penny Hock and magistrates Jan Stevenson and Graeme Henson. A big shout-out to the courts' media managers – Sonya Zadel, Lisa Miller, Felicita Benedikovics, Georgie Loudon and Angus Huntsdale – for all their years of unflagging assistance.

I am eternally grateful to my agent, Fiona Inglis, the ever-patient Meredith Curnow from Penguin Random House and the sharp eye and deft hand of editor Catherine Hill.

I also have a decade of editors at the *Sydney Morning Herald* to thank for allowing me the time to pursue this story: Peter Fray, Amanda Wilson, Darren Goodsir and Lisa Davies; and our lawyers Richard Coleman (whose number I had on speed dial) and his successor, Larina Alick.

To my wonderful friends, especially my Sunday morning coffee pals, who propped me up with humour and wisdom and gossip, my bridge-playing mates and my journo buddies – I thank you all.

But most of all I would like to thank my children, Phoebe, Jack and Sophie. You three make everything so much more fun.

Discover a
new favourite